CHINESE LEGALITY

Chinese Legality focuses on the concept of "legality" as a lens through which to look at Chinese legal reforms, making a valuable contribution to the argument that law has historically been used as a tool to control society in China.

This book discusses how Chinese legality in the Xi Jinping era is defined from a theoretical, ideological, historical, and cultural point of view. Covering vitally important events such as Xi's term limit issue, the Hong Kong protests, and the Covid-19 pandemic, the book examines how legality is reflected and embodied in laws and constitutions, and how legality is realized through institutions, with particular focus on how the CCP interacts with the legislature, the judiciary, the procuratorate, and the police.

As a study of the legal reforms under Xi Jinping, this book will be of interest to students and scholars of Chinese politics and law.

Shiping Hua is Calvin and Helen Lang Distinguished Chair in Asian Studies, Director of the Asian Studies Program, and Professor of Political Science at the University of Louisville, US.

Routledge Studies on Comparative Asian Politics

Editor: Shiping Hua, *the Calvin and Helen Lang Distinguished Chair in Asian Studies, Director of the Asian Studies Program and Professor of Political Science at the University of Louisville, USA.*

Books in this series will cover such areas as political institutions and systems, political economy, political culture, political thought, political psychology, public administration, law, and political histories of Asia. The studies may deal with Asia as a whole, a single country, or a group of countries in Asia. Those studies that have a clear comparative edge are especially welcome.

The Authoritarian Public Sphere
Legitimation and Autocratic Power in North Korea, Burma, and China
Alexander Dukalskis

An East Asian Challenge to Western Neoliberalism
Niv Horesh and Kean Fan Lim

China's Global Political Economy
Managerial Perspectives
Robert Taylor and Jacques Jaussaud

Japanese Contemporary Politics
Igarashi Akio

Social Cohesion in Asia
Historical Origins, Contemporary Shapes and Future Dynamics
Edited by Aurel Croissant and Peter Walkenhorst

The Evolving Relationship between China, the EU and the USA
A New Global Order?
Edited by Jing Men, Simon Schunz and Duncan Freeman

China's Grand Strategy Under Xi Jinping
How History Complicates Beijing's Global Outreach
Niv Horesh

Chinese Ideology
Shiping Hua

US-China-Taiwan in the Age of Trump and Biden
Towards a Nationalist Strategy
Dean P. Chen

Democratic Governance in Taiwan
Edited by John Hsieh and Robert Henry Cox

Chinese Legality
Ideology, Law, and Institutions
Edited by Shiping Hua

For more information about this series, please visit: www.routledge.com/Routledge-Studies-on-Comparative-Asian-Politics/book-series/RSCAP

CHINESE LEGALITY

Ideology, Law, and Institutions

Edited by Shiping Hua

Routledge
Taylor & Francis Group
LONDON AND NEW YORK

First published 2023
by Routledge
4 Park Square, Milton Park, Abingdon, Oxon OX14 4RN

and by Routledge
605 Third Avenue, New York, NY 10158

Routledge is an imprint of the Taylor & Francis Group, an informa business

British Library Cataloguing-in-Publication Data
A catalogue record for this book is available from the British Library

ISBN: 978-1-032-27992-3 (hbk)
ISBN: 978-1-032-27994-7 (pbk)
ISBN: 978-1-003-29488-7 (ebk)

DOI: 10.4324/9781003294887

Typeset in Times New Roman
by Apex CoVantage, LLC

CONTENTS

FIGURES

TABLES

CONTRIBUTORS

Chun-Chih Chang is Associate Professor of Political Science at Xiamen University, China. His research interests encompass Chinese politics, legislative study, political sociology, and internet politics. He has coedited a volume *Evolutionary Governance in China: State-Society Relations under Authoritarianism* with Szu-chien Hsu and Kellee S. Tsai. His articles have appeared in several journals, including *Social Science & Medicine*, *Democratization*, *Journal of Contemporary China*, and *Issues and Studies*.

Chien-Min Chao is Distinguished Chair Professor at the Graduate Institute for National Development and Mainland China Studies and also Dean of the College of Social Sciences at the Chinese Culture University. Between 2008 and 2012, Dr. Chao served as Deputy Minister for the Mainland Affairs Council in the ROC government. Dr. Chao was Visiting Distinguished Professor at the George Washington University and Visiting Teaching Professor at the University of Wisconsin-Madison. Dr. Chao has written and edited 13 books, including Decision-making in China: Leadership, Process and Mechanism (in Chinese) (2014). The book has won him a distinguished award in Taiwan and has been translated into Korean. Other publications include Introduction to China and Cross-Strait Relations (2010); Lee Teng-hui's Legacy (2002); Rethinking the Chinese State, 2001; Analysis to Contemporary Chinese Politics (1997); and Authoritarian Politics (1994). Dr. Chao has also produced over 100 articles in academic journals such as the *Asian Affairs*, *Asian Survey*, *the China Quarterly*, *Journal of Contemporary China*, *Pacific Affairs*, *Issues & Studies*, *Chinese Law and Government*, and *Zhongguo dalu yanjiu*.

Ming Du is Professor of Law and Director of the Centre for Chinese Law and Policy at Durham Law School in the UK. He holds an LLB from Tsinghua University in Beijing, an LLM from Harvard Law School, and a DPhil from the University of Oxford. His current research focuses on the theoretical and structural issues of global governance, China's approach to international law, and the development of the rule of law in contemporary China. His works have appeared or are forthcoming in leading international law journals, including *International and Comparative Law Quarterly*, *Journal of International Economic Law*, *Georgetown Journal of International Law*, *European Law Journal*, *Yearbook of European Law*, *German Law Journal*, and *Journal of Environmental Law*. His Monograph *The Regulation of Product Standards in World Trade Law* was published in 2020.

Michael R. Fowler is Professor of Political Science at the University of Louisville with academic and professional interests in Asia and the Pacific. He has published seven books and served as a two-time Fulbright Scholar to Japan at the University of the Ryukyus in Okinawa. Professor Fowler lectured at Bond University in Australia and presented a two-week seminar for professors from across China at the China Foreign Affairs University. Through the Program for International Studies in Asia, he has taught on multiple occasions at the training wings of the Ministries of Foreign Affairs of Vietnam and Laos. Fowler published an edited volume, *Envisioning Reform: Enhancing UN Accountability in the Twenty-first Century*, alongside former UN Assistant Secretary-General Sumihiro Kuyama. A graduate of Harvard Law School as well as the University of Virginia and Dartmouth College, he practiced law for several years with Mintz, Levin, a large Boston law firm with various clients in Asia. His best-known works, both co-authored with Julie Bunck, are *Law, Power, and the Sovereign State: The Evolution and Application of the Concept of Sovereignty*, and *Bribes, Bullets, and Intimidation: Drug Trafficking and the Law in Central America.*

Shiping Hua is Calvin and Helen Lang Distinguished Chair in Asian Studies, Professor of Political Science, and Director of Asian Studies Program at the University of Louisville, US. He has published 14 books in English, edited or single-authored, including Chinese Legal Culture and Constitutional Order, Chinese Utopianism: A Comparative Study of Reformist Thought with Japan and Russia (1898–1997), and Scientism and Humanism: Two Cultures in Post-Mao China (1978–1989). He edited two book series, "Asia in the New Millennium" with University Press of Kentucky and "Comparative Asian Politics" with Routledge.

Bin Liang (PhD/JD) is Professor of Sociology at Oklahoma State University. His research interests include globalization and its impact on the Chinese legal system, crime and deviance in China, and comparative studies in criminology and criminal justice. He is the author of five books, including *The Changing Chinese Legal System, 1978—Present: Centralization of Power and Rationalization of the Legal System* (2008), *China's Drug Practices and Policies: Regulating Controlled Substances in a Global Context* (2009, coauthored), *Jurisprudence* (2012, co-edited, in Chinese), *The Death Penalty in China: Policy, Practice and Reform* (2016, co-edited), and *Chinese Netizens' Opinions on Death Sentences: An Empirical Examination* (2021, coauthored). In addition to the aforementioned books, his works also appeared in many peer-reviewed journals in the US and other nations, including *Journal of Criminal Justice*, *British Journal of Criminology*, *The China Quarterly*, *European Journal on Criminal Policy and Research*, *Australian and New Zealand Journal of Criminology*, and *Asian Journal of Criminology*.

Stephan Ortmann is Adjunct Assistant Professor in the Department of Politics and Public Administration of the University of Hong Kong. He has worked on various issues related to political change and protest movements in Hong Kong, Singapore, China, and Vietnam. His publications have appeared in many reputable journals including *Asian Survey, Administration and Society, Asia Pacific Law Review, China Quarterly, Journal of Democracy, Government and Opposition, and Pacific Review*. He is the author of *Politics and Change in Singapore and Hong Kong: Containing Contention* (2010) and *Environmental Governance in Vietnam: Institutional Reforms and Failures* (2017). Most recently, he has co-edited a volume with Mark R. Thompson titled *China's "Singapore Model" and Authoritarian Learning* (2020).

Haig Patapan is Professor in the School of Government and International Relations, Griffith University. His research interests are in democratic theory and practice, political philosophy, political leadership, and comparative constitutionalism. Professor Patapan is Fellow of the Academy of Social Sciences in Australia. He has received a number of awards, including an Australian Prime Ministers Centre Fellowship, a Senior Fulbright Scholarship at the Center for Public Leadership, Harvard Kennedy School of Government, and an Isaac Manasseh Meyer Fellowship at the National University of Singapore. In his recent work, Professor Patapan examines the nature of leadership and judgment in democracies, a theme he has explored in the co-authored book *The Democratic Leader* (2012) as well as the co-edited collections *Dispersed Democratic Leadership* (2009) and *Good Democratic Leadership* (2014). His latest book, *A Dangerous Passion* (2021), examines the importance of honor in contemporary politics.

Suzanne E. Scoggins is Associate Professor of Political Science and Director of Asian Studies at Clark University. Her research focuses on policing in reform-era China and explores themes of state legitimacy, local governance, and authoritarian control. Her new book, Policing China: Street-Level Cops in the Shadow of Protest, examines the paradox of China's self-projection of a strong security state while having a weak police bureaucracy. Dr. Scoggins holds a PhD in political science from the University of California, Berkeley, and was previously a predoctoral fellow at Stanford University's Center on Democracy, Development and the Rule of Law. She is currently a Public Intellectuals Program Fellow at the National Committee on US–China Relations.

Zheng (Sophia) Tang is Professor at Wuhan University, Institute of International Law in China, and Associate Dean at Wuhan University Academy of International Law and Governance in China. Additionally, she is a barrister, arbitrator, and mediator. She specializes in private international law, international commercial arbitration and mediation, consumer law, and internet law. Professor Tang obtained her BA in International Law from Wuhan University, an LLM in International Law from Manchester University, and a PhD in International Law from Birmingham University. She formerly held the positions of Full Professor at Newcastle University, Associate Professor at the University of Leeds, Lecturer at the University of Aberdeen, and Senior Visiting Scholar at the Duke University and the Max Planck Institute of Comparative and International Private Law.

Jeffrey E. Thomas is Daniel L. Brenner Faculty Scholar, Professor of Law, and Associate Dean for Strategic Initiatives and Graduate Programs at the University of Missouri—Kansas City School of Law. He earned his Bachelor of Arts degree from Loyola Marymount University (*magna cum laude*) and his Juris Doctor degree from Berkeley Law at the University of California, Berkeley. His research focuses on the interaction between law and culture, the rule of law, and insurance law. His rule of law work has been published in the *Asia Pacific Law Journal* (Hong Kong), the *Frontier of Science of Society* (China), the *Indonesian Journal of International Law* (Indonesia), *Law Text Culture* (Australia), and the *UCLA Law Review* (US). Comparative law works have been published in Europe, Russia, Singapore, Turkey, the UK, and the US. He was Bigelow Teaching Fellow and Lecturer in Law at the University of Chicago Law School, Adjunct at Loyola Law School (Los Angeles), and Summer Visitor at the University of Connecticut School of Law. In 1999–2000, he was Fulbright Fellow at Nankai University (Tianjin, China) and in 2010 at Immanuel Kant Baltic Federal University (Kaliningrad, Russia).

Andrew Wedeman is Professor of Political Science at Georgia State University, where he heads the China Studies Initiative. Previously, he was Professor of Political Science at the University of Nebraska-Lincoln. He has held posts as Fulbright Research Professor at Taiwan National University, Visiting Associate Professor of Political Science at the Johns Hopkins Nanjing University Center for Sino-American Studies, Visiting Research Professor at Beijing University, and Research Fellow at the Woodrow Wilson Center for International Scholars. His publications include *From Mao to Market: Rent Seeking, Local Protectionism, and Marketization in China* and *Double Paradox: Rapid Growth and Rising Corruption in China.* He is currently completing a book on China's ongoing anti-corruption crackdown entitled *The Third Paradox: Rapid Growth, Rising Corruption and China's Never Ending Battle with Corruption.*

Xinxin Zhang is a PhD candidate at the Wuhan University, Institute of International Law. Her research interests include personal data protection laws and empirical studies of Private International Law in China. Before her current research program, she received a master's degree in Law from Wuhan University in 2021 and a bachelor's degree in Law from Nankai University in 2018.

Guobin Zhu, PhD, is Professor of Law, School of Law, City University of Hong Kong; Director, Public Law and Human Rights Forum, School of Law, City University of Hong Kong; and Co-Associate Director, Centre of Public Affairs and Law, City University of Hong Kong. He received BA, MA, LLM (RenminU of China, Beijing), LLM (Hong Kong University), PhD, and HDR (*Diplôme d'Habilitation à Diriger des Recherches*) (Aix-Marseille University, France). He is Titular Member of the International Academy of Comparative Law, Council Member of the Chinese Association of Constitutional Law, and Chinese Society of Judicial Studies, Executive Council Member of the Association of the Hong Kong Basic Law and Macau Basic Law, as well as an Arbitrator (Zhuhai, Qingdao, Wuhan & SCIAHK). His research interests cover Chinese and comparative constitutional law, the Basic Law of Hong Kong, law of human rights in Hong Kong and China, and public administration of China. He has published widely on various topics in the areas relevant to his research. He also has extensive engagement in community services, including serving as Advisor to Our Hong Kong Foundation, Vice-Chairman of Steering Committee for Undergraduate Legal Education of Colleges and Universities of Guangdong Province, China, and Trustee of the Legal Education Trust Fund, Hong Kong.

1

INTRODUCTION TO CHINESE LEGALITY

Ideology, Law, and Institutions

Shiping Hua

The book discusses how Chinese legality is defined from theoretical, ideological, historical, and cultural perspectives; how the legality is reflected and embodied in laws and constitutions; and how the legality is realized through institutions, especially how the CCP interacts with the legislature, the judiciary, the procuratorate, and the police.

The focus of the book is the concept of "legality" that ties together the different parts of the book, since the editor believes that it is a clearer lens through which to look at the Chinese legal reforms. The title of the book is "Chinese Legality," instead of "Legality in China," with the former indicating some kind of subjectiveness, i.e., legality Chinese style, and the latter implying that legality is something neutral. The time frame is the last decade of the Xi Jinping era.

In the last two decades, China's rule of law has improved in a general sense. According to World Bank rule of law data, China's score had improved from −0.55 in 1996 to −0.27 in 2019. But compared with liberal democracies such as that of Finland of 2.03 in 2019, China's record is still lagging far behind. In addition, China's rule of law index dropped in the last few years because of Xi's tightening of political control.

The Xi administration came into power in 2012 with a louder voice on law that is different from the rule of law in the context of the West. In the last decade, the Chinese government passed some very crucial legal documents, such as the Fifth Constitutional Amendment, that include granting virtual tenure to Xi as the top leader, emphasizing ideology and the role of the Chinese Communist Party, and the National Security Law that tightened the CCP's political control. The Fifth Amendment and the National Security Law apparently restored some of the ideological trends of the pre-reform era.

However, the picture is far from a clear one. For instance, the Xi administration also promulgated the Civil Code that took the PRC 60 years to accomplish. The

DOI: 10.4324/9781003294887-1

Civil Code reflects the regime's desire to give the public more breathing space in those areas that don't hurt the state's monopoly of power, e.g., protecting the civil rights among non-state actors.

These documents transmitted complex political and ideological messages to the public. Although the Fifth Amendment and the Civil Code seem to move in different directions, they may serve the purpose of complementing each other: Tightened control in politics goes hand in hand with providing some breathing space to the people in the socio-economic sphere. This strategy seems similar to that after the 1989 Tiananmen incident: tightened political control went hand in hand with economic reform and opening up to the outside world.

The complexity of the situation called for accurate terminologies in describing the law situation in China. Exactly what does "rule of law" mean in the Chinese context? The direct translation of the Chinese official version is "rule according to law," which is different from the commonly used term of "rule of law." Some legal scholars increasing started to use another term to describe the current situation in law in China, "rule by law," which is supposed to be rooted in Qin (221–206 BCE).

Because of this complex situation, some useful studies have been conducted to look at the Xi regime from legal perspectives. The topics of research on legal reforms in the Xi administration include the meaning of "rule according to law" (Peerenboom 2014; Trevaskes 2018); how centralization was achieved through the legal system (Li 2016); how lawyers struggled under the Xi administration (He 2021), the justice system under Xi (Biddulph, Nesossi, and Trevaskes 2017); the international law and the rise of China (Cai 2019); how the working class was impacted upon by the authoritarian legality (Gallagher 2017); and the complaint system (Fang 2013). This volume joins this flow of studies on legal reforms in the last decade.

1. How Is Chinese Legality Defined?

The book is divided into three parts with the first one dealing with how Chinese legality is defined, i.e., those theoretical, ideological, and historical issues related to the definition of legality. Legality, the quality and state of being in accordance with the law, is often a key to understanding the Chinese law and society (Smith 2020). Legality is defined along the perspectives of the legality of imperial China (Patapan) and the legality of state socialist China (Thomas). The third chapter of this part deals with the debates on the legality (Zhu).

The legality of traditional China. The Chinese legal system laid its foundation in Qin (221–206 BCE). Law was pragmatic and instrumentalist to serve the purpose of the state. On the basis of theories developed by Legalists like Han Fei (280–233 BCE) that advocated relying on law and eliminating the privileges of the aristocrats, Qin effectively strengthened the power of the state and eventually defeated all the other six rival kingdoms. But with the eventual dominance of Confucianism over Legalism after the unification of China by Qin, law is viewed as the last resort for governance. A good ruler relied on morality for effective governance, e.g., the Emperor setting an example for people to follow. Those who encourage litigation can go to jail. Law was not as important as morality, such as filial piety. For instance, in Qing (1644–1912), it was legal for the son to cover up for the father who had committed a crime. Traditional Chinese court "judged persons according to their concrete qualities and in terms of the concrete situation, or according to equity and the appropriateness of the concrete result" (Hua 2019, 149). China does not have the tradition of natural law. There was no separation of power. In the last decade, there seems to be a revival of certain elements of the Chinese cultural tradition. Xi is believed to stress China's cultural tradition more than any of his predecessors. Many Chinese universities recently established the School of Chinese Studies (Guo Xue Yuan).

In this book, Haig Patapan explores the extent to which Han Fei and Chinese Legalism inform Xi Jinping Thought and therefore contemporary Chinese politics. Han Fei theorized the legalist school of thought that was adopted by Qin. This chapter examines Xi's China Dream and specific policy initiatives including the concentration of power in his hands, the anti-corruption campaigns against officials, the use of law as an instrument of the state, and the significant investment in the military to argue that all these initiatives follow closely Han Fei's advice on how to make a state wealthy and powerful. It concludes by noting that Xi is not unique in this respect—Chinese leaders have historically resorted to Legalism in times of political instability and uncertainty.

The legality of state socialism. Theoretically speaking, Marxism de-emphasizes the role of law, because it is part of "superstructure" that is not essential as the "economic base." In the history of both the former Soviet Union and the PRC, sometimes there was no law as was the case with the Soviet Union for the first few years after the Bolshevik Revolution and for the first few years after 1949. In 1954, the PRC had the first constitution that was based on the 1937 Soviet constitution. The first PRC constitution was used for only three years that was followed by waves after waves of leftist movements such as the Anti-Rightist Movement in 1957 and the lawless Cultural Revolution from 1966 to 1976. The emphasis on law during the reform era was rooted in at least two origins. First, the veteran cadres suffered a lot during the lawless Cultural Revolution, including the PRC President Liu Shaoqi (White 1992, 48–51). Second, the opening up to foreign investment called for law.

The imperial legal culture and the communist one share at least the following characteristics: pragmatism, i.e., law serves a pragmatic purpose of the regime, not based on some moral principles; instrumentalism, i.e., law is a stool of the regime that can be picked up when it is useful and dropped when it is not; statism, i.e., the focus is on the state.

In this volume, Jeffrey E. Thomas uses World Justice Project data on rule of law to demonstrate that while China has made some progress toward the rule of law, it is far short of reaching the rule of law ideal as measured by the western standard. He analyzes the ambiguous impact of the Chinese culture on rule of law and believes that although Chinese culture may hinder the development of rule of law in the short rule, China may eventually develop into a legal system similar to other Asian countries, such as Japan or Singapore. In other words, it is possible for China to realize some thin "constitutionalism." The argument of Thomas was shared by scholars such as Lynn T. White (2009).

Guobin Zhu divides Chinese legal scholars into two camps, "socialist constitutionalism" and "liberal constitutionalism" with the former being a combination of imperial legal thought, state socialist, and some elements of the west, while the latter refers to the western notion of rule of law. The first group of legal scholars is people like Qiang Shigong, who argues that constitutionalism Chinese style had its legality (Qiang 2014, 119–32). The second group includes legal scholars such as He Weifang (He 1998, 2012).

2. How Legality Is Reflected and Embodied in Laws and Constitutions?

In the second part of the book, the authors discuss issues related to how legality is reflected and embodied in laws and constitutions. When the reform started in 1978, China had almost no law. An enormous number of laws and regulations have been promulgated in the last four decades. The Chinese government announced that China had established its comprehensive legal system in 2010. This part of the book includes studies of those laws that deal with some of the most pressing issues that China faced: national security (Du), international relations (Tang), and civil rights (Hua).

Ming Du takes a critical look at the prevailing narratives on how international trade and investment norms may impact domestic governance and the rule of law of a nation state. This chapter argues that, although international economic norms and institutions have played a positive role in advancing the rule of law in China, such a role has long been exaggerated. The prevailing narratives were based on misunderstandings of the nature and function of international economic law as well as deeply flawed assumptions.

Zheng Sophia Tang and Xinxin Zhang discusses the recent extraterritorial legislation attempts in China and assesses how they are going to serve China's international strategy. Historically speaking, China suffered humiliation in the past because Western countries use it to encroach on China's sovereignty. How, with the country's rise as an economic and political power, does China use it to protect its own overseas interest and to strengthen the country's foreign policy? In the past, the Eight Foreign Powers such as Great Britain, France, and Germany used extraterritoriality in China to protect their interests. This time China used it in dealing with foreign countries to protect Chinese interests.

On the issue of civil rights, Shiping Hua argues that at least in principle, the Civil Code is a step forward from the previous civil laws in protecting private properties, privacy, and contractual relations. Nevertheless, the rights are by and large among individuals and other non-state actors, not vis-a-vis the state. Restricting the state rights is mostly in an abstract sense. When it involves concrete issues, it is mostly in small areas, such as "Lost & Found." When the state is a party vis-a-vis the legal persons or natural persons, it is mostly in the areas of economics, not politics. This does not contradict the Fifth Amendment that strengthens the party leadership and personality cult. This is civil rights Chinese style, not rule of law as we understand it in the west.

3. How Is Legality Realized Through Institutions?

The third part of the book discusses the issues related to how legality is realized through such institutions as the legislature, the courts, as well as the police. This part explores issues related to the role played by NPC vis-a-vis the party (Chao/Chang), policing (Scoggins), the Hong Kong protests (Ortmann); corruption and organized crime (Wedeman); and the police mishandling of the case of Li Wenliang during the pandemic (Liang).

One key issue is the relations between the party and these institutions and how the laws and the constitution justify them. In the 1982 PRC constitution, there was an attempt to separate the party from the daily operations of the government. There was also an attempt to encourage the judiciary to become more independent. With the Fifth Amendment that emphasizes the party's role and the top leader's personal role, this situation seems to have been reversed. This is reflected in the observations of some of the authors in this part of the book.

On the role played by the National People's Congress, Chien-Min Chao and Chun-Chih Chang argue that the problem of bureaucratic interests is likely to be soothed by introducing more transparency and input channels into the lawmaking process. In this regard, the role of the Chinese People's Congress may be underlined as a collector of diverse interests in the political system. This was done against the background of the increased power by the CCP. The 1982 constitution was to increase the power of the NPC and separate the CCP from the daily operations of the government. Theoretically speaking, NPC is supposed to be the ultimate powerful body.

On policing, Suzanne E. Scoggins takes a historical perspective on the developing notion of legality for policing in China, using path dependency as the methodological framework for understanding the shifting use of the rule of law to justify state goals that range from restrictions on guns and use of force to detention of suspects. The author talks about the improvement of China's policing: in the 1980s, the police did not follow rules/laws closely. Now the situation gets better. It is better governance. In other words, there is a stronger legal base for police actions in China compared with what it was in the 1980s. Using law is more efficient than not using law as in the 1980s in policing. She did not explicitly argue whether the Chinese way is in the sense of the west or not.

On the Hong Kong protests/law, Stephan Ortmann noted that following months of unrest, on June 30, 2020, the Chinese government introduced the National Security Law directly into the Basic Law, thus circumventing the explicitly stated legal process that basically eroded the territory's autonomy by introducing institutions outside the rule of law and undermining civil liberties while allowing extraterritorial prosecutions. Moreover, an electoral reform to ensure the election of only "patriots" basically disabled the limited democracy. As such, not only has the protesters' worst nightmare become reality, but the principle of legality has also become imperiled. He uses the western standard, and the Chinese NSL is not legal.

According to the Hong Kong National Security Law, the Hong Kong police establish institutions to deal specifically cases involving national security, then the procuratorate handles it, and finally, the judges appointed by the Hong Kong Special Administrative Region Executive handle it. Beijing's police, procuratorate, and supreme court can also get involved.

On anti-organized-crime and corruption, Andrew Wademan argues that the fact that the regime has been willing and able to attack the official/police-criminal nexus, however, suggests that the regime is far from crippled and headed toward a potentially serious governance crisis. This chapter addresses the contradictory possibilities. People like Cai Xia have been talking about the possibility that the regime is going to collapse. Wademan does not believe so. He believes that the regime's efforts are effective, which shows the governance is pretty good. Dealing with organized crimes involves not only the police but also the court and the party.

On the police handling of the case of Li Wenliang during the pandemic, Bin Liang believed that overall, Li Wenliang's experience shows how the legality of policing and/or social control is subject to contest and different interpretations, and how public trust may have affected its interpretation and application amid the pandemic in China. This chapter talks about how the regime handles the case of Li Wenliang, the man who blew the whistle during the pandemic. He was reprimanded by the policy and confessed "wrong doing." But he died. This case tests the legality of how the police handles the case. He did not make a clear connection between the authorities' handling of the case and whether it has legality problems.

References

Biddulph, Sarah, Elisa Nesossi, and Susan Trevaskes. 2017. "Criminal Justice Reform in the Xi Jinping Era." *China Law and Society Review* 2 (1): 63–12.

Cai, Congyan. 2019. *The Rise of China and International Law: Taking Chinese Exceptionalism Seriously, Law And Global Governance*. New York: Oxford Academic. Online edn, Oct 24, 2019. https://doi.org/10.1093/oso/9780190073602.001.0001.

Fang, Qiang. 2013. *Chinese Complaint Systems: Natural Resistance*. London: Routledge.

Gallagher, Mary E. 2017. *Authoritarian Legality in China: Law, Workers, and the State*. Cambridge: Cambridge University Press.

He, Weifang. 1998. *Sifa de linian yu zhidu "Legal ideals and institutions*." Beijing: Zhongguo Zhengfa Daxue Chubanshe.

———. 2012. *In the Name of Justice: Striving for the Rule of Law in China*. Washington, DC: Brookings Institution Press.

He, Xin. 2021. "Pressures on Chinese Judges Under Xi." *The China Journal* (85).

Hua, Shiping. 2019. *Chinese Legal Culture and Constitutional Order, 149.* London: Routledge.
Li, Anthony H. F. 2016. "Centralisation of Power in the Pursuit of Law-Based Governance, Legal Reform in China Under the Xi Administration." *China Perspectives* (2): 63–68.
Peerenboom, Randall. 2014. "The Battle Over Legal Reforms in China: Has There Been a Turn Against Law?" *The Chinese Journal of Comparative Law* 2 (2): 188–212.
Smith, Ewan. 2020. "The Concept of Legality Under Xi Jinping." In *Law and the Party in China: Ideology and Organization*, edited by Rogier J. E. H. Creemers and Susan Trevaskes. Cambridge: Cambridge University Press.
Qiang, Shigong. 2014. "Written and Unwritten Constitutions." *Modern China* 2 (40): 119–32.
Trevaskes, Susan. 2018. "A Law Unto Itself: Chinese Communist Party Leadership and Yifa Zhiguo in the Xi Era." *Modern China* 44 (4): 347–73.
White, Lynn T. III. 1992. "Ch'en Po-ta" and "Liu Shao-ch'i." In *Historical Dictionary of Revolutionary China*, edited by Edwin Pak-Wah Leung, 48–51, 230–33. Westport, CT: Greenwood Press.
———. 2009. "Chinese Constitutional Currents." *Modern China* 1 (36): 100–14.

PART 1

How Is Legality Defined? Theories and Ideologies

2

RULE OF LAW WITH CHINESE CHARACTERISTICS

Jeffrey E. Thomas

Introduction: Definition of the Rule of Law

One of the biggest challenges of the concept of rule of law is to define it. There is considerable uncertainty about what "rule of law" means (Belton 2005; Peerenboom 2004, 1–2; Orts 2001, 50–51). This uncertainty has led some to argue that the phrase is devoid of meaning and is simply a rhetorical device used to suggest that a country is using law in some fashion that makes a positive contribution to society (Sarsfield 2010, 3).

This chapter does not try to address this challenge but instead adopts the operational definition of rule of law used by the World Justice Project (WJP). The WJP defined the rule of law by reviewing international standards, national constitutions, and the scholarly literature for rule of law which led to a statement of four general principles that were vetted and refined by international experts (Agrast et al. 2012–13, 7–8). The four general principles are as follows:

1. The government and its officials and agents as well as individuals and private entities are accountable under the law.
2. The laws are clear, publicized, stable, and just, are applied evenly, and protect fundamental rights, including the security of persons and property.
3. The process by which the laws are enacted, administered, and enforced is accessible, fair, and efficient.
4. Justice is delivered in a timely way by competent, ethical, and independent representatives and neutrals who are of sufficient number, have adequate resources, and reflect the makeup of the communities they serve.

(Agrast et al. 2012–13, 9 Box 2; World Justice Project 2021, 14).

DOI: 10.4324/9781003294887-3

To measure the adherence to these four principles, the WJP uses eight factors:

1. Constraints on Government Powers
2. Absence of Corruption
3. Open Government
4. Fundamental Rights
5. Order and Security
6. Regulatory Enforcement
7. Civil Justice
8. Criminal Justice.

(World Justice Project 2021, 14)

These eight factors each have between four and seven sub-factors, for a total of 44 (World Justice Project 2021, 15–19). Data for the sub-factors are drawn from a general population poll using a representative sample of 1,000 respondents in each country analyzed in the index, and qualified respondents' questionnaires obtained from in-country legal practitioners, experts, and academics (World Justice Project 2021, 12; Botero and Ponce 2011). The WJP has been collecting and analyzing rule of law data since 2009.

1. WJP Assessment of China and the Rule of Law

Although China has made a commitment to moving toward rule of law (see Zhang 2010; Peerenboom 2002), using the WJP methodology, China does not do very well on rule of law measures. In the 2021 WJP rule of law index, China received an overall rule of law score of 0.47 on a scale between 0 and 1. This gave China a global rank of 98 out of 139 countries ranked (WJP 2021, 23), about the 30th percentile. By comparison, the top ten countries for rule of law scored between 0.81 and 0.90 (WJP 2021, 22). Compared to other East Asian and Pacific countries (which includes Australia and New Zealand), China's rank was 12 out of 15, or about the 20th percentile (though Hong Kong, which is a special administrative region of China that was returned to China by the UK in 1997, ranked fifth) (WJP 2021, 24). Compared to other countries with upper-middle-income economies (defined as Gross National Income per capita between $4,046 and $12,535 (WJP 2021, 26 n.*)), China ranked 33 out of 40 countries, or about the 18th percentile, immediately behind Belarus and just ahead of the Russian Federation (WJP 2021, 27).

Of the eight factors used for rule of law assessment, China scored the highest on Order and Security, receiving a score of 0.81 in 2021, up three points from the prior year. On this factor, China is ranked 36th globally, 7th regionally, and 2nd among the upper-middle-income countries (WJP 2021, 64). This factor has three sub-factors, absence of crime, absence of civil conflict, and absence of violent redress. China scored 1.00 on absence of civil conflict, a "perfect" score.[1] Its score for absence of crime was 0.81, and the score for absence of violent redress was 0.62.

China's lowest score was 0.27 for the factor of Fundamental Rights. This score is very low; it ranked 136th out of 139 counties globally, 14th out of 15 for the East Asia and Pacific region, and 39th out of 40 for upper-middle-income countries (WJP 2021, 64). This factor has eight sub-factors: non-discrimination, right to life and security, due process of law, freedom of expression, freedom of religion, right to privacy, freedom of association, and labor rights. Of these eight sub-factors, China scored reasonably well (0.52) on due process of law. This score was higher than the average for upper-middle-income countries, and just below the average for East Asia and the Pacific. China's scores for freedom of expression (0.11), freedom of religion (0.16), right to privacy (0.14), and freedom of association (0.11) were very low. For the other three sub-factors, China's scores were not quite as low: non-discrimination, 0.46; right to life and security, 0.33; and labor rights, 0.31 (WJP 2021, 64).

China's score for the factor of Constraints on Government Powers was somewhat higher, 0.31 (compared to 0.27), but that was still very low compared to other countries. On this factor, China was ranked 133rd out of 139 countries globally, 14th out of 15 countries in East Asia and the Pacific region, and 37th out of 40 countries in the upper-middle-income countries (WJP 2021, 64). This factor has six sub-factors: limits by legislature, limits by judiciary, independent auditing, sanctions for official misconduct, non-governmental check, and lawful transition of power. China's score on the non-governmental checks sub-factor is very low, 0.11. The sub-factors for limits by the legislature (0.35), limits by the judiciary (0.28), and lawful transition of power (0.24) are also quite low. Constraints on government power by independent auditing (0.42) and by sanctions for official misconduct (0.47) are somewhat better. China's score on sanctions for official misconduct (0.47) is above the average for upper-middle-income countries (WJP 2021, 64).

China's score for the factor of Open Government was also quite low, 0.38. On this factor, China ranked 111th out of 139 countries globally, 13th out of 15 countries in East Asia and the Pacific, and 36th out of 40 countries in the upper-middle-income group (WJP 2021, 64). This factor has four sub-factors: publicized laws and government data, right to information, civic participation, and complaint mechanisms. China's score on publicized laws and government data was 0.46, which was above the average for upper-middle-income countries. The score for the right to information, 0.48, was also nearly at the average for upper-middle-income countries. The score for complaint mechanisms, 0.42, was well below average compared to the region and countries of that income level. The lowest sub-factor score was 0.18 for civic participation, which is a very low score (WJP 2021, 64).

China's scores on the factors that address the administration of justice (Regulatory Enforcement, Civil Justice, and Criminal Justice) were pretty close to the overall rule of law score of 0.47. For Regulatory Enforcement, China scored 0.49, which is 76th globally, 10th regionally, and 19th among upper-middle-income countries. The score for Civil Justice was a little higher, 0.52, which was 74th

TABLE 2.1 WJP 2021 Rule of Law Index Factor Scores and Rankings for China

Factor	*Score*	*Global Rank (Out of 139)*	*Regional Rank (Out of 15)*	*Upper-Middle-Income Rank (Out of 40)*
Overall	0.47	98	12	33
Order and security	0.81	36	7	15
Absence of corruption	0.53	55	8	11
Civil justice	0.52	74	9	22
Regulatory enforcement	0.49	76	10	19
Criminal justice	0.45	69	10	18
Open government	0.38	111	13	36
Constraints on government power	0.31	133	14	37
Fundamental rights	0.27	136	14	39

Source: Created by the author from World Justice Project data.

globally, 9th regionally, and 22nd among upper-middle-income countries. On the Criminal Justice factor, China scored 0.45, which is lower than the other two factors, but placed China higher by comparison to other countries globally (69th out of 139) and by income level (18th out of 40), and about the same regionally (10th out of 15) (WJP 2021, 64).

The final factor is absence of corruption, where China did reasonably well, scoring 0.53, which placed it 55th globally, 8th regionally, and 11th out of 40 middle-income countries (WJP 2021, 64). The sub-factors for this factor consider different organs of government, the executive, the judiciary, the police and military, and the legislature. China scored 0.67 in absence of corruption in the police and military, which put it above the average for the region and the middle-upper-income group. The scores for executive branch (0.52) and legislature (0.41) were both above average compared to other upper-middle-income countries, but below average for the region. The lowest score was for the sub-factor about the judiciary, where the score was still reasonably good (0.53), but the average scores in the region and for upper-middle income were higher (WJP 2021, 64).

Table 2.1 summarizes the data for China overall and for each factor from the 2021 WJP rule of law index. It has been organized by the score for each factor, from highest to lowest.

2. Chinese Characteristics and the Rule of Law

On the basis of the scores on the WJP rule of law index, one might conclude that China does not adhere to the rule of law as that concept is operationally defined. Being ranked 98th out of 139 countries puts China in the bottom third of the countries assessed, which include a broad array of legal and political systems. Nevertheless, China seems to aspire to something akin to the rule of law but wants to have that concept adapted to have Chinese (as opposed to Western) characteristics. What might those characteristics be?

This chapter answers this question by looking at characteristics of Chinese culture and how those interact with the rule of law. For the characteristics of Chinese culture, this chapter relies on the work of social psychologist Geert Hofstede who developed metrics to measure dimensions of national culture while working with IBM on problems of cross-border management (Hofstede 1980, 2001). The initial framework was developed on the basis of data from more than 116,000 questionnaires administered to IBM employees and business school students in 72 countries (Hofstede 2001, 41). In the first iteration, Hofstede identified four dimensions: power distance, uncertainty avoidance, individualism, and masculinity (Hofstede 2001, 58). Subsequent work done with Michael Harris Bond, who was exploring Asian cultures as compared to Western bias, resulted in the identification of a fifth dimension: long-term orientation (Hofstede 2001, 69–71).

Of these five dimensions, two are most immediately relevant to rule of law: power distance and individualism. The power distance dimension measures the cultural attitudes about the distribution of power in a society. A high score on the power distance dimension shows that those who are less powerful members of society are likely to accept and expect that power is distributed unequally (Geerthofstede.com, n.d., 6-D model). In more technical terms, "Power distance is a measure of the interpersonal power or influence between B [boss] and S [subordinate] as perceived by the less powerful of the two, S" (Hofstede 2001, 83). This chapter suggests that the power distance dimension of culture has some bearing on the willingness of a culture to accept highly centralized governmental power. It hypothesizes that countries like China that have a high score, and therefore high tolerance of centralized power, are more likely to have fewer constraints on governmental power.

The individualism dimension is a comparison of the cultural importance placed on the individual compared to the collectivity. "It describes the relationship between the individual and the collectivity that prevails in a given society" (Hofstede 2001, 209). A high score on individualism reflects a cultural value toward individual independence as opposed to being an interdependent member of a larger whole (Geerthofstede.com, n.d., 6-D model). This chapter suggests that the individualism dimension of culture has some influence on a country's protection of fundamental rights. Although not all the fundamental rights are, strictly speaking, individualistic, non-discrimination, due process of law, freedom of expression, and right to privacy tend to emphasize the protection of the individual over the collective. In addition, while other rights such as freedom of religion and freedom of association have a collectivist aspect to them, those rights are often protected for minority groups against the wishes of the majority and in that respect are a kind of aggregation of individual rights for a group, but not the entire collective of the society.

This chapter will also briefly discuss long-term orientation, the fifth dimension of culture. It was originally based on data gathered in the Chinese Value survey of students in 23 countries (Hofstede 2001, 351). A long-term orientation is one that believes the world is in flux and therefore that preparing for the future is needed. A short-term orientation does not embrace change in the same way but believes that the world is more static and that the past provides a moral compass for future behavior (Geerthofstede.com, n.d., 6-D model). This chapter will reference this long-term orientation when it considers the future of rule of law in China.

We will begin with the individualism dimension because that is such a strong feature of Chinese culture and has a significant bearing on fundamental rights assessed in the rule of law index. We will then turn to the power distance dimension. We will come back to the long-term orientation dimension in a later section of the chapter.

Individualism and the Rule of Law

Chinese culture has a strong commitment to collectivity and a relatively weak commitment to the individual. Consequently, as a cultural matter, China is unlikely to reach the levels of protection for individual rights as countries in the West, which have a much stronger cultural commitment to individualism.

China has a score of 20 on the individuality dimension, which is in the bottom 20% of the 78 countries assessed (Geerthofstede.com, Dimension).[2] Not surprisingly, other Asian countries, which also tend to be more collectivist in their cultural orientation, also scored fairly low on this dimension: Indonesia (14), Pakistan (14), Taiwan (17), South Korea (18), Singapore (20), Vietnam (20), Thailand (20), Malaysia (26), and Philippines (32) (Geerthofstede.com, Dimension). Hong Kong, which was a British Colony for over a century, is culturally closer to China on the individuality dimension than to Great Britain. Hong Kong's score on Individuality is 25. Great Britain's score is 89 (Geerthofstede.com, Dimension).

Not too surprisingly, the highest individuality dimension score in the world was 91 for the US. Countries with similar cultural traditions also have high scores: Australia (90), Great Britain (89), and Canada (80) (Geerthofstede.com, Dimension). On the European continent, the countries with the highest individuality dimension scores are the Netherlands (80) and Hungary (80) (Geerthofstede.com, Dimension). The top three countries in the 2021 rule of law index (Denmark, Norway, and Finland), which were also the top three countries for protection of fundamental rights in the 2021 index (WJP 2021, 31), also have fairly high scores on the individuality dimension: 74 (Denmark), 69 (Norway), and 63 (Finland) (Geerthofstede.com, Dimension).

Figure 2.1 provides a visual presentation of these countries on the individuality dimension.

Because of China's cultural commitment to collectivity over individuality, it seems unlikely that China will ever reach the level of protection for fundamental rights in countries that have a much stronger commitment to individualism. In general, there is a strong correlation (0.663) between a country's individualism dimension score and its rule of law fundamental rights score (Thomas 2014, 16). Although China's cultural commitment to collectivity will provide some limit on its progress toward protection of fundamental rights, there is plenty of room for progress. Singapore, which has the same score as China for individualism (20),

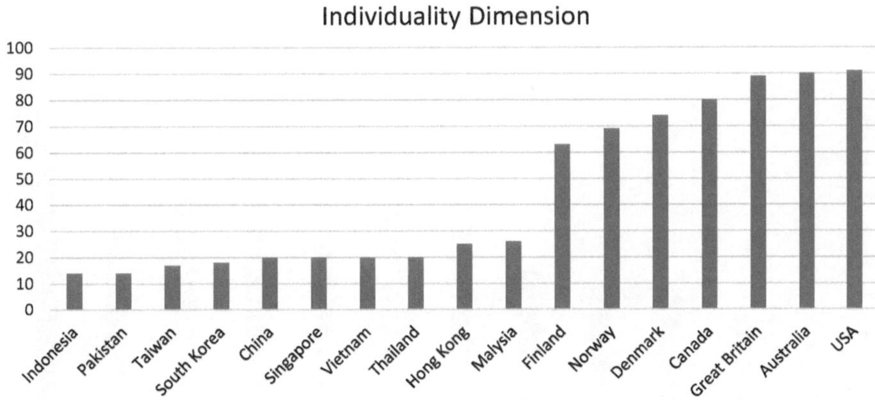

FIGURE 2.1 Individuality Dimension Scores for Selected Countries

Source: Created by the author from data available on geerthostede.com downloaded from https://geerthofstede.com/research-and-vsm/dimension-data-matrix/, *last visited April 19, 2022.*

has a score of 0.67 on fundamental rights in the 2021 rule of law index (WJP 2021, 31). China's score on fundamental rights was only 0.27, so that leaves substantial room for China to improve in protection of fundamental rights even though it may never the levels of protection of Western countries (see Thomas 2014, 14–15).

Power Distance and the Rule of Law

A second cultural dimension that has bearing on the rule of law is power distance. This measures the cultural tolerance of centralized and unequal distribution of power. In a culture with a high score on the power distance dimension, people will likely have less power and role in governance and will have a higher tolerance for strong governmental power which can conflict with rule of law. Because Chinese culture has a high tolerance for centralized and unequal power, Chinese people are more willing to accept a powerful unitary government.

China's score on the power distance dimension of culture is 80, which is quite high, roughly in the 80th percentile. Singapore, with a large Chinese population that has significant power over governance, scored 74. Other Asian countries have high scores as well: the Philippines (94), Bangladesh (80), Indonesia (78), and Vietnam (70) (Geerthofstede.com, Dimension). Hong Kong was treated as a separate country from China for purposes of this assessment but has returned to China as a special administrative region. As noted earlier, notwithstanding many years as a British colony, Hong Kong has cultural similarities to China. Hong Kong's score on the power distribution dimension is 68. Great Britain's score is 35 (Geerthofstede.com, Dimension).

Countries that are high in the rule of law index scores have relatively low power distance scores. The top three countries for the rule of law in the 2021 index (Denmark (90), Norway (90), and Finland (88)) (WJP 2021, 22) had some of the

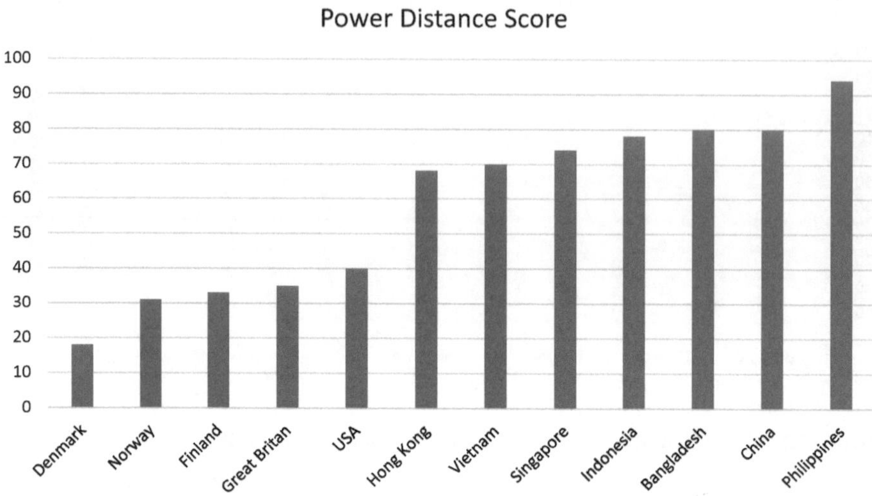

FIGURE 2.2 Power Distance Dimension Scores for Selected Countries

Source: Created by author from data available at geerthofstede.com.

lowest scores for power distance: Denmark, 18; Norway, 31; and Finland, 33 (Geerthofstede.com, Dimension). As a point of reference, the US, which has a rule of law score of 0.69 (ranked 27th), has a power distance score of 40 (Geerthofstede.com, Dimension). Low scores on the power distance dimension are strongly and negatively correlated (−0.6548) with higher scores on the Government Accountability to Law factor[3] for the rule of law index (Thomas 2014, 17).

Figure 2.2 provides a visual representation of these power distance dimension scores.

Because Chinese culture, as reflected by the power distance dimension score, has a high tolerance for a centralized and unequal power distribution, culturally, it is more difficult to hold the government accountable to the law. Over thousands of years, Chinese people have come to expect that power will be distributed unequally. Consequently, they are less likely to demand government accountability than people from countries that expect a less centralized, more equal distribution of power.

Although Chinese tolerance for unequal distribution of power limits the extent to which the government may be held accountable by rule of law, as with fundamental rights, China has plenty of room for improvement. Singapore, which has a power distribution dimension score of 74 (just six points lower than China's score of 80), achieved a score of 0.67 (and a 32nd global ranking) on the constraints on government powers factor in the 2021 rule of law index (WJP 2021, 28). Similarly, Hong Kong, which has a score of 68 on the power distribution index, achieved a score of 0.61 (ranked 45th globally) on the constraints on government power factor. Thus, while rule of law with Chinese Characteristics probably means that the Chinese government will never be as accountable to the law as European and North American countries, China, which has a score of 0.31, can make significant progress in that direction notwithstanding its cultural tendency regarding power distribution.

Long-Term Orientation: Hope for the Future

China's cultural long-term orientation provides some basis for optimism that China will make progress toward rule of law in the future. The long-term orientation of Chinese culture makes China somewhat more pragmatic than other countries and more open to change over time. China's score on the long-term orientation is 87, only surpassed by three other Asian countries: Japan (88), Taiwan (93), and South Korea (100). Several European countries also have high scores on this dimension: Ukraine (86), Germany (83), Estonia (82), Belgium (82), and Lithuania (82) (gerthofstede.com).

Figure 2.3 provides a visual representation of the countries with high scores on the long-term orientation dimension.

While long-term orientation does not necessarily correlate with rule of law generally or any particular rule of law factor, it suggests a culture openness to change and could support greater movement in China toward the rule of law. The other Asian countries with long-term orientation have significantly higher rule of law scores.[4] Japan scored 0.79 overall and is ranked 15th globally. South Korea scored 0.74 and is ranked 20th (WJP 2021, 10). The European countries with a long-term orientation also have higher rule of law scores than China. Germany scored 0.84 overall and is ranked fifth globally. Estonia, formerly part of

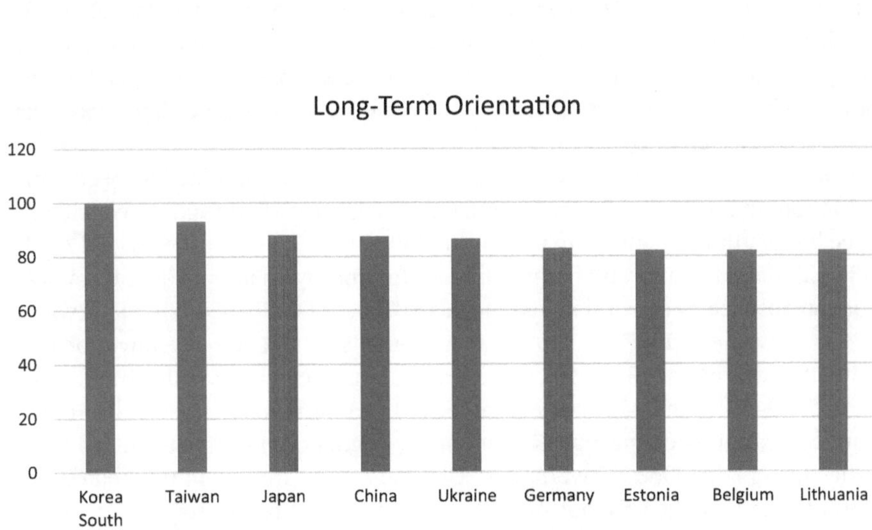

FIGURE 2.3 Long-Term Orientation Scores for Selected Countries

Source: Created by the author from data available at geerthofstede.com.

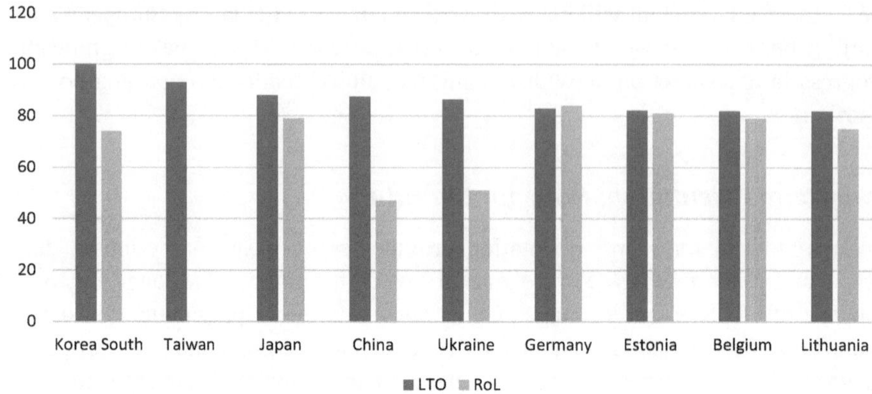

FIGURE 2.4 Long-Term Orientation and Rule of Law Scores for Selected Countries

Source: Created by the author from data available at geerthofstede.com and from the World Justice Project 2021 Rule of Law Index.

the Soviet bloc, scored 0.81 and ranked 11th. Belgium scored 0.79 and is ranked 14th (WJP 2021, 10). Lithuania scored 0.75 and is ranked 18th (WJP 2021, 11).

Figure 2.4 adds the rule of law scores (using a 100-point scale to be similar to the cultural dimension scale) to the long-term orientation scores.

Ukraine is the lowest scoring of these countries with long-term orientation (other than China), with a score of 0.51 and a rank of 74th, but Ukraine has improved its rule of law ranking over time. In 2014, Ukraine's overall score was 0.47 (WJP 2014, 173).[5] Although the overall score was not calculated in 2012–13, Ukraine's 2014 score was an improvement over 2012–2013 (same in most areas, but up in order and security) (WJP 2014, 33). If one averages the individual scores for the eight factors from 2012 to 2013, Ukraine's average rule of law score was 0.45 (see Agrast et al. 2012–13, 148).

One of the most significant areas of improvement for Ukraine has been anti-corruption. In 2012–13, Ukraine scored 0.25 in absence of corruption, which was in the bottom three countries in the world (94th out of 97) (Agrast et al. 2012–13, 148). Although Ukraine still has much room for improvement, in 2021, Ukraine's score on absence of corruption had increased to 0.33 (WJP 2021, 29). This was a 32% improvement from 2012 to 2013. Although still ranked quite low globally, 115th, that was out of 139 countries so was an improvement from the 3rd percentile in 2012–13 to the 17th percentile in 2021, up 14 points. Ukraine also made significant progress on the Open Government, Regulatory Enforcement, and Civil Justice factors. On Open Government, Ukraine moved from 0.44 (ranked 62 out of 97) to 0.57 (ranked 51 out of 139). On the Regulatory Enforcement factor, Ukraine moved up from 0.35 (ranked 91/97) to 0.44 (102/130). For Civil Justice, Ukraine progress was more modest, but still positive, from 0.52 (56/97) to 0.54 (64/139) (see Agrast et al. 2012–13, 148; WJP 2021, 168).

Figure 2.5 shows Ukraine's overall rule of law score and scores on the absence of corruption, open government, regulatory enforcement, and civil justice factors from 2012 to 2021.

Perhaps, China's long-term orientation, like Ukraine's, will allow it to make progress toward rule of law over the long run. Unfortunately, China's rule of law score has eroded some in the past few years. Its highest overall score came in 2017, a score of 0.50 with a global rank of 75th (WJP 2017, 17), putting it in the 33rd percentile. China's overall score went down to 0.47 in 2021 with a global ranking of 98th (WJP 2021, 23), putting it in the 29th percentile (out of 139 countries included in the index). A significant part of this erosion is attributable to the decline in protection of fundamental rights. In 2012–13, China's score on fundamental rights was 0.35 (Agrast et al. 2012–13, 77), which declined to 0.27 in 2021, giving China a global rank of 136th (WJP 2021, 64). This is the bottom 2 percentile for the index. This score can certainly improve and still be consistent with the Chinese cultural tendency toward collectivity. Singapore, with a similar cultural tendency, scored 0.67 on Fundamental Rights (WJP 2021, 149), which is more than double China's score of 0.27.

China's anti-corruption efforts tell a more positive story. In 2021, China's score on absence of corruption was 0.53, giving China a global rank of 55th (WJP 2021, 29), which put China in the 60th percentile. This is China's highest score on any factor other than Order and Security. Xi Jinping has made anti-corruption efforts a significant part of his rule (Zhang and Ginsburg 2019, 385–86). China's anti-corruption efforts were even more successful a few years ago when China achieved scores of 0.55 (WJP 2019, 23; WJP 2017–18, 33).

These anti-corruption efforts have made the Chinese government somewhat more accountable to law, have promoted greater legality, and have improved

FIGURE 2.5 Ukraine Rule of Law Score and Selected Factors, 2012–2021

Source: Created by the author from World Justice Project Current and Historical Data, accessed April 19, 2022, available at https://worldjusticeproject.org/our-work/research-and-data/wjp-rule-law-index-2021/current-historical-data.

China's scores on some other factors and sub-factors in the rule of law index. For example, China's score on the civil justice factor has improved significantly providing evidence of greater legality. In 2012–13, China's civil justice score was 0.43, ranked 82nd out of 97 countries (Agrast et al. 2012–13, 77). In 2021, China's score was 0.52 with a global rank of 74 out of 139 (WJP 2021, 64). This is an improvement of 21% and represents movement from the 15th percentile to the 38th.[6] Similarly, China improved on regulatory enforcement from 0.41 in 2012–13 (ranked 80 out of 97 globally) (Agrast et al. 2012–13, 77) to 0.49 in 2021 (ranked 76 out of 139). This was an improvement of 20% and represents movement from the 21st percentile to the 45th. Although China's score for constraints on government powers factor has eroded over time from 0.36 (Agrast et al. 2012–13, 77) to 0.31 (WJP 2021, 64), China's scores on the sub-factors of independent auditing and review and sanctions against officials for misconduct have improved from 0.35 to 0.42 and 0.37 to 0.47 respectively (Agrast et al. 2012–13, 77; WJP 2021, 64).

Figure 2.6 provides a visual representation of these data on China's scores overall and on selected factors and sub-factors.

The figure shows a more complicated picture for China than for Ukraine, but it shows some progress and that scores for some factors and sub-factors have improved (though in some cases, the improvements have been followed by some erosion or offset by lower scores on other factors or sub-factors). It may be that the decline in China's rule of law scores is temporary due to the pandemic and other global and political considerations. On the other hand, it may be that China is not willing to make a full commitment to the rule of law as defined by the WJP and its metrics. It is possible that China seeks to invoke rule of law "with Chinese

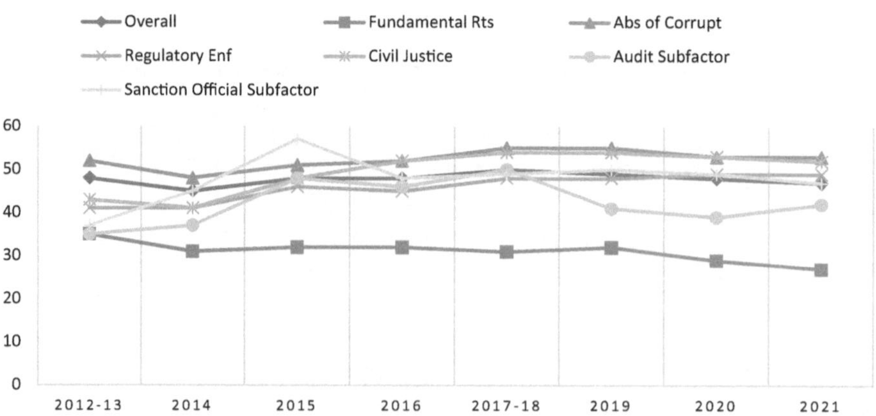

FIGURE 2.6 China Rule of Law Score and Selected Factors and Sub-Factors, 2012–2021

Source: Created by the author from World Justice Project Current and Historical Data, accessed April 19, 2022, available at https://worldjusticeproject.org/our-work/research-and-data/wjp-rule-law-index-2021/current-historical-data.

characteristics" to achieve "rule by law," rather than rule of law (see Tushnet 2014). The legal system may be used as an effective tool for governance and management of the economy (Zhang and Ginsburg 2019, 373–80). It may be that rule of law with Chinese characteristics is really just "rule by law" with the Chinese Communist Party remaining independent of legal restrictions. Efforts to control the government bureaucracy and Party members, which could be important to maintaining the public perception of legitimacy (Zhang and Ginsburg 2019, 380–90), could in the long run help to move toward rule of law with meaningful constraints on government power. With China's Long-Term Orientation resulting in a more pragmatic and open attitude, the anti-corruption efforts could perhaps evolve into meaningful limits on government powers and greater governmental openness.

3. Conclusion

Rule of law with Chinese characteristics may not be rule of law at all. It may be rule by law or even rule by man. Using the cultural dimensions developed by Geert Hofstede, this chapter has shown that Chinese culture has a strong commitment to collectivity (and a weak commitment to individualism) which correlated with weaker performance on the fundamental rights factor from the WJP rule of law index. This cultural dimension makes it unlikely that China will ever reach the level of protection for fundamental rights in Europe and North America. The top ten scores on protection of Fundamental Rights are all European countries.[7] While Chinese culture will likely prevent China from ever reaching those levels, other Asian countries with a similar cultural commitment to collectivity have performed much better than China and so provide evidence that China can certainly improve while still being committed to collectivity.[8]

China's cultural tolerance of centralized and unequal distribution of power, as reflected by its high score on the Power Distance dimension of culture, reduces the incentive for the Chinese government (and the Chinese Communist Party) to significantly limit governmental power. In the long run, this may prevent China from ever achieving what many in the West consider the essence of the rule of law. Using other Asian countries as benchmarks, however, China can certainly improve its score on the Constraints on Government Powers factor.[9] In addition, China's commitment to anti-corruption, and perhaps the need to promote government legitimacy, may, in the long run, help to move China toward greater constraints on government power.

It is impossible to know whether China will improve on the rule of law metrics used by the WJP, whether it will stagnate at its current levels, or whether it will further erode in its performance and commitment to the rule of law. While Chinese culture likely limits the upper end of China's potential for rule of law performance on the WJP metrics, the performance of other Asian countries with similar cultural dimensions shows that China can do much better notwithstanding its commitment to collectivity and its high power distribution score. With China's Long-Term

Orientation and with the efforts to use law to reduce corruption, improve efficient administration, and build governmental legitimacy, perhaps China's cultural pragmatism and openness will in the long run bring China closer to the rule of law performance of other Asian countries such as Japan, Singapore, and South Korea.

Notes

1 Although a score of 1.0 is excellent on this sub-factor, dozens of other countries also scored 1.0 on it. See World Justice Project, Current & Historical Data, accessed April 11, 2022, https://worldjusticeproject.org/our-work/research-and-data/wjp-rule-law-index-2021/current-historical-data.

2 These scores come from data provided on geerthofstede.com. The website has two versions of verified dimension scores, one that uses a 100-point scale and one that allows some scores that are higher than 100. I have used the scaled version. These data were last reviewed in 2015. *See* https://geerthofstede.com/research-and-vsm/dimension-data-matrix/, last visited April 19, 2022.

3 This was the name for this factor in the WJP 2012–13 Rule of Law Index that was used for the correlation analysis (see Thomas 2014, 5). The name of this factor has been changed to Constraints on Government Power in the 2021 index (WJP 2021, 28).

4 Unfortunately, Taiwan is not included in the Rule of Law index.

5 Ukraine was ranked 68th in 2014 (WJP 2014, 173). Although this is higher than the 2021 ranking of 74th in 2021, this ranking was out of 99 countries, so was in the 31st percentile. The 2021 ranking was out of 139 countries, so a ranking of 74th was much better comparatively, in the 46th percentile, 15 points higher.

6 Although this was significant improvement, it should be noted that China's most recent scores on the Civil Justice factor have eroded from the high point in 2017–2019, the same time when the absence of corruption scores were the highest. The Civil Justice scores were 0.54 during that period (WJP 2019, 28, 2017–18, 38), and went down to 0.53 in 2020 (WJP 2020, 28).

7 Denmark, Norway, Finland, Sweden, Austria, Germany, Luxembourg, Netherland, Belgium, and Ireland (WJP 2021, 31).

8 Japan scored 0.78 and was ranked 18th globally. South Korea scored 0.75 and was ranked 23rd. Hong Kong, a special administrative region of China, scored 0.61 and ranked 54th globally (WJP 2021, 31).

9 Japan was the Asian country with the highest score on Constraints on Government Power factor. It scored 0.72 and was ranked 22nd globally. South Korea scored 0.71 and was ranked 25th. Singapore scored 0.67 and was ranked 32nd. Hong Kong, part of China but a special administrative region, scored 0.61, ranking 45th globally (WJP 2021, 28).

References

Agrast, Mark David, Juan Carlos Botero, Joel Martinez, Alejandro Ponce, and Christine S. Pratt. 2012–2013. *The World Justice Project Rule of Law Index*. Washington, DC: World Justice Project. https://worldjusticeproject.org/our-work/publications/rule-law-index-reports/wjp-rule-law-index-2012–2013-report.

Belton, Rachel Kleinfeld. 2005. *Competing Definitions of the Rule of Law: Implications for Practitioners*. Washington, DC: Carnegie Endowment for International Peace.

Botero, Juan Carlos, and Alejandro Ponce. 2011. "Measuring the Rule of Law." WJP Working Paper No. 1. https://papers.ssrn.com/sol3/papers.cfm?abstract_id=1966257.

Geerthofstede.com. n.d. "Dimension Data Matrix." Accessed April 19, 2022. https://geerthofstede.com/research-and-vsm/dimension-data-matrix/.

———. "The 6-D Model of National Culture." Accessed April 19, 2022. https://geerthofstede.com/culture-geert-hofstede-gert-jan-hofstede/6d-model-of-national-culture/.

Hofstede, Geert. 1980. *Culture's Consequences, International Differences in Work-Related Values*. Beverly Hills: Sage.

———. 2001. *Culture's Consequences: Comparing Values, Behaviors, Institutions and Organizations Across Nations*, 2nd ed. Thousand Oaks: Sage.

Orts, Eric W. 2001. "The Rule of Law in China." *Vanderbilt Journal of Transnational Law* 34: 43–115.

Peerenboom, Randall. 2002. *China's Long March Toward Rule of Law*. Cambridge: Cambridge University Press.

———. 2004. "Varieties of Rule of Law." In *Asian Discourses of Rule of Law: Theories and Implementation of Rule of Law in Twelve Asian Countries, France and the U.S.*, edited by Randall Peerenboom. London: Routledge.

Sarsfield, Rodolfo. 2010. "What Is the Rule of Law (and Is Not)? Accessed April 19, 2022. https://papers.ssrn.com/sol3/papers.cfm?abstract_id=1667682.

Thomas, Jeffrey E. 2014. "Rule of Law With Chinese Characteristics: An Empirical Cultural Perspective on China, Hong Kong and Singapore." *Asia Pacific Law Review* 22 (2): 115–46.

Tushnet, Mark. 2014. "Rule by Law or Rule of Law?" *Asia Pacific Law Review* 22 (2): 79–92.

World Justice Project. 2014. *Rule of Law Index*. Washington, DC: World Justice Project. https://worldjusticeproject.org/sites/default/files/files/wjp_rule_of_law_index_2014_report.pdf.

———. 2015. *Rule of Law Index*. Washington, DC: World Justice Project. https://worldjusticeproject.org/sites/default/files/roli_2015_0.pdf.

———. 2016. *Rule of Law Index*. Washington, DC: World Justice Project. https://worldjusticeproject.org/sites/default/files/documents/RoLI_Final-Digital_0.pdf.

———. 2017–18. *Rule of Law Index*. Washington, DC: World Justice Project. https://worldjusticeproject.org/sites/default/files/documents/WJP-ROLI-2018-June-Online-Edition_0.pdf.

———. 2019. *Rule of Law Index*. Washington, DC: World Justice Project. https://worldjusticeproject.org/sites/default/files/documents/WJP-ROLI-2019-Single%20Page%20View-Reduced_0.pdf.

———. 2020. *Rule of Law Index*. Washington, DC: World Justice Project. https://worldjusticeproject.org/sites/default/files/documents/WJP-ROLI-2020-Online_0.pdf.

———. 2021. *Rule of Law Index*. Washington, DC: World Justice Project. https://worldjusticeproject.org/sites/default/files/documents/WJP-INDEX-21.pdf.

———. n.d. "Current & Historical Data." Accessed April 19, 2022. https://worldjusticeproject.org/our-work/research-and-data/wjp-rule-law-index-2021/current-historical-data.

Zhang, Mo. 2010. "The Socialist Legal System With Chinese Characteristics: China's Discourse for the Rule of Law and a Bitter Experience." *Temple International and Comparative Law Journal* 24: 1–64.

Zhang, Taisu, and Tom Ginsburg. 2019. "China's Turn Toward Law." *Virginia Journal of International Law* 59: 313–65.

3

A HUNDRED SCHOOLS OF THOUGHT CONTENDING ON CONSTITUTIONALISM—THE SHORT LIFE OF THE GREAT DEBATE OF CONSTITUTIONALISM REMEMBERED

Guobin Zhu[1]

Introduction

The dissemination of the concepts, thoughts, and theories of Western constitutionalism in China first appeared in the 1980s during the reform and opening up era. We can observe that after the Tiananmen Square Incident in the Summer of 1989, the Chinese theoretical and academic circles, including legal circle certainly, experienced a period of regression, confusion, and stagnation for about a decade.

At the turn of the new century, precisely, it should be after 1999 that the legal circle, especially the constitutional circle, began to systematically discuss the concepts and theories of constitutionalism in China again, when in this year, China revised its Constitution and wrote in it that "the People's Republic of China implements the rule of law and builds a socialist country under the rule of law" (Article 5). Thus, people saw reform and progress in sight. Constitutionalism (the Chinese translation is *Xianzheng* 憲政, *Xianzhengzhuyi* 憲政主義, or *Lixianzhuyi* 立憲主義, being used interchangeably depending on the preference of scholars) was one of the hot and attractive topics of contention in Chinese academia. It was not an exaggeration to state that national academia was mobilized, and scholars from law, political science, economics, and other related social sciences fields, and even politicians and officials in charge of the ideological work of the Communist Party of China ("the CPC"), actively participated in the debate on constitutionalism and continued reform of political and economic systems. A large number of academic works including translated works of important foreign authors were published around this period, and various academic trends and schools of thought emerged and initially formed. The impact of this academic blossoming, if not qualified yet as an academic movement calling for constitutionalism, was immense and far-reaching on the definition and understanding of constitutionalism and the realization of it in China.

DOI: 10.4324/9781003294887-4

Unfortunately, this debate of great significance was halted due to the dramatical adjustment of the leading ideology of the ruling party and in the meanwhile, owing to the changeover of the political leadership between 2012 and 2013. In May 2013, Yang Xiaoqing, a professor of jurisprudence from Renmin University of China Law School all of a sudden published an article criticizing and opposing constitutionalism. "One stone stirred up a thousand waves" as a Chinese expression demonstrates; it officially launched a nationwide campaign opposing constitutionalism and political reform in China.

This chapter retrospectively records the sudden change of wind and the event following Yang's article and introduces the main academic schools that formed before and around 2013, in hopes to leave an as authentic as possible record of this glorious, although short-lived, academic history of constitutional studies. I want to make a disclaimer here that in view of the length limit, it is not possible for me to include every single representative author and his/her works in this record. Roughly speaking, constitutionalism is a thing of the past after 2013.

1. The Countercurrents Against Constitutionalism

1.1 How Did This Sudden U-Turn Take Place in 2013?

On December 4, 2012, Xi Jinping, the Secretary General of the CPC, delivered a speech on constitutionalism on the occasion of celebrating 30 years of promulgation and implementation of the current Constitution. Xi stressed that "the full implementation of the Constitution is the primary task and fundamental work for the construction of Socialist state under the rule of law" and "the life of the Constitution lies in its implementation and so does the authority of the Constitution" (Xi 2012). It seemed that Xi was enthusiastic about constitutionalism and supportive of advancing constitutionalism in China.

When many intellectuals and scholars were still deeply immersed in this enthusiastic and encouraging high-profile speech on the implementation of constitution and constitutionalism by the chief leader of the Chinese Party and state, the publication of a propaganda style journal article in May 2013 suddenly poisoned this joyful atmosphere and overthrew the situation. This explosive article, named "A Comparative Study of Constitutionalism and People's Democratic Regime," was authored by Yang Xiaoqing, a retired professor of jurisprudence at Renmin University of China School of Law, and published in one of the CPC's theoretical fora, the semimonthly journal *Red Flag Manuscripts* (*Hongqi Wengao*, 紅旗文稿) on May 21, 2013. It bluntly declared that "constitutionalism only belongs to capitalism, and it is not compatible with socialist people's democracy" (Yang 2013). Yang's opinion ostensibly ran counter to the official position on constitutionalism.

A round of seemingly organized debate aiming at fighting against constitutionalism immediately emerged in China. On the basis of a review of the focuses and contents of the articles published since May 2013, I roughly divide this several-month-long tense polemic into three phases/rounds.

The first phase of the debate was located from May to June 2013, whose main focus was placed on the denial of constitutionalism as generally applicable value and particularly, on its non-applicability in China. Yang's aforementioned article blew the horn. On the next day on May 22, the populist newspaper *Global Times* (*Huanqiu Shibao*, 環球時報) first supported Yang with its Editorial entitled "Constitutionalism Is Tantamount to a Denial of the Chinese Development Path." The Editorial pointed out that constitutionalism essentially stands opposite to the current PRC constitution (HQSB 2013). On May 29, an article entitled "Clearly Understanding the Essence of Constitutionalism," authored by Zheng Zhixue, was published in another CPC's theoretical journal *Party Building* (*Dang Jian*, 黨建), arguing that the concept of constitutionalism is only suitable for bourgeois capitalism, and it is a covert call for the end of the Party leadership and the subversion of socialism, and a "discourse trap" that must be avoided at all costs in China (Zheng 2013). Following the increasingly heating polemic, the *Red Flag Manuscripts* continued to publish more articles that aimed at systematically counterattacking constitutionalism, which was represented by Wang Youting's "Some Viewpoints on Constitutionalism" (Wang 2013) and Yu Zhong's "'Chinese Dream' and the Choice of the Path of Democratic Politics" (Yu 2013). The former took an entire denial of both socialist constitutionalism and capitalist constitutionalism, and the latter claimed that the "Chinese dream" is higher than the dream of constitutionalism.

The second phase of the debate basically took place in August 2013. During this tense period, a number of articles were published, first of all, attempting to draw the lessons from the collapse of the USSR, and secondly and mainly, targeting the American promoted "universal values"—constitutionalism, and the American idea of human rights and its practice. The representative works were, just to name three: Ma Zhongcheng's "The American Constitutionalism is a Misnomer" in *People's Daily Overseas Edition* (*Renmin Ribao Haiwaiban, 人民日報海外版*) (Ma 2013), Yang Yunguang's "Interpreting American Idea of Human Rights and Practice of Human Rights" in the aforementioned *Red Flag Manuscripts* (Yang Y 2013), and Xie Xiaoguang's "Why is the U.S. so Keen to Promote 'Universal Value'" in the *Red Flag Manuscripts* too (Xie 2013). The core point of view is, as demonstrated in Xie's article, that "the purpose of promoting 'universal value' in China is very clear; it aims at guiding the direction of China' development toward the well-set capitalist track, overthrowing the fundamental political system of China, and ending the State power system under the leadership of the CPC" (Xie 2013).

From September to October (actually to early 2014), the polemic entered its third wave, during which the attention of propaganda works turned to the ideological front and several local party leaders joined this campaign against constitutionalism. Suffices it to quote two articles to illustrate this tendency: the first is "A Profound Understanding of the Extreme Importance of Ideological Work" which was authored by Yin Hanning, Director of Propaganda Department of the Hubei Provincial Party Committee (Yin 2013), and the second "Leading Cadres

Must Strengthen their Political Determination," signed by Yuan Chunqing, the Party Secretary of Shanxi Province (Yuan 2013). [Ironically, Yuan was ordered to step down in early September 2014 due to his alleged deep involvement in corruption saga in Shanxi, where he served as Secretary of the Party during 2010–2014.]

Judging from the sporadic articles and comments, we can discover that this politically motivated polemic gradually slowed down and then cooled down close to the end of 2013 to a lower level in terms of the number of clearly pointed articles against constitutionalism and the "fire force" of these publications. And judging from the quantity of works and their impact on the academia and theoretical circle, we also have reason to believe that a strong allied force of anti-constitutionalism has taken form in China. This force successfully gathered both officials and academics mainly from areas of Marxist studies, political science, and law, and most of their works are still present today on the Internet and other public spaces, including journals and newspapers, and new media such as Weibo (Micro-blog).

Before concluding, it might be interesting to include in this factual account the article published by Wang Weiguang, then President of China Academy of Social Sciences, in the 2014 September Issue of *Red Flag Manuscripts*. Entitled "Adhering to the People's Democratic Dictatorship Is Not Unjustified," this article asserted that it was impossible for class struggle within the country to extinguish on its own and the people's democratic dictatorship must absolutely not be abolished (Wang 2014). Soon after the publication of Wang's article, *Study Times* (*Xuexi Shibao*, 學習時報) of the Central Party School, a weekly newspaper, published an article calling for a complete rejection of "taking class struggle as the key line/guiding principle" ("以階級鬥爭爲綱") (Han 2014); it didn't mention the name of Wang, but commentators believed it was written as a response to Wang's extremely orthodoxy (and in my view, obviously leftist) position. Despite the strong support from the old and hardliners, needless to say, Wang's article has troubled the water of ideology. Not only is it because he was the President of China Academy of Social Sciences, the chief advisory institution, but also the main points he put forward in the article contradicted the main ideological themes and thus created some confusion in the field of ideological work of the Party. On September 29, 2014, the Academy of which Wang was the President published a one-page article on its official website trying to clarify the meaning of "taking class struggle as the key line" and to face the relentless criticism.

1.2 Understanding Counter-Constitutionalism in a Larger Setting

The fact that the countercurrent against constitutionalism has taken form in such a short period of time, roughly from May to October 2013, was not surprising and can only be understood in association with the long-lasting theoretical and ideological debate on the Chinese path of development and also the internal struggle regarding the formation of the central political line within the CPC. The latter does not constitute a focus of this chapter even though it is of direct relevance to approaching the controversy over constitutionalism, and I will leave it aside.

It is believed that the authors who have contributed to the countercurrent aiming at refusing or denying constitutionalism in China were specifically encouraged by the "Communiqué on the Current State of the Ideological Sphere of the Central Committee of the CPC," representing the new Party line on ideological work, circulated within the Party by its General Office in April 2013, in addition to their conservative political stance. This Communiqué, being the ninth Working Paper issued in 2013, has once been called "Document No 9" (*Jiuhao Wenjian*, 九號文件). The Editors of *China File* observed that (China File 2013):

> President Xi Jinping has signaled that a significant new wave of economic liberalization may be in the works. But in the realm of political reform, Xi also has signaled a deep reluctance. In fact, many of the actions taken and techniques used under his year of leadership suggest a return to ideas and tactics that hark back to the days of Mao Zedong.

The Editors further noted that:

> What suggests the significance of Document 9 is the fact that a worrisomely harsh crackdown against human rights lawyers, media outlets, academics, and other such independent thinkers has followed. But, whether Document 9 is the expression of one faction or that of the central Chinese leadership itself is still uncertain.
>
> *Mingjing* Magazine, a U.S.-based Chinese-language magazine, obtained and published the full text of the document in September 2013 in print. We are confident it is authentic and translate and re-publish it here with *Mingjing*'s permission.

In the Document, it was summarized that "the Party leadership was being urged to guard against seven political 'perils', including constitutionalism, civil society, 'nihilistic' views of history, 'universal values', and the promotion of 'the West's view of media'." The Document also called on Party members to strengthen their resistance to "infiltration" by outside ideas, renew their commitment to work "in the ideological sphere," and handle with renewed vigilance all ideas, institutions, and people deemed threatening to unilateral Party rule (China File 2013).

The Communiqué stated that:

> "Currently, the following false ideological trends, positions, and activities all deserve note":
>
> i. Promoting Western constitutional democracy: an attempt to undermine the current leadership and the socialism with Chinese characteristics system of governance;

ii. Promoting "universal values" in an attempt to weaken the theoretical foundations of the Party's leadership;
iii. Promoting civil society in an attempt to dismantle the ruling party's social foundation;
iv. Promoting neoliberalism, attempting to change China's basic economic system;
v. Promoting the West's idea of journalism, challenging China's principle that the media and publishing system should be subject to Party discipline;
vi. Promoting historical nihilism, trying to undermine the history of the CPC and of New China;
vii. Questioning reform and opening-up and the socialist nature of socialism with Chinese characteristics.

Since Document 9 urged to guard against seven political "perils," Chinese scholars often summarize it as "prohibiting the spreading and promotion of seven ideas" and simply call it "Seven No-Mentions" (*Qi Bujiang*, 七不講).

On the surface, we have strong reasons to believe that the so-called "Seven No-mentions" was directly derived from the previously promoted "Five No-doings" (*Wu Bugao*, 五不搞), first pronounced by Wu Bangguo and then the Chairman of the National People's Congress Standing Committee (NPCSC) on March 10, 2013, at the NPC Session. Wu declared that "we should solemnly pronounce that, based on the Chinese national situation, we must not adopt the following: the multi-party alternation of power, diversity of guiding ideology, separation of three powers and bicameralism, federalism, and privatization" (Wu 2011).

The last official document of the Party that urged to strengthen the ideological work was the speech pronounced by Xi Jinping, the Secretary General of the Party, during the National Conference on Propaganda and Ideological Work held on August 19–20, 2013, in Beijing (Xi 2013). Interestingly, only the summary, but not the whole text, of this Speech was widely made public. Scholars have often named it "August 19 Speech" (8.19 *Jianghua*, 8.19講話).

Comparing the "August 19 Speech" with "Document No 9," one can see that in the former, Xi Jinping not only proclaimed his stance on the ideological work of the Party but also gave instructions on relevant important aspects concerning the Party building and the Chinese characteristics (Xi 2013).

1.3 So, the Wind Has Changed

All the aforementioned have brought about confusion and disorders among academics and officials in charge of the Party's ideological work. What did this mean actually? The general feel we obtain from reading and observation can be described as follows.

First of all, the majority of intellectuals have since then become skeptical about the intention of this policy move and preferred to adopt a "wait and see" attitude based on the past experiences of struggle, particularly the ones acquired in the eras of Mao Zedong and Deng Xiaoping during the Anti-Rightist Movement in 1956–1957, the Campaign of Clearing Capitalist Spiritual Pollution in 1983, and the Political Campaign anti-Bourgeois Liberalization in 1986. They did have reasons to doubt and verify if this was a game of "drawing snakes out of their holes" (*Yin She Chu Dong*, 引蛇出洞) as once played by Mao prior to the Anti-Rightist Movement.

Second, scholars and some general public might think and believe that there was no consensus reached yet at the top level of the Party nomenclature regarding the next direction to march for the Party. Against this backdrop, the direction was defined later in mid-November 2013 by the Party in "The Decision on Major Issues Concerning Comprehensively Deepening Reforms," a document of great importance adopted at the third Plenum of the Central Committee of the 18th Congress of the CPC ("the Decision," CC 2013). In this Decision, the Party surprised the public by adopting a much-shrunk version of (a formalist, or to say, a thin version of) constitutionalism and the rule of law. In Part IX "Rule of Law," the relevant measures have been highlighted (CC 2013):

> Efforts are to be made to deepen the reform of the justice system, to protect the people's rights and let the masses feel equality and justice in every court verdict.
>
> 30. Uphold the Constitution and laws;
> 32. Ensure independence and fairness in courts and prosecuting bodies;
> 33. Let the judicial system be more transparent;
> 34. Boost the judicial system to protect human rights.

Compared with a common understanding of constitutionalism, the aforementioned is certainly far below the widely agreed standard, even to moderate intellectuals. Compared with the previously cited other official documents of the Party, the terms of constitution and the rule of law continued to exist in the political discourses. Given that Xi Jinping and his team had just taken power for less than two years from 2012 onward, we could argue that Xi and his entourage needed time to explore and adjust the direction and political line to take in the future, and this explained the zigzag of ideological policy-making. [It has been proven that this observation was rather optimistic in the light of the strengthened control of ideology and the censorship over publications today.]

In the end, people speculated, but did not express in writing, that the chaotic situation during May to early 2014 reflected the continued political struggle within the Party between the two major factions that are "Second Generation of the Red Revolutionaries" (*Hong Er Dai*, 紅二代, whose parents are professional revolutionaries and generals) and "Cadres from the Communist Youth League" (*Tuan Pai*, 團派, most of whom grew up from grassroots after the founding of the People's Republic), and these two factions were disagreeable to each other before the making of general policy insofar as the political line and the reform to undertake were concerned. The outcome of the political compromise, as some people so believed, has been written into the aforementioned Decision.

Looking back at the history of this short period today in early 2022, it is all clear to conclude that the Chinese Party state has obviously abandoned the original ideas and doctrine of constitutionalism in their official discourses, and furthermore, the leadership has taken a rather hardline toward political reform. A milestone marking this change is obviously the constitutional amendment in 2018 which has exerted a far-reaching impact on China's political construct and social development. Many commentators have expressed similar views on it.

2. Hundred Flowers Blooming and Hundred Schools Contending

Around this period of time, advocates and supporters of constitutionalism ("擁憲派") have together put forward various counterarguments that openly oppose the views of the counter-constitutionalism camp ("反憲派," hereafter referred to as CCC). However, they were neither unified nor sharing major ideas promoting and/or backing up constitutionalism. They represent different currents of thought in favor of (their version of) constitutionalism.

Broadly speaking, there were/are two major schools/currents from among the advocates of constitutionalism: the self-proclaimed Socialist Constitutionalism School (SCS, often abbreviated as *She Xian Pai*, 社憲派) and Liberal Constitutionalism School (LCS, *Zi Xian Pai*, 自憲派). Tong Zhiwei named the latter 泛憲派, and its English translation is "Universal Constitutionalism Faction (UCF)" on his Sina Weibo (Tong 2014), which literally means Pan-constitutionalism School. The theories advanced by these two major schools, however, demonstrate enormous differences between them. Thus, there appeared a situation of tripartite contention and confrontation in the controversy of constitutionalism. In retrospect, SCS, LCS, and CCC came under the spotlight as protagonists in this significant academic (as well as political) debate under the heading of constitutionalism. The aforementioned three schools evidently cannot encompass all the academic positions and currents on constitutionalism.

In addition to SCS and LCS, we can state that there existed two other currents of thought also advocating constitutionalism, which can be named Statist Constitutionalism School (SCSc, *Guo Xian Pai*, 國憲派) and Confucian Constitutionalism School (CCS, *Ru Xian Pai*, 儒憲派), respectively. Confucian constitutionalism was being promoted, but it occupied a rather marginal position due to its size and academic influence, but interestingly, it had a wider spreading overseas, while Statist/nationalist constitutionalism mainly focused its central attention on building a constitutional theory aiming at justifying the leadership of the CPC in China.

During 2016–2017, the City University of Hong Kong Press published a series of eight original works on constitutionalism by either well-established Chinese scholars or rising stars of constitutional law and jurisprudence. The Series, under my direction, is named Constitutionalism in China (*Xianzheng Zhongguo*, 憲政中國), and the principal objective of the publication is to record theoretical achievements, pass on academic heritage from our generation to the next generation, and preserve the valuable academic and cultural legacy. They include works on liberal/libertarian constitutionalism, socialist constitutionalism, political constitutionalism, Confucian constitutionalism, and new realistic theory of constitutionalism. A complete list of them is presented as follows: (i) *Common Sense of Constitutionalism* (*Xianzheng Changshi*, 憲法常識, authored by Zhang Qianfan and published in 2016); (ii) *Essentials of Constitutionalism* (*Xianzheng Yaoyi*, 憲政要義, authored by Wang Jianxun and published in 2017); (iii) *Reform of Chinese Constitutional System* (*Zhongguo Xianzhi Zhi Weixin*, 中國憲制之維新, authored by Tong Zhiwei and published in 2016); (iv) *Research on Socialist Constitutionalism* (*Shehui Zhuyi Xianzheng Yanjiu*, 社會主義憲政研究, authored by Qin Qianhong & Ye Haibo and published in 2017); (v) *Political Constitution and Future Constitutional System* (*Zhengzhi Xianfa Yu Weilai Xianzhi*, 政治憲法與未來憲制, authored by Gao Quanxi and published in 2016); (vi) *Chinese Road to Political Constitution* (*Zhengzhi Xianfa de Zhongguo Zhidao*, 政治憲法的中國之道, authored by Tian Feilong and published in 2017); (vii) *On Confucian Constitutionalism* (*Ruja Xianzheng Lun*, 儒家憲政論, authored by Yao Zhongqiu and published in 2016); and (viii) *What is the Constitution of China?* (*Xianfa Heyi Zhongguo*, 憲法何以中國, authored by Zhai Zhiyong and published in 2017). I want to add to this list another book authored by Tong Zhiwei, which is published outside the Series by the same Press in Spring 2022, and it is *The Search for the Path to Chinese Constitutionalism* (*Zhongguo Lixian Zhuyi Daolu Qiusuo*, 中國立憲主義道路求索).

The following parts basically describe and present the central ideas of each of the schools or camps, in hopes that after this review, we would be able to achieve a better and deeper understanding of this nationwide polemics and the representative outcomes.

2.1 Socialist Constitutionalism School: Seeking Consensus and Solution Within the Subsisting Constitutional Order

Without any doubt, the front runners of the Socialist Constitutionalism School, i.e., SCS, were/are Tong Zhiwei, a professor from East China University of Politics and Law in Shanghai, and Qin Qianhong, a professor from Wuhan University Law School. Tong once worked at Wuhan University for years before moving to Shanghai. Both always held sharp ideas and together played an irreplaceable, or to say, leading role in the debate. As early as 2008, Qin already co-authored a book titled *A Study of Socialist Constitutionalism* (Qin and Ye 2008). In the "Postscript," the authors claimed the ownership of "Socialist constitutionalism," a formulation first put forward by them in 2003. Tong also believed that the formulation of "Socialist constitutionalism" as a school of thought was established in 2008 (Tong 2013a, 2022).

Even so, as criticized by an academic, "the SCS is actually constructed out of the need to fight against the emergence of the foresaid anti-constitutionalism force, rather than a spontaneous scholarly integration" (Chen 2013). For this, Tong also admitted frankly that

> there is no such a unified socialist constitutional jurist groups in China. The advocates distinguish themselves by their rather different points of view, but their common ground is that they all cherish and respect the existing constitution (this does not exclude criticism over it), and they are determined to support any development toward constraining public power, and protecting fundamental rights of citizens under the overall framework of the existing Constitution.
>
> *(Tong 2013a, 2022)*

2.1.1 Tong Zhiwei and His Main Ideas

Tong strongly advocated his main proposition of SCS in the course of defining Socialist constitutionalism and insisted on the efficient and comprehensive implementation of the current Constitution which, to him, has the fully recognized legitimacy. "Socialist constitutionalism," as defined by Tong, should refer to this situation where:

> whilst not denying the constitutional legitimacy of the CPC's long-term rule, [we assert that] in the Constitution, the scope of the Party's power shall be limited and the ways of functioning of these powers shall be specifically regulated, the fundamental rights of citizens shall be protected, and the Constitution shall be fully and effectively implemented.
>
> *(Tong 2013b)*

Tong further supported his definition in this manner: although a rather large proportion of people in China were not ardent supporters or even reserved about the long-term ruling of the CPC, they showed no objection or hedge to this issue. Members of SCS must endeavor to win back the endorsement of these people or at least, persuade them not to oppose, so as to expand their social identity (Tong 2013b).

It is already evident to us that Tong's definition of Socialist constitutionalism could be approached from the following perspectives.

First and the foremost, it is about the constitutional legitimacy of the CPC's ruling. Tong elaborated on the reasons why the CPC's constitutional status should not be challenged nowadays from three different angles (Tong 2013b):

> In the first place, the CPC's long-term ruling status is a result of the confrontation of political forces and will not shift with man's will. The CPC will never give up its existing ruling power in accordance with its

> self-maintaining theories and value system. In the second, the widespread social basis and strengths which the CPC owns should not be ignored. To be specific, the CPC now enjoys the support of the overwhelming majority from the following classes: in-service or retired Party and governmental cadres, officers and soldiers of armed forces, personalities from the democratic parties and groups and from the Chinese People's Political Consultative Conference, senior intellectuals, all of whom are enjoying a variety of preferential treatments; senior and middle-rank managers in state-owned enterprises and public institutions with high wages, a portion of private entrepreneurs whose freedom and private-property rights are guaranteed by the authorities, and other social classes who have acquired practical benefits and advantages from the implementation of opening-up policy. In the third and last, from the pragmatist and progressive perspective, there is simply no need to challenge the constitutional status of CPC's long-term ruling, which absolutely matters to the CPC and concerns with its bottom line, and the violation of it would trigger the sense of defence and counter-attack of the ruling party. Therefore, a consensus should be reached between all the sectors of intellectuals and the CPC, this is: intellectuals support the CPC, and the CPC actively and vigorously pushes forward the political reform.

Second, as far as the relationship between the CPC and the current Constitution is concerned, Tong quoted Gao Kai, the former Director of Research Division of the Legislative Work Commission of the NPC, as having expressed the following standpoints in "The Constitution is as the Flag of Political Structure Reform": "There is no 'the Communist Party' but 'all political parties' in the text of the Constitution. Treating the CPC as one of 'all political parties' reflects the idea of 'all political parties are equal'" (Tong 2013c, 2022). Tong insisted that his stance of "the CPC under the Constitution" was based on and derived from Article 5 (3) (4) of the Constitution which reads:

> All state organs, the armed forces, all political parties and public organizations and all enterprises and institutions must abide by the Constitution and the law. All acts in violation of the Constitution or the law must be investigated. No organization or individual is privileged to be beyond the Constitution or the law.

In his opinion, "all state organs" should include, of course, the CPC. The principle of "the CPC under the Constitution" should imply that there is a boundary that helps define the CPC's ruling power. In such a sense, Tong concluded that "the CPC should well define the scope of its Party power in strict accordance with the Constitution, and practice a self-restraint via legislation or even constitutional amendments" (Tong 2013c, 2022).

Third and the last, as regards safeguarding citizen's fundamental rights, Tong pointed out that, in view of the fact that the current constitutional law has been widely confirmed and justified as a good law by the mainland constitutional scholars, the focus of constitutional implementation therefore lied largely in whether the constitutional clauses of fundamental rights were workable or not. Thus, to realize constitutional rights, the CPC ought to actively facilitate the constitutional practice in the following aspects (Tong 2013b):

First and fundamentally, citizen's freedom of speech, freedom of association, and freedom of religion should be implemented and guaranteed by national legislation, and especially, citizen's right to supervise public authorities and their agents shall be protected. Second, based on the premise that the CPC's representation predominates local people's congresses at all levels, the CPC should legally embark on a more direct, open, and competitive election and extend the direct election to a higher level. Third, it was a pressing need to establish a trial system based on the judge's independent adjudicative power and a system that assures that the judge can work responsibly and incorruptibly. Finally, a mechanism of strict restraint of power from the exterior of the agencies of public security, public prosecution, and national security should be constructed, and the activities of these agencies should be subject to strict control in order to protect citizen's liberty and freedom of communication better and in a feasible way.

Tong believed that there was ample reason for the CPC, the ruler of China, to implement those constitutional rights. As stressed by him,

> Safeguarding clauses on fundamental rights in the current Constitution are the most formal promise given by the CPC to protect citizens' rights and liberties. The CPC definitely understand that it will confront immense risk of political and moral failure if it breaks the promise, which will, in the end, cause severe damage to its governance and reign.
>
> *(Tong 2013c, 2022)*

2.1.2 Qin Qianhong and His Theory

As a professor of constitutional law at Wuhan University and then a local lawmaker from Wuhan Municipal People's Congress Standing Committee, Hubei Province, Qin systematically elucidated his basic ideas on Socialist constitutionalism as early as 2004 in this very first paper "On Socialist Constitutionalism" (Qin and Ye 2004). He aimed at providing China, a socialist state, with logical and theoretical support for its constitutionalism construction. Nearly a decade after that, Qin wrote again two more articles on this theme, and they were "Discussion again on Socialist Constitutionalism" (Qin 2013a) and "Restatement of My Viewpoints on Socialist Constitutionalism" (Qin 2013b), attempting to further consolidate the theory of Socialist constitutionalism so as to draw forth the general consensus.

Compared with Tong, a precise definition of Socialist constitutionalism has not been generated and according to Qin, should not be given hastily. In Qin's mind, the reason why Socialist constitutionalism could not be meticulously defined attributed to its "open quality" (Qin 2013a), and specifically, to its actual meaning of "Socialist/m" in the context of the present China and to the vagueness of "constitutionalism" (Qin 2013b). In Qin's wordings, Socialist constitutionalism was primarily a historical concept or "a new political idea coping with social governance failure and dysfunction of power restraint mechanism" (Qin 2013b). Meanwhile, when it comes to the uncontrollable institutional corruption which has acted as the greatest challenge to Chinese politics, Qin asserted that "constitutionalism," as a check of political power, not only was the best choice for anti-corruption enterprise but also indicated the orientation of political reform (Qin 2013b), and these were realistic and necessary parameters of Socialist constitutionalism.

How did Qin formulate his theory of Socialist constitutionalism? Grounded on the classical Marxist theory, Qin framed a compatible relationship between socialism and constitutionalism based on this logic (Qin and Ye 2004).

First, constitutionalism was, and would be, both the necessity of socialist construction and the feature in identifying socialism. Second, only socialism could effectively activate the substantial constitutionalism. Determined by the historical stage and social reality in which the Socialist China is situated now, the first aspect covered the following four propositions: (i) "only constitutionalism-construction can achieve the fundamental value of socialism"; (ii) "constitutionalism is a vitally significant part for identifying socialism and building socialist political civilization"; (iii) "considering this contemporary environment where the initial stage of socialism and capitalism are existing side by side, it is proven absolutely necessary for socialist China to construct constitutionalism"; and (iv) "constitutionalism-construction in socialist China has unique historical significance." The second aspect of his rhetoric can be approached with reference to the intrinsic relevance between the constitution and the rule of law, which briefly mirrors the logical relation between socialism and the realization of substantial constitutionalism. According to Qin's theory, socialism is initially pertinent to constitutionalism. This notwithstanding, he has never neglected the universal value of constitutionalism or socialist constitutionalism.

> After human rights as primary value have been included as one of the Socialist core values, the "socialist quality" of Chinese constitutionalism and the "capitalist quality" of constitutionalism of the Western countries become different only in terms of language usage and in form, they constitute two different branches in the genealogy of constitutionalism, and then converge to become the common civilization of mankind.
>
> *(Qin 2013a)*

The universal value of Socialist constitutionalism was expressly based on the consensus regarding the understanding of constitutionalism. The approach adopted by SCS is conveniently equipped with a methodological function in reaching consensus from all camps. On this matter, Tong and Qin, even the whole group of Socialist constitutionalists, would agree with each other. For instance,

Han Dayuan, a professor of constitutional law and then Dean of Law School of Renmin University of China, once put forward his viewpoint of "using the idea of Socialist constitutionalism to reach consensus" in an interview with *China News Weekly* (*Zhongguo Xinwen Zhoukan, 中國新聞周刊*) (Shen 2012).

Following Qin's point, the reasons why Socialist constitutionalism was capable of formulating or even achieving a comprehensive consensus were presented as follows: primarily, after the rule of law clause and human rights protection clause have been added to the Constitution, Socialist constitutionalism would inevitably follow this tendency. Second, it would be more likely to reach a consensus between the authorities and the people under the banner of Socialist constitutionalism, thereby arriving at a constitutional moment. Third, SCS took the current Constitution as the premise and the basis of discussion (Qin 2013a).

In a word, reaching a consensus would require the society to respect the existing constitutional order as a premise, which meant that a rational path toward constitutionalism would need deference [to the current order], or even adoption of "a conservative attitude" (Qin 2013b). The resilience of Qin and the whole SCS were obvious. "SCS, which unalterably recognizes the constitutional legitimacy of the CPC, appeals to facilitate the advancement of constitutionalism with the greatest deference and resilience; meanwhile, it hopes that the ruling party is able to honestly guard and observe the Constitution" (Qin 2013c).

2.2 Liberal Constitutionalism School: Constitutionalism Without the Current Constitution

The Liberal Constitutionalism School (LCS), which builds on libertarian doctrine, or British–American political philosophy, held an entirely different proposal compared with SCS in vowing constitutionalism. It refused to recognize China's present political order, challenged the legitimacy of the current Constitution as well as the leadership of the CPC, and furthermore, was skeptical about the likelihood of a "constitutionalist China" under socialism. Thereby, following the essential elements of universal constitutionalism, LCS adopted an approach to the constitutionalism construction in China that could be called "uprooting" or a kind of "shock therapy." Zhao Chu, Zhang Xuezhong, and He Weifang were/are the three fervent promoters of LCS.

As Tong mentioned previously, one of SCS's argumentative presuppositions was based on the truly dormant but well-drafted current Constitution (Tong 2013c, 2022). Different from SCS's applause, LCS has sharply challenged the legitimacy of the Constitution since the beginning of the debate. Zhao Chu, an active critic in the Chinese public sphere, who unswervingly stood on LCS's side, held that

> the current document in the name of Constitution is a unique political document produced under the authoritarian regime. Its making did not comply with the constitution-making process, its basic theory and contents contradict the spirit of constitutionalism, . . . it has been against constitutionalism since its birth. It is merely a modern political trick with a view to strengthen

> its own power of the new ruling class of the Republic, and with the purpose of perpetually consolidating the dictatorship and the system of power monopoly of this class.
>
> *(Zhao 2013)*

The legitimacy of the current Constitution has been constantly questioned by LCS, and the conclusion that it was "a constitution without constitutionalism" has thus been reached. Zhao further elaborated that "the past 60 year's history has already eloquently evidenced that the current Constitution would never result in neither constitutionalism, nor effective guarantee of constitutional rights" (Zhao 2013).

According to Zhao, the text of the current Constitution fully expounded the incontestable quality of one party ruling which was the basic spirit of it. Moreover, the reality has never sustained any procedure in constitutional law protection. Fang Shaowei, who can be regarded as a member of the LCS, also said that "socialism in China means and only means the CPC's ruling, or rather, other implications are just textual" (Fang 2013a), and "there exist 'constitutional system' but no 'constitutionalism' under socialism" (Fang 2013b). Since then, impugnation of the legitimacy of the current Constitution has transformed into a challenge to socialist China and the compatibility between the CPC's long-term ruling and the implementation of the Constitution. As Zhao said,

> During the formation of China's current power system, dictatorship is the core connotation and concept. That is to say, power itself is the primary goal of so-called proletarian revolution, which is a theoretical difficulty for all the scholars who are trying to discuss the possibility and feasibility of the transformation of constitution under the so-called socialistic theory. Since the 'red ideology' politics is a supper-moral utopia based on self-arguing history in a circle, it needs no support from social contract. Therefore, it is the most unlikely for standard institution like constitutionalism to have other status. . . . What cannot be neglected is that the factor that directly leads to China's current situation is the ruling party who creates all of this.
>
> *(Zhao 2013)*

This implies that only if China got rid of "one party ruling" could it start the development of constitutionalism. In this sense, the proposal of the LCS possesses the distinct "revolutionary quality" characteristic. Just as Zhang Xuezhong audaciously put forward that "the realization of constitutionalism in a dictatorial society must be premised on the disintegration of the dictatorial system" (Zhang 2013a). Obviously, Zhao, Fang, and Zhang all held the standpoints of "revolutionary quality" in relation to constitutionalism and stood on the radical side of LCS. [Due to his liberal speeches on constitutionalism and other sensitive matters, Zhang was dismissed by his university in 2013 in Shanghai, his license as a lawyer was canceled in 2019, and was once arrested in 2020.]

Pursuant to libertarian doctrine or jurisprudence, constitutionalism is a set of legal insurances for protecting the fundamental rights and freedoms of people and checking the power of authorities. Largely based on these, LCS preferred to illustrate its standpoints by presupposing a well-formed Western-style political model or a legal regime as the standard. Such kinds of argumentations were typically reflected in Zhang's article "I Want to Draw a Circle with Angles: An Assessment of the Standpoints of SCS." Zhang noticed that

> if socialist constitutional system can be regarded as constitutionalism, it must have the elements of constitutionalism; otherwise, it only has the name of constitutionalism, but has nothing to do with constitutionalism. It is generally believed that the elements of constitutionalism include: government established in accordance with the constitution; separation of powers and checks and balances; popular sovereignty and democratic government; review of unconstitutionality; independent judiciary; limited government abiding by the Bill of Rights; control over police power; civil control of army; and, no or very limited and strictly demarcated governmental power to suspend the operation of a constitution or an entire constitution.
>
> *(Zhang 2013b)*

Similar discourse subsequently stayed alive on He Weifang's Weibo (Microblog) for a while, China's equivalent of Twitter, which disappeared for obvious reasons in the end. He, a notable liberal scholar from Peking University School of Law and a widely respected public intellectual, and a somewhat mild scholar compared to Zhao and Zhang, wrote that

> if the foundation of constitutionalism is democracy, separation of powers and checks and balances, then one-party governance would have to be subject to the choices made by the people through ballots, then confirming the long-term rule of one party in the Constitution is a denial of democracy, and the implementation of such a Constitution is itself an act of anti-constitutionalism.
>
> *(He 2013)*

On LCS, a commentator noted and believed that:

> The essence of the standpoints of LCS (including the way of justifying its presupposed indicators) demonstrates that a group of scholars, intellectuals and people deeply influenced by the Western traditional constitutionalism, with worries about China's reality and with aspirations for a better future, hope to learn from the mature Western developmental models of constitutionalism to quickly and effectively improve China's democracy, freedom and the rule of law, and improve people's well-being.
>
> *(Ding 2013)*

2.3 Statist/Nationalist Constitutionalism School: Realizing Constitutionalism on the Basis of State Power

We should not leave aside Statist/Nationalist Constitutionalism School (SCSc) when discussing the representative schools/currents of constitutionalism in China. Although SCSc has not intervened in the debate over constitutionalism in the public sphere, one cannot ignore the strong discourse-formulating power and influence possessed by this school. In this regard, a commentator believed that SCSc "is in a position of invisible dominance" among the trends of constitutionalism in China, and he was surprised by the fact that SCSc was actually indifferent to the "provocation" by the counter-constitutionalism camp (Chen 2013).

Statism is a trend of thought that originated in Germany in the early 19th century. It advocates that the state is the core, the state is supreme, and that individual interests must be absolutely subordinate to national interests. In general terms, statism still belongs to nationalism (Ma 2012). One of the ideological lines of statism is Schmidtism (Ma 2012). Based on this, the basic requirement of Statist constitutionalism is to deny and reject universal values as the accepted standard for measuring constitutionalism and to clearly recognize that China itself has a "Chinese-style" constitutional system.

The importance of this theoretical paradigm lies in its efforts in and contribution to the justification of the legitimacy of the leadership of the CPC. Interestingly, major scholars all come from Peking University Law School, and no doubt, the key figure representing this school is Jiang Shigong. Equally interesting is that Jiang found an ideological soulmate on the other side of the Pacific; he is Larry Catá Backer, a professor of law and international affairs from Pennsylvania State University the Dickinson School of Law.

Jiang, long being considered by Chinese constitutional scholars to be a statist constitutional scholar, was not interested in constructing a school of constitutionalism, nor was it on his academic agenda. He made his efforts to justify the legitimacy of the CPC leadership in China and, in this way, contributed to constitutional debate. Jiang, when commenting on the 2004 Ukrainian "Colour Revolution," once asserted that

> the key to political issues is not the question of right or wrong, but the question of obedience and disobedience. As long as you disobey political authority, you will be wrong even you are not wrong, and you will be wrong even you are right. The primary problem in politics is to distinguish between enemies and friends. Between enemy and friend, there is no question of freedom, only violence and conquest, which is the essence of politics.
>
> *(Ma 2012)*

Jiang still considered that "the will of Chinese state stands for the will of the Party-state, the CPC is the soul as well as the state takes the flesh body" (Ma 2012). Jiang's taking jungle laws for the foundation of politics has reflected the doughty logic of SCSc. Statist constitutionalists oppose the definition of constitutionalism by Socialist or Liberal constitutionalists and believe that constitutionalism is a kind of national spirit, state structure, or supreme rule (Chen 2013).

Since the Statist constitutionalists refuse to imitate other countries or a certain universal model of constitutionalism, this means that scholars of this School tend to explore new ideas of Chinese-style constitutional order from the perspective of practice and history outside of form and text. Taking Jiang as an example, he believed that although China's constitutional system was born under a special political and social background, it still has the general function of constitutionalism, namely, managing political sects and promoting social harmony and stability. Under these constitutional commonalities, the only special feature of Chinese constitutionalism is that China is a one-party state (Backer 2013). Jiang also attempted to solve this constitutional dilemma by repositioning the Communist Party's position and role in China's constitutional order.

As observed and commented by Backer, "at this point," to Jiang,

> the most important thing was not to confuse the CPC with the Western concept of "party." This is because Chinese traditional culture emphasizes the political philosophy of "family-universe under the Heaven" (*Jia Tianxia*, 家天下), and "under the Heaven" means "under the whole world/universe" (*Putian Zhixa*, 普天之下), which symbolizes a universality. In ancient China, the emperor was the 'Son of Heaven' (*Tianzi*, 天子), and the symbol of "Son of Heaven" transcended factional interests or national interests in a narrow sense. The "Son of Heaven" upholds the mandate of the Heaven to govern the world, and it represents a universal political function. Jiang believes that the function of the Communist Party is closer to the "Son of Heaven" than a general political party, because the Communist Party is not a political interest group. In this way, the Communist Party must fulfill its "Mandate of Heaven" (*Tianming*, 天命) and govern the world, with public welfare as the top priority, and to maintain the connection between the party and the people. Based on this, Jiang concluded that the Communist Party and Chinese history are the two core elements that constitute the constitutional order in China.
>
> *(Backer 2013)*

The theory of "Mandate of Heaven" which was deduced by Jiang embodies that SCSc pursues the methodology of "everything real is rational" (*Cunzai Ji Heli*, 存在即合理); in other words, SCSc believes that

> ruled under the current Constitution in the past 30 years, China marvels the whole world since its booming economy as a rising power, which evidences that we must have done something right. Surely, the answer is that this is thanks to our living constitutionalism.
>
> *(Chen 2013)*

Moreover, Jiang has created a number of new concepts in the context of Chinese politics, such as "unwritten constitution in the PRC Constitution" (Jiang 2010) and "indirect soft governance of the CPC" (Jiang 2012), in order to theorize and normalize the legitimacy for the constitutional order of contemporary China.

On the other side of the earth, Backer published in 2009 an interesting and important article comprehensively examining the constitutional practice in the world, in which he formulated his value-based theory of constitutionalism and divided various constitutionalist systems into five types: traditional nationalist constitutionalism, transnational constitutionalism, natural law constitutionalism, theocratic constitutionalism, and rationalist constitutionalism (Jiang 2012; Backer 2009a). In his view expressed in an early article, there are currently three constitutionalist models in the world, and the first one is the "transnational constitutionalism" established under the leadership of the US after World War II. This "transnational constitutionalism" was first manifested in the constitutional reconstruction of Germany and Japan after World War II. The second model is the "theological constitutionalism" represented by Iran's 1979 constitution. This constitutional model establishes a Western-style state apparatus and even establishes constitutional systems such as human rights protection and checks and balances of power. However, its constitution clearly stipulates that the most fundamental and highest substantive norm of value of the country is not the secular values such as freedom and human rights, but the norm of value established by Islam. The third is China's "state-party" constitutional system. This constitutional system is derived from Marxism Leninism, which Backer classified as "rationalist constitutionalism." However, in Backer's specific discussion, China's constitutional model has similarities with Iran's theocratic constitutional model, i.e., the CPC represents the highest social normative value that transcends the constitution. It belongs to the ancient statist constitutional government, which advocates the supremacy of national sovereignty and transcends international legal norms (Jiang 2012; Backer 2008).

On the basis of the aforementioned theoretical construct, Backer further viewed Chinese constitutional system from a rather original perspective, and he believed that the CPC has constituted the core of China's constitutional system, and China has thus formed a "constitutional government model based on "state-party'" that is different from the Western liberal constitutional government model, i.e., a "single-party constitutionalist state" (Jiang 2012; Backer 2009b).

Jiang and Backer made a good pair of soulmates. Observing the traces of cross-introduction and referencing, we can see that Jiang and Backer inspired each other and echoed in each other's works. However, it is still hard to tell who has fueled whom. It is not important and necessary to clarify this point as long as we know that they have left their primordial influence in the course of formation of the trend of thought.

2.4 Confucian Constitutionalism School: Resorting to China's Ancient Past to Shape Its Political Future

Confucian constitutionalism got its current name around 2010, and its predecessor was political Confucianism, which was based on Gongyang Studies (Gongyang Xue, 公羊學) (Xu 2012). Similar to the SCSc, scholars from CCS advocate finding solutions to Chinese politics in the local historical and cultural resources, especially to explore the source of China's political legitimacy in the polemical dichotomy of "democracy, or authoritarianism" (Jiang and Bell 2012; Xu 2012). As Jiang Qing, the principal promoter of CCS, said: "The biggest problem facing Chinese contemporary politics is to establish a reasonable political order; and in order to establish a reasonable political order, we must establish a Chinese-style political system" (Xu 2012). Then, how should we establish a reasonable political order? What about a Chinese-style political system? Undoubtedly, the Confucian tradition, which represents the ancient Chinese wisdom, is naturally the local cultural resource that this school must rely on to plan a political blueprint for contemporary China.

Jiang believed that in Chinese history, the legitimacy of the political order was bestowed by Confucianism. Specifically, Confucianism provided the standard of legitimacy for political order through the "three-fold legitimacy of kingly politics" (王道政治三重合法性) (Jiang Q 2012). In the discourse system constructed by Jiang, the "three-fold legitimacy of kingly politics" includes three sources of legitimacy: the legitimacy of the divine heaven way (神聖天道的合法性), the legitimacy of history and culture (歷史文化的合法性), and the legitimacy of the people's will (人心民意的合法性). He also believed that a political order must have three sources of legitimacy at the same time to be completely legitimate; otherwise, the legitimacy will be compromised (Jiang Q 2012). Jiang advocated that "the kingly politics is the development direction of today's Chinese politics" for two reasons: first, foreign culture, especially Marxist ideology, as China's dominant culture, is difficult to be regarded as the foundation of political legitimacy in the long run (Bei 2010). Second, the kingly politics itself is a system with Chinese cultural characteristics, and its triple legitimacy is superior in content to the single legitimacy possessed by a democratic system (Jiang Q 2012). "The single legitimacy," in Jiang's discourse, refers to the legitimacy of authority obtained through people's ballots. Jiang's political philosophy is actually based on his interpretation of Gongyang Zhuan (公羊傳)—a commentary on a Confucian classic, "political power can be justified through three sources: the legitimacy of heaven (a sacred, transcendent sense of natural morality), the legitimacy of earth (wisdom from history and culture), and the legitimacy of the human (political obedience through popular will)" (Jiang and Bell 2012).

In order to implement the top-level constitutional arrangement of kingly politics, Jiang designed a tricameral legislature, or a parliamentary model of "three houses," each house representing a source/layer of legitimacy: a House of

Exemplary Persons (*Tong Ru Yuan*, 通儒院; a scholar translated it as House of *Ru*) that represents sacred legitimacy; a House of the Nation (*Guo Ti Yuan*, 國體院) that represents historical and cultural legitimacy; and a House of the People (*Shu Min Yuan*, 庶民院) that represents popular legitimacy. Another scholar interpreted the structure in this way: "a House of Ru (通儒院), which represents the legitimacy of heaven; a House of the Nation (國體院), which represents the legitimacy of earth; and a House of the People (庶民院), which represents the legitimacy of the human"; and "political power must fulfill the demands of the heaven, earth and human (天、地、人) to be considered legitimate" (Wang 2015).

Jiang and Bell further explained that the leader of the House of Exemplary Persons should be a great scholar. The leader of the House of the Nation should be a direct descendant of Confucius. Finally, members of the House of the People should be elected either by popular vote or as heads of occupational groups. In their view,

> this system would have checks and balances. Each house would deliberate in its own way and not interfere in the affairs of the others . . . the House of Exemplary Persons would have a final, exclusive veto, but its power would be constrained by that of the other two houses.
>
> *(Jiang and Bell 2012; Jiang Q 2012)*

Jiang's Confucian constitutionalism, which takes Gongyang Studies as the core and the basis, is more of a fundamentalist color (Xu 2012). In Jiang's view, "the so-called Confucian constitutional government is Chinese-style constitutional government; to be precise, it is a constitutionalism with Chinese historical and cultural characteristics, and is another way of political development for human beings apart from liberal and democratic politics" (Xu 2012). Because of this, some commentators regard this highly impactful theory of constitutionalism as "rigid Confucian constitutionalism" (Xu 2012).

In contrast, the advocates of "soft Confucian constitutionalism" are also a branch that cannot be ignored in today's Confucian constitutionalism, represented by Qiu Feng (this is believed to be the penname of Yao Zhongqiu). Qiu chose to use the concept of "Confucian constitutionalist people's livelihood" or "people's livelihood of Confucian constitutionalism" (儒家憲政民生主義) to express his Confucian constitutionalism idea and believed that Confucianism possesses in it a tradition of constitutionalism, in terms of both political and ideological tendencies, and in the structure of governance it conceived (Qiu 2011). In addition, from a historical perspective, Confucianism also represents an ideal of constitutionalism. Throughout history, Confucianism has constructed at least three systems of varying degrees of constitutionalism, namely, feudalism, co-governance system (共治體制), and modern constitutionalism (Qiu 2011).

Qiu's argumentative method is to "find the traces of freedom and constitutionalism from the traditional Chinese political system in order to provide a historical basis for the realization of constitutionalism in the future" (Ma 2012). This approach has been demonstrated in his article "Confucius You May Not Know" in *Southern People Weekly* (*Nanfang Renwu Zhoukan, 南方人物周刊*). In this sense, through the grafting of constitutionalism, Confucianism and the universal values of liberty, equality, and democracy have extensive intercommunication and deep connection. It is worth noting that Qiu's comprehensive development of his idea of Confucian constitutionalism is recorded in his book *On Confucian Constitutionalism* (*儒家憲政論*) (Yao 2016).

In addition to Qiu Feng, Chen Ming also had a similar proposition. Chen believed that Confucianism emphasizes public opinion, so Confucianism has the idea of constitutionalism. Constitutionalism advocates establishing a civil society, limiting government power, and protecting citizens' rights and property, which is consistent with the Confucian principle of respecting morality and protecting the people (Chen 2009). Chen also said that the Confucian tradition is a positive aid to China's constitutionalist goals. China's political reform requires compromise and should take into account various needs, especially to find a combination with Chinese culture to reduce shocks (Chen 2009). It can be seen from this that the task of "soft Confucian constitutionalism" is to extract the cultural essence that can be used in modern times from the traditional Confucian ideas, aiming to achieve a "soft landing" of the current political transformation in China.

3. Concluding Remarks

The article authored by Yang Xiaoqing in May 2013 triggered the great debate on constitutionalism that swept the Chinese academic circles and led to the publication of a good number of academic articles, official papers, and articles on social media mainly against constitutionalism. After one year or so, its presence in China quickly died down.

In fact, the discussion on constitutionalism, and the formation of the trends of thought or schools of constitutionalism occurred far before this particular year, and it can be traced back to the time when the Constitution was amended to incorporate the concept of "rule of law" (*Yifa Zhiguo, 依法治國*) in 1999 and to include the provisions of "the State respects and protects human rights" in 2014. That is to say, the dissemination of the concepts and ideas of constitutionalism actually occurred between the beginning of this century and 2014. Roughly during this period of over ten years, a large number of legal scholars, political scholars, and economists actively participated in the discussion of constitutionalism in China, subsequently published a large number of academic works, and gradually formed different academic currents and created such a situation as "a hundred flowers bloom, and a hundred schools of thought contend." The discussion on constitutionalism provided different theoretical paradigms and useful theoretical sets for the practice of constitutionalism in China and made its own contribution to popularizing the knowledge of constitution and constitutionalism as well as to theoretical design for future reform of the political system.

Looking around at today's academic circles, the discussion of constitutionalism has passed away, and the political scrutiny and censorship of publications and academic research have been very strictly implemented. Even the terms 憲政 (*Xianzheng*, a translation of constitutionalism) and 憲政主義or 立憲主義 (*Xianzheng Zhuyi* and *Lixian Zhuyi*, another translations of constitutionalism) have been banned and been generally replaced by the term 憲制 (*Xianzhi*, the literal translation of constitutional system). However, this short period of history is worth remembering because it represents not only a milestone in the development of Chinese legal academic research but also a record of China's political and constitutional reform. Maybe in one day, people will have the opportunity to reopen this precious page of the history book, learn from it, and make it known to the light of day. I believe that, as long as China hopes to make progress and pursue universal values in the future, constitutionalism shall be an inevitable option, or to say, constitutionalism shall be a must-be solution.

Note

1 First, I would like to record my sincere thanks to Dr Deng Kai and then a PhD candidate under my direction, who helped me collect and sort out the primary and original materials in 2014 when I prepared my presentation on the still ongoing constitutional debate in China for the symposium on Chinese law at Oxford University organized by the European Association of Chinese Law. The materials have multiple sources, and a few of which from websites have disappeared for obvious reasons of censorship. I must also thank Prof. Hua Shiping, the Editor of this Book, who kindly advised me to complete the incomplete work, without his encouragement the publication of this chapter would not have been possible indeed.

References

Backer, Larry Catá. 2008. "God(s) Over Constitutions: International and Religious Transnational Constitutionalism in the 21st Century." 27 *Mississippi College Law Review* 1. Accessed July 12, 2022. https://dc.law.mc.edu/lawreview/vol27/iss1/3.

———. 2009a. "From Constitution to Constitutionalism: A Global Framework for Legitimate Public Power Systems." 113 *Penn State Law Review* 101.

———. 2009b. "The Party as Polity, the Communist Party, and the Chinese Constitutional State: A Theory of State-Party Constitutionalism." *Penn State Legal Studies Research Paper No. 05–2009*, January 10, 2009. Accessed July 12, 2022. https://ssrn.com/abstract=1325792 or http://dx.doi.org/10.2139/ssrn.1325792.

———. 2013. "Creating and Developing a Sound Theory of Chinese Constitutionalism: Jiang Shigong's Discussion on the Formalism and Legitimacy of Chinese Constitutionalism." In Chinese, First Published on Larry Backer Sina Weibo on August 16, 2013. Accessed July 12, 2022. www.aisixiang.com/data/73300.html.

Bei, Danning (Bell, Daniel A.). 2010. *New Confucianists in China (中國新儒家)*, 190. Shanghai: Shanghai Sanlian Publishing House.

CC of the CPC. 2013. "The Decision on Major Issues Concerning Comprehensively Deepening Reforms." A Brief of the Decision in English Was Published at: www.china.org.cn/china/third_plenary_session/2013-11/16/content_30620736.htm; and the Full Text in Chinese. Accessed July 12, 2022. www.fmprc.gov.cn/ce/cemx/chn/gdxw/t1100200.htm.

Chen, Hongguo. 2013. "China's Current Trends of Constitutionalism: The Debate Over Goals and Paths." First Published on Chen Hongguo's Sina Blog on June 20, 2013. Accessed July 12, 2022. www.aisixiang.com/data/65355.html. Text Available Upon Request.

Chen, Ming. 2009. *Cultural Confucianism: Speculation and Debate (文化儒學：思辨與論辯)*, 119. Chengdu: Sichuan People's Publishing House.

China File. 2013. "Document 9: A China File Translation: How Much Is a Hardline Party Directive Shaping China's Current Political Climate?" Authored by the Editors. Accessed July 12, 2022. www.chinafile.com/document-9-chinafile-translation#start.

Ding, Dong. 2013. "China's Current Constitutional Controversy Over Constitutionalism and Its Essence." ("中國當前的憲政之爭及其實質") First Published on Dingdong Sohu Blog on June 23, 2013. Accessed July 12, 2022. https://wenku.baidu.com/view/dfc39a7c561252d380eb6e45.html.

Fang, Shaowei. 2013a. "Don't Refer China's 'Constitutional System' to as 'Constitutionalism'." ("不能把中國的'憲制'說成'憲政'") May 31, 2013 and Cited from Tong Zhiwei. 2016. *The Innovation of the Chinese Constitutional System* (*Zhongguo Xianzhi zhi Weixin, 中國憲制之維新*), 116–22. Hong Kong: City University of Hong Kong Press.

———. 2013b. "There Is Constitutional System but No Constitutionalism Under Socialism." ("社會主義有'憲制'無'憲政'") June 9, 2013. Accessed July 12, 2022. https://bnn.co/cgi-bin/news/gb_display/print_versiOn.cgi?art=/gb/pubvp/2013/06&link=201306091442.shtml.

Han, Gang. 2014. "The Most Fundamental Restoration of Things to Order: Rejection of 'Taking Class Struggle as the Key Link'." *Xuexi Shibao (Study Times, 學習時報)*, September 29, 2014.

He, Weifang. 2013. Sina Weibo (Microblog) Text, May 26, 2013. The Text Is No Longer Available Online. Permission for Citation Obtained from the Blog Author.

HQSB. 2013. *Huanqiu Shibao (Global Times, 環球時報)*. "The Editorial," May 22, 2013. Accessed July 12, 2022. http://opinion.huanqiu.com/editorial/2013-05/3957200.html.

Jiang, Shigong. 2010. "Written and Unwritten Constitutions: A New Approach to the Study of Constitutional Government in China." *Modern China* 36 (1): 12–46.

———. 2012. "China's Constitutionalist Model? – Baker's Research on China's 'Single Party Constitutional State' System." *Sino-Foreign Law Review (Zhongwai Faxue, 中外法學)* (5). Accessed July 12, 2022. http://lawdata.com.tw/tw/detail.aspx?no=144496.

Jiang, Qing. 2012. "What Is the Use of Confucianism in Today's China." In *Confucian Constitutionalism and China's Future（儒學憲政與中國未來）*, edited by Fan Ruiping, Bei Danning and Hong Xiuping, 10–16. Shanghai: East China Normal University Press.

Jiang, Qing, and Daniel A. Bell. 2012. "A Confucian Constitution for China." *New York Times*, July 11, 2012.

Ma, Licheng. 2012. *Eight Social Trends of Thought in Contemporary China" (Dangxia Zhongguo Bazhong Shehui Sichao,* 當下中國八種社會思潮*)*, 80–81, p. 196. Beijing: Social Sciences Literature Publishing House.

Ma, Zhongcheng. 2013. "The American Constitutionalism Is a Misnomer." *Renmin Ribao Haiwaiban (People's Daily Overseas Edition, 人民日報海外版)*, August 6, 2013. Accessed July 12, 2022. http://opinion.cntv.cn/2013/08/06/ARTI1375761052276531.shtml.

Qin, Qianhong. 2013a. "Discussing Again Socialist Constitutionalism." May 5, 2013, Cited from Hua Bingxiao, "Theoretical Poverty of the School of Counter-Constitutionalism and Its Achilles' Heel – Part 1 of a Series in Response to the Viewpoints of the School of Counter-Constitutionalism." Accessed July 12, 2022. https://m.aisixiang.com/data/65356-4.html.

———. 2013b. "Restatement of My View on Socialist Constitutionalism." July 5, 2013. www.hybsl.cn/zonghe/zuixinshiliao/2013-07-05/38417.html. Permission for Citation Obtained from the Blog Author.

———. 2013c. Sina Weibo (Microblog) Text, May 28, 2013. Permission for Citation Obtained from the Blog Author.

Qin, Qianhong, and Ye Haibo. 2004. "On Socialist Constitutionalism." *Journal of National Procurators College* (2).

———. 2008. A Study of Socialist Constitutionalism (Shehui Zhuyi Xianzheng Yanjiu, 社會主義憲政研究). Jinan: Shandong People's Press.

Qiu, Feng. 2011. "Confucian Constitutionalist People's Livelihood." *Open Times (Kaifang Shidai,* 開放時代*)* (6).

Shen, Xinwang. 2012. "Building Consensus Using the Concept of 'Socialist Constitutionalism' – Interview with Han Dayuan, President of Chinese Association of Constitutional Law." *China News Weekly (Zhongguo Xinwen ZHoukan, 中國新聞週刊*) (9).

Tong, Zhiwei. 2013a. "The Year of 2008 for Socialist Constitutionalism School, Counter-Constitutionalism Camp, and Pan-Constitutionalism School: A Law Professor' Recollection Based on his Personal Experiences." June 14, 2013, in His Column at http://blog.21ccom.net/ and Sina Weibo. This Article Is Included in His Book *the Innovation of the Chinese Constitutional System* (Zhongguo Xianzhi zhi Weixin, *中國憲制之維新*), City University of Hong Kong Press, 2016, 168–76.

———. 2013b. "A Supplementary Explanation of the Concept of Socialist Constitutionalism." June 3, 2013, Available on Several Websites. This Article Is Included in His Book *the Innovation of the Chinese Constitutional System (Zhongguo Xianzhi zhi Weixin,* 中國憲制之維新*)*, City University of Hong Kong Press, 2016, 110–16.

———. 2013c. "The Pan-Constitutionalists Must Eliminate Misunderstandings About the Constitution and Constitutional Principles – A Reply to Professor He Weifang." June 15, 2013, a Series of Four Blog Articles. These Blog Articles Are Included in His Book *the Innovation of the Chinese Constitutional System (Zhongguo Xianzhi zhi Weixin, 中國憲制之維新)*, City University of Hong Kong Press, 2016, 203–20.

———. 2014. Sino Weibo Text Dated March 22, 2014; Incorporated in His Discussion on the Debate on Constitutionalism in China, and Included in His Book *the Innovation of the Chinese Constitutional System (Zhongguo Xianzhi zhi Weixin, 中國憲制之維新)*, City University of Hong Kong Press, 2016, 184–90.

———. 2022. *A Search for the Path to Chinese Constitutionalism* (*Zhongguo Lixian Zhuyi Daolu Qiusuo, 中國立憲主義道路求索*). Hong Kong: City University of Hong Kong Press.

Wang, Binfan. 2015. "Jiang Qing's Confucian Constitutionalism: A Meaningful Fantasy." March 28, 2015, in CORN March 2015 Edition. CORN Stands for China Open Research Network, a Network Established at the Department of Political Science of the University of Toronto. The Author of This Chapter Has the Article in PDF format, and It Is Available Upon Request.

Wang, Tingyou. 2013. "Some Viewpoints on Constitutionalism." Accessed July 12, 2022. www.wenming.cn/ll_pd/zz/201306/t20130613_1288751.shtml.

Wang, Weiguang. 2014. "Adhering to the People's Democratic Dictatorship Is Not Unjustified." *Red Flag Manuscripts (Hongqi Wengao, 紅旗文稿*), Issue September 2014. Accessed July 12, 2022. http://news.sina.com.cn/c/2014-09-24/145630907684.shtml.

Wu, Bangguo. 2011. "We Must Not Adopt the Multi-party Alternation of Power, Federalism, and Privatization." Accessed July 12, 2022. www.npc.gov.cn/zgrdw/npc/dbdhhy/11_4/2011-03/10/content_1640332.htm.

Xi, Jinping. 2012. "Xi Jinping's Speech at the Commemoration of the 30th Anniversary of the Promulgation and Implementation of the Current Constitution." December 4, 2012. The Speech Was Widely Reported in the Chinese Media. Accessed July 12, 2022. www.gov.cn/ldhd/2012-12/04/content_2282522.htm.

———. 2013."Ideological Work Is an Extremely Important Work of the Party." August 20, 2013. Accessed July 12, 2022. http://politics.people.com.cn/n/2013/0820/c1024-22634056.html. An Unofficial Publication of the Full Text of Xi Jinping's Speech Is Available Overseas. Accessed July 12, 2022. www.boxun.com/news/gb/china/2013/11/201311042254.shtml. However the Authenticity of It Is Open to Double-Check.

Xie, Xiaoguang. 2013. "Why Is the U.S. So Keen to Promote 'Universal Value'." *Red Flag Manuscripts (Hongqi Wengao, 紅旗文稿)*, August 7, 2013. Accessed July 12, 2022. www.71.cn/2013/0808/726976.shtml.

Xu, Jiling. 2012. "The Reality and History of Confucian Constitutionalism." *Open Times (Kaifang Shidai, 開放時代)* (1).

Yang, Xiaoqing. 2013. "A Comparative Study of Constitutionalism and People's Democratic Regime." *Red Flag Manuscript (Hongqi Wengao, 紅旗文稿)*, May 21, 2013. Accessed July 12, 2022. http://theory.people.com.cn/n/2013/0522/c40531-21566974.html.

Yang, Yunguang. 2013. "Interpreting American Idea of Human Rights and Practice of Human Rights." *Red Flag Manuscripts* (*Hongqi Wengao, 紅旗文稿*), August 7, 2013. Accessed July 12, 2022. www.71.cn/2013/0808/726826.shtml.

Yao, Zhongqiu. 2016. *On Confucian Constitutionalism (儒家憲政論)*. Hong Kong: City University of Hong Kong Press.

Yin, Hanning. 2013. "A Profound Understanding of the Extreme Importance of Ideological Work." *Seeking Truth (Qiushi, 求是)*, September 16, 2013. Accessed July 12, 2022. http://theory.people.com.cn/n/2013/0916/c40531-22935925.html.

Yu, Zhong. 2013. "'Chinese Dream' and the Choice of the Path of Democratic Politics." Accessed July 12, 2022. http://zt.cyu.edu.cn/zqxxw/llwz/xzxl/201306/t20130620_46761.html.

Yuan, Chunqing. 2013. "Leading Cadres Must Strengthen Their Political Determination." *People's Daily*, September 24, 2013. Accessed July 12, 2022. http://politics.people.com.cn/n/2013/0924/c1001-23009079.html.

Zhang, Xuezhong. 2013a. Sina Weibo (Microblog) Text, June 2013. The Text Is No Longer Available Online. Zhang Xuezhong, a Political Dissident, Has Been Under Residential Surveillance Since Late 2013. All His Publications Have Been Removed from the Websites. He Now Is Not Reachable to the Author of This Chapter. The Author of This Chapter Has with Him a Word File of This Blog Text Downloaded from the Blog and It Is Available Upon Request.

———. 2013b. "I Want to Draw a Circle with Angles: An Assessment of the Standpoints of Socialist Constitutionalism School." May 2013, Originally Published at http://blog.sina.com.cn/s/blog_67e0832b0101b7gc.html. It Is No Longer Available Online. However, the Citation Can Be Found in Tong Zhiwei. 2016. *The Innovation of the Chinese Constitutional System (Zhongguo Xianzhi zhi Weixin, 中國憲制之維新)*, 188. Hong Kong: City University of Hong Kong Press.

Zhao, Chu. 2013. "A Common Sense Reflection of Constitutionalism." May 28, 2013. Accessed July 12, 2022. https://m.aisixiang.com/data/64355.html.

Zheng, Zhixue. 2013. "Clearly Understanding the Essence of Constitutionalism." *Party Building (Dan Jian,* 黨建), May 29, 2013. Accessed July 12, 2022. http://theory.people.com.cn/n/2013/0529/c83855-21652535.html?mType=Other.

4

LEGALISM AND XI JINPING THOUGHT

Han Fei's Influence on Contemporary Chinese Politics and Law

Haig Patapan

China's economic and military rise presents profound questions concerning the character of the Chinese state and its international ambitions. For some, an important source for exploring these questions is the leadership of Xi Jinping, who became General Secretary of the Communist Party of China (CPC) in 2012 (see, for example, Brown 2016; Lampton 2014; Li 2016). Xi's influence on contemporary China can be seen in the prominence of "Xi Jinping Thought on Socialism with Chinese Characteristics in the New Era," simply known as Xi Jinping Thought, first mentioned by him in the third part of the opening day report delivered to the 19th Party Congress in October 2017. It was subsequently incorporated in the Constitution of the CPC in 2017 and in the state Constitution in 2018 and thus became the guiding political doctrine. As one of the only two leaders with a "Thought" (the other is Mao Zedong, the founder of the People's Republic of China), Xi Jinping rises above his two most recent predecessors Hu Jintao with his "scientific development perspective" and Jiang Zemin with his "important thought of the Three Represents," and even Deng Xiaoping who only had a "theory."[1] Given its significance, this doctrine will therefore shape China's domestic development and global engagement for the foreseeable future. Yet the exact substance of this Thought and the ideals and policies it elaborates and advocates, especially the meaning of "Chinese Characteristics," remains obscure.

One possible answer to the meaning of Xi Jinping Thought is provided by Xi's frequent references to the classical Chinese Legalist philosopher Han Fei, who is critical of Confucian thought and whose ideas were instrumental in the founding of imperial China and its first Qin Dynasty (see, for example, MCLC Resource Center 2015; Zwagerman 2016; Buckley 2014; Hilton 2015; Lin 2017). To what extent is Xi Jinping Thought informed by Legalism? And what are the practical implications of such influence on contemporary Chinese law and politics? These are the core questions we will examine in this chapter. These questions are

DOI: 10.4324/9781003294887-5

important theoretically because they reveal the extent to which Chinese classical thought is consistent with and can accommodate western socialism, allowing us to assess the CPC's claim of socialism with Chinese characteristics.[2] Their practical significance is that if Xi Jinping Thought is indeed indebted to Han Fei, it may allow us to explain in a more predictable manner, beyond the vagaries of factional contestation and unpredictable exigencies of domestic and international politics, the influential and guiding principles and potential directions of China's contemporary politics.

In the discussion that follows, I first outline the nature of Legalism in China, with a particular focus on the influential work of Han Fei. I then show the powerfully influential role of Legalism in Chinese history, noting how Chinese leaders have resorted to Legalism in times of change or crisis. Having shown the character and historical significance of Legalism in China, the chapter will then focus on contemporary Chinese political and legal questions to examine the extent to which Xi's policies are consistent with Han Fei's counsels. It will examine Xi Jinping's "China Dream," in particular his decisions to concentrate power in his hands, initiate a comprehensive anti-corruption initiative, as well as his use of law as a state instrument and investment in the military to show how in these major respects Xi's actions are explicable in terms of Han Fei's Legalism. It concludes by reflecting on the role of Legalism in understanding Xi Jinping Thought and how Chinese leaders have historically resorted to Legalism in times of political instability and uncertainty.

1. What Is Chinese Legalism?

Legalism was an intellectual school that appeared in the latter half of the Warring States period (453–221 BCE), a time of war and great economic, military, and social instability. Though one of the "Hundred Schools" that sought the path to peace and stability through unity of *Tianxia* or "All-under-Heaven," it was distinctive by its emphasis on political practice. Its origins can be traced to Shang Yang and Shen Buhai, but we will focus on its most influential exponent, Han Fei (280–233 BCE), who drew on these thinkers in writing his influential work, the *Han Feizi*.[3] The overall aim of the Legalists was the attainment of *fu guo qiang bing* or a "rich state with a powerful army," which would make the unity of *tianxia* possible, while Han Fei himself was more ambitious, seeking a world of *zhi an zhi shi* or absolute peace, where the "ruler can rest in peace and his subjects can be happy with their undertakings."[4]

What is distinctive about Han Fei's Legalism is its fundamental repudiation of the Confucian approach that looked to past examples for models of virtuous leaders who could ensure political stability.[5] Han Fei does not deny the existence of virtuous individuals but argues that as they are so few in number, it would be foolish to rely on them, as ridiculous as the silly Song farmer who had seen a rabbit kill itself on a stump waiting there for another.[6] Thus Confucius and his virtuous disciples, all ten or so, would not be sufficient for the modern state. This problem of the small number of virtuous individuals manifests itself in another respect—the inability of most to discern these individuals. Most people lack judgment, according to Han Fei, which means those who govern would have to do more than "win the hearts of the people."

But the people's wisdom is useless because it is like the mind of an infant. . . . In order to shave its head or lance its boil, one person must hold it down while the kind mother cures it, but it whoops and hollers unceasingly, for the infant does not know the great benefits brought about by this small discomfort.

(Chen 2000, ch 19, v 50, 1147)

The people do not recognize what is best for them because they cannot see how small discomforts will lead to gains. They also lack knowledge of important things, whereas the ruler oversees four great enterprises: colonization of new land, penal law, taxation, and military service. Though all these enterprises contribute to order and security, "the people do not know enough to rejoice in them" (Chen 2000, ch 19, v 50, 1147). Consequently, one cannot rely on virtue for political peace and stability, because there is no assurance that any particular ruler is a sage since it is hard to see virtue unless one is virtuous, while the people tend to dissemble, appearing virtuous when they are merely self-seeking. Instead, Han Fei proposes a novel means that can be understood and applied by anyone, guaranteeing success.

The *Han Feizi*, as a radically innovative teaching, has to deploy a complex rhetorical strategy for its success. It will speak directly to rulers who are capable of understanding his teaching. At the same time, however, it will instruct advisers, who may counsel or even replace rulers who lack the ability and judgment to understand the new teaching. It will also bolster its teaching by making it appear consistent with "Daoism," comforting those who may still want to rely on cosmic forces rather than their own abilities.[7] What, then, is the character of this teaching? It is based on the view that it is safer to assume all want to pursue *si*, what they think is good for them, rather than *gong* or the public good. This focus on individual interest is the source of political instability because as we have noted individuals are, according to Han Fei, generally incapable of seeing what is in their long-term interests. True, these passions result in political institutions and structures that distinguish between rulers and ruled. But this exacerbates the situation, with rulers exploiting the ruled. Han Fei will therefore use this basic human disposition and political structures to secure peace and prosperity. He will do so by teaching a few simple rules, rather than hoping for the unreliable fruits of years of Confucian education in history and rituals to yield the sage ruler.

To make a state most powerful (*ba wang*) by making it rich with a potent army, Han Fei advocates the combined use of *shi* or position (势), *shu* or tactics (术), and *fa* or law (法). An essential foundation for this proposed solution is the primacy of the ruler because it is only through the ruler's pre-eminence that all the other parts can function productively. It would seem that the self-interest of the ruler, properly instructed by Han Fei to show how the interest of others benefits the rulers, comprehends the welfare of all, even if it is not identical to a notion of a disinterested pursuit of the public good. Put somewhat differently, Han Fei counsels rulers on what they no doubt desire—how to keep their authority and how to counter challenges to their power. But in doing so, he shows how their actions will indirectly benefit the many, so that the ruler's self-interest, properly directed by Han Fei, becomes the foundation of a version of the public good. In any case, as Han Fei warns, it is not in the ruler's interest to mistreat the people, since they may become embittered and be exploited by others in conspiracies. Consequently, his advice concerns above all the concentration of power in the hands of the sovereign who is described as a deadly dragon who can nevertheless be tamed as long as one does not accidentally brush against the scales under its throat.[8]

In addition to this general counsel, Han Fei reminds rulers that one of the greatest dangers they will face will come from those who are unavoidable and indeed necessary for rule, his counselors and officials. He therefore provides extensive advice on the use of specific tactics to manage them. As *Han Feizi*'s "*Wudu*" or "Five Vermin" chapters show in detail, the interests of the ministers and the ruler are diametrically opposed. Ministers hope for a comfortable career, while the ruler has to look to a more comprehensive good.[9] All officials will be likely to seek private gain at the expense of the public, and they will attempt to dissemble, disguising their private interests as the general interest to take advantage of the ruler. They will also form cliques to benefit each other and their families at the expense of the state. These insights help explain Han Fei's teaching on tactics. Thus, the ruler should ensure all power comes from his office and not from his advisors, which means, for example, all powers to reward and punish should remain in his hands. Also, rulers should not reveal what they think and what they like and don't like, even to their closest members of the family to ensure that officials do not exploit these sentiments for personal gain. Importantly, Han Fei thinks selecting officials for specific tasks and offices based on their abilities exposes rulers to manipulation. Instead, he proposes *Xingmin* that officials should initiate projects and that they should be judged by what they promise and what they deliver, rather than what the ruler orders and instructs. "One who speaks spontaneously produces a 'title'; one who acts spontaneously produces a 'performance.' When 'performance and title' match identically, then everything returns to its essence without any action on the part of the ruler" (Chen 2000, ch 1, v 5, 66). The enlightened ruler therefore domesticates his ministers as follows:

> ministers cannot attain merit by overstepping their offices or failing to match the words they put forth. If they overstep their offices, they are to die; if they fail to match [their words], they are to be convicted. If they keep to their offices and remain faithful to their words, the thronging ministers will be unable to form cliques and act in one another's behalf.
>
> *(Chen 2000, ch 2, v 7, 126; cf. also ch 18, v 5, 330)*

Yet these tactics are not, by themselves, sufficient for controlling advisors or the many. More comprehensive and far-reaching control requires the use of *fa* or law (法): "If the ruler does not know the tactics of control there will be problems at the top; if the officials do not follow the law, there will be chaos at the bottom."[10] Tactics without law allows officials to exploit inconsistencies to defy the orders of the ruler. But what is law? It is the decree of the ruler, a form of communication to everyone regarding how they should order their desires.[11] Laws are effective because rather than attempting to educate people about their passions, the ruler will use passions against passions, employing *erbing* or "the two handles" (二柄)—rewards and punishments—to direct and control them. According to Han Fei,

> If the lord makes use of such techniques, the great ministers will not be able to make decisions on their own authority; those who are familiar [with the ruler] will not dare to sell their influence. If the administration carries out *fa*, vagabond commoners will have to rush to their tilling and knights-errant will have to brave danger at the battlefront. Thus the techniques of *fa* are a disaster for thronging ministers and men-of-service.
>
> *(Chen 2000, ch 13, 273)*

Law also gives the ruler clear and public standards to measure the talents, merits, and mistakes of the people and provide for rewards and punishments. Properly designed laws applied to all will therefore encourage favorable and prevent harmful behavior: "In applying the law to transgressions, one does not pardon great ministers; in rewarding good conduct, one does not pass over commoners" (Chen 2000, ch 2, v 6, 111). Law is applied equally not because of a fundamental endorsement of the principle of equality, but for its efficacy:

> For this reason, those whose accomplishments are real must be rewarded, even if they are lowly and base; those whose transgressions are real must be punished, even if they are close and beloved. Then the lowly and base will not become insolent nor the close and beloved haughty.
>
> *(Chen 2000, ch 2, v 5, 81)*

The source of the law is therefore the ruler, who is exempt from the law, and not the people, even though a prudent ruler will consider what is good for them, which may not always be what they desire.

Law is distinctive because it aids rulers and ultimately advances the general good. Since laws, unlike tactics, need to be widely followed, applied, and enforced, they need to be made public, which means they need to be disseminated widely, written in plain language to be comprehensible to common people, and promulgated extensively so that the ordinary people are familiar with them. They should also be stable and remain consistent to guide behavior though change is permitted if circumstances warrant. Importantly, laws need to provide heavy punishments, even for minor misbehavior, since severe punishments are more effective to deter undesirable acts of the people. Laws that advance the strength and wealth of the state will be designed to save the people from disorder by preventing the strong from attacking the weak and the majority from oppressing the minority, to allow the old to live in peace and the young to have a chance to grow and to secure peaceful borders. Law will establish the standards to measure behavior just like the compass and the scales determine roundness and weight. As the hammer and anvil and timber-bending device are used to shape metal and wood, the law, according to Han Fei, can be used to change people, transforming them into what they ought to be. The ruler should therefore unify the *fa* instead of seeking out the wise and consolidate his techniques instead of admiring the trustworthy so that *fa* will not fail, and among the thronging ministers, there will be no treachery or machination (Chen 2000, ch 19, v 49, 1109; cf. ch 19, v 50, 1141–42).

Legalism closely resembles influential theoretical approaches in western thought that developed much later.[12] It should therefore not surprise us that significant ambiguities in these approaches are also evident in Han Fei's teaching. The first concerns the role of the leader and the nature of leadership required by Legalism. This puzzle becomes manifest in the practical question of whether rulers need prudence or judgment, a distinctive quality possessed unequally, and one that can be nurtured and developed through education and training, or whether ruling is simply a matter of mastering certain techniques and applying fundamental principles. The second concerns the ambiguous character of the state for Han Fei. Han Fei appears at the same time to be an elitist, suggesting a difference between the few who rule and advise and the many, and also an egalitarian, suggesting that there is no significant difference between humans, who all seek their self-interest. Thus, in emphasizing the importance of individuals, as leaders and members of the public, Han Fei appears to endorse a democratic or republican regime. Yet the radical elevation of the ruler, whose authority does not come from the people, and who appears unconstrained by conventional, ethical, or legal limitations suggests a preference for legal positivism and extreme authoritarianism. It is therefore not clear whether Han Fei has a political conception of the common good that is distinct from the common interest.[13] Finally, there is an ambiguity regarding the aim of politics more generally. Han Fei suggests security and prosperity are the *summum bonum* of political life. This assessment seems to deny any significant place for the family, religion, and patriotism, let alone poets and the gods in politics. Whether these material concerns are sufficient to banish the human longing for the noble, the good, and the divine remains an unresolved question in his thought.

2. Confucius-Legalist Influence in China

Imperial China was founded on Legalism. During the later phase of the Warring States period, King Zhang of Qin was so impressed by Han Fei that he implemented a series of reforms based on his writings.[14] As Qin became economically rich and militarily powerful, it subdued its six rivals and unified China in 221 BCE after five centuries of interstate warfare. Though the Legalists were influential in the formation of Qin and the first empire after Qin, the severe penal system that was implemented led to the collapse of the Qin dynasty in 207 BCE only 14 years after its founding, discrediting Legalism in the eyes of subsequent literati and emperors. Consequently, Confucianism became dominant, with followers of Legalism banned from holding public offices under the reign of Emperor Wu of the Han (141–87 BCE) (see generally Pines and Defoort 2016; Chang 2016). Yet Legalism continued to be influential, and indeed subsequent history shows a complex relationship between Confucianism and Legalism, with Confucianism dominant during periods of peace, while Legalism with its emphasis on innovations and new solutions reasserting itself in times of change. For example, reform-oriented politicians of various dynasties, such as Zhuge Liang (181–234), Wang Anshi (1021–1086), and Zhang Juzheng (1525–1582), showed a keen interest in Legalism to pursue economic growth and military power. But more generally, both Confucianism and Legalism (as well as other schools of thought) were applied selectively by the rulers throughout Chinese history to suit their purposes. Though Confucianism's humanity favored it as orthodoxy, emperors had reservations about some of its teachings and, in fact, secretly resorted to teachings of Legalism to maintain their rule. This came to be understood as *yang ru yin fa* (阳儒阴法), "Confucianism as Yang and Legalism as Yin" or "Confucianism on the outside and Legalism on the inside." For example, while denouncing Legalism, Emperor Wu of the Han dynasty adopted many assertive policies that were comparable to those of the Qin dynasty. In fact, the emperors resorted to both Confucianism as the orthodox ideology and Legalism to maintain their rule for over two millennia.[15] Knowing which was favored by the emperor was an essential skill for capable advisors:

> If the audience seeks for a good name while you try to persuade him of big profit, you will be considered low bred. You will be treated basely and kept at a distance. If the audience strives after big profit while you persuade him to seek a good name, you will be considered mindless and unable to adapt to practical situations. You will never be put in an important position. If the audience's true motive is to strive after big profit but pretends to seek a good name while you try to persuade him to seek a good name, you will be accepted on the surface but kept at a distance in actuality; and if you persuade him to strive for big profit, your advice will *be adopted in secret* but you will *not* be accepted openly.
>
> *(cited in Lu 1993, 112; emphasis added)*

This Confucian–Legalist dynamic and its influence can be seen in the subsequent history of China.[16] "Lagging behind leaves one vulnerable to attacks" (落后就要挨打) became the influential lesson learned from China's military defeats in the Opium Wars and the loss to Japan in 1885.[17] Consequently, influential intellectuals at the time such as Liang Qichao claimed that only Legalism offered solutions to these contemporary problems (Liang 1999, 1255). Similarly, Chen Qitian maintained that a new Warring States period had arrived in which powerful states conquer weak ones so that a poor state without a powerful army could not survive (Chen 1936, 112–14). Legalism was also praised by famous scholars like Shen Jiaben, Zhang Taiyan, Liu Shipei, and Chang Yansheng.[18] Even leading liberal thinkers such as Hu Shi (1891–1962) praised Han Fei and Li Si for their "brave spirit of opposing those who 'do not make the present into their teacher but learn from the past'" (cited in Pines 2018). The prominence of Legalism in the first half of the 20th century can be seen in its use by politicians such as Hu Hanmin (1879–1936), one of the most influential leaders of KMT (Kuomintang), who wrote a preface to a new edition of the *Book of Lord Shang* (Hu 1933).

This was a view endorsed by Mao Zedong (1893–1976), who as a high school student had written an essay praising Shang Yang.[19] Mao did not waver from his early assessment of Legalism as "progressive" so that in 1957, he half-jokingly called himself a combination of the First Emperor of Qin and Karl Marx (Xu 2009). He especially endorsed Han Fei's views of officials, advising Ho Chi Minh that all officials are corrupt, only to a different extent.[20] This perspective explains in part why he initiated the Cultural Revolution and mobilized common people to prosecute the corrupt in power. In Mao's last years, he started the notorious "anti-Confucian" movement, openly denouncing Confucianism and praising Legalism.

With Mao's death, Legalism seemed to lose its official endorsement. Deng Xiaoping assumed power in 1978 after Hua Guofeng, Mao's loyal follower stepped down, and as Deng endorsed both Jiang Zemin and Hu Jintao who largely followed his policies, it is arguable that the Deng era lasted until 2012, when Xi Jinping assumed office. Domestically, Deng himself together with many other high-ranking officials like Xi Zhongxun, Xi Jinping's father, had suffered Mao's attacks on officials. For Deng, corrupt officials are the exception rather than the rule, so that there was no need to control the officials on a large scale, let alone have officials prosecuted by the masses. Internationally, Deng judged that there would be no major wars in the future, allowing China to concentrate on economic development. Deng's international policy was therefore *tao guang yang hui*, literally hide one's capacities and bide one's time maintaining friendly international relationships and above all not challenging the dominant position of the US. There was therefore no need to resort to Legalism during this period.

3. China Dream and Legalism

Having presented an account of Legalism and its influential role in Chinese thought and practice, we now turn to the question of whether it represents an important aspect of the "Chinese Characteristics" that constitute Xi Jinping Thought. Though endorsing Han Fei, Xi has not provided an extensive theoretical treatment of the way Legalism informs and shapes his conception of socialism. In the spirit of Legalism, I will therefore approach this question by examining actual political practice, to see the extent to which contemporary Chinese politics, both domestic and international, is consistent with or can be explained sufficiently by Legalist principles. I do so by looking at the "China Dream," Xi's overarching ambition for China, and the specific policy initiatives as a practical manifestation of Xi Jinping Thought. My overall argument, as we will see, is that these otherwise unexpected and seemingly disparate developments can, individually and taken as a whole, be seen to follow Han Fei's counsel on how to make a state powerful and wealthy. Legalism therefore helps explain Xi's leadership and ambitions for modern China.

In a visit to the National Museum of China in November of 2012, soon after he had been elected General Secretary of the Central Committee of the Communist Party of China (CCP) and Chairman of the CCP Central Military Commission, Xi Jinping announced his vision of the "Chinese Dream." Reminiscent of the "American Dream," Xi declared, "I firmly believe that the great dream of the renewal of the Chinese nation will come true." In doing so, he called for the new leadership to enhance the study and practice of the theory of socialism with Chinese characteristics, accelerate the construction of a moderately prosperous society, improve the people's livelihoods, strengthen Party building, and deepen reform and opening up. An important part of the Chinese Dream was the rule of law, with Xi calling on CPC members to take the lead to ensure the implementation of the Constitution and act in accordance with the law. Soon after this announcement, Xi was elected President of People's Republic of China (PRC) and Chairman of the PRC Central Military Commission on March 14, 2013, becoming "paramount leader" who leads the Party and the state. Since then, the "Chinese Dream" has become widespread in official announcements and has come to define Xi's leadership. More recently, it seems that the "China Dream of Great Rejuvenation" (*weida fuxing* 伟大复兴) is being augmented with the "Four Comprehensives," first raised by Xi in a trip to Jiangsu Province in December 2014. The "Four Comprehensives," according to official media, means "comprehensively building a moderately prosperous society, comprehensively deepening reform, comprehensively implementing the rule of law and comprehensively strengthening party discipline."

China Dream as a rejuvenation of the Chinese nation and the restoration of China's former leading place in the world represents the practical expression of Xi Jinping Thought. As we have seen, Legalism is not the only important tradition or theoretical approach influential in contemporary China. Confucius continues to be significant in both theory and practice.[21] China Dream itself appears to draw on diverse historical sources, open to Confucius as well as Marxist-Leninism.[22] To what extent are the China Dream and the "Four Comprehensives" consistent with Han Fei's counsel? Han Fei recommended the combined use of position, tactics, and law to make a state predominant by becoming rich and making its army powerful. We therefore will examine specific initiatives such as Xi's recent accumulation of power, control of officials, the deployment of law, and finally his more assertive foreign policy to assess the influence of Han Fei in contemporary China.

3.1 Power Concentration

As we have seen, in Legalist thought, it is important for the ruler to hold all the power in his own hands and guard it against the ambitious and self-serving officials in order to ensure the smooth functioning of the entire political system. From the founding of PRC in 1949 to his death in 1976, Mao Zedong, a keen follower of Legalism, reserved to himself the final word in Chinese politics. Alarmed by the catastrophic consequences of such power concentration, his successor Deng Xiaoping pushed forward the separation between the Party and the government (*dang zheng fen kai*) so that powers were shared by several state and Party offices such as General Secretary of the CPC, Premier of State Council, and Chairman of the Central Military Commission. This dispersal of power gave rise to other problems, such as lack of consensus on how to handle the student protests in 1989, suggesting that power decentralization could not adequately address crises. Consequently, the new consensus after 1989 was the desirability of power concentration so that it has now become an unwritten rule that the General Secretary of the CPC also holds the offices of the President and the Chairman of the Central Military Commission. Similarly, the separation between the Party and the government was no longer seriously advocated, and indeed, the precedence of Party organs over the state became the rule. Thus, from 1989 on, the Politburo Standing Committee of the Central Committee of the CPC, which practices collective leadership, retained the power to make the most important decisions in Chinese politics.

After Xi Jinping took power in 2012, he initiated major changes. He assumed leadership of newly established committees responsible for important matters like the economy and national security, accumulating more power at the cost of his colleagues in the Politburo Standing Committee. As a result of the consolidation of Xi Jinping's status as a paramount leader, the leadership of the Party is now closely linked to or even reinterpreted in terms of Xi's leadership. It is in this spirit that a document issued by the General Office of the CPC Central Committee in 2019 states:

> To uphold and strengthen the party's overall leadership, the most important thing is to firmly uphold the authority and centralized leadership of the Party Central Committee. The key is to resolutely safeguard the status of General Secretary Xi Jinping as the core of Party Central Committee and of the whole party.[23]

The 2018 constitutional amendments repealing the term limits for the President and Vice President of the PRC represented the legal manifestation of such concentration of power.[24] These changes are consistent with Legalism, which views the concentration of power in the ruler as essential for a well-functioning state. From the Legalist perspective, this kind of power concentration is not a usurpation of power for personal aggrandizement but a necessary corrective to the instability caused by dispersed leadership.

3.2 Control of Officials

The CPC is fully aware that some officials are not loyal and pose a challenge to the authority of the Party. According to Xi, some officials are double-dealers (*liang mian ren*, literally "double-faced" people) who follow in appearance but in fact oppose the Party leadership, foster their own followers and supporters within the Party, and form factions to snatch political power. Some officials ignore rules and discipline, appoint their trusted subordinates and exclude outsiders, hand out official posts, and make promises to grant special favor. Some officials do not respect or fear rules and do not abide by them, changing the rules as they see fit. Others dare not change them but try their best to evade the restraints and supervision of rules to exploit loopholes.[25] These accounts are certainly in the spirit of Han Fei's disparagement of the "Five Vermin" and how seriously he took the threat of counselors and officials who would pursue their private advantage at the expense of the state. As Xi warned,

> if the Central Committee does not have authority, the theories, line and policies may be put aside arbitrarily, if everybody does or leaves what he freely chooses, the Party will be like a heap of loose sand lacking cohesion, and will become a "private club" where everyone goes his own way, and the leadership of the Party will be empty talk.
>
> (*Xi 2017, 21*)

Han Fei's harsh measures to solve the problem of self-interested officials can also be seen in Xi's anti-corruption initiatives. First of all, since 2012 Xi has to public acclaim pursued a ruthless anti-corruption campaign aimed at both the "flies" and the "tigers." The campaign has been justified as necessary to protect the legitimacy of the Party.[26] The establishment of a state supervisory system based on internal bodies of the CPC as an anti-graft task force was another major measure to control the officials. In the past, disciplinary authorities of the CPC responsible for fighting corruption, being internal organs of the CPC, exercised investigatory powers reserved to state organs, giving rise to criticism due to the extra-legal nature of this practice. Through the amendment of the Constitution in 2018, these disciplinary authorities were essentially awarded the status of state organs and thus completely legalized. According to the amended Constitution, supervision commissions at various levels function as the state supervisory organs, which are equal to the government, the prosecuting authorities, and the courts. On the national level, the National Supervision Commission acts as the highest supervisory organ. It is listed along with the State Council, the Supreme People's Court, and the Supreme People's Procuratorate in the Constitution.[27] Under the Constitution, supervision commissions exercise "independent supervisory power" in accordance with laws and "shall be free from any interference from any administrative organ, social organization, or individual."[28] After this institutional reform, the disciplinary bodies of the CPC, previously only responsible for disciplinary supervision of Party members, act at the same time as state organs and have acquired jurisdiction over all persons exercising public power. This supervisory system, similar to Han Fei's "dragon's scales," poses a genuine threat to the officials and causes them to refrain from graft, though it might also have the unintended chilling effect of making bureaucracy cautious and reluctant to innovate. As we can see from this brief overview of Xi's assessment of the seriousness of official corruption and the means for addressing it, Xi has adopted the Legalist diagnosis of the dangers of officials as well as the recommended remedial measures.

3.3 Rule of Law

The CPC's position on law had evolved since 1949. After the founding of the PRC, the Party leaders did not rely on the legal system to govern the country. Although great importance was attached to the passage of the Constitution in 1954, this Constitution and the whole legal system were put aside in the subsequent turbulent political changes. Mao Zedong himself held that it was more expedient to govern the country by decrees instead of laws and constitutions. The resulting state of lawlessness contributed to political instability and mass violation of rights, especially in the Cultural Revolution. After the end of the Mao era, Deng Xiaoping came to the conclusion that there must be rules to maintain order in the society, ensuring that the legislature enacted statutes to establish a legal regime (*you fa ke yi*). In the 1980s, there was a profound debate over the rule of law versus the rule of man. In the end, advocates of rule of law prevailed so that "Ruling the country by law" became a governing strategy of the state in the 1990s, incorporated into the Constitution as Section 1 of Article 5: "The People's Republic of China practices ruling the country by law (*yi fa zhi guo*) and building a socialist country of law." As a consequence, law is a fundamental aspect of modern Chinese politics, but in the spirit of Legalism, it is essentially a tool of the state to ensure compliance, order, and efficiency.[29]

Xi Jinping Thought stands in this Legalist tradition concerning the role of law. For him, law has "played an important role in promoting social fairness and justice, maintaining social harmony and stability, ensuring the long-lasting rule and security of the Party and the state."[30] But unlike Jiang Zemin and Hu Jintao's emphasis on institutionalizing a socialist rule of law through legislative reform, Xi's *Yifa xhiguo* is also a political initiative, a leading *tifa* or "narrative hook," propaganda or political signal for the integration of the Party into the state.[31] This concept of law is identical to the Legalist notion of *fa* as the technique for ensuring peace and stability in the state. It is no coincidence that the social harmony and stability that law is said to promote is reminiscent of Han Fei's world of absolute peace. In the contemporary context, Xi Jinping Thought sees law as a valuable instrument, comparable to Han Fei's allusion to compass, scales, hammer, and anvil to serve two related goals: the promotion and realization of the Chinese Dream of the great rejuvenation of the Chinese Nation, and to raise the governing capabilities of the CPC.[32]

3.4 Strong and Wealthy State

Han Fei promised that his counsel would lead to a rich state. But he also argued a wealthy state made possible a powerful army, which was essential for national security because states are necessarily in tension with each other, and that a backward country is doomed to be beaten (*luo hou jiu yao ai da*). It is true that it's not always possible to separate national security or defense from more ambitious foreign policy. We should recall that the Qin Dynasty came into being by defeating six other kingdoms. There is therefore a core ambiguity in Han Fei regarding foreign policy—does it favor a powerful state for stability and defensive security, or do its psychological presuppositions and the primacy it accords to national prosperity envisage a more ambitious or assertive international relations? This tension or ambiguity has special salience given the tumultuous history of modern China.

All states desire prosperity and security. This is especially true of China given its recent history.[33] See, for example, the Preamble of the Chinese Constitution:

Under the leadership of the Communist Party of China . . ., the Chinese people of all nationalities will build China into a great modern socialist country that is rich, powerful, democratic, civilized, harmonious, and beautiful and achieve the grand rejuvenation of the Chinese nation.

(Section 7).

Domestically, the Chinese suffered extraordinary economic and political instability from the founding of the People's Republic of China in 1949 until the end of the Cultural Revolution in 1976. These included the Anti-Rightest Campaign of 1967, the Great Leap Forward in 1958, and the subsequent great famine of 1959–1961, followed by the Cultural Revolution from 1966 to 1976. After Deng Xiaoping took charge in 1978, it became widely accepted that stability should be maintained at all costs. This led to the opening up of its economy, resulting in increased wealth and prosperity during the leadership of Deng, Jiang, and Hu. This unprecedented economic transformation would soon find expression in China's foreign policy.

China shares borders with 14 countries and faces three chains of islands to the east. Between 1840 and 1949, it faced an existential threat from Japan and western powers. Since 1949, China has fought wars against the US in the Korean War, defeated India in the 1962 border war, faced confrontations and even a threat of a surgical nuclear attack by the USSR, and fought Vietnam in 1979. It is therefore tempting for some to see China in a Global Warring States Period, justifying greater investment in its military.[34] Thus, the rise of China has inevitably been accompanied by increased military strength, as anticipated by Han Fei. What is interesting about this development has been the change in the way China has presented this transformation to the world. Deng's emphasis on socialist modernization meant a foreign policy where China should never take the lead and favor a strategy of biding one's time. In contrast, Xi's "new era" seems to have turned this on its head. For Xi, the Chinese Dream includes the "Dream of a Powerful Army."

We can see this in the range of new initiatives, from the Belt and Road to the more assertive policy in the South China Sea, the recent border skirmishes with India, and the latest constitutional amendments to the Hong Kong Basic Law. This new approach was anticipated to some extent by Xi's recent speeches, such as his 2019 exhortation to officials that they needed to display a "fighting spirit" to overcome challenges ranging from security concerns to financial risks.[35] It has recently been dubbed "Wolf Warrior Diplomacy," named after popular movies depicting Chinese special operation forces.[36] It is not clear whether this is simply the continuation of the CPC promotion of a form of nationalism such as the "four confidences" (in our chosen path, in our political system, in our guiding theories, and in our culture) or if it presages greater Chinese ambition, recalling its historical regional pre-eminence. As we have seen, there is an ambiguity in Han Fei regarding the character of the foreign policy he advocates.[37] In either case, it is clear that this new form of diplomacy is consistent with Han Fei's insight that national wealth and military strength are inextricably and essentially interconnected.

4. Conclusion

Contemporary China has entered a "new era" under the leadership of Xi Jinping. What this new era entails philosophically and politically therefore requires a better appreciation of the substance of "Xi Jinping Thought on Socialism with Chinese Characteristics for a New Era." Based on the frequent references to Han Fei by Xi, this chapter has explored the extent to which Legalism, an influential Chinese political and legal school of thought, informs Xi Jinping Thought and therefore contemporary Chinese politics. Our examination of Xi's China Dream shows how in a diverse range of specific policy initiatives and laws Xi's actions are consistent with Han Fei's counsel. Xi appears to be following closely Han Fei's advice to have power concentrated in the hands of the ruler, to ensure that advisors, counselors, and bureaucrats are under strict control, to use law and its "two handles" to control and shape subjects, and finally, to make a nation wealthy and powerful. Clearly, Legalism is not the only theoretical influence on Xi Jinping Thought; many strains of thought and tradition come together to shape the political reality throughout China's long history. As we have seen, there is a long tradition of Confucian and Legalist thought forming a yin-yang dynamic in Chinese politics. But what our discussion reveals is that in times of unpredictability and instability Chinese leaders have sometimes openly and more often quietly resorted to Legalism to determine their politics. It is therefore not surprising that Han Fei's counsel continues to shape and influence contemporary China, just as it did at its origin and founding.

Notes

1 On the evolution of ideology since Xi's accession, see Minzner (2014) and Lin and Trevaskes (2019).

2 According to Politburo Standing Committee member Yu Zhensheng, this Thought "represents the latest achievement in adapting Marxism to the Chinese context, and is an important component of the system of theories of socialism with Chinese characteristics." See *Xinhua* (2017).

3 There is an extensive scholarship on Legalism and Han Fei. See, for example, Cheng (2011), Dreher and Crump (1952), Moody (2011), Goldin (2011, 2013), Harris (2014), Haitas (2018), Fu (1996), Pines and Defoort (2016), and Schneider (2011).
4 References to *Han Feizi* are to the translations in Chen (2000) by chapter, verse and page. I have also consulted the translation by Watson (2003).
5 On the differences between Legalism and Confucianism, see Cheng (1981), Harris (2013), Hutton (2008), and Cunshan (2016).
6 Han Fei thinks old advice goes out of date and needs to be reconsidered. "Those who know nothing of rulership always say: 'Do not change old ways; do not alter what has endured.' Sages do not pay attention to whether there should be change or no change; they do no more than rule correctly" (Chen 2000, ch 5, v 18, 334).
7 The Daoist influence on Hai Fei is a complex question. See Goldin (2013), who makes a persuasive case that Daoism is a supplement to Legalism.
8 See generally the discussion of persuasion in Chapter 12.
9 See the discussion in Goldin (2001) on *gong* and *si* and how ministers will always pursue what is in their self-interest.
10 Chen 2000.
11 Or as Goldin (2011, 68) puts it, *fa*, is "an impersonal administrative technique of determining rewards and punishments in accordance with a subject's true merit."
12 For comparative scholarship that notes similarities in Machiavelli and Hobbes, see Moody (1979), Martinich (2011), and He (2011).
13 On the moral implications of Han Fei's Legalism, see Ivanhoe (2011), Winston (2005), and Schneider (2013).
14 It is ironic, and perhaps revealing, that Han Fei, who left his Han Kingdom to advise Zhang who had read and admired his writings, was imprisoned and persuaded to kill himself by the secretive manipulations of Li Si, his friend and chief minister to Qin.
15 See the discussion in Sun (2012).
16 See the discussion of Fu (1996) and Lin (2017) regarding the role of Confucianism and Legalism in contemporary China.
17 This sentence is attributed to Stalin. It is, however, one of the most repeated slogans in China and has arguably become second nature for Chinese, as can be seen from baidu (11.7 mil.) and google (1.3 mil.) search results.
18 See the overview by Yu (2015).
19 See Pines (2018) who refers to Schram (1992–2004, Vol. 1, 5–6).
20 Excerpt from the Conversation between Mao Zedong and Ho Chi Minh, available at https://ccradb.appspot.com/post/1094.
21 For a thoughtful overview of the recent theoretical debates, see Jiang (2018). On the contemporary use of ancient Chinese thought, see Yan (2011). Thus, Confucian conceptions of virtue and morality have been deployed in recent law reform initiatives (Lin 2017). Officially, the rule according to law (依法治国 *yi fa zhi guo*) is often mentioned together with the rule of virtue (以德治国 *yi de zhi guo*), a Confucian understanding that runs diametrically counter to the propositions of Legalism. See also Lin and Trevaskes (2019) on the contemporary emphasis on "pan-moralism." Similarly, Confucian Institutes have been promoted as an aspect of Chinese "soft power" in international relations: see Lahtinen (2015) for a critical overview.
22 See generally Chai and Chai (2013) on *ming* or "dream" in Chinese culture, Carrai (2020) on the strategic use and manipulation of history in the formulation of the China Dream, and more generally Peters (2017). On Xi's attempt at "strengthening belief" through the use of history, see https://en.gmw.cn/2021-04/29/content_34810161.htm.
23 Zhonggongzhongyang Guanyu Jiaqiang Dang de Zhengzhi Jianshe de Yijian [Opinions of the CPC Central Committee on Strengthening the Party's Political Construction], issued by General Office of the CPC Central Committee on January 31, 2019. http://en.dfgjjt.com.cn/m/NewsDetail.aspx?ID=1391.

24 Article 45 repealed Article 79 of the Constitution, which stated the President and Vice President could not serve more than two consecutive five-year terms.
25 On the various forms of corruption, from double-dealers to those who misuse their office see generally "Opinions of the CPC Central Committee on Strengthening the Party's Political Construction," issued by General Office of the CPC Central Committee on January 31, 2019. http://en.dfgjjt.com.cn/m/NewsDetail.aspx?ID=1391.
26 For an overview and evaluation of these campaigns, see Li (2017).
27 Constitution articles 3, 123, 125.
28 Article 127.
29 For an overview of Chinese constitutionalism, see Wang (1977), Schneider (2011), and Harris (2011).
30 See www.gov.cn/xinwen/2019-11/30/content_5457206.htm and Creemers (2015).
31 On the nature of this new dimension of *Yifa Zhiguo*, see Trevaskes (2018, 368): "As made clear through the meanings embedded into *yifa zhiguo* as a central *tifa* of the current governance narrative, socialist rule of law in China (thin, thick, or otherwise) is not the teleological end-game of nearly four decades of legal development, but an ideology that works for perfecting clean and virtuous party rule to fulfill its endgame of national and party rejuvenation."
32 See Zhonggongzhongyang Guanyu Quanmian Tuijin Yifazhiguo Ruogan Zhongda Wenti de Jueding [CCP Central Committee's decision concerning some major questions in comprehensively moving ruling the country according to the Law Forward], passed by the fourth Plenary Session of the 18th Central Committee of the CPC from October 20 to 23, 2014.
33 See generally Schell and Delury (2013), who show the persistent theme of restoration for Chinese leaders.
34 See Liff and Erikson 2013 for an evaluation of Chinese military spending.
35 For the 2019 speech to cadres, see *The Print* 2019.
36 On the movie and its social and political impact, see Shi and Liu (2020).
37 As there are in western versions of Legalism, for example, on the striking differences between Machiavellian and Hobbesian foreign policy, and even in Hobbes who is used to justify both offensive and defensive realism in international relations thought.

References

Brown, Kerry. 2016. *CEO, China: The Rise of Xi Jinping*. London: I. B. Tauris.

Buckley, Chris. 2014. "Leader Taps into Chinese Classics in Seeking to Cement Power." *The New York Times*, October 11. www.nytimes.com/2014/10/12/world/leader-taps-into-chinese-classics-in-seeking-to-cement-power.html.

Carrai, Maria Adele. 2020. "Chinese Political Nostalgia and Xi Jinping's Dream of Great Rejuvenation." *International Journal of Asian Studies* (2021): 18, 7–25.

Chai, Winberg, and May-Lee Chai. 2013. "The Meaning of Xi Jinping's Chinese Dream." *American Journal of Chinese Studies* 20 (2): 95–97.

Chang, Wejen. 2016. *In Search of the Way: Legal Philosophy of the Classic Chinese Tinkers*. Edinburgh: Edinburgh University Press.

Chen, Qitian. 1936. *Zhongguo Fajia Gailun* [Introduction of Legalism in China]. Shanghai: Shanghai Zhonghua Shuju [Shanghai Zhonghua Press].

Chen, Qiyou. 2000. *Han Feizi*, with New Collations and Commentary. Shanghai: Guji.

Cheng, Chung-Ying. 1981. "Legalism Versus Confucianism: A Philosophical Appraisal." *Journal of Chinese Philosophy* 8 (3): 271–302.

———. 2011. "Preface: Understanding Legalism in Chinese Philosophy." *Journal of Chinese Philosophy* 38 (1): 1–3.

Creemers, Rogier. 2015. "China's Constitutionalism Debate: Content, Context and Implications." *China Journal* 74 (1): 91–109.
Cunshan, Li. 2016. "*Book of Lord Shang* and Elevation of Confucianism in the Han – Including the Discussion of the Conflict Between Shang Yang, His School, and the Confucians." *Contemporary Chinese Thought* 47 (2): 112–24.
Dreher, John, and James I. Crump Jr. 1952. "Pre-Han Persuasion: The Legalist School." *Communication Studies* 3 (2): 10–14.
Fu, Zhengyuan. 1996. *China's Legalists: The Earliest Totalitarians and Their Art of Ruling*. Armonk: M.E. Sharpe.
Goldin, Paul. 2001. "Han Fei's Doctrine of Self-Interest." *Asian Philosophy* 11 (3): 151–59.
———. 2011. "Persistent Misconceptions About Chinese Legalism." *Journal of Chinese Philosophy* 38 (1): 88–104.
———. 2013. "Han Fei and the *Han Feizi*." In *Dao Companion to the Philosophy of Han Fei*, edited by Paul R. Goldin, 1–21. Dordrecht: Springer.
Haitas, Daniel. 2018. "Shang Yang and Legalist Reform in the Ancient Chinese State of Qin." *Lex et Scientia* XXV (1): 100–11.
Harris, Eirik Lang. 2011. "Is the Law in the Way: On the Source of Han Fei's Laws." *Journal of Chinese Philosophy* 38 (1): 73–87.
———. 2013. "Constraining the Ruler: On Escaping Hen Fei's Criticism of Confucian Virtue Politics." *Asian Philosophy* 23 (1): 43–61.
———. 2014. "Legalism: Introducing a Concept and Analysing Aspects of Han Fei's Political Philosophy." *Philosophy Compass* 9 (3): 155–64.
He, Pen. 2011. "The Difference of Chinese Legalism and Western Legalism." *Frontiers of Law in China* 6 (4): 645–69.
Hilton, Isabel. 2015. "Ancient Origins of President Xi's Harsh Brand of Justice in China." *Financial Times*, August 17. www.ft.com/content/4c1ba05c-4295-11e5-b98b-87c7270955cf.
Hu, Hanmin. 1933. "Shang Jun Shu Xu" [Foreword of the Book of Lord Shang], *Shang Jun Shu Jianzheng* [Notes on the Book of Lord Shang]. Rpt, Taibei: Guangwen Shuju [Guangwen Press, 1975].
Hutton, Eric. 2008. "Han Feizi's Criticism of Confucianism and Its Implications for Virtue Ethics." *Journal of Moral Philosophy* 5 (3): 423–53.
Ivanhoe, Philip. 2011. "Hanfeizi and Moral Self-Cultivation." *Journal of Chinese Philosophy* 38 (1): 31–45.
Jiang, Yi-Huah. 2018. "Confucian Political Theory in Contemporary China." *Annual Review of Political Science* 21: 155–73.
Lahtinen, Anja. 2015. "China's Soft Power: Challenges of Confucianism and Confucius Institutes." *Journal of Comparative Asian Development* 14 (2): 200–26.
Lampton, David M. 2014. *Following the Leader: Ruling China, From Deng Xiaoping to Xi Jinping*. Oakland: University of California Press.
Li, Cheng. 2016. *Chinese Politics in the Xi Jinping Era: Reassessing Collective Leadership*. Washington, DC: Brookings Institution.
Li, Shaomin. 2017. "Assessment of and Outlook on China's Corruption and Anticorruption Campaigns: Stagnation in the Authoritarian Trap." *Modern China Studies* 24 (2): 139–57.
Liang, Qichao. 1999. *Liang Qichao Quanji* [Works of Liang Qichao]. Beijing: Beijing Chubanshe [Beijing Press].
Liff, Adam P., and Andrew S. Erickson. 2013. "Demystifying China's Defence Spending: Less Mysterious in the Aggregate." *The China Quarterly* 216: 805–30.
Lin, Delia. 2017. "The CCP's Exploitation of Confucianism and Legalism." In *Routledge Handbook of the Chinese Communist Party*, edited by Wo-Lap Lam, 47–58. London: Routledge.

Lin, Delia, and Susan Trevaskes. 2019. "Creating a Virtuous Leviathan: The Party, Law, and Socialist Core Values." *Asian Journal of Law and Society* 6 (1): 41–66.
Lu, Xing. 1993. "The Theory of Persuasion in Han Fei Tzu and Its Impact on Chinese Communication Behaviours." *Howard Journal of Communications* 5 (1–2): 108–22.
MCLC Resource Center. 2015. "Xi Jinping and Han Feizi." Ohio State University, January 16. https://u.osu.edu/mclc/2015/01/16/xi-jinping-and-han-feizi/.
Minzner, Carl. 2014. "Old Wine in an Ancient Bottle: Changes in Chinese State Ideology." *China Brief* 14 (6), The Jamestown Foundation.
Martinich, A. P. 2011. "The Sovereign in the Political Thought of Hanfeizi and Thomas Hobbes." *Journal of Chinese Philosophy* 38 (1): 64–72.
Moody, Peter Jr. 1979. "The Legalism of Han Fei-Tzu and Its Affinities With Modern Political Thought." *International Philosophical Quarterly* 19 (3): 317–30.
———. 2011. "Han Fei in His Context: Legalism on the Eve of the Qin Conquest." *Journal of Chinese Philosophy* 38 (1): 14–30.
Peters, Michael A. 2017. "The Chinese Dream: Xi Jinping Thought on Socialism With Chinese Characteristics for a New Era." *Educational Philosophy and Theory* 49 (14): 1299–304.
Pines, Yuri. 2018. "Legalism in Chinese Philosophy." In *Stanford Encyclopaedia of Chinese Philosophy*, edited by Edward N. Zalta. https://plato.stanford.edu/entries/chinese-legalism/.
Pines, Yuri, and Carine Defoort. 2016. "Chinese Academic Views on Shang Yang Since the Open-Up-and-Reform Era." *Contemporary Chinese Thought* 47 (2): 59–68.
The Print. 2019. "Xi Jinping Asks Communist Party Officials To Show 'Fighting Spirit' to Overcome Risks." September 4. https://theprint.in/world/xi-jinping-asks-communist-party-officials-to-show-fighting-spirit-to-overcome-risks/286273/.
Schell, Orville, and John Delury. 2013. *Wealth and Power*. New York: Random House.
Schneider, Henrique. 2011. "Legalism: Chinese Style Constitutionalism." *Journal of Chinese Philosophy* 38 (1): 46–63.
———. 2013. "Han Fei, De, Welfare." *Asian Philosophy* 23 (3): 260–74.
Schram, Stuart R., ed. 1992–2004. *Mao's Road to Power: Revolutionary Writings 1912–1949*, 8 vols. Armonk, NY: M. E. Sharpe.
Shi, Wei, and Shih-Diing Liu. 2020. "Pride as Structure of Feeling: Wolf Warrior II and the National Subject of the Chinese Dream." *Chinese Journal of Communication* 13 (3): 329–43.
Sun, Yanqing. 2012."Rufa Liangdao de 'xianxing xuanyang' yu 'niming yunyong' [On 'Open Advocacy' and 'Hidden Use' of Confucianism and Legalism]. *Kongzi Yanjiu* [Confucius Studies] (5): 165–66.
Trevaskes, Susan. 2018. "A Law Unto Itself: Chinese Communist Party Leadership and *Yifa zhiguo* in the Xi Era." *Modern China* 44 (4): 347–73.
Wang, Hsiao-po. 1977. "The Significance of the Concept of 'Fa' in Han Fei's Thought System." *Philosophy East and West* 27 (1): 35–52.
Watson, Burton. 2003. *Han Feizi: Basic Writings*. New York: Columbia University Press.
Winston, Kenneth. 2005. "The Internal Morality of Chinese Legalism." *Singapore Journal of Legal Studies* 2005 (2): 313–37.
Xi, Jinping. 2017. *Xi Jinping Tan Zhiguo Lizheng* (di er juan) [Xi Jinping on Governance (vol. II)]. Beijing: Waijiao Chubanshe [Foreign Relations Press].
Xinhua. 2017. "CPC Creates Xi Jinping Thought on Socialism With Chinese Characteristics for a New Era." October 19. www.xinhuanet.com//english/2017-10/19/c_136689808.htm.
Xu, Quanxing. 2009. " 'makesi jia qinsihuang' de chuchu he benyi." [The Source and Original Meaning of 'A Combination of the First Emperor of Qin and Karl Marx'] *Hunan*

Kejidaxue Xuebao (shehui kexue ban) [*Journal of Human University of Science and Technology* (Social Science Edition)] (3): 5–8.

Yan Xuetong. 2011. *Ancient Chinese Thought, Modern Chinese Power*. Princeton: Princeton University Press.

Yu, Zhong. 2015. "Fajia Disanqi: Quanmian Tuijin Yifazhiguo de Sixiangshi Jieshi" [Third Phase of Legalism: Explaining Overall Promotion of Ruling the Country According to Law from the History of Idea Perspective]. *Faxue Luntan* [*Forum on Law*] (1): 74.

Zwagerman, Alexander. 2016. "The Chinese Hobbes – Xi Jinping's Favourite Philosopher." *Hong Kong Free Press*, June 13. www.hongkongfp.com/2016/06/13/chinese-hobbes-xi-jinpings-favorite-philosopher/.

PART 2

How Is Legality Reflected and Embodied in Laws?

5

DASHED HOPES? THE LIMITS OF INTERNATIONAL ECONOMIC NORMS IN PROMOTING THE RULE OF LAW IN CHINA

Ming Du

Introduction

For a long time, Western elites were enthusiastic about the prospect that China's integration into the liberal international economic order would not only boost international trade and investment and encourage China's restructuring toward a market economy but also discipline China's domestic legal system and strengthen the rule of law in China (Barshefsky 2000, 367; Lamy 2000). Indeed, besides the tremendous economic benefits of accessing a giant market with 1.3 billion consumers, the expectation that China's adherence to strict global trade and investment norms would instill in China a sense of the rule of law that is the basis of democratic reform figured prominently in the debate whether the US should support China's entry into the World Trade Organization (WTO) two decades ago (Clinton 2000). Such optimism was also shared enthusiastically among reform-minded senior Chinese Communist Party (CCP) officials (Cao 2002, 379). After China's entry into the WTO, the positive impact of China's WTO membership on China's progress in rule of law and good governance was praised as a prominent example of how the WTO may promote good governance norms in the domestic context (Stewart and Badin 2011, 573).

In the same vein, when the assertion of international investment treaties leading to increased foreign direct investment has become increasingly untenable in view of the empirical evidence (Bonnitcha, Skovgaard, and Michael 2017, 155–60), the narrative of investment treaties securing and promoting the rule of law has been advanced to provide another raison d'être to legitimize the existence and operation of the international investment regime (Sattorova 2018, 7–9). The argument was that, out of their desire to avoid draconian liability for breaches of investment treaties, host states will internalize their international investment law obligations and reform their policy-making process. Crucially, norms in

DOI: 10.4324/9781003294887-7

international investment treaties are said to embody core rule of law requirements such as transparency, due process, and protection against discrimination and arbitrariness (Schill 2010, 159–71). By internalizing and implementing international legal obligations in investment treaties, the rule of law in host states is improved accordingly. Since its first bilateral investment treaty (BIT) with Sweden in 1982, China has entered into more than 100 international investment treaties over the past four decades. It is therefore only a natural conclusion that China's extensive network of BITs has had a positive and palpable impact on China's rule of law (Hadley 2013, 310).

More recently, however, a new consensus has emerged that China's increased participation in the liberal international economic order had not effectuated China's deeper engagement with market economy transformation or respect for the rule of law. The first National Security Strategy issued by the Trump Administration in December 2017 painted a pessimistic picture:

> For decades, U.S. policy was rooted in the belief that support for China's rise and for its integration into the post-war international order would liberalize China. Contrary to our hopes, China expanded its power at the expense of the sovereignty of others. China gathers and exploits data on an unrivaled scale and spreads features of its authoritarian system, including corruption and the use of surveillance. . . . China is determined to make economies less free and less fair, to grow their militaries, and to control information and data to repress their societies and expand their influence.
>
> *(the White House 2017, 25)*

Reflecting on the limited impact of the WTO on China's economic and political reforms, the Trump Administration called the US support for China's entry into the WTO 18 years ago "a mistake" (Donnan 2018). The enthusiasm for utilizing economic ties as a driver for China's rule of law and political reform China has been substantially reduced. The prospect of concluding the China–US BIT negotiations remains dim given the strategic rivalry between the two powers. Members of the European Parliament voted overwhelmingly on May 20, 2021, in support of freezing the legislative process for ratifying the landmark EU–China Comprehensive Agreement on Investment because of alleged human rights violations in Xinjiang (Ewing 2021).

The purpose of this chapter is to take a critical look at the prevailing narratives on how international trade and investment norms may impact domestic governance and the rule of law of a nation state. Tracing the rule of law development in China over the past two decades, this chapter argues that, although international economic norms and institutions have played a positive role in advancing the rule of law in China, such a role has long been exaggerated. The prevailing narratives were based on misunderstandings of the nature and function of international economic law as well as deeply flawed assumptions.

The chapter is structured as follows. Section 1 clarifies the concept of rule of law and reviews major theoretical propositions on the relationship between the rule of law and liberal international economic norms. Section 2 discusses the rule of law development in China over the past two decades. Section 3 reflects on why more integration of China into the international economy has not been successful in performing the expected catalyst role in promoting the rule of law in China. Section 4 concludes the chapter.

1. International Economic Norms and the Rule of Law: Representations of a Relationship

1.1 Defining the Rule of Law

Rule of law is an "essentially contested concept," meaning many different things to different people (Radin 1989, 791). Consequently, the precise meaning and content of the rule of law remain deeply ambiguous and progress in rule of law performance is difficult to measure. Theoretical formulations of rule of law can be roughly divided into two general types, formal/thin and substantive/thick (Tamanaha 2004, 91). The formal conception of the rule of law tends to focus on the proper sources and form of legality. It is concerned with the instrumental aspects of the rule of law that a state must possess in order to effectively function as a system of law, such as the manner in which the law is promulgated, the clarity of the ensuing norms, and the temporal dimension of the enacted norm (was it prospective or retrospective) (Craig 1997, 467). There are different formulations of the formal conception of the rule of law, and the most influential articulation is probably the list drawn up by Lon Fuller which also constitutes what he called the "internal morality" of law. These characteristics include publicity, prospectivity, generality, clarity, consistency, performability, stability over time, and congruity between the rules that are announced and the enforcement of them in actual practice (Fuller 1977, 46–73). Fuller's aspirational list of characteristics for the rule of law is not exhaustive. In addition to purely formal qualities, institutional elements such as the existence of an independent judicial system and open and effective law-enforcement agencies applying the rules with due process are also seen as emblematic of a commitment to effectuate the rule of law in practice (Hachez and Wouters 2013, 7).

The fundamental feature of the formal conceptions of the rule of law is that it does not seek to pass judgment upon the actual content of the law itself. They are not concerned with whether the law was in that sense a good law or bad law, provided that the formal precepts of the rule of law were themselves met (Craig 1997, 467). In other words, all the basic characteristics of a formal rule of law are consistent with an instrumental view of law, i.e., the use of legal rules by a government to achieve whatever substantive ends chosen by the government. Thus, the rule of law in its formal conception is a version of judging that values the systemic virtues of regularity, predictability, and certainty over the concern with substantive justice in particular instances (Hutchinson 1999, 199). It is possible for a legal system to comply with the formal conception of the rule of law and still be undemocratic, unjust, and in gross violation of human rights (Raz 1979, 214).

Critics of the formal conception of the rule of law theories often argued that it is devoid of political and economic morality. In the absence of substantive moral content, a formal conception of the rule of law could be used instrumentally by an authoritarian government to strengthen the regime and deprive individuals of their rights (Peerenboom 2002, 69). But this would run counter to the long tradition of the rule of law, which has essentially been protecting the rights of citizens from arbitrary infringement from state actors (Fegen 2012, 1197). Therefore, a formal conception of rule of law has a lot in common with the idea of "rule by law." There is no guarantee that the formal conception of the rule of law will change the life of society members for the better. As one theorist argues, "a state which savagely represents or persecutes sections of its people does not genuinely follow the rule of law simply because it undertakes those acts according to detailed laws duly enacted and scrupulously observed" (Shuker 2010, 220–22). Still, it must be emphasized that even a formal conception of the rule of law has many important virtues. It promises at least some degree of predictability of how citizens should plan their actions and imposes some constraint on arbitrary wield of state power, and hence provides some protection of individual rights and freedoms As Neil MacCormick observed:

> There is always something to be said for treating people with formal fairness. . . . Where it is observed, people are confronted by a state which treats them as rational agents due some respect as such. It applies fairly whatever standards of conduct and of judgment it applies. This has real value, and independent value, even where the substance of what is done falls short of any relevant ideal of substantive justice.
>
> *(MacCormick 1992, 123)*

In view of the criticisms leveled at formal legality as "an impoverished account of the rule of law" (Waldron 2008, 61), some scholars espouse a thick, substantive approach to defining rule of law that attempts to provide additional normative elements of political morality or justice to the formal aspects of the rule of law. They argue that certain substantial rights are said to be based on, or derived from, the rule of law. The concept of rule of law is used as the foundation for those rights, which are then used to distinguish between "good" laws which comply with these rights and "bad" laws which do not (Craig 1997, 467). For example, the United Nations defines the rule of law as follows:

> A principle of governance in which all persons, institutions and entities, public and private, including the State itself, are accountable to laws that are publicly promulgated, equally enforced and independently adjudicated, and *which are*

> *consistent with international human rights norms and standards*. It requires, as well, measures to ensure adherence to the principles of supremacy of law, equality before the law, accountability to the law, fairness in the application of the law, separation of powers, participation in decision-making, legal certainty, avoidance of arbitrariness and procedural and legal transparency.
>
> *(United Nations 2004)*

Like formal conceptions of the rule of law, there are competing forms of substantive conceptions of the rule of law. Regardless of what form of substantive theory one prefers, what is in common about all substantive conceptions of the rule of law is that, in addition to the formal attributes identified by the formal conception, they seek to impose very specific normative and political theories of the relationship between the state and a legal system. For example, within Western liberal democracies, the most common substantive version includes democracy and individual rights within the rule of law (Bingham 2011, 67). Other versions include freedom, equality, dignity, fairness, free market capitalism, and even various social welfare rights to establish necessary social, economic, educational, and cultural conditions (Dworkin 1986, 407–10).

In spite of the desirability of these substantive elements of the rule of law, they cannot be justified as the necessary or inherent meaning of the rule of law but only as a common understanding within Western societies. Moreover, there are potential clashes among the variegated substantive rule of law attributes advocated, for instance, the conflicts among individual rights and between individual rights and democracy (Tamanaha 2004, 113). Precisely because substantive theories of the rule of law require "a complete moral and political philosophy" as Raz argued, they present particular challenges to cross-cultural dialogues because of cultural differences between nations and across regions and to persons with different political persuasions (Teitel 2004, 231). This challenge explains why the World Bank and other development agencies are more likely to employ a formal conception of the rule of law in their development aid activities (Tshuma 1999, 83).

In summary, it would be simplistic to suggest that there is an overarching coherence to the rule of law concept. At its core, the rule of law requires not only formal legality or the thin conception of the rule of law but also the notion that state and its officials must operate within a limiting framework of the law. In this respect, "rule of law" is distinct from "rule by law" or "rule by man." Under the rule of law, the law constrains all members of society, including government actions. Rule by law, by contrast, means the state uses law to control its citizens but never allows law to be used by the people to control the state (Waldron 2019, 3–4). Moreover, in addition to the requirement that government officials must abide by the currently valid positive law, there are legal limits on the government's law-making power so that the state cannot mold the positive law to its will. While in the past, divine law or some type of "natural law" provided the limits, human rights declarations are said to be the common phraseology in western liberal societies today (Tamanaha 2004, 118).

1.2 The Relationship Between Liberal International Economic Norms and the Rule of Law

The conventional accounts of how international trade and investment norms may have a positive impact on the rule of law have been extensively outlined in the literature (Lam 2009; Ostry et al. 2002, 121–208). According to the account, international economic norms can contribute to the rule of law both directly and indirectly. Take the WTO as an example. Over the past 60 years, the WTO has evolved from a system based on reciprocal bargaining and mutual concessions among WTO Members to a system that promotes rules of good governance norms in both the transnational and domestic contexts (Ala'I 2008, 780). Article X of the General Agreement on Tariffs and Trade of 1994 (GATT 1994) requires that trade-related measures be promptly published, administered in a uniform, impartial, and reasonable manner and provide for an independent review of administrative measures that impact international trade. Article X is significant because it goes to the heart of a country's legal infrastructure and more precisely to the nature and enforcement of its administrative law regime. In the recent two decades, Article X has developed into a provision of fundamental importance as the embodiment of the principles of transparency and due process, which impose limitations on the exercise of executive discretion (Ostry 1998, 2; WTO Appellate Body 1997). Notably, the requirements provided in Article X embody some of the same principles required by the formal theory of the rule of law (Wang 2004, 377). Thanks to the clarity and strength of these rule of law requirements, the WTO's near universal membership, and its compulsory dispute settlement mechanism, the WTO was expected to play a direct role in promoting at least a formal conception of the rule of law in China.

Likewise, in international investment law, the narrative of investment treaties securing and promoting the rule of law has taken a prominent place in legitimizing the existence and operation of the international investment regime (Sattorova 2018, 7–9). For example, the fair and equitable treatment (FET), a core investment law concept in all modern BITs and likely to be found in almost all investment disputes, has been said to offer the best example for the interlinkage of investment protection and the rule of law. Schill identifies seven rule of law requirements that emerged in investment awards on FET, all of which also figure prominently as expressions of the broader concept of the rule of law in domestic legal systems: (1) the requirement of stability, predictability, and consistency of the legal framework; (2) the principle of legality; (3) the protection of legitimate expectations; (4) procedural due process and denial of justice; (5) substantive due process and protection against discrimination and arbitrariness; (6) transparency; and (7) the principle of reasonableness and proportionality (Schill 2010, 159–71). These developments have also been codified in the new generation of investment agreements, such as the Comprehensive and Progressive Agreement for Trans-Pacific Partnership, US–Mexico–Canada Agreement, and Canada–EU Comprehensive Economic and Trade Agreement. The concretizations of the FET standard effectively translate the declaratory rule of law commitments of states into palpable requirements whose breach can entail costly consequences (Zivkovic 2019, 522–24).

More significant are the expected indirect wide social, legal, and political implications of international trade and investment norms. The WTO and investment treaties promote a neoliberal economic paradigm—low tariffs, limited government subsidies, minimal government regulation, and strong protection of private property rights that reflects conventional wisdom about the role of government (Hartwick and Peet 2003, 190–92). They are thus a channel through which neoliberal commitments are formalized and key norms of good governance are spread. For a state like China, with a long history of official intervention in all aspects of life, from economic activity to social policy, the neoliberal paradigm challenges core ideas about the proper role of the Chinese government in society (Fewsmith 2001, 584–86). Therefore, the induction of China into the WTO and investment treaties is part of a larger strategy of massive and fundamental economic and socio-legal reform in China.

Moreover, WTO and investment treaties represent the rule of law in trade and investment, respectively. The rule of law, however, is not easily compartmentalized or confined to a single sector. Once there is a rule of law in trade and investment, it will have spillover effects on China's legal system in general. In the end, it will strengthen the accountability of institutions and generally improve the protection of rights of individuals (Murck 2002). Indeed, the potential for spillover effects is the most important aspect of the American trade agreement with China. As President Clinton asserted:

> By joining the WTO, China is not simply agreeing to import more of our products; it is agreeing to import one of democracy's most cherished values: economic freedom. The more China liberalises its economy, the more fully it will liberate the potential of its people. . . . And when individuals have the power . . . they will demand a greater say.
>
> *(Clinton 2000)*

The idea that norms of international society profoundly affect or even transform state behavior has a distinguished intellectual tradition in social sciences. For example, the international constructivist theory contends that state identity and state interests are defined by forces unleashed by the norms of behavior embedded in international society. Therefore, international norms promoted by international organizations can teach states what their interests should be, decisively influence national policies by pushing states to adopt these norms, and help them learn good behavior in international society (Finnemore 1996, 2). From this perspective, China's accession to the WTO and entering into international investment treaties could help socialize China to conform to global legal norms, including the rule of law (Steinberg 2013, 186–88).

Similarly, a new institutional economics school has long argued China's WTO membership would orient China toward its official policy of the development of a market economy. However, a flourishing market economy requires not only physical facilities but also the rule of law (Coase 1988, 10). The Chinese government's desire for fast economic growth would require China to create a framework of rules and institutions to secure investment and attract capital and develop a judicial branch capable of enforcing binding legal rules. Otherwise, it would risk the loss of international capital and significant foreign trade (Silverstein 2003, 427). In the same vein, political scientists have long termed the process of using WTO membership as a lever to improve domestic good governance as "policy anchoring" (Ferrantino 2006, 3). Once China becomes a formal member of the WTO, it will be difficult for China to renege on its commitments without incurring considerable political and economic costs. The reform-minded Chinese leaders could then wield the WTO accession as an external force to lock in and further domestic economic and political reforms (Rajapatirana 2001, 78–95).

2. The Rule of Law Development in China: From Theory to Practice

It is well known that the rule of law has been weak in traditional Chinese legal culture. The two dominant intellectual traditions of Confucianism and legalism are more accommodating to the notion of "rule of man" and "rule by law" respectively, as opposed to "rule of law" (Fang and Forges 2008, 103). In particular, law was traditionally viewed as an instrument of governance for the rulers to impose their will on the people and not something that protects the weak individual from the state. This is fundamentally different from the Western notion of the rule of law, in which law has the capacity to serve as an independent source of restraint on government behavior (Sheehy 2006, 238–45).

How should we evaluate the progress of China's long march toward the rule of law? On the one hand, there is no denying that law has been playing an increasingly significant role in supporting economic development and preserving social order in contemporary China. China has advanced from "rule by law" in the imperial period and the Mao era and has been transitioning toward at least a "thin" or "formal" version of the rule of law (Zhang and Ginsburg 2019, 348). The Chinese government's proclamation that it is committed unwaveringly to pushing forward the project of "ruling the country according to law" has triggered much enthusiasm (Wang Yuhua 2015, 3–4). On the other hand, the formal version of the rule of law is only partially achieved in China with varying degrees of adherence in different regions and domains. It remains the case that law and legal procedure are sometimes being used selectively and inconsistently in China (Chen 2016, 35). Moreover, the Chinese government's conception of law remains highly instrumentalist (DeLisle 2017, 79). The substantial conception of the rule of law in China remains a "bird in a cage" due to various institutional, cultural, and ideological limitations (Lubman 2000, 389–410). Some even argue that China is moving away from the rule of law, because it does not comply with the core elements of the rule of law, such as the separation of powers, the supremacy of law, an independent judiciary, and the protection of human rights (Blasek 2015; Carl Minzner 2016). The World Justice Project's Rule of Law Index ranked China 98th among the 139 jurisdictions in its 2021 report (World Justice Project 2021).

Specifically, what impact have international trade and investment norms brought on the rule of law in China? To evaluate the role of international economic law in shaping the rule of law in China, one needs to appreciate the broad legal reforms China has undertaken to implement and comply with its commitments under the WTO and investment treaties. In this section, we will take a look at the WTO's requirements of transparency, uniform administration of law, and independent judicial review as they had a direct impact on a formal/thin conception of the rule of law in China. Then we will proceed to assess to what extent the WTO has also shaped the rule of law in China in its substantive conception.

Transparency is one of the vital elements of trade liberalism, underpinning all substantive areas of the WTO (WTO 2001). It requires that all laws, regulations, judicial decisions, and administrative decisions affecting the trade of a WTO Member should be made public. Transparency is also one of the most crucial aspects of the formal conception of the rule of law, encompassing mainly its key principle of promulgation but also relevant to the principles of clarity, stability, and prospectivity (Wang 2004, 380). The issue of transparency was among the top concerns of China's major trading partners in negotiations leading up to China's accession to the WTO as China's administrative legal system was not designed for transparency. One typical example was a body of regulatory documents grouped together under the heading "normative documents," which are not part of the formal system of laws, not available in the public domain, and changing frequently (Farah 2006, 278–80). However, they are extensively used by Chinese government ministries and they affect the rights and duties of business actors to the extent that they define the ways in which state agencies carry out their work and implement the law.

China has committed to extensive transparency commitments in the Accession Protocol. After 20 years of full WTO Membership, one can fairly say that China has largely complied with its transparency obligations. This is particularly the case for the Chinese central government and those central government ministries with a primary or significant responsibility for international trade-related issues (Gao 2018, 26). Nevertheless, there remains much room for China to improve, in particular with regard to local governments and internal normative documents. It is still less common for some central government measures such as opinions, circulars, orders, directives, and notices to be published, even though they are all binding legal measures with implications for international trade (USTR 2020, 114). Moreover, China rarely publishes certain types of trade-related measures and sub-central government measures in official journals. A typical example is China's complex and extensive subsidy programs. The US has frequently accused China of severely under-reporting important programs and significantly over-reporting irrelevant or minor programs (WTO 2019, 1).

In its WTO accession agreement, China also committed to apply, implement, and administer its laws, regulations, and other measures relating to trade in goods and services in a *uniform, impartial, and reasonable manner* at all levels of government throughout China. This uniform administration commitment is significant because if successful, it could reduce a major obstacle—local and departmental protectionism—to strengthening at least a formal conception of the rule of law in China, ensuring generality and non-contradictory of rules enforced (Lubman 2014). Nevertheless, foreign investors continue to voice concerns about inconsistent enforcement of laws and regulations in different areas including customs trade administration, taxation, investment, and intellectual property rights (USTR 2020, 168). One example is the alleged China's selective enforcement of the Anti-Monopoly Law (AML) against foreign companies in merger reviews to advance China's industrial policy goals and boost national champions, while the law has rarely been applied to powerful Chinese state-owned enterprises. In fact, a review of China's AML enforcement activities since the law took effect in 2008 shows that all transactions blocked or conditionally approved to date have involved foreign companies (United States Chamber of Commerce 2014, 2).

Independent courts are widely seen as an institution emblematic of a commitment to the rule of law (Balasubramaniam 2009, 405). Under Article 2(D) of the Accession Protocol, China is committed to giving foreign investors in all cases an opportunity for an impartial and independent judicial body to review specified administrative actions (Hung 2004, 79). This requirement has also been frequently referred to as an example that WTO law embodies various substantive constitutional law principles (Petersmann 2006, 32–33).

Chinese courts have come a long way in their reforms (Information Office 2012). There is no doubt that the Chinese government is committed to improving judicial professionalism, making the rule of law in the Chinese context more transparent, taking meddling by local officials out of the judicial process, improving the fairness of judicial decisions, and ensuring better implementation of laws (Minzner 2015, 6–7). However, based on the standards and jurisprudence laid down by the WTO and other international legal instruments, it remains doubtful whether China's judicial system can pass the scrutiny of the WTO requirements (Wu 2012, 119–26). Chinese judges continue to be influenced by political, government, or business pressures, particularly outside of China's big cities (USTR 2020, 168). In particular, there are serious concerns about the independence of China's judiciary from the CCP. Ample evidence shows that despite all the reforms, the party retains systematic and structural control over the courts. More specifically, the party has the power to command courts to develop judicial policies consistent with its political objectives and priorities and to instruct courts regarding specific decisions in individual cases or categories of cases that the party deems important (Li 2016, 72). The Chief Justice Zhou Qiang, China's top judicial official, publicly denounced the idea of an independent judiciary and warned judges not to fall into "the trap of western ideology" (Forsythe 2017). Consequently, though judicial power in China is separate from other state powers, it is always a pliant agent to the supreme power of the party. Indeed, As President Xi Jinping stated unequivocally, the cornerstone of socialist rule of law with Chinese characteristics is the leadership of the party. Discussion of judicial independence from the party at the central level is currently a forbidden subject in China (Cohen 2016).

In summary, it is fair to say that China has gradually moved away from a purely instrumental conception of law toward a substantial conception of rule of law where law is meant to protect human rights, binding not only citizens but also government officials and the party (Chen 2007, 735–36). However, it remains true that similar formal commitments to more democratic governance, protection of individual civil and political rights, and effective control of the state and its actors are widely dismissed as largely empty words. Numerous accounts have emphasized the supremacy of the party's rule and suggested that even if China is making progress in extending some form of governance by law, the system cannot be regarded as following the rule of law because the rule of law has so far failed to reach political sensitive domains where party's important interests are at stake (Pils 2015). Consequently, even though the CCP has become more confident in using sophisticated legal tools to achieve policy goals; it is also one in which China travels further away from the Western rule of law (Ye 2021, 1861). To the extent one expects to see the profound indirect impact of WTO membership in terms of moving China toward a western-style liberal democratic version of rule of law, that hope was completely dashed (Chen 2016, 10–11). The primary motivation for undertaking legal reform in China was economic, and it was not a question to bring the rule of law to China at least in the western sense of separation of powers, human rights, and democracy (Woo 2017, 244–51).

3. Explaining the Limits of International Economic Norms in Shaping Rule of Law in China

3.1 The Limited Mandate of International Economic Law

To begin with, despite all the enthusiasm about the direct and potential role of international economic norms in improving the rule of law in China, both WTO law and international investment law have actually very little to say about the rule of law in China except for some sporadic provisions and specific sectors and most of these obligations, if they exist after all, are procedural in nature. They do not address substantive justice or any structural issues that have hindered China from being a rule of law country.

Around the time when China was about to join the WTO, some prominent legal scholars argued that China's WTO entry was at root a fundamental challenge to China's politics and governance and that consequently China was required to revamp virtually all aspects of its legal and regulatory systems in order to comply with its WTO obligations. When assessing legal institutional reform that the WTO requires, one commentator wrote:

> In order to meet the transparency and rule of law requirements of the GATT... constitutional provisions permitting control by the Chinese Communist Party in the operation of the legal system may have to be revised. . . . This may also require deletion or amendment of the term "socialism" in the constitutional references to the rule of law. . . . This is a basic rule of law concept contained in GATT Article X(3)(b), on independent adjudication and review of trade regulation matters.
>
> *(Potter 2001, 603)*

But this argument is seriously flawed as it erroneously paints the GATT/WTO legal system as an anti-socialism, anti-authoritarianism, and liberal democracy-oriented machine (Wang 2004, 375). In fact, there is even no requirement under the WTO Agreement that the judicial system of a WTO Member must be independent and free from political interference, let alone a liberal democratic rule of law (Clarke 2003, 111). This realistic observation takes us back to the fundamental nature of WTO law: it is a multilateral regime designed to facilitate reciprocal market access for goods and services by reducing tariff and non-tariff barriers (Kyle Bagwell, Mavroidis, and Staiger 2002, 59). It does not envision the rule of law with constitutional and political values.

Furthermore, there is a growing perception that the current GATT/WTO rules are incapable of constraining China's unique state-led development model (The European Commission 2018; WTO 2018). While some problematic policies and practices being pursued by the Chinese government have been found to be inconsistent with China's WTO obligations after an expensive and long litigation process, many other interventions fall into a gray area: they violate the spirit, if not always the letter, of WTO rules (Rodrik 2018). Consequently, they are not directly and effectively disciplined by WTO rules. The allegation that Chinese government officials force foreign enterprises to transfer technology as a condition for securing investment approvals, a trigger of the ongoing China–US trade war, is one of such examples (USTR 2018, 23–43). But unless a WTO Member has made specific commitments, ownership restrictions on foreign investment are not regulated by WTO disciplines, nor are they generally prohibited by international investment treaties (Mavroidis and Andre 2021, 162–166). Some developing countries even argue that the market for technology policy such as a joint venture requirement is a perfectly legitimate tool for economic development (Qin 2020, 753–58).

The same may be said with regard to international investment law. Since its origin, investment treaties have always been promoting international investment and economic growth through the protection of foreign investments against expropriation and regulatory uncertainty in host countries. They typically will specify standards of treatment for foreign investors and provide for extra-jurisdictional dispute resolution and enforcement, lowering the risk of bias in the host state jurisdiction. More recent BITs go further to require substantial liberalization, for example, by requiring market access and prohibiting technology transfer, as well as provisions on environment, labor protection, and sustainable development (OECD 2021, 8–13). Though it may have a bearing on rule of law and good governance, that relationship is indirect and flimsy at best. The reality is that the international trade and investment rules were not formulated with a state-led economy in mind. It is not effective in addressing China's regime that many argue broadly conflicts with the fundamental underpinnings of the WTO system (Hillman 2018).

Finally, to the extent that we see improvements in certain aspects of the rule of law in either a formal or substantive conception in China, it is not entirely clear whether the key driver of change in the Chinese legal system is the influence of international economic norms, the internal developments within China, or simply a convergence of interests between the Chinese government and other foreign stakeholders. It seems plausible that the Chinese government's decision to pursue WTO Membership and investment treaties was because they are consistent with China's domestic reform agenda. They not only opened more markets for Chinese products, services, and investments but also gave the Chinese leadership extra leverage to overcome domestic obstacles in the domestic economic and legal system (Clarke 2003, 97–98). To be sure, this claim is not to downplay the positive influence of the WTO and BITs, but more of a plea to pin down the causal mechanisms and to provide sufficient evidence demonstrating that China has indeed internalized the international norms and that these norms are primary drivers underlying the progress in the rule of law in China.

3.2 The Limits of International Dispute Settlement Processes

The WTO dispute settlement system is widely considered as an independent judiciary and the "jewel in the crown" of the global trade architecture. Nevertheless, the WTO Appellate Body appears to be very conscious of its legitimacy when it passes judgment over domestic policies in sensitive areas (Picciotto 2005, 477–503). Through various issue-avoidance techniques and a number of crucial jurisprudence moves, the Appellate Body has been largely successful in avoiding the charges of judicial activism and the appearance that it is the agent of the neo-liberal project or inspired by the deep liberalization telos reflected in the WTO Agreement (Howse 2016, 13). However, the WTO judiciary's conservativism renders itself a reluctant guardian for values of rule of law that are not explicitly embodied in WTO Agreements.

Take *China—Publications and Audiovisual Products* as an example. China argued that it would need to censor the content of imported foreign cultural products because some contents may be harmful to public morals in China. The Appellate Body accepted the panel's assumption, with no further investigation, that China's submission was true. Ironically, in the same case, the Appellate Body criticized the panel for relying on "an assumption arguendo" when the panel had simply "assumed" without making a proper legal finding (WTO Appellate

Body 2014). As a consequence of such a hasty assumption, the fact that China's content review mechanism may be violating basic principles of freedom of speech, arguably an essential element of the rule of law in liberal societies, was not even mentioned (Joost Pauwelyn 2010, 133).

Moreover, as an ancient Chinese saying goes, law is not enough for oneself. Having rules on paper does not mean that they are fairly enforced in practice. It is only meaningful to talk about WTO's impact on the rule of law if China has faithfully and promptly implemented its WTO commitments, including adverse WTO rulings against it. It is widely acknowledged that China has an overall good record in complying with the WTO rulings in a timely and qualitatively sound manner (Webster 2014, 572). However, China's implementation record also suggests that China has done what is necessary to achieve compliance with the WTO norms, but it may drag its feet in particularly sensitive areas and matters that it considers vital to its national interest. The point is simply that it is unrealistic to believe that WTO enforcement actions alone can have a significant impact on an economy as large as China's economy unless the Chinese government is truly committed to market-based competition and the rule of law. With the paralysis of the WTO Appellate Body at the moment, the impact of the WTO dispute settlement on the rule of law in China will be further diminished.

Compared to the WTO dispute settlement processes, investor–state dispute settlement has had even less impact on the rule of law in China up to date. For some time, international investment lawyers have been debating the puzzle of the so-called "China disequilibrium" in international investment arbitration. Despite the fact that China is a signatory of almost 150 bilateral investment treaties in which comprehensive ISDS procedures are a common feature, there are only few investor–state investment disputes involving the Chinese government, Chinese investors, or Chinese BITs. According to public records, the Chinese government was the respondent in seven reported cases by December 2021 and China has never lost one case in ISDS (Du 2022).

Several reasons were offered to explain the Chinese Government's absence from investment arbitration (Hong and Lee 2018, 47–51). One explanation is that the Chinese government has always appreciated the important role of foreign investment in Chinese economic development and offered sufficient investment protection to foreign investors (Zhang 2008, 159). Therefore, the risk of the Chinese government violating its BIT obligations is very low. Opposite to this optimistic explanation, a competing argument holds essentially that a dearth of ISDS claims against China is precisely due to the lack of the rule of law in China. Foreign investors may fear that their ISDS claim could jeopardize their relationship with the Chinese government and in turn put their business dealings in China at risk. By contrast, foreign investors may gain more from non-adversarial means such as negotiation and mediation to resolve their disputes with the Chinese government in view of its preference to settle disputes informally. Initiating arbitration against the Chinese government is therefore only the last resort (Trakman 2015, 279).

3.3 The Resilience of the Chinese State

In hindsight, much of the original optimism about the profound impact of international commitment devices, such as bilateral investment treaties, international arbitration, and multilateral trade commitments, on China's rule of law construction, in both formal and substantial conceptions, seems to be founded on flawed assumptions. International economic norms and commitments may have a powerful spillover effect on domestic rule of law or can even substitute for domestic institutions (The Economist 2000; Ginsburg 2005, 118–22). However, contrary to what many people hoped for, the economic liberalization—rule of law process is not at all automatic but heavily dependent on the existence of many other pre-conditions such as political will, expertise, funds, and an independent judiciary benefitting from the existence of embedded judicial authority and an established tradition of broad interpretation of judicial rules and doctrines (Silverstein, 430). Moreover, increased economic and cultural exchange deriving from WTO membership will not necessarily lead to political pressure for democratic reform and a western liberal conception of the rule of law. Policymakers may at times be unwilling or unable to effectively change behavior, institutions, and culture. Instead, the cultural disruption ensuing from economic globalization and trade liberalization may encourage a greater exertion of central government authority to maintain societal stability and national identity (Orts 2001, 109).

This is arguably the case in China. After 40 years of reform and opening policy, China's remarkable economic liberalization stands in marked contrast to political conservativeness, featuring the monopoly of political power by the CCP and the blurring line between Chinese national interests and the security of the CCP regime (Yang 2017, 88–90). When the CCP perceives potential threats to its grip of power, it is very easy for it to slow or even block any spillover effects that the WTO may have on the rule of law effectively, efficiently, and constitutionally, at no discernible cost to its economic standing in the world community (Silverstein, 442).

It is further submitted that the root problem with regard to trade and investment liberalization and rule of law nexus is that it implicitly assumes nation states as rational, docile, and readily receptive to all direct and indirect influences of economic globalization, and their national policies and identities could be easily mounded along liberal democratic lines. Indeed, the rule of law thesis is rooted in a traditional, rational-choice theory of the state as an actor making preference-maximizing decisions on the basis of cost–benefit analyses. Given the benefits of compliance with international obligations and the costs of violation, a rational choice model predicts that states, on balance, will gain more from internalizing their obligations and complying with them (Calamita 2015, 16). The reality is, as Ian Hurd puts it, "states are both socialised to norms and strategic calculators that manipulate them" (Hurd 2007, 209). State power co-exists with global governance institutions. It may retreat under exogenous normative forces, but it is equally possible that the pendulum may swing toward the opposite direction. In short, it is not surprising that China's WTO membership and extensive BIT network do not automatically bring rule of law to China. Although there is a solid theoretical foundation for the claim that trade liberalization may ultimately lead to rule of law, it is not a guaranteed outcome.

4. Conclusion

The conventional wisdom has it that China's WTO membership and its extensive investment treaty networks constituted an unprecedented opportunity to put China's economic, legal, and political system under strict scrutiny and to push China to reform its legal system toward the rule of law. In contrast, the alternative narrative argues that China undertakes minimum commitments to the international legal regime while extracting the benefits of global institutions and that China only selectively incorporates international norms most conducive to its economic growth and preferable to its elites (Kim 1994, 419; Potter 2007, 701). In particular, it is claimed that China's increased participation in international organizations has not effectuated deeper engagement with, or respect for, rule of law. Though rhetoric about law has been prominent in official statements, reality has fallen short of official promises (DeLisle 2017, 70).

While it is undisputed that China has made great strides in rule of law construction, it is less clear that the locomotion which gives impetus to China's positive behavioral evolution was primarily supplied by international trade and investment norms. My contention is by no means a rejection of the positive role that the WTO and investment treaties have played in promoting the rule of law in China. There is indeed some evidence showing that the Chinese regions in which the rule of law is better realized are those in which foreign investors play a considerable role in their economic development (Wang 2004, 3–4). Rather, the purpose of this chapter is to interrogate the degree, depth, and scope of such effects. To be sure, international economic law is not a magic formula for converting a member government into a rule of law country.

References

Ala'i, Padideh. 2008. "From the Periphery to the Centre? The Evolving WTO Jurisprudence on Transparency and Good Governance." *Journal of International Economic Law* 11 (4): 779–802.

Balasubramaniam, Ratna Rueban. 2009. "Judicial Politics in Authoritarian Regimes." *University of Toronto Law Journal* 59: 405–16.

Barshefsky, Charlene. 2000. "Trade Policy and the Rule of Law." *Minnesota Journal of Global Trade* 9: 361–68.

Bingham, Tom. 2011. *The Rule of Law*. New York: Penguin Press.

Blasek, Katrin. 2015. *Rule of Law in China: A Comparative Approach*. Heidelberg: Springer.

Bonnitcha, Jonathan, Poulsen Lauge N. Skovgaard, and Waibel Michael. 2017. *The Political Economy of the Investment Treaty Regime*. Oxford: Oxford University Press.

Calamita, N. Jansen. 2015. "The Rule of Law, Investment Treaties, and Economic Growth: Mapping Normative and Empirical Questions." In *The Importance of the Rule of Law in Promoting Development*, edited by J. Jowell, C. J. Thomas, and J. Van Z. Y. L. Smit, 1–18. Singapore: Singapore Academy of Law.

Cao, Jianming. 2002. "WTO and the Rule of Law in China." *Temple International and Comparative Law Journal* 16: 379–90.

Chen, Albert H. Y. 2016. "China's Long March Towards Rule of Law or China's Turn Against Law?" *Chinese Journal of Comparative Law* 4: 1–35.

Chen, Jianfu. 2007. "The Transformation of Chinese Law: From Formal to Substantial." *Hong Kong Law Journal* 37: 689–739.

Clarke, Donald. 2003. "China's Legal System and the WTO: Prospects for Compliance." *Washington University Global Studies Law Review* 2: 97–118.

Clinton, William J. 2000. Speech on China Trade Bill at the Paul H. Nitze School of Advanced International Studies of the John Hopkins University.

Coase, Ronald H. 1988. *The Firm, the Market, and the Law*. Chicago: University of Chicago Press.

Cohen, Jerome A. 2016. "A Looming Crisis for China's Legal System." *Foreign Policy*, February 22, 2016.

Craig, Paul. 1997. "Formal and Substantive Conceptions of the Rule of Law: An Analytical Framework." *Public Law*: 467–87.

DeLisle, Jacques. 2017. "Law in the China Model 2.0: Legality, Developmentalism and Leninism Under Xi Jinping." *Journal of Cotemporary China* 26: 68–84.

Du, Ming. 2022. "Explaining China's Approach to the Investor-State Dispute Settlement Reform." *European Law Journal* 27: 1–29.

Donnan, Shawn. 2018. "US Says China WTO Membership Was a Mistake." *Financial Times*, January 19, 2018.

Dworkin, Ronald. 1986. *Law's Empire*. Cambridge, MA: Harvard University Press.

The Economist. 2000. "Vote for China's Freedom." *The Economist*, May 20, 2000.

The European Commission Concept Paper. 2018. "WTO Modernisation: Future EU Proposals on Rulemaking." June 2018.

Ewing, Jack. 2021. "European Lawmakers Block a Pact With China, Citing Human Rights Violations." *New York Times*, May 20, 2021.

Fang, Qiang, and Roger Des Forges. 2008. "Were Chinese Rulers Above the Law? Toward a Theory of the Rule of Law in China from Early Times to 1949 CE." *Stanford Journal of International Law* 44: 101–46.

Farah, Paolo D. 2006. "Five Years of China's WTO Membership: EU and US Perspectives on China's Compliance with Transparency Commitments and the Transitional Review Mechanism." *Legal Issues of Economic Integration* 33 (3): 263–304.

Ferrantino, Michael J. 2006. "Policy Anchors: Do Free Trade Agreements and WTO Accessions Serve as Vehicles for Developing Country Reform?" Office of Economics Working paper, U.S. International Trade Commission.

Fegen, Nicolas. 2012. "Thick or Thin? Defining Rule of Law: Why the "Arab Spring" Calls for a Thin Rule of Law Theory." *UMKC Law Review* 80: 1187–210.

Fewsmith, Joseph. 2001. "The Political and Social Implications of China's Accession to the WTO." *China Quarterly* 167: 573–91.

Finnemore, Martha. 1996. *National Interests in International Society*. Ithaca: Cornell University Press.

Forsythe, Michael. "China's Chief Justice Rejects an Independent Judiciary, and Reformers Wince." *New York Times*, January 18, 2017.

Fuller, Lon L. 1977. *The Morality of Law*. New Haven: Yale University Press.

Ginsburg, Tom. 2005. "International Substitutes for Domestic Institutions: Bilateral Investment Treaties and Governance." *International Review of Law and Economics* 25: 107–23.

Hachez, Nicolas, and Jan Wouters. 2013. "Promoting the Rule of Law: A Benchmark Approach." Leuven Centre for Global Governance Studies Working Paper No. 105.

Hadley, Kate. 2013. "Do China's BITs Matter – Assessing the Effect of China's Investment Agreements on Foreign Direct Investment Flows, Investor Rights, and the Rule of Law." *Georgetown Journal of International Law* 45 (1): 255–321.

Hartwick, Elaine, and Richard Peet. 2003. "Neoliberalism and Nature: The Case of the WTO." *Annals American Academy Political and Social Science* 590: 188–211.

Henry, Gao. 2018. "The WTO Transparency Obligations and China." *Journal of Comparative Law* 12 (2): 1–28.

Hillman, Jennifer. 2018. Testimony Before the U.S. Senate Foreign Relations Committee Hearing on Multilateral Economic Institutions and U.S. Foreign Policy, November 27, 2018.

Hong, Dae Un, and Ju Yoen Lee. 2018. "Why Are There So Few Investor-State Arbitrations in China? A Comparison with Other East Asian Economies." *China & WTO Review*: 35–65.

Howse, Robert. 2016. "The World Trade Organization 20 Years On: Global Governance by Judiciary." *European Journal of International Law* 27 (1): 9–77.

Hung, Veron Mei-Ying. 2004. "China's WTO Commitment on Independent Judicial Review: Impact on Legal and Political Reform." *American Journal of International Law* 52 (1): 77–132.

Hurd, Ian. 2007. "Breaking and Making Norms: American Revisionism and Crises of Legitimacy." *International Politics* 44 (2): 194–213.

Hutchinson, Allan C. 1999. "The Rule of Law Revisited: Democracy and Courts." In *Recrafting the Rule of Law: The Limits of Legal Order*, edited by David Dyzenhaus, 196–224. Oxford: Hart Publishing.

Information Office of the State Council. 2012. "Judicial Reform in China." www.mfa.gov.cn/ce/cezw/eng/zgjj/t977471.htm.

Kim, Samuel S. 1994. "China's International Organization Behavior." In *Chinese Foreign Policy: Theory and Practice*, edited by Thomas W. Robinson and David Shambaugh, 401–34. Oxford: Oxford University Press.

Kyle Bagwell, Petros C. Mavroidis, and Robert W. Staiger. 2002. "It Is a Question of Market Access." *American Journal of International Law* 96 (1): 56–76.

Lam, Esther. 2009. *China and the World Trade Organization: A Long March Towards the Rule of Law*. London: Kluwer Law International.

Lamy, Pascal. 2000. "Remarks at the China – Britain Business Council Conference." London, October 2, 2000.

Li, Ling. 2016. "The Chinese Communist Party and People's Courts: Judicial Independence in China." *American Journal of Comparative Law* 64: 37–74.

Lubman, Stanley. 2000. "Bird in a Cage: Chinese Law Reform After Twenty Years." *Northwestern Journal of International Law & Business* 20 (3): 383–423.

———. 2014. "A Key Move to Protect Courts in China." *The Wall Street Journal*, July 30, 2014.

MacCormick, Neil. 1992. "Natural Law and the Separation of Law and Morals." In *Natural Law Theory: Contemporary Essays*, edited by Robert P. George, 105–33. Oxford: Oxford University Press.

Mavroidis, Petros C., and Sapir Andre. 2021. *China and the WTO: Why Multilateralim Still Matters*. Princeton: Princeton University Press.

Minzner, Carl. 2015. "Legal Reform in the Xi Jinping Era." *Asia Policy* (20): 4–9.

———. 2016. "The Great China Crackdown Is Here (and Why You Should Worry)." *The National Interest*, April 25, 2016.

Murck, Christian. 2002. *Testimony to the Congressional-Executive Commission on China Hearing on WTO: Will China Keep Its Promises? Can It?*, June 6, 2002. https://www.cecc.gov/events/hearings/wto-will-china-keep-its-promises-can-it.

OECD. 2021. *The Future of Investment Treaties: Background Note on Potential Avenues for Future Policies*. Paris: OECD Publishing.
Orts, Eric W. 2001. "The Rule of Law in China." *Vanderbilt Journal of Transnational Law* 34: 43–115.
Ostry, Sylvia. 1998. "China and the WTO: The Transparency Issue." *UCLA Journal of International Law and Foreign Affairs* 3 (1): 1–22.
Ostry, Sylvia et al., eds. 2002. *China and the Long March to Global Trade: The Accession of China to the World Trade Organization*. Abingdon-on-Thames: Routledge.
Pauwelyn, Joost. 2010. "Squaring Free Trade in Culture With Chinese Censorship: The WTO Appellate Body Report on *China-Audiovisuals*." *Melbourne Journal of International Law* 11: 119–40.
Peerenboom, Randall. 2002. *The Long March Towards Rule of Law*. Cambridge: Cambridge University Press.
Petersmann, Ernst U. 2006. "Multilevel Trade Governance in the WTO Requires Multilevel Constitutionalism." In *Constitutionalism, Multilevel Trade Governance and Social Regulation*, edited by C. Joerges and E. U. Petersmann, 5–59. Oxford: Hart Publishing.
Picciotto, Sol. 2005. "The WTO Appellate Body: Legal Formalism as a Legitimation of Global Governance." *Governance* 8 (3): 477–503.
Pils, Eva. 2015. *China's Human Rights Lawyers: Advocacy and Resistance*. Abingdon-on-Thames: Routledge.
Potter, Pitman. 2001. "The Legal Implications of China's Accession to the WTO." *The China Quarterly* 167: 592–609.
———. 2007. "China and the International Legal System: Challenges of participation." *China Quarterly* 191: 699–715.
Qin, Julia Ya. 2020. "Forced Technology Transfer and the US-China Trade War: Implications for International Economic Law." *Journal of International Economic Law* 22: 743–62.
Radin, Margaret Jane. 1989. "Reconsidering the Rule of Law." *Boston University Law Review* 69: 781–819.
Raz, Joseph. 1979. *The Authority of Law – Essays on Law and Morality*. Oxford: Clarendon Press.
Rodrik, Dani. 2018. "The WTO Has Become Dysfunctional." *Financial Times*, August 5, 2018.
Sarath, Rajapatirana. 2001. "Developing Countries' Trade Policies in the 1990s: Back to the Future." In *Trade, Development and Political Economy: Essays in Honour of Anne O. Krueger*, edited by D. Lai and R. H. Snape, 78–95. New York: Palgrave Publisher.
Sattorova, Mavluda. 2018. *The Impact of Investment Treaty Law on Host States: Enabling Good Governance*. Oxford: Hart Publishing.
Schill, Stephan W. 2010. "Fair and Equitable Treatment, the Rule of Law, and Comparative Public Law." In *International Investment Law and Comparative Public Law*, edited by Stephan W. Schill, 151–82. Oxford: Oxford University Press.
Sheehy, Benedict. 2006. "Fundamentally Conflicting Views of the Rule of Law in China and the West and Implications for Commercial Disputes." *Northwestern Journal of International Law & Business* 26 (2): 225–66.
Shuker, Daniel. 2010. "Review of 'Rule of Law' by Tom Bingham." *Yale Journal of International Law* 36: 219–22.
Silverstein, Gordon. 2003. "Globalization and the Rule of Law: A Machine That Runs of Itself? *International Journal of Constitutional Law* 1 (3): 427–45.
Steinberg, Richard H. 2013. "International Trade Law as a Mechanism for State Transformation." In *Back to Basics: State Power in a Contemporary World*, edited by Martha Finnemore and Judith Goldstein, 177–95. Oxford: Oxford University Press.

Stewart, Richard B., and Michelle Ratton Sanchez Badin. 2011. "The World Trade Organization: Multiple Dimensions of Global Administrative Law." *International Journal of Constitutional Law* 9: 556–86.

Tamanaha, Brian. 2004. *On the Rule of Law: History, Politics. Theory*. Cambridge: Cambridge University Press.

Teitel, Ruti. 2004. "Global Rule of Law: Universal and Particular." In *Human Rights With Modesty – The Problem of Universalism*, edited by Andras Sajo, 231–47. Leiden: Martinus Nijhoff Publishers.

Trakman, Leon E. 2015. "Geopolitics, China, and Investor-State Arbitration." In *China in the International Economic Order*, edited by Lisa Toohey, Colin B. Picker, and Jonathan Greenacre, 268–92. Cambridge: Cambridge University Press.

Tshuma, Lawrence. 1999. "The Political Economy of the World Bank's Legal Framework for Economic Development." *Social and Legal Studies* 8: 75–96.

United Nations Security Council. 2004. *Report of the Secretary-General on the Rule of Law and Transitional Justice in Conflict and Post-Conflict Societies*. https://www.un.org/ruleoflaw/blog/document/the-rule-of-law-and-transitional-justice-in-conflict-and-post-conflict-societies-report-of-the-secretary-general/.

United States Chamber of Commerce. 2014. *Competing Interests in China's Competition Law Enforcement: China's Anti-Monopoly Law Application and the Role of Industrial Policy*. https://www.uschamber.com/assets/archived/images/aml_final_090814_final_locked.pdf

United States Trade Representative. 2020. *2019 Report to Congress on China's WTO Compliance*. https://ustr.gov/sites/default/files/2019_Report_on_China%E2%80%99s_WTO_Compliance.pdf.

USTR. 2018. *Findings of the Investigation Into China's Acts, Policies and Practices Related to Technology Transfer, Intellectual Property, and Innovation Under Section 301 of the Trade Act of 1974*. https://ustr.gov/sites/default/files/Section%20301%20FINAL.PDF.

Waldron, Jeremy. 2008. "The Concept and the Rule of Law." *Georgia Law Review* 43: 1–61.

———. 2019. "Rule by Law: A Much Maligned Proposition." NYU School of Law Public Law & Legal Theory Research Paper Series Working Paper No. 19–19.

Wang, Jiangyu. 2004. "The Rule of Law in China." *Singapore Journal of Legal Studies*: 347–89.

Webster, Timothy. 2014. "Paper Compliance: How China Implements WTO Decisions." *Michigan Journal of International Law* 35 (3): 525–78.

The White House. 2017. "National Security Strategy of the United States of American." December 2017.

Woo, Margaret Y. K. 2017. "Court Reform With Chinese Characteristics" *Washington International Law Journal* 27: 241–71.

World Justice Project Rule of Law Index. 2021. https://worldjusticeproject.org/rule-of-law-index/global/2021/ranking.

WTO Appellate Body Report. 1997. "United States – Restrictions on Imports of Cotton and Man-Made Fiber Underwear." WT/DS24/R, February 25, 1997.

———. 2014. "China-Measures Affecting Trading Rights and Distributions Services for Certain Publications and Audiovisual Products (China-Publications and Audiovisual Products)." WT/DS363/AB/R, December 21, 2014.

WTO Committee on Subsidies and Countervailing Measures. 2019. "Questions from the United States Regarding the New and Full Notification of China." G/SCM/Q2/CHN/75, January 30, 2019.

WTO Communication from the United States. 2018. "China's Trade Disruptive Economic Model." WT/GC/W/745, July 16, 2018.

WTO, Doha Ministerial Declaration, WTO Doc. WT/MIN(01)/DEC/1(2001), November 20, 2001.

Wu, Chien-Huei. 2012. *WTO and the Greater China: Economic Integration and Dispute Resolution*. Leiden: Brill.

Yang, Xiangfeng. 2017. "The Anachronism of a China Socialized: Why Engagement Is Not All Its's Cracked Up to Be." *The Chinese Journal of International Politics* 10 (1): 67–94.

Ye, Ruiping. 2021. "Shifting Meanings of Fazhi and China's Journey Toward Social Rule of Law." *International Journal of Constitutional Law* 19 (5): 1859–1881.

Yuhua Wang. 2015. *Tying the Autocrat's Hands: The Rise of the Rule of Law in China*. Cambridge: Cambridge University Press.

Zhang, Taisu, and Tom Ginsburg. 2019. "China's Turn Toward Law." *Virginia Journal of International Law* 59: 306–89.

Zhang, Yuqing. 2008. "The Case of China." In *Investor-State Arbitration – Lessons for Asia*, edited by Michael Moser. New York: Juris Publishing.

Zivkovic, Velimir. 2019. "Fair and Equitable Treatment Between International and National Rule of Law." *Journal of International Investment and Trade* 20: 513–52.

6

LEGALITY OF CHINESE EXTRATERRITORIAL JURISDICTION[1]

Zheng Sophia Tang and Xinxin Zhang

Introduction

Extraterritorial jurisdiction allows states to use their domestic law and instruments to regulate overseas events. This "long arm" exercise of domestic legislative power challenges the traditional international law that makes territoriality the basic principle of jurisdiction (Ryngaert 2015, 35–38). Many commentators have studied the definition (Born 1992; Colangelo 2014; Cohen-Tanugi 2015), principles (Ryngaert 2015), and limitations (Colangelo 2007; Stigall 2012) of extraterritorial jurisdiction, as well as extraterritorial jurisdiction in specific fields, such as competition law (Lwssambo 2020), criminal law (Doyle 2016), securities law (Morgut 2012), export control (Bowman 2014), and personal data protection law (Scott 2014). Although international law permits extraterritorial prescriptive jurisdiction as far as it is not executed abroad,[2] such legislation, *per se*, makes other countries, especially countries where the regulated entities situate, or activities occur, uncomfortable. Although extraterritorial jurisdiction is not an unusual practice, it is controversial as to how to coordinate conflicts arising from it.

In contrast to the proliferation of materials on the general principles and concepts of extraterritorial jurisdiction, there are limited works of literature on extraterritorial jurisdiction in China. China has, for a long time, held a critical view of extraterritorial jurisdiction. As a result, past research was primarily on the extraterritorial privilege, which was a type of consular jurisdiction, given to some Western Powers in the 19th and 20th centuries (Quigley 1926; Sheehan 2012). Entering the 21st century, China only includes extraterritorial jurisdiction provisions in the criminal law and anti-monopoly law. However, because the US extraterritorial jurisdiction inevitably affects China and Chinese enterprises, more research focuses on the "long-arm" jurisdiction of the US (Guo and Gan 2000; Peng 2011). Chinese mainstream rhetoric criticizes the US extraterritorial

DOI: 10.4324/9781003294887-8

jurisdiction for interfering in other countries' internal affairs (China Daily 2019). However, the relationship between China and the Western world, especially the USA, turned increasingly rivalrous since 2017, and a series of sanctions were imposed against China. As a response, Chinese central authorities changed the official narrative and made establishing a Chinese system of extraterritoriality one of its priorities to counteract the foreign sanctions. More recent publications by Chinese scholars start to examine the Chinese system of extraterritorial jurisdiction from the macro level (Huo and Yip 2021; Liao 2019b) and extraterritorial jurisdiction in the specific legal field from the micro level, such as securities law (Shi 2014), labor law (Sun 2021), anti-monopoly law (Wang and Wu 2017), and personal information protection law (PIPL) (Zhang and Qi 2021). At the same time, Chinese scholars also focus on the Chinese path to defend or block the unjustified extraterritoriality of other countries (Xiao 2019; Li 2019; Huo 2020; Shen 2021; Sun 2021).

It is doubtful whether China's approach to extraterritoriality shows the double standard, namely, China criticizes the US' exercise of extraterritorial jurisdiction but adopts extraterritorial jurisdiction of its own. While some commentators describe China's recent adoption of extraterritorial jurisdiction as an instrument for hegemonic rivalry (Slawotsky 2021, 427–28), other commentators argue that the Chinese system of extraterritoriality is fundamentally different from the US because China does not use extraterritoriality to suppress other countries, but to protect genuine national interests and adopt multilateralism as a cornerstone (Huo and Yip 2021, 26). Theories and ideologies influence policies and law. China's legal theories and ideologies are reflected in legislation and implemented through specific legal systems. At this stage, China proposed to build a system of extraterritoriality, which is in line with its current policies, economic strength, international status, and international role. This chapter analyzes the recent extraterritorial legislation attempts in China and assesses its legality.

1. The Background for China to Adopt Extraterritorial Jurisdiction

1.1 Direct External Pressure

China has been holding a cautious and conservative policy against extraterritoriality until recently. Since taking office in 2017, the Trump Administration propagandized the "America First", blamed China for trade surplus, forced technology transfers, intellectual property theft, and other matters (Zhang, Zhang, and Yang 2021, 36). As a consequence, the US has launched direct sanctions against China and Chinese entities, and passed a series of law and orders, such as the Chinese Military Industrial Complext Sanctions Regulations, Hong Kong Human Rights and Democracy Act, Hong Kong Autonomy Act, and the Uyghur Human Rights Policy Act. A large number of Chinese entitites were included in the "Entity List' and "Specially Designated Nationals List". On the other hand, numerous Chinese entities were also attacked by the US secondary sanctions as many other states' sanctions by the US, such as Iran, Russia, Venezuela, and North Korea, have a close political and economic relationship with China. For example, in 2018, ZTE was charged a USD 1.4 billion penalty for violation of the US sanctions on Iran,[3] and Huawei came under investigation by the US authority for similar allegations.[4]

The effect of the US extraterritorial law on non-US entities alerted China. Chinese central authorities were made aware of the threat to China and its entities by such an instrument, as well as its effective impact on overseas enterprises and individuals. China's policymakers proposed to build the "system of extraterritorial application of domestic law," which in fact means China intends to adopt a systematic and comprehensive extraterritorial jurisdiction system. The tit-for-tat extraterritorial jurisdiction may bring similar pressure on the US and the US entities, which may be a strategic way to force the US to restrain from imposing more sanctions on China. It would send out the signal to overseas companies, which may have to think twice before directly complying with the US sanctions against Chinese firms.

1.2 The Regulation Needs

The external pressure is not the only reason for China to exercise extraterritorial jurisdiction. The rising economic power makes extraterritorial jurisdiction necessary to protect China's interests (Huo and Yip 2021). Since China adopted the Open Door Policy to reform its economic system and open up to the outside world, and especially after China joined the World Trade Organization (WTO) in 2001, China has integrated into the international trade and economic system. The reforms resulted in rapid economic growth. In 2010, China's total GDP overtook that of Japan and China became the second-largest economy in the world. China is also the world's leading exporter, a significant destination for, and increasingly a source of foreign direct investment (Jenkins 2019, 16). Since China is integrated into the global market, economic activities occurring abroad could lead to an impact on the Chinese market. China cannot effectively regulate its market without regulating overseas commercial activities that may result in an effect in China. As a result, China has the incentive to grant extraterritorial effects to its domestic law in the area of economic and market regulation.

With China's economic power grows, China is also showing its ambition to play a more active role in international governance and to actively participate in the reform and construction of the global governance system. China's One Belt One Road (OBOR) aims to cast Chinese economic power and influence abroad. In the mean time, China need an effective instrument to ensure the overseas projcts and investment can meet its original purpose. In the process to converting from an international rule follower to an international rule maker, China realise extraterritorial jurisdiction is an effective way to spill its regulatory power overseas (Liao 2019a).

Furthermore, XI Jinping, the general secretary of the Communist Party of China Central Committee, stressed prusing a holistic approach to national security. Chinese central authority believes prominent destabilizing factors and uncertainties in security, such as hegemonism, power politics, unilateralism and constant regional conflicts and wars, remain to threaten security of the international community and individual states. China faces diverse and complex security threats and challenges, including the "Taiwan independence", "Tibet independence", "East Turkistan", territorial sovereignty, maritime demarcation, international turmoil, terrorism, cyber attack, natural disasters, and major epidemics.[5] Threat to China's security may come from both within and outside of China. Combating overseas threat on China's security has been givern priority in China's legislation and policy. It is unrealistic to rely on other countries to act actively in protecting Chinese interests and security and, as a result, China need to adopt a more proactive approach to utilize extraterritorial jurisdiction.

2. Chinese Extraterritorial Regulatory Law by Category

2.1 Protection of Human Rights and Personality

Personal information is the data representation of the personal and behavior status of an individual, including any information related to a natural person whose identity has been identified or identifiable, including personal name, address, date of birth, ID number, medical record, personnel record, and so on. Article 12 of the Universal Declaration of Human Rights adopted in 1948 regards privacy as a fundamental right of human beings.[6] Protection of personal information and privacy is articulated in both Constitution and Civil Code in China.[7] Following the development of telecommunication technology, personal information is easily collected, transferred, processed, analyzed, and commercialized, both domestically and transnationally (Daskal 2018, 181). In 2018, there were more than 6,500 data breaches worldwide, with about 2 billion pieces of data leaked,[8] and this number is still growing. By the end of 2020, 142 countries (including self-governing territories) enacted data privacy laws (Greenleaf and Cottier 2020, 24–16). Due to the natural convenience of the cross-border flow of data and the virtuality and universality of the network, the traditional protection of personal information limited to the territory can no longer effectively protect the personal information, and the expansion of the extraterritorial application of domestic laws has become an inevitable trend (Kong and Yu 2020, 76).

By June 2021, China's total number of Internet users has reached 1.011 billion.[9] The cross-border flow of personal information and the transnational operation of multinational commercial companies make it necessary for China to exercise extraterritorial jurisdiction in personal information protection. In addition, China advocates data sovereignty, which extends state sovereignty to the Internet and allows a state to control data generated in cyberspace (Pohle 2020, 4).

When multinational enterprises collect, control, and transfer personal data of Chinese residents, it threats the personal rights of these data subjects and also challenges the state's sovereignty to regulate the use of data in cyberspace. It also causes concerns about state interests and national security if the collective interests of mass individuals are damaged. The expansion of extraterritorial effect of data protection legislation, therefore, is an important way for China to safeguard its national interests and protect its citizens (Zhang and Qi 2021, 5).

What's more, China lists data as one of five major production factors,[10] makes the development of the digital economy one of its economic strategic priorities, and has the intention to cultivate a data factor market. The prerequisite for a digital economy is a scientific and effective data protection institution, which makes development sustainable and inclusive.[11] Such an institution certainly has to deal with overseas entities for actions done abroad to collect and process data of individuals located in China, without which the internationalization nature of cyberspace can easily evade the implementation of the law and undermine its effectiveness. Extraterritorial jurisdiction can propel China's network power strategy, national big data strategy, and digital China construction.

As a result, China adopted the PIPL in 2021, on the basis of adhering to the territoriality principle, which stipulates the extraterritorial effects of the law. Article 3(2) provides that the PIPL shall apply to the processing outside the territory of China of the personal information of natural persons within the territory of China, (1) for the purpose of providing products or services for natural persons inside the PRC; (2) for analyzing or evaluating the behaviors of natural persons within the territory of the PRC; and (3) in any other circumstance as provided by any law or administrative regulation.[12] This law is based on the principle of effect, i.e., the overseas activity causes effects on individuals' rights and interests in China (Cohen-Tanugi 2015), and the principle of passive nationality, i.e., a state can regulate any conduct targeting or victimizing its nationals or residents (Ryngaert 2015, 49).

2.2 National Security

National security is the core and primary interest of a State protected by international law. States have the liberty, under international law, to enact the law to protect such core interests, which forms one of the jurisdictional grounds—the principle of protection. Extraterritorial conduct that threatens a state's national security creates a link between the actor and the regulating state, regardless of the nationality of the actor or any effect on the state's territory (Bialostozky 2014, 622–23). In other words, where extraterritorial conduct endangers certain national security interests, states may assert jurisdiction. China takes national security very seriously and enacted a series of national security protection laws with extraterritorial effects, all based on the principle of protection. For example, the Counterterrorism Law 2018 provides this law applies to terrorist crimes committed against the state, citizens, or institutions of China outside its territory or terrorist crimes stipulated in international treaties concluded or acceded to by China. Both the Cybersecurity Law 2016 and the Data Security Law 2021 authorize Chinese law enforcement authorities to sanction actors for attacking or damaging the critical information infrastructure of China[13] or any data processing activities that damage China's national security, public interests or lawful rights, and interests of individuals and organizations.[14] In 2020, China adopted the Hong Kong National Security Law (the HKNSL), which applies to any individuals or entities in the world for committing offenses in the law irrespective of where the act is carried out, planned, and participated.[15]

These laws, especially the HKNSL, cause loud criticism (BBC 2020; TIME 2020). Especially, Chinese law defines national security broadly, including security of a country's government, sovereignty, unity, territorial integrity, population, economy, and society;[16] the action deemed dangerous is also broad to include assistance and abetting; and the penalty is usually harsh. However, taking the face value of the principle of protection, it is within a state's power to define both what interests are the core interests to protect and how such protection shall be executed. International law, unfortunately, does not impose clearer principles to restrict the exercise of legislative jurisdiction to protect national core interests. Although the scope of national security is broad, it does not violate international law which leaves the concept of core interests for states to define. Challenges to national-security-related laws, especially HKNSL, rarely successfully build on its extraterritorial effect, but on the substantive provisions that do not provide clear rules to distinguish legitimate criticisms and protests, from inciting and abetting a crime (Clift 2020, 6), or government transparency and press freedom from unauthorized obtaining and leaking state secrets (Datt 2021; Tang and Huang 2021).

2.3 Economic Regulations

China also adopts the "effect principle" to regulate foreign economic activities that may have an impact in Chinese individuals and market. This principle enables states to assert jurisdiction over acts committed abroad by foreign persons when these acts have effects in the territory of the regulating state (Cohen-Tanugi 2015, 4). Although the effect principle has been subject to controversy and criticism after it was invented by the US, it has been gradually followed by many other countries and become an important principle in prescription. After World War II, as the transnational flow of goods, capital, technology, and labor became a common phenomenon, multinational corporations also became very active (Bagheri, Jafar, and Jahromi 2016, 394–95). With the further expansion of economic globalization and China's open-door policy, China's economy has been increasingly integrated with the international market. Under such circumstances, enterprises outside China reach monopoly agreements and abuse their dominant market positions, which may have an impact on the Chinese market. Article 2.2 of the Anti-Monopoly Law 2007 provides this law is applicable to the monopolistic conducts outside the territory of the PRC, which serve to eliminate or restrict competition in the domestic market of China. In the past, this provision has rarely been used by courts, though administrative agencies are more proactive in applying it (Huo and Yip 2021, 20). More recently, it has been implemented more by Chinese Courts. For example, in *Huawei v. Inter Digital Inc (IDC)*.,[17] and *OPPO v. Sisvelinternationals. et al.*,[18] the courts relied on the effect principle and applied the Chinese Anti-Monopoly Law to overseas anti-competition activities.

The more recent example of Chinese law falling within this category is the new Securities Law 2019. Because of the globalization of the securities industry, many enterprises decide to cross-list on numerous exchanges and investors trade on foreign markets (Morgut 2012, 547). At the same time, globalization has made the financial markets of various states integrated and inseverable. Confining the jurisdiction of a country's securities laws to its own territory cannot effectively protect domestic investors or maintain the order of the domestic securities market (Zhang 2020, 41). Article 2.4 of the PRC Securities Law[19] provides where the issurance and transaction of securities outside the territory of China have disrupted the market order within the territory of China and damaged the legitimate rights and interests of investors within the territory, such activities shall be handled and investigated for legal responsibility in accordance with the relevant provisions of this law. The extraterritorial effect of the Securities Law is based on the effect principle. China's capital market is constantly opening up and moving toward the world and in line with international standards. China needs an effective law that can regulate overseas activities that disrupts the Chinese market and harms the rights of Chinese investors.

China's Export Control Law also has extraterritorial effect. Any organization or individual outside the territory of the PRC violates the administration of export control, endangers the national security and interest of China, or obstructs fulfillment of non-proliferation and other international obligations; the organization or individual shall be held legally liable and be punished.[20] Second, re-export means controlled items or foreign products containing a certain percentage of the value of the controlled items of the PRC exported from abroad to other countries (regions). Article 16 provides the end user of a controlled item shall undertake not to change the end use of the relevant controlled item or transfer it to any third party without the consent of the state export control authorities. The application scope of the Law expands to the overseas end user.

2.4 Blocking and Counteracting

The category that generates most discussion is the blacking and counteracting laws with extraterritorial effect to tackle the US sanctions against China and Chinese individuals and entities, including Rules on Counteracting Unjustified Extra-territorial Application of Foreign Legislation and Other Measures (Blocking Law),[21] Unreliable Entity List (UEL),[22] Anti-foreign Sanctions Law of the PRC,[23] and Export Control Law, to defend the US sanctions.

UEL permits Chinese authorities to adopt measures, in response to a foreign individual, enterprise, or organization in international economic, trade, and other relevant activities, which either endanger national sovereignty, security, or development interests of China or suspend normal transactions with an enterprise, other organization, or individual of China or applying discriminatory measures against an enterprise, other organization, or individual of China.[24] The Anti-Foreign Sanctions Law provides that if foreign states violate international law and the basic norms of international relations contain and suppress China under various pretexts or take discriminatory restrictive measures against Chinese citizens and organizations, and interfere in China's internal affairs, China has the right to take corresponding countermeasures.[25] The Blocking Law prohibits any individuals or entities from complying or enforcing unjustified extraterritorial foreign sanctions either against China or third states.[26] Finally, although the Export Control Law aims to regulate foreign economic sales activities, export restriction on foreign entities or end users can be applied as a reciprocal and retaliation measure against foreign states or regions that abuse export control measures to harm China's national interest and security.[27]

3 Legality of China's Extraterritorial Jurisdiction

3.1 Legality of Extraterritorial Legislation

Although China showed objection to the concept of "extraterritoriality," the situation is changing. China has already adopted various laws and regulations with extraterritorial effects. These laws cover a wide range of fields, from national security and economic regulations to privacy and human rights protection. In general, China has taken international law seriously and has employed a conservative approach to handling extraterritorial jurisdiction. This is demonstrated in that although the *Lotus* judgment seems to suggest in the absence of international law prohibitive rules, a state has the freedom to exercise extraterritorial jurisdiction to prescribe,[28] which is the power to enact a law with extraterritorial effects; China has rarely exercised this power without a customary international law basis of extraterritorial jurisdiction. Therefore, if one takes a close observation of the existing Chinese law with extraterritorial effect, one can usually find the customary jurisdictional ground, being it the principle of nationality, protection, or effect.

If there is an exception, it is the counteraction against foreign sanctions. Chinese sanctions will be imposed if overseas entities have complied with the US law by refusing to supply goods or services to Chinese firms. From this perspective, it is like they are based on the principle of passive nationality. However, this principle usually applies to activities that the actors are free to conduct, instead of activities caused by external pressure or compulsion, or force majeure. When an American company stopped transactions with a Chinese company because of the US sanction, it is hard to argue it has the freedom of choice, but it will be punished by the Chinese law. Furthermore, the Anti-Foreign Sanctions Law and Export Control Law also suggest that China will be free to issue proactive sanctions against "innocent" foreign entities based on reciprocity. However, it does not suggest China has adopted a more aggressive approach to exerting power overseas. The Legal Affairs Committee of the Standing Committee of the National People's Congress in its press conference on the Anti-Foreign Sanctions Law stated that Chinese extraterritorial sanctions are counteracting and defensive measures, which are fundamentally different from the "unilateral sanction" (Fabre 2016, 261). The Chinese sanctions can only be initiated when other countries adopt discriminatory measures to suppress Chinese and Chinese entities.[29] These measures may be legalized as countermeasures in international law, unless foreign sanctions against China are consistent with international law and authorized by the United Nations (Alland 2010, 1127–36; Paddeu 2015).

Furthermore, the earlier countermeasures, such as the Blocking Law and UEL, are all administrative regulations, instead of national statutes. The Anti-Foreign Sanctions Law provides a catch-all principle to guide future administrative measures with extraterritorial effects for anti-sanction purposes. This shows that Chinese legislators at least attempt to legalize prescriptive extraterritorial jurisdiction in the area of economic sanctions.

In addition, these laws serve clear political purposes. They are instruments to defend China against foreign powers. Different from the past, when the foreign relations were left exclusively for the Ministry of Foreign Affairs to handle, China now had adopted legal instruments to affect foreign affairs. It shows the trend of legalization of politics. From this perspective, it is a positive sign because political matters and international disputes are regulated by law instead of treated randomly by politicians. The clear risk and liability provided by the black-letter law would enable international players to adjust their activities to mitigate the risk, instead of facing detriments in surprise. On the other hand, it may also relieve politicians from accountability because the political decisions are now replaced by judicial and administrative enforcement of law. More importantly, these counteracting laws show a clear sign of political will instead of factual enforceability as ordinary laws. Many provisions are statements of principles and doctrines, instead of detailed rules that can be readily implemented by courts or followed by individuals and entities. There is a lot of ambiguity as to when, how, and to whom sanctions may be imposed. It has been argued by commentators that these laws serve more political purposes than the legal purpose to be an enforceable law.

Finally, although China attempts to use national statutes to legalize extraterritorial countermeasures, it is not enough to simply find one of the customary jurisdiction grounds. To enact extraterritorial law, a state should consider not only the need to protect domestic interests but also the interests of foreign countries that may be affected by this law. Extraterritorial jurisdiction faces an inevitable conflict of interests between the regulating state and other states. Unfortunately, international law does not provide clear rules and principles to settle this conflict (Ryngaert 2015, 146). As a new comer in extraterritorial regulations, China has not enough experience in how this power is exercised. Therefore, the relevant Chinese law largely imitates the law and practice in other countries. For example, the extraterritorial application provision of China's PIPL learns from the European Union's General Data Protection Regulation (EU GDPR);[30] the Chinese Blocking Statue draws on the blocking law of the EU, which both deny and set off the extraterritorial effect of foreign laws (Lefeber 1997, 1); China's UEL, Securities Law, and Export Control Law all borrow from the US legislation (Morgut 2012, 552). China's Anti-Monopoly Law is similar to US and EU competition laws (Lwssambo 2020, 133–65). There is no coherent, underlying principle to guide the overall extraterritorial legislation in China. The element of rule of law does include not only the existence of clear law that can be enforced and obeyed but also the predictability of legislation activities. It is thus suggested that China should adopt the law on foreign relation, which establishes a clear guidance for extraterritorial jurisdiction, including the jurisdiction bases (nationality, protection, effect, universality), the restriction (such as comity, reciprocity, reasonableness and proportionality) (Maier 1982, 281–300), and special measures to address the conflict (such as the presumption against extraterritoriality, foreign sovereign compulsion, and double criminality) (Bu 2015, 431–36).

3.2 Legality of Extraterritorial Adjudicatory Jurisdiction

Besides legislation, extraterritoriality also includes adjudication and execution. Extraterritorial adjudicative jurisdiction refers to the courts' power to adjudicate disputes against foreign actors. Although China started to build its extraterritorial jurisdiction system, the current work primarily exists in legislation. In adjudication, Chinese courts demonstrate clear caution. In terms of jurisdiction, Chinese courts cannot exert jurisdiction over foreign defendants in the absence of a legal basis. Chinese criminal law does not state when Chinese courts have jurisdiction over foreign actors. In practice, adjudicatory jurisdiction is exercised when the Chinese criminal law applies to the overseas actor, in other words, the foreign actor's conduct falls within the remit of the prescriptive jurisdiction, and the offender is physically under the control of the Chinese law enforcement agency, such as the public security bureaus, state security bureaus, and police. Unless a foreign offender voluntarily enters into China's territory, such a control cannot occur without the cooperation and judicial assistance of foreign states by extradition. In *Shantou Municipal People's Prosecutor v. Naim Atan et al.*,[31] China arrested and prosecuted Indonesian gang members. On June 8, 1999, Atan Naim and his nine gang members, all Indonesian citizens, committed piracy and armed robbery in Malaysian waters. On 16 June, they were arrested by the Chinese coast guard when they entered the Chinese territorial sea. Naim and his gang members were prosecuted for robbery before the Intermediate People's Court of Shantou. The trial court ruled that the defendants committed the criminal offences stipulated in article 3(1)(a) of the Rome Convention for the Suppression of Unlawful Acts against the Safety of Maritime Navigation (SUA) to which China was a contracting State. Chinese court has universial jurisdiction.

In terms of civil jurisdiction, there is no such concept of *foreign necessitates* that grants Chinese courts the discretion to take jurisdiction even if no jurisdictional grounds are found (Mora 2018, 155). If Chinese law intends to regulate foreign actors, but the defendant does not have relevant connections with China to justify jurisdiction (such as the place of domicile, the place of representative, the place of contracting or performance, the place of tort, and the place of disposable assets), Chinese courts cannot take jurisdiction just because they find it necessary to give effect to the legislative purpose. Furthermore, even if Chinese courts take jurisdiction, they have taken caution when applying the law. In the absence of explicit asserting of extraterritorial effects in the law or legislative interpretation, Chinese courts take a conservative approach of "presumption against extraterritoriality." There is not yet a reported judgment that interprets a domestic law to have extraterritorial effects if the law does not explicitly provide so.

Although the judicial practice may undermine the purpose of extraterritorial legislation, it is believed to be consistent with the rule of law. In terms of jurisdiction, a defendant has the due process right not to be subject to an unexpected forum. Only when the defendant has done something that indicates its intention to target a country and thus subject to the regulation and governance of this country's judicial system, taking jurisdiction is justifiable (Hartley 2015, 155). Although extraterritorial legislation generally requires the "genuine connection" between the regulated activity and the regulating state,[32] this connection may not coincide with the connection in judicial jurisdiction. For example, a state may enact a law to tackle foreign anti-competition activities that affect the local market. However, the foreign player may not "target" the local market and foresee such an effect to justify jurisdiction. Furthermore, the civil law tradition does not mean to give courts semi-law-making power, which allows a court to give the law substantive interpretation beyond its text, such as extending the scope of application.

Therefore, although some Chinese commentators criticize that the role of Chinese courts in the extraterritorial jurisdiction has not yet been highlighted (Sheng 2015, 94), it is not rational to empower the courts to take a more active role in implementing extraterritorial regulations. The judiciary is the weakest institution in China, and it operates under the macro-supervision and guidance of the Party and (sometimes) of the government (Li 2016, 41). Although the judicial reform has managed to untie the court from the government and improve independent trial (not judicial independence), the court's status is still vulnerable. If we require courts not to strictly apply the law, but to take the politics and policy into consideration when implementing the law, it would make the court a dangerous arm of politics. It is thus argued that China should not extend the courts' power in terms of extraterritorial jurisdiction but make the court a "check and balance" body (Huo and Yip 2021, 30).

3.3 Legality of Extraterritorial Executive Jurisdiction

Executive jurisdiction means the administrative authority enforces laws against foreign actors for actions done abroad. Unlike prescriptive jurisdiction, international law clearly refines executive jurisdiction within the territory of the regulating state. Sovereign equality prevents a government from exercising its power in the territory of other states. In other words, executive jurisdiction is exclusively territorial (*Lotus*).[33]

However, administrative agents in China are more ready to enforce Chinese law on overseas actors. For example, in the field of antitrust, most of the cases where the Chinese Anti-Monopoly Law was applied extraterritorially were handled by the Chinese antitrust agencies (NDRC, State Administration for Market Regulation, and Ministry of Commerce PRC) instead of the courts (Huo and Yip 2021, 20). A more recent example is the utilization of the Anti-Foreign Sanctions Law by the Chinese government to impose new sanctions on US defense contractors Raytheon Technologies and Lockheed Martin due to their arms sales to Taiwan (Wang 2022). These administrative decisions were not controversial in that the enforced law explicitly grants extraterritorial effects and the antitrust agencies exercised their power in China. However, controversy exists in more recent administrative decisions. In 2018, the Civil Aviation Administration of China (CCAC) sent letters to 36 foreign airlines demanding them to correct their website information that lists Taiwan, Hong Kong, and Macau as "countries" instead of regions in the PRC. This has been argued by some commentators as examples of extraterritorial execution (Huo and Yip 2021, 23–24). However, although the CCAC has sent official letters to entities abroad, this may not be viewed as "execution of official powers." The foreign entities may not comply with the requests and the CCAC cannot enforce any penalties abroad. This letters also have no legal, executive effects and can only be treated as notice.

Therefore, although Chinese administrative authorities are more active in enforcing Chinese extraterritorial regulations, they do not exercise extraterritorial executive jurisdiction. Chinese administrative authorities can only exercise power domestically, including supervision, inspection, investigation, collecting evidence, imposing compulsory measures, seizing assets, imposing penalties, and travel and entry restrictions. Arguably, these compulsory executive measures can only be done in Chinese territory against entities located in China and may not have a significant impact on entities abroad. However, impact can exist in two circumstances. First, if the foreign entities are controlled by Chinese individuals or entities, such as shareholders, associated companies, and principals, Chinese administrative authorities can impose pressure directly on these Chinese entities that will control the activities of foreign entities through internal corporate governance. Second, if the foreign entities have commercial interests in China, Chinese administrative authorities can effectively prevent those entities from accessing the Chinese market and obtaining Chinese products and technology. Since China is the second largest economy in the world, this measure would be effective for overseas companies that aim to explore commercial profits in China. However, if overseas actors that the law intends to regulate have no direct interests in China, enforcement will be difficult.

4 Conclusion

The aforementioned analysis shows that China is very careful not to breach international law. Nearly all Chinese extraterritorial regulations can be justified by international law principles, or find international law bases. China uses legal methods to enforce its foreign policy and realize its political will. Weaponizing the law in international relations becomes a new trend in the current China–US tension.

However, the weak enforcement of extraterritorial regulations may question whether this practice is consistent with the rule of law. As an important element of the rule of law, the enacted law should be complied and effectively enforced. Although extraterritorial regulations intend to regulate overseas actors and activities, they cannot be effectively enforced either by the Chinese courts or by administrative authorities. This is not a specific challenge for China, but for nearly all countries that attempt to utilize extraterritorial regulations to protect domestic interests. States either base for example, the US utilizes its economic, financial, and technology hegemony, by imposing control on the US entities that will naturally pass the pressure abroad. The EU, on the other hand, uses a more conservative approach in its legislation, by only regulating foreign actors whose activities have a more permanent and stable connection with the EU, or requiring foreign actors to establish representatives in the EU; both can help enforcement (Joanne 2014, 96–102). China has followed the US approach but does not have as strong economic power as the US, which will put Chinese extraterritorial regulations in an awkward situation. More importantly, the most recent development in China is to use the extraterritorial regulations to fight against the US sanctions. It forces entities to take a side: either comply with the US law and accept the Chinese penalty or vice versa. The decision of entities is directly affected by the power balance between two countries. Enforceability of Chinese extraterritorial regulations, thus, faces an inevitable dilemma.

Declaration

This chapter is a mid-term output of the Project (20BFX193) supported by the National Social Science Fund of China.

Notes

1 Declaration: This chapter is a mid-term output of the Project (20BFX193) supported by the National Social Science Fund of China.
2 PCIJ, *SS Lotus (Turkey v France)*, PCIL Reports, Series A, No 10 (1927).
3 The US Department of Justice. "ZTE Corporation Agrees to Plead Guilty and Pay Over $430.4 Million for Violating U.S. Sanctions by Sending U.S.-Origin Items to Iran (March 7,2017)." Accessed January 16, 2022. www.justice.gov/opa/pr/zte-corporation-agrees-plead-guilty-and-pay-over-4304-million-violating-us-sanctions-sending.
4 US v. HUAWEI TECHNOLOGIES CO, LTD.
5 Xinhuanet. "China's National Defense in the New Era (24 July, 2019)." Accessed Feburary 22, 2022. eng.mod.gov.cn/publications/2019-07/24/content_4846452.htm.

6 Article 12, the Universal Declaration of Human Rights.
7 Article 40, the Constitution of the PRC; Articles 111, 127, 990, 1032, Civil Code of the PRC.
8 China Academy of Information and Communications Technology. "White Paper on Internet Law (2019)." Accessed January 11, 2022. www.caict.ac.cn/kxyj/qwfb/bps/201912/t20191219_272126.htm.
9 China Internet Network Information Center. "The 48th Statistical Report on China's Internet Development."
10 Macro-economic Structural Reform Optimization of Doing Business. "Opinions of the CPC Central Committee and the State Council on Improving the Systems and Mechanisms for Market-based Allocation of Factors of Production" (March 30, 2020). Accessed January 11, 2022. www.gov.cn/zhengce/2020-04/09/content_5500622.htm.
11 Macro-economic Structural Reform Optimization of Doing Business. "Opinions of the CPC Central Committee and the State Council on Accelerating the Improvement of the System of Socialist Market Economy in a New Era" (May 11, 2020). Accessed January 11, 2022. www. gov.cn/zhengce/2020–05/18/content_5512696.htm.
12 Article 3(2), Personal Information Protection Law.
13 Article 75, Cybersecurity Law (2016).
14 Article 2.2, The Data Security Law (2021).
15 Article 38, The HKNSL.
16 The National Security Law (2015).
17 Shenzhen Intermediate People's Court Shenzhong Fazhi Minchuzi, No. 858 (2011).
18 The Supreme People's Court of The PRC zuigaofa minxiazhong. No. 392(2020).
19 The Securities Law (2019).
20 Article 44, The Export Control Law (2020).
21 Rules on Counteracting Unjustified Extra-territorial Application of Foreign Legislation and Other Measures. Order No. 1 [2021] of the Ministry of Commerce of the People's Republic of China.
22 Provisions on the Unreliable Entity List. No.4 [2020] Order of the Ministry of Commerce of the People's Republic of China.
23 The Anti-foreign Sanctions Law (2021).
24 MOFCOM Order No.4 of 2020 on provisions on the Unreliable Entity List. MOFCOM September 19,2020.
25 Article 3, The Anti-foreign Sanctions Law.
26 The blocking law was recently discussed in a foreign arbitral award enforcement case: *Macquarie Bank Limited v. Wanda Group Co. Ltd.* Shanghai Financial Court, Hu 74 Xie Wai Ren No 1(2021).
27 Article 48, The Export Control Law (2020).
28 PCIJ, *SS Lotus (Turkey v France)*, PCIL Reports, Series A, No 10 (1927).
29 The State Council Information Office of the PRC. "The Legislative Affairs Committee of the Standing Committee of the National People's Congress answers reporters' questions on the Anti-Foreign Sanctions Law." Accessed February 8, 2022. www.scio.gov.cn/xwfbh/rdzxxwfbh/xwfbh/wjb44184/Document/1706314/1706314.htm.
30 Guidelines 3/2018 on the territorial scope of the GDPR (Article 3). The application of the "targeting criterion" toward data subjects who are in the Union can be triggered by processing activities carried out by a controller or processor not established in the Union which relate to two distinct and alternative types of activities provided that these processing activities relate to data subjects that are in the Union.
31 *Shantou Municipal People's Prosecutor v. Naim Atan et al.*, Shantou Municipal People's Court, Shan Zhong Fa Min Yi Chu Zi no 22 (2000).
32 Restatement of the law fourth (2018) The foreign relations law of the United States. Section 407, comment.
33 PCIJ, *SS Lotus (Turkey v France)*, PCIL Reports, Series A, No. 10 (1927).

References

Alland, Denis. 2010. "The Definition of Countermeasures." In *The Law of International Responsibility*, edited by James Crawford, Alain Pellet, and Simon Olleson, 1127–36. Oxford: Oxford University Press.

Bagheri, Mahmood, Mohammad Jafar, and Ghanbari Jahromi. 2016. "Globalization and Extraterritorial Application of Economic Regulation: Crisis in International Law and Balancing Interests." *European Journal of Law and Economics* 41: 393–429.

BBC. 2020. "Hong Kong Security Law: What Is It and Is It Worrying?" June 30, 2020. www.bbc.com/news/world-asia-china-52765838.

Bialostozky, Noah. 2014. "Extraterritoriality and National Security: Protective Jurisdiction as a Circumstance Precluding Wrongfulness Columbia Journal of Transnational Law." *Columbia Journal of Transnational Law* 52: 617–87.

Born, Gary B. 1992. "A Reappraisal of the Extraterritorial Reach of U.S. Law." *Law and Policy in International Business* 24 (1): 1–100.

Bowman, Gregory W. 2014. "A Prescription for Curing U.S. Export Controls." *Marquette Law Review* 97 (3): 599–693.

Bu, Qingxiu. 2015. "Neither Rock Nor Hard Place? The Foreign Sovereign Compulsion Defence in Antitrust Litigation." *Journal of International Dispute Settlement* (6): 427–53.

China Daily. 2019. "US Long-Arm Jurisdiction a Blatant Violation of International Law." *China Daily.com.cn*, June 26, 2019. www.chinadaily.com.cn/a/201911/25/WS5ddb3162a310cf3e35579a51.html.

Clift, Brendan. 2020. "Hong Kong's Made-in-China National Security Law: Upending the Legal Order for the Sake of Law and Order." *Australian Journal of Asian Law* 21 (1): 1–23.

Cohen-Tanugi, Laurent. 2015. "The Extraterritorial Application of American Law: Myths and Realities." *Social Sciences Research Network*. https://papers.ssrn.com/sol3/papers.cfm?abstract_id=2576678.

Colangelo, Anthony J. 2007. "Constitutional Limits on Extraterritorial Jurisdiction: Terrorism and the Intersection of National and International Law." *Harvard International Law Journal* 48 (1): 121–201.

———. 2014. "What Is Extraterritorial Jurisdiction." *Cornell Law Review* 99 (6): 1303–52.

Daskal, Jennifer. 2018. "Borders and Bits." *Vanderbilt Law Review* 71 (1) (Spring): 179–240. https://vanderbiltlawreview.org/lawreview/2018/01/borders-and-bits/.

Datt, Angeli. 2021. "The Impact of the National Security Law on Media and Internet Freedom in Hong Kong." *Testimony and Remarks*, October 19, 2021. https://freedomhouse.org/article/impact-national-security-law-media-and-internet-freedom-hong-kong.

Doyle, Charles. 2016. "Extraterritorial Application of American Criminal Law: An Abbreviated Sketch." *Congressional Research Service, Library of Congress*: 1–69.

Fabre, Cecile. 2016. "Secondary Economic Sanctions." *Current Legal Problems* 69 (1) (Winter): 259–88.

Foreign Airlines List Taiwan, Hong Kong and Macau as "Country." 2020. "Ministry of Foreign Affairs of the PRC: There Is Only One China in the World – (ccaonline.cn)." Accessed February 8, 2022. www.ccaonline.cn/news/top/411501.html.

Greenleaf, Graham, and Bertil Cottier. 2020. "2020 Ends a Decade of 62 New Data Privacy Laws." *Privacy Laws & Business International Report* 163: 24–26.

Guo, Yujun, and Yong Gan. 2000. "The 'Long Arm Jurisdiction' of American Courts – the Reasonableness Principle for Jurisdiction in International Civil Cases." *Journal of Comparative Law* (3): 266–76.

Hartley, Trevor C. 2015. *International Commercial Litigation*. 2nd ed. Cambridge: Cambridge University Press.

Huo, Zhengxin. 2020. "Extraterritoriality of Domestic Law: American Model, Jurisprudential Deconstruction and Chinese Approach." *Tribune of Political Science and Law* 38 (2): 173–91.

Huo, Zhengxin, and Man Yip. 2021. "Extraterritoriality of Chinese Law: Myths, Realities and the Future." *Chinese Journal of Comparative Law* (May): 1–31. https://doi.org/10.1093/cjcl/cxab004.

Jenkins, Rhys. 2019. *How China Is Reshaping the Global Economy Development Impacts in Africa and Latin America*. New York and Oxford: Oxford University Press.

Kong, Qingjiang, and Huayi Yu. 2020. "The Extraterritorial Application of Data Law and China's Countermeasures." *Law Science Magazine* 8: 76–88.

Lefeber, Rene. 1997. "Frontiers of International Law: Counteracting the Exercise of Extraterritorial Jurisdiction." *Leiden Journal of International Law* 10 (1): 1–7.

Li, Ling. 2016. "The Chinese Communist Party and People's Courts: Judicial Dependence in China." *American Journal of Comparative Law* 64 (1): 37–74.

Li, Qingming. 2019. "The Extraterritorial Jurisdiction of the United States: Concept, Practice and China's Response." *Chinese Review of International Law* (3): 3–23.

Liao, Shiping. 2019a. "The Extraterritorial Application of Domestic Law and Countermeasures Thereof: Taking the Extraterritorial Application of the US Law as an Example." *Global Law Review* (3): 166–78.

———. 2019b. "The Legal System of Extraterritorial Application of Chinese Law: Status, Problems and Completion." *China Law Science* (6): 20–38.

Lwssambo, Felix I. 2020. "Extraterritorial Competence of the United States, the EU, and China Competition Laws." In *Mergers in the Global Markets*, edited by Palgrave Macmillan, 133–65. Cham: Palgrave Macmillan.

Maier, Harold G. 1982. "Extraterritorial Jurisdiction at a Crossroads: An Intersection Between Public and Private International Law." *The American Journal of International* 76 (2): 280–320.

Mora, Paul David. 2018. "Universal Civil Jurisdiction and Forum Necessitatis: The Confusion of Public and Private International Law in Nait-Liman v Switzerland." *Netherlands International Law Review* 65: 155–83.

Morgut, Milosz. 2012. "Extraterritorial Application of U.S. Securities Law." *European Business Law Review* 23 (4): 547–63.

Paddeu, Federica I. 2015. "Countermeasures." In *Max Planck Encyclopedia of Public International Law*, edited by Rudiger Wolfrum and Margret Solveigardottir. New York: Oxford University Press. https://opil.ouplaw.com/view/10.1093/law:epil/9780199231690/law-9780199231690-e1020.

Peng, Yue. 2011. "Latest Advances in Extraterritorial Jurisdiction Under US Securities and Their Enlightenment." *Modern Law Science* 33 (6): 139–47.

Pohle, Julia, and Thorsten Thiel. 2020. "Digital Sovereignty." *Internet Policy Review* 9 (4): 1–18.

Quigley, Harold Scott. 1926. "Extraterritoriality in China." *American Society of International Law* 20 (1): 46–68.

Ryngaert, Cedric. 2015. *Jurisdiction in International Law*. 2nd ed. New York and Oxford: Oxford University Press.

Scott, Joanne. 2014. "Extraterritorality and Territorial Extension in EU Law." *American Journal of Comparative Law* 62 (1): 87–126.

Sheehan, James J. 2012. *Extraterritoriality and Imperial Power in Nineteenth-Century China and Japan*. New York and Oxford: Oxford University Press.

Shen, Wei. 2021. "Legal Warfare in the US-China Trade Friction: Understanding the Unreliable Entity List System and Blocking Regulations." *Journal of Comparative Law* (1): 180–200.

Sheng, Jin. 2015. "Private Securities Litigation in China: Passive People's Courts and Weak Investor Protection." *Bond Law Review* 26 (1): 94–147.

Shi, Jiayou. 2014. "A Study of Extraterritorial Effect of China's Security Law." *Science of Law* (5): 129–37.

Slawotsky, Joel. 2021. "U.S. Extraterritorial Jurisdiction in an Age of International Economic Strategic Competition." *Georgetown Journal of International Law* 52 (3) (Winter): 427–68.

Stigall, Dan E. 2012. "International Law and Limitations on the Exercise of Extraterritorial Jurisdiction in U.S. Domestic Law." *Hastings International and Comparative Law Review* 35 (2): 323–82.

Su, Changhe. 2014. "The Five Principles of Peaceful Coexistence and China's Thinking System of International Law." *World Economics and Politics* (6): 3–22.

Sun, Nanxiang. 2021. "The Origin and Modernization of Extraterritoriality in the American Judiciary: With Reflections on the Extraterritorial Application of Chinese Laws." *Journal of Comparative Law* (3): 167–78.

Tang, Zheng, and Huang Xu. 2021. "State Secrets in the Hong Kong National Security Law." In *Hong Kong National Security Law*, edited by Hualing Fu. https://ssrn.com/abstract=3779153.

Time. 2020. "'It's So Much Worse Than Anyone Expected.' Why Hong Kong's National Security Law Is Having Such a Chilling Effect." July 23, 2020. https://time.com/5867000/hong-kong-china-national-security-law-effect/.

Wang, Wenbin. 2022. "According to the 'Anti-Foreign Sanctions Law', China Has Implemented Countermeasures Against the Infringing Acts of U.S. Companies." February 21, 2022. www.mfa.gov.cn/web/sp_683685/wjbfyrlxjzh_683691/202202/t20220221_10644053.shtml.

Wang, Xiaoye, and Qianlan Wu. 2017."International Cartel and Extraterritorial Application of Chinese Antimonopoly Law." *Journal of Comparative Law* (3): 132–45.

Xiao, Yongping. 2019. "Jurisprudential Analysis and Countermeasures of 'Long-arm Jurisdiction'." *China Law Science* (6): 39–65.

Zhang, Mai. 2020. "Extraterritorial Jurisdiction Standards and Applicable Conditions of China's Securities Law." *Financial Law Forum* 104 (4): 40–58.

Zhang, Yueran, Xiaolei Zhang, and Jijun Yang. 2021. "The Extraterritorial Abuse of US Long-arm Jurisdiction and China's Countermeasures." *International Trade* (3): 36–43.

Zhang, Zhe, and Aimin Qi. 2021. "On the Construction of Extraterritorial Effect System of Personal Information Protection Law." *Journal of Chongqing University (Social Science Edition)* (3): 3–20.

7

CIVIL RIGHTS CHINESE STYLE

The Politics and Ideology of the New *Civil Code*

Shiping Hua

This is a study of the newly promulgated Civil Code of the People's Republic of China that went into effect on January 1, 2021. The Civil Code consists of seven parts, i.e., General Rules, Property Rights, Contracts, Personality Rights, Marriage and Family, Right of Inheritance, and Tort Liability with a total of 1,260 Articles.

In the last half a decade, the West has become increasingly concerned about the direction in which China has been moving, with almost consensus that the reversal of the post-Mao reform, at least in some key areas, such as personality cult, more emphasis on ideology, and more political control, has occurred (Zhao 2016; Hua 2019). Yet, in communist countries, such as the former Soviet Union, the promulgation of civil laws usually indicates a relaxing of communist fanaticism. What kind of messages of policy orientation and ideological trends that the regime has sent through this Civil Code?

This is the fifth time that the PRC has tried to make the civil code: the four previous failed attempts were made in 1954, 1962, 1979, and 2001. Why this time was it successful? In comparison with the previous civil laws, what is new in this Civil Code that protects civil rights? How serious is this Civil Code in restricting the state rights? To what extent that Civil Code reflects the Chinese tradition? To what extent that Civil Code reflects the regime's attitudes toward foreign experiences? Western scholars have noted such terms as civil rights, freedom, democracy, equality, and rule of law have different meanings when used in the Chinese context (Gow 2017, 92–116). How is this reflected in the Civil Code?

It is not a systematic introduction to the Civil Code that is a conglomeration of civil laws promulgated over the years in the past. In addition, some fruitful studies have been done that tried to explain the various civil laws, such as the general provisions (Wen 2018), contracts laws (DiMatteo 2017), and private property laws

DOI: 10.4324/9781003294887-9

(Kielsgard and Chen 2014), and the impact of civil laws on sustainable development (Zhai and Chang 2019, 294). This project focuses on the issue of human rights by highlighting those new provisions that have political and ideological connotations. My approach is similar to some of the most recent studies on the Civil Code that focuses on one particular dimension of the large document (Ling 2020, 558–634).

This study shows that the Civil Code has successfully been completed in the midst of the situation when China's economy had experienced a decline of growth for half a decade and an increasingly challenging international environment exemplified by the US–China trade war. The regime intends to give the public more breathing space in those areas that don't hurt the state monopoly of power, e.g., protecting the civil rights among non-state actors. This situation is similar to the post-1989 Tiananmen Massacre period when the political control was tightened, while other areas such as the control of the economy were loosened, symbolized by Deng Xiaoping's 1992 Southern Tour (Zhao 1993, 739–56). The promulgation of the Civil Code is also a reflection of a more modernized Chinese society.

At least in principle, the Civil Code is a step forward from the previous civil laws in protecting private properties, privacy, and contractual relations. It looks even more significant if we take a retrospect perspective of four decades when the idea of the public–private divide, property rights, and even individualism had no root in the Chinese legal academia yet then. Nevertheless, the rights as stipulated in the Civil Code are by and large among individuals and other non-state actors, not vis-a-vis the state. Restricting the state rights is mostly in an abstract sense. When it involves concrete issues, it is mostly in small areas, such as "Lost & Found." When the state is a party vis-a-vis the legal persons or natural persons, it is mostly in the areas of economics, not politics.

Some new contents in the Civil Code seem to indicate that the economic reform will continue. For instance, the so-called "exploitation" was cut from the previous civil laws, indicating that "exploitation" such as stocks is allowed in state socialism; "a variety of forms of ownership" was added, indicating private ownerships are considered to be part of state socialism; the party's dominant theory of "primary stage socialism[1] that was formulated at the beginning of the reform was cut in some places, indicating that the allowance of "exploitation" and "private ownership of the means of production" will be part of the Chinese system for a long time, not merely a part of the transition. This does not contradict the fact that under Xi Jinping, China's political control has tightened, not loosened.

The Civil Code is also to decrease social tension, e.g., to protect the middle class and the poor in terms of properties. This was against the background that the new party constitution in 2017 changed the policy of "letting a few to become rich" in the 1980s to "more equality" (CCP General Outline).

The Civil Code also reflects the regime's pragmatic attitudes toward the Chinese tradition and the foreign experience. Some aspects of the Chinese tradition such as the strong emphasis on family were protected; others such as dowry were banned. While endorsing some foreign experiences, especially in contract laws, the Civil Code seems to have distanced itself from some of the other foreign experiences.

The chapter is divided into four sections. It first lays down the historical background against which the Civil Code was promulgated, such as that of the communist countries' past experience including that of the USSR and China in drafting civil laws. The second section discusses civil rights as included in the Civil Code for a legal person and a natural person. The third section discusses the Civil Code's limitations in restricting the rights of the state. The fourth section discusses the regime's pragmatic attitudes toward the Chinese tradition and the foreign experience, as reflected in the Civil Code. The conclusion part is reflections on some historical and theoretical issues related to the Civil Code.

1. China's Previous Attempts for the Civil Code

Modern law came from the West and all laws in modern China are connected with foreign experiences. China's first attempt to promulgate a civil code began as early as 1911, with the Draft Civil Code of the Great Qing Dynasty that was accomplished with the help of Japanese scholars Yoshimasa Matsuoka and Kotaro Shida (Chen 2009).

This situation is consistent with the fact that the Qing constitution, China's first, was also based on that of Japan, i.e., the Meiji constitution. The Chinese elites in the early 20th century believe that learning from Japan is a "short cut" for China's modernization, because of Japan's success in learning from the West. Japan accomplished its modernization drive in three or four decades after the Meiji Restoration in 1868. The Qing court was also fond of the Japanese elites' attitudes of being in favor of modernization without eliminating the monarchy.

In communist countries, the promulgation of civil laws usually signals taking a break from communist fanaticism, i.e., reform that promoted private initiative, personal stimuli of labor and energy, and free accumulation of private property. The promulgation of the Soviet Civil Code went hand in hand with the New Economic Policy in 1921–1924 that was a "retreat" from communist ideals, in the words of Vladimir Lenin. The Soviet Civil Code was passed in October 1922, taking effect in January 1923. The code intended to uphold and regulate private property relations which was a departure from War Communism in the first few years after the October Revolution in 1917 (Service 1997, 124–25).

Compared with its communist neighbor of Russia, China is rather late in adopting a civil code. In fact, China under Mao was reluctant to adopt even a constitution. It was under pressure from Joseph Stalin that China adopted its first constitution in 1954 (Li 2001, 28–47). Although the Chinese 1954 constitution was largely modeled after the 1937 Soviet constitution, it gave people less rights than the Soviet one. This is consistent with the fact that the late Qing Constitution, although modeled after the Meiji constitution, also gave the people less rights than the Japanese one (Hua 2019).

China's first attempt in 1954 to make a civil law went hand in hand with the first PRC constitution that was promulgated in the same year. It was partly based on the 1922 Civil Code of the then Soviet Union. The attempt was aborted because the country went into turmoil two years later first with the Hundred Flowers movement and then the Anti-Rightist Campaign (Chung 2011, 391–411). The 1954 constitution itself was cast aside a few years after its promulgation.

The second attempt for a civil code was in 1962. It went hand in hand with Liu Shaoqi/Deng Xiaoping's "responsibility system," which was supposed to give people a break from leftist fanaticism as demonstrated during the Great Leap Forward that was responsible for the deaths of millions of Chinese. It was aborted because the country went into another round of leftist fanaticism with the first being the Four Cleanings in 1964 and then the Cultural Revolution in 1966 (MacFarquhar 1999).

The third one started following the 1978 Third Plenum of the CCP Central Committee that started the post-Mao reform (Schram 1984, 417–61). The NPC Standing Committee re-commenced the drafting of a civil code in an attempt to meet the needs of building a market-oriented economy in 1979. In 1982, they worked out a fourth draft of the civil code after drawing on the experience of civil codes in the Soviet Union and Hungary. The foreign connection is obvious in that the 1982 constitution was also based on the PRC constitution of 1954 that was in turn based on the Soviet one in 1937. Apparently, the complexity of the Chinese society unleashed by the reform made it harder for the civil law to go into completion.

Since the 1980s, a series of standalone civil laws was enacted with the expectation of codifying them in the future. Those separate statutes include the 1980 Marriage Law [婚姻法] (amended in 2001); 1985 Inheritance Law [继承法]; 1986 General Principles of Civil Law [民法通则] (amended in 2009); 1991 Adoption Law [收养法] (amended in 1998); 1995 Security Law [担保法]; and 1999 Contracts Law [合同法].

The fourth attempt for a civil code was made when China joined the World Trade Organization in 2001. China's legislature submitted it for review in late 2002. It was not approved. China was probably too preoccupied with raising the productivity and GDP to enact the large and complex civil code. Therefore, China continued with the piece-by-piece approach instead of the codification of the civil laws. The 2007 Rights in Rem Law [物权法] and 2009 Tort Liability Law [侵权责任法] were introduced.

The fifth attempt to codify the civil law coincided Xi's ascendance to power in 2012, when the Communist Party's 18th NPC called for progress in drafting the unified civil code. The NPC passed the General Provisions in 2017. The Civil Code in its finalized form was thus presented to and adopted by the NPC at its annual session on May 28, 2020, concluding the country's six-decade journey to enacting a comprehensive civil code.

The successful enabling of the Civil Code resembles the previous attempts that occurred in the correction of extreme politics. The Hu Jintao era witnessed a substantial increase in both registered and unregistered social organizations, with registered social organizations doubling in number, from 244,509 to over 499,268, between 2002 and 2012 (Howel 2019, 58–81). Despite Hu's emphasis on "harmony," some estimated that "mass incidents" in China had grown to approximately 180,000 in 2010 compared to 90,000 back in 2006 (Chen 2021). The Hu regime reportedly spent more money on the maintenance of social order than its military expense (Buckley 2011).

It also coincided with Xi regime's louder voice on the market and law, because the heightened political control made the private sector worried. In the new party constitution, the role of the market has been changed from "essential role" to "decisive role," implying a more important role by the market (CCP General Outline).

The principle of "rule according to law" was emphasized. In the Civil Code, "rule according to law" was added at least three times (Articles 237, 238, and 262, compared with the 2007 law).[2] In Xi's report to the 19th National Party Congress in 2017, he mentioned "rule according to law" 55 times.

Without legal protection, private businessmen don't feel safe. The survey showed that they think there is a 22.5% chance of danger to themselves and a 26.8% chance that their assets are at risk (Zhai, Crossley and Tian 2020). Private sector investment in China slowed sharply from more than 20% growth when Xi assumed power to single digits in recent years. It fell 13% during the coronavirus-battered first four months of 2020, compared with a 7% decline for state-owned companies (Zhai 2020).

China under Xi had experienced seven years of decline in economic growth (World Bank 2021). To make the matters worse, the US started a trade war against China in 2017 soon after President Donald Trump came to power. China needs the private sector to boost up the country's economy, and it needs foreign investment as well.

The fifth attempt to codify the civil code also coincided with Xi's more assertive stands in foreign policy, e.g., in 2014, China started to militarize the South China Sea by building artificial islands that could be used for military airports (Chung 2016). It also went hand in hand with Xi's slogans of China Dream and *Bainian weiyou zhi dabianju* (a great change that has not happened in a hundred years). In a departure from the Hu regime that was noted for its emphasis on "harmony" and "stability," Xi wants to do something great.

The codification of the Chinese civil laws was viewed by Chinese scholars as significant as the French Civil Code of 1804 that embodied a legacy of the Napoleonic era. It was also regarded as significant as the German Civil Code of 1896 that grew out of a desire for a national law that would override the various customs and codes of the German territories. The Chinese Civil Code was also viewed as important as the Japanese Civil Code of 1898 that was the result of the modernization drive following the Meiji Restoration (Huo 2020).

The inspirational vision of the codification of the Chinese civil laws did not finish here. Ten years after the codification of the Napoleonic law, the dictator was defeated in 1814. Two decades after the promulgation of the German Civil Code, Germany was defeated in World War I. The Japanese Civil Code surely ushered Japan into the modern era with remarkable success including its defeat of Russia six years later. Nevertheless, the Japanese were defeated during World War II. It is not settled if the analogy of the Chinese civil code and that of these powers bears good or bad omens for China.

Civil laws and other lesser laws such as criminal laws and election laws are complements of the constitution, including the five constitutional amendments. Generally speaking, the Four Amendments in 1988, 1993, 1999, and 2004 were largely for the reform. The Civil Code is not a good reconfirmation of such principles as rule of law, human rights, and private property, as embodied in the first four constitutional amendments. The Fifth Amendment serves as a correction of the previous four amendments in the sense that it restored some of the pre-reform policies such as a stronger emphasis on personality leadership, the emphasis on communist ideology, and centralization of power. It deviated from the quasi-capitalism of the "primary stage capitalism," which was more prominent in the first Four Constitutional Amendments, but less so from the Fifth Constitutional Amendment (Hua 2019).

The Civil Code could be viewed as a correction or complement of the Fifth Constitutional Amendment in that the tightening of political control is complemented with the protection of certain individual rights, especially economic rights, on the condition that it did not threaten the political monopoly of power of the CCP.

2. Civil Rights

2.1 Rights of a Legal Person

Regarding the rights of a legal person, the Civil Code is highly pragmatic in the sense that it strives to deal with the most urgent problems of the Chinese society today, i.e., housing. "Implementation of the code, which incorporates existing laws including those covering property, contracts and torts, reflects concerns among business owners over protection of personal and property rights" (Zhai 2020).

From 2007 to 2017, city dwellers grew from around 42–57% of the population. China's urban population now accounts for around 820 million people, and by 2030, the number will be over one billion, meaning almost another 200 million people will be living in cities (Chen 2021). In China, more than 90% of households own homes, with 87% in urban and 96% in rural areas (Huang, He and Gan 2021).

Among those housing issues, one of them is what the house owners should do after the 70-year land-use right expires for their home. In China, the state owns all land, and residents have a 70-year land usage right. As expirations approaches, people are worried about what they should do with their homes.

Homeowners need legal protection for their properties. Although the previously promulgated *PRC Property Law* allows the automatic renewal of construction land use for residential property upon the expiry of the contractual term, it does not have the stipulations on the requirements for such renewal. The Civil Code (Article 359) makes it clear that when construction land use rights for residential property are automatically renewed, the payment and the reduction or exemption of relevant renewal fees shall be made.

Another example of the Civil Code to protect the rights of the property owners is that in terms of the repair fees of buildings, the new Civil Code raised from two-thirds to three-quarters of property owners' agreement (Article 278 of the Civil Code as compared with Article 76 of 2007 law).

The codification of "change of circumstances" (most comparable to a disruption to the business foundation) is another issue in protecting the interest of property owners. In particular, during the Covid-19 crisis and the legal problems caused by disruptions in supply chains, and the invocation of force majeure and change of circumstances in particular, numerous legal disputes arose. In this respect, the corresponding legal regulation on the change of circumstances, which was previously only addressed in a corresponding Interpretation of the Supreme People's Court on the contract law, can now provide more legal certainty (Rödl and Partner 2021).

In addition, the provisions related to contracts and property could impact on foreign companies operating in China. For example, in the areas of factoring, guarantee contracts, property management contracts, partnerships, mortgages, and pledges, provisions were introduced (Rödl and Partner 2021). Enacting the civil code that was labeled as "the basic law of a market economy" shows that the Chinese leadership wants to continue to open to the outside world (Huo 2020).

2.2 Rights of a Natural Person

On the rights of a natural person, the provisions with regard to the right to reside were added compared with the 2007 law. This is in response to the fact that more people are renting now. It is to protect the poor who can't buy houses as against the property owners. Property owners can't cut water, electricity, and so on to urge the tenants to pay rent (Articles 366–371). Legal experts called to separate the rights of property occupation and ownership to protect the rights of renters for a long time.

The Civil Code also made the attempt to protect the interest of villagers regarding collective property. The provision was added that members have the right to check and copy the financial record (Article 264, compared with the 2007 version).

Consumers domestic and international have long complained about the quality of Chinese products (Guo 2021). In response to this situation, the provision was added to the effect that those who sell commodities that have defects are legally liable (Article 1206).

Intellectual property rights violation in China is another area that irritates lots of people domestic and international. For instance, in 2015, China and Hong Kong reportedly represented 86% of the global counterfeit industry, which is around

400 billion USD each year. About 80% of the world's counterfeit goods reportedly come from China, and many of the market's consumers are in China as well (Daxue Consulting 2021). The Civil Code added a provision to ban intellectual property rights violations (Article 1185).

The Civil Code not only codifies the rights of a natural person on business and commercial matters but also strengthens the protection of the rights of privacy and personal information (Reedsmith 2020). These things were unimportant when China was poor. Now a large middle class has emerged in China and people have started to care not only about their material life, but also increasingly about a decent spiritual life. China's middle class has been among the fastest growing in the world, swelling from 39.1 million people (3.1% of the population) in 2000 to roughly 707 million (50.8% of the population) in 2018 (CSIS 2021). The Civil Code added the provision that those who suffer spiritual damage can sue for compensation (Articles 996 and 1183).

It also added the provision that allows people to choose to die with dignity (Article 1002). This is in response to the situation where some long-suffering patients cannot die with dignity because the medical workers don't want to take the responsibility of letting those patients who have no hope of survival die and the children of the patients don't want to be blamed for not having the proper behavior of piety that is supposed to be the top moral requirement for children in the Confucian tradition.

The Civil Code has more detailed regulations on sexual harassment, not restricted to the workplace (Article 1010). The concept of "sexual harassment" is defined for the first time. Employers are now required to be proactive in preventing sexual harassment and to implement concrete procedures to handle complaints and take disciplinary action accordingly. According to the new code, a person may be held liable "for speech, words, images or bodily actions that have been used to carry out sexual harassment against a person's wishes" (Article 1010). As a social phenomenon, sexual harassment is a relatively new thing in the last three decades. Before the reform, with the Maoist sexual asceticism, it rarely happened in China (Hua 1998, 53–65).

It also has more detailed protection of privacy (Article 1032). Provisions were added that if the media don't use personal information properly, such as name, portrait, and other personal information, the person involved can sue the media (Article 999). Therefore, the new Civil Law may have a positive impact on famous foreigners looking to protect their rights in China. For example, Bruce Lee's heir sued a fast food chain for portrait right infringement and Michael Jordan has several disputes with Qiaodan Sports Co., Ltd. (Qiaodan is the Chinese pronunciation of Jordan) over use of his name and likeness and recently won a victory on the trademark side.

But there are also compromises in the code's efforts to protect privacy. Compared with the EU GDPR, which is considered the toughest privacy and security law in the world, China's new civil code falls short in regulating how long data collectors can keep people's information and under what circumstances they must delete data (Shan and Wei 2020).

3. Civil Rights and the State

3.1 Key Concepts

The Civil Code indicates the regime's new definition of socialism. It defines socialism as the following:

> The country sticks to the principle that the public ownership of the means of production is the base, while a variety of ownerships coexist; to each according to his/her contribution is the base, while a variety of the form of distributions co-exist; socialist market economy, etc. These are characteristics of a socialist system.
>
> *(Article 206)*

Some key differences in this definition are noted in comparison with the 2004 Constitution's description of China's "socialist system." First, the term "exploitation" was cut, indicating an endorsement of such economic mechanism as stocks that by nature are supposed to be exploitative (Cohen 1979, 338–60). Stocks were not allowed under the Maoist regime or the Soviet regime before Mikhail Gorbachev.

Another item to be noted is that "a variety of ownerships co-exist" was added, because the Chinese economy has become more diverse. According to the official *China Daily*, the number of private companies accounted for 84.1% of all enterprises in 2018 in China (Yang 2019b). In addition, the phrase "primary stage socialism" was cut, indicating the current regime's judgment that regards the current Chinese society as more established, not in transition from one mode of production, i.e., pre-socialist, to the next, i.e., socialist (compared with the 2004 Constitution, Article 6).

Another key conceptual issue is how to define "civil rights." "Civil law modulates the personal and property relationships between natural persons, legal persons, and non-legal-person organizations that are equal entities" (Article 2). Civil rights are defined as "natural persons enjoy the right to life, body rights, the right to health, name rights, image rights, reputation rights, honor rights, privacy rights, the right to marital autonomy and other such rights." For legal persons and unincorporated organizations, they "enjoy name rights, reputation rights, honor rights and other such rights" (Article 110).

But the bottom line is this does not involve the state rights. It does not include political rights, whereas civil rights in the western setting do include political rights such as voting rights or the rights for a fair trial (Hamlin 2021). In the west, the concept of civil rights is defined as "the rights that constitute free and equal citizenship and include personal, political, and economic rights"(Stanford

2021). In China, the official explanation of the term of "civil rights" is separated from "political rights." Therefore, it does not contradict the Fifth Constitutional Amendment that strengthens the state power, state ideology, and personality cult. The civil code is largely to clarify the rights and interests, mostly in economic setting, among non-state entities.

3.2 Relations with the State

In the West, the protection of civil rights inevitably involves restricting the state's rights. In the Civil Code, however, restricting the state's rights is either in an abstract sense (slogans) or on some economic rights, or on some trivial matters, such as Lost & Found, not in restricting the state's rights in politics.

Equal protection of state and private properties was included in the civil code. Noticeably, the word "equally" was added to the code (Article 207 as compared with the 2007 Property Law Article 4).

This is significant that in the eyes of some Chinese legal scholars, the implementation of the principle of equal protection of public property and private property as was stipulated in the earlier Property Law (Draft) was unconstitutional (Jiao 2006).

But this is largely in the area of economics. For instance, subpart III: a usufruct is one person's right to "possess, use, or benefit from" another's property (Article 323). After setting forth some general provisions, the Subpart prescribes more detailed rules on various types of usufructs: right to land contractual management; right to the use of land for construction (e.g., businesses' right to use state-owned land for real estate development); and right to the use of house sites (e.g., rural residents' right to use land to build homes). This is important in the Chinese text because of the state and collective ownership of all lands.

It also includes some small things that the individual's rights are protected vis-a-vis the state. For instance, with Lost/Found, if nobody claims it belongs to the state, the time period was changed from six months to one year (Article 318, compared with Article 113 in the 2007 law).

Examples of limitations in restricting the State's rights include that those who infringe upon the name, likeness, reputation, or honor of a hero, martyr, harming the societal public interest, shall bear civil liability (Article 185).

The Civil Code also added that for the property owners' meeting and the election of the owners' committee, both the local government and the residents' committee shall provide guidance and assistance (Article 277).

This situation made legal experts worry that the new civil code will apply only to disputes between private parties. It does not grant businesses any added privacy rights or legal protections in cases of criminal charges or asset seizure by the state (Ikeda 2020).

Legal experts added that "since the Civil Code only covers civil disputes, it does not help protect property rights against seizure of assets by the state, a most important concern among entrepreneurs" (Zhai, Crossley and Tian 2020).

> For individuals, the civil code carves out the country's first definitions of private spaces and private information. However, as with the business terms, this applies only to private individuals and organizations. It does not enumerate any new privacy rights that apply to state snooping.
>
> *(Ikeda 2020)*

Experts also noted the civil code won't protect entrepreneurs in criminal cases—they can still have assets seized by the state. This is one reason that some say the code can be more symbol than substance, although there is also hope that it will reduce bureaucratic meddling and abuse (Gill 2020).

Another difficulty is the implementation of those provisions that are supposed to protect civil rights. For instance, the Civil Code imposes civil liability on illegally confining others and illegally searching others' bodies (Article 1011). But legal experts noted that although China has a comprehensive system of laws, people are concerned about their enforcement rather than the laws themselves (Zhai, Crossley, and Tian 2020).

"Though the civil code is a step in the right direction for privacy rights, the fact that it does not establish independent courts means that it will be enforced at the pleasure of the government" (Ikeda 2020). As courts are not independent and ultimately answer to the party, legal reforms in recent years have aimed to give judges more independence and rein in local officials' influence over courts (Zhai, Crossley, and Tian 2020). Experts noted that there are fairly strong privacy laws on the books, but it is entirely at the discretion of the government as to whether they will be respected and enforced; it is unclear to what extent the new civil code will change that state of affairs (Ikeda 2020).

Another area of ambiguity is that with China's use of artificial intelligence and the thousands and thousands of surveillance video cameras installed in large cities, protection of personal information, including somebody's whereabouts, becomes questionable (Article 1034) (Yang 2019a, 62–82).

Contradictions in the different legal documents have also been noted. The Civil Code added the new provision that people can sue for illegal detention (Article 1011). However, this contradicts the National Security Law in the Fifth Constitution Amendment about *Liu Zhi*, which allows the government to detain people without going through proper legal procedures.

4. Modernization: Chinese Cultural Tradition and Foreign Experience

The regime has taken a pragmatic attitude in the Civil Code toward Chinese cultural tradition in the sense that some aspects of the Chinese tradition were endorsed, such as stable marriages, and others were discouraged, such as dowry.

Stable families are important for the stability of the Chinese society (Wang 2020, 1–32). However, Chinese families have become less and less stable in recent decades. Last year, some 4.15 million Chinese couples divorced—up from 1.3 million in 2003, when couples were first allowed to divorce by mutual consent without going to court. Before then, divorce had to be obtained by one spouse suing another in court (Gill 2020).

In response to the rise of divorce in China in recent decades, the Civil Code added a cooling-off period of 30 days. Within that time, either party can withdraw the divorce application (Article 1077). In addition, one year within a child was born, the husband can't divorce the wife. Within half a year after abortion, the husband can't divorce the wife. The provision of promoting morality within the family was also added (Article 1043).

On the other hand, the provision of forbidding dowry was added to the Civil Code (Article 1042). Dowry is part of the Chinese tradition when girls were more or less treated by the parents as their properties for sale. In recent decades, dowry in different forms existed for different reasons, one being China's one-child policy adopted in 1979 that resulted in the unbalanced ratio of gender. There are reportedly 118 men for every 100 women in China, with an "extra" 40 million males in the country. Consequently, in some areas, the bride price has skyrocketed, especially in the countryside (BBC 2021).

The Civil Code is pragmatic in the sense that it did not try to deal with all the problems that the Chinese society has. For instance, the legalization of same-sex marriage was not included. Relatedly, there is no provision for non-marital cohabitation. These issues are controversial and the lawmakers were not sure how to deal with them at this moment.

On foreign experiences, the Civil Code also takes a pragmatic attitude in emphasizing some foreign experiences such as the contract laws and rejecting others. Contract laws are a large part of the Civil Code. Lots of the provisions in the contract laws are borrowed from foreign countries. The structure of the Civil Code is believed to be an adoption of the German Pandekten system, which contains an introductory section about general principles, followed by several specific sections (Lu 2020). To ensure that the new code contributes to a better business environment, lawmakers used the criteria in the World Bank's "Doing Business" report as reference for drafting articles related to business guarantees (Shan and Wei 2020).

However, regarding foreign companies operating in China, the following is cut: for those cases involving foreign parties, if domestic laws are not available, the law that another country used in the most similar circumstances can be used (Article 467). This is part of the regime's efforts to show its *Wenhua Zixin* (confidence in the Chinese culture).

The Civil Code also de-emphasizes "primary stage socialism," as was the case with Fifth Amendment. "Primary stage socialism" was based on the Soviet version of Marxism. This is part of the efforts by the regime to reflect the official characterization of the so-called "Xi Jinping New Era Socialism with Chinese Characteristics"(Moody 2021; Buckley 2017) *Lilun zixin* (confidence in theories).

5. Conclusion: Some Historical and Theoretical Considerations

In communist countries, the promulgation of civil codes usually occurred when the leaders wanted to take a break from revolutionary fanaticism. The recent promulgation of China's Civil Code came out in the midst of the country's economic slowdown, the US–China trade war, and other social tensions. Compared with the previously promulgated civil laws, the *Civil Code* has made it clearer about the protection of non-state actors' rights, such as property rights and citizens' privacy. It has taken a pragmatic attitude toward Chinese tradition and foreign experiences.

However, the "civil rights" in the Civil Code do not include political rights. Other difficulties include the poor implementation of these laws with the Chinese Communist Party's dominance and its inconsistency with some provisions in other legal documents such as the Fifth Constitutional Amendment. The regime is willing to yield some rights to its citizens, mainly in the areas of economics, among the non-state actors such as natural persons, legal persons, and unincorporated organizations, as long it does not threaten the dominance of the party.

The promulgation of the Civil Code needs to be comprehended in comparison with other important legal documents such as the recently promulgated Fifth Constitutional Amendment which include some policies similar to those prior to the reform. These documents complement each other: the regime intends to give the republic some breathing space in those less political, non-state areas, as is the case with the Civil Code, while tightening the state's political control of society, as is the case with the Fifth Constitutional Amendment.

The emphasis on the state did not start with Xi or the CCP in general. For instance, Sun Yat-sen in the early 20th century provided China with a recipe for a mobilizational guardianship rather than democracy. Sun was adamant in holding that the state will significantly regulate the market. He also portrayed ordinary citizens as impetuous, unjustifiably confident in their claims to understand political matters based on their experiences, and unable to grasp fully the knowledge necessary to make policy on a routine basis (Lorenzo 2021).

The promulgation of Civil Code is also a result of the Xi administration's strong emphasis on law. In Xi's report to the 19th National Party Congress in 2017, he mentioned "rule according to law" 55 times. But Xi's "rule according to law" is certainly not rule of law in the Western sense. The emphasis of law can go hand in hand with centralization of power (Li 2016). It is rule by law, not rule of law (Dowdle 1999).

Rule by law was practiced in China as early as in the Warring States (481/403 BCE–221 BCE) when the Legalists such as Han Fei (ca. 280–233 BCE) advocated the idea of governance with law instead of rule of man. The central idea of the Legalists was that the state guarantees the people's safety and material necessities, but the people need to give up their political rights in return. This kind of governance was ensured not by personal dictatorship, but through law (Watson 2003, 2).

China's legal reform also needs to be viewed in comparison with the former Soviet Union's experiences. In the eyes of the Chinese leaders, the collapse of the USSR was because of Mikhail Gorbachev's simultaneous push for not only economic reform but also political reform. Following the transitional period of Boris Yeltsin who was more liberal minded, Vladimir Putin seems to turn back to the Russian tradition, the Orthodox Church, to remold the political consciousness of the Russians. Now, again, the two countries seem to follow similar paths: authoritarianism rooted in the indigenous cultural tradition.

Comparatively speaking, China always gives the people less freedom than USSR. Although both the 1954 Chinese constitution and the Soviet one in 1937 were based on the Marxist theory of historical materialism, the Soviet constitution gives people more freedom than the Chinese one (Hua 2019). The current situation is similar. Although both Putin and Xi intend to stay in power as long as they wish, the former held a referendum, while the latter does not feel the need to do so.

To what extent are Xi's policies an ideological departure from his predecessors? It is hard to cut an ideological line among Jiang Zemin, Hu Jintao, and Xi Jinping. Jiang Zemin said to Wallace on TV that the uneducated peasants should be blamed for China not to have democracy (Jiang and Wallace 2000, Sept. 3). Wen Jiabao said the same thing in 2004. Both seemed to suggest China's condition for democracy was not ripe, although value-wise, democracy is good. But on other occasions, the ideological line is not clear. For instance, Jiang Zemin asserted that the CCP would make entrepreneurs bankrupt (Wong 2021).

Xi glorified the peasants by ordering the cadres to go back to such communist bases of the earlier times as Jing Gangshan and Yan'an for revolutionary education, *bu wang chu xin* (never forget about the original goals of the CCP). As the domestic and international situation of China had become more challenging, the way that the Xi regime handles law had become more political. Legal experts noted that if the law did not stipulate clearly, then the court can rule based on ideological considerations (Chen, Guangchen 2021). Previously, the Chinese law ruled that in those cases involving foreign parties, if domestic laws are not available, the law of another country in similar circumstances can be used.

However, even for the Xi regime, the ideological line is not always clear. This is reflected in the regime's inconsistency in treating the Cultural Revolution. Sometimes, the Cultural Revolution was regarded not as a total disaster, but as a hard exploration by the CCP to look for the path of socialist development (Radio France International 2021). Sometimes, the interpretation is similar to that of the 1978 Third Plenum in which the Cultural Revolution was totally renounced (Yu 2020).

Theoretically speaking, the separation between economic rights and political rights as demonstrated in the Civil Code is not properly explained by Marxist theories. Marxism is known for its strong emphasis on the close relations between the economic base and superstructure to such an extent that before Deng's reform in 1978, there was no economics as a social science discipline. There was "political economy" though.

The Civil Code's emphasis on economics to the neglect of political rights is also inconsistent with the modernization theory that holds a large middle class will demand to defend not only their economic rights but also political rights (Peerenboom 2008; So 1990). For modernization theory, economic prosperity will bring about a large middle class that is well educated and they naturally would want to have a voice in the governance of the country. Democracy will by necessity follow substantial economic development. The theory was influential also because it demonstrated validity in the developments of some other countries, such as South Korea, Taiwan, and Singapore (Huntington 1993).

Accidentally, the present promulgation of Civil Code at the theoretical level provides intellectual support to those who disfavor the American legal model that advocates the idea that law should be understood from the perspectives of social sciences such as history, sociology, and economics, and to endorse the European continental model, because they are specifics and concrete laws, and legal theoreticians don't have to debate about the fundamental nature about the Chinese legal system. During much of the reform era, Chinese law transplantation was pre-dominantly Anglo-American (Zhu, Qu, and Zhai 2021).

Scholars have viewed the Chinese experience from different perspectives. Some argue that human rights, including political rights, are interrelated, i.e., private property law will promote human rights, including political rights, in general (Kielsgard and Chen 2014). These scholars are not alone that have taken an apologist position toward the Chinese way (Gottfried Wilhelm Leibniz admired the rational social order of China, the respect for law, the social stability, and the moral system; Lach 1945, 436–55). Others disagree by saying that China's path of legal development has to follow the path of major industrialized societies. Therefore, the Chinese legal system needs much improvements (Zhang 2016).

Notes

1 "Primary stage socialism" is based on the historical materialism's belief that human society progresses through different stages, from lower level to higher level of development: from slavery society, to feudal society, to capitalist society and then finally to communist society. Socialism is the primary stage communism. Chinese theoreticians at the beginning of the reform believed that Mao made the mistakes of trying to skip the stage of capitalism and jump into communism prematurely (Ai 1983).

2 "Rule according to law" differs from the Western notion of "rule of law," in the sense that the former sometimes places the party above the law. "Rule according law" has some similarities with China's imperial tradition in premodern times.

References

Ai, Siqi. 1983. *Bianzheng weiwu zhuyi, lishi weiwu zhuyi (Dialectical Materialism and Historical Materialism)*. Beijing: Renmin chubanshe.

BBC. 2021. "The Rising Cost of a Chinese Bride Price." *BBC*. Accessed May 1, 2021. www.bbc.com/news/blogs-trending-35727057.

Buckley, Chris. 2011. "China Internal Security Spending Jumps Past Army Budget." *Reuters*, March 4.

———. 2017. "China Enshrines 'Xi Jinping Thought,' Elevating Leader to Mao-Like Status." *The New York Times*, October 24.

Chen, Charlie. 2021. "Waiting for China's Precarious Housing Bubble to Burst." *The Politic*. Accessed April 25, 2021. https://thepolitic.org/waiting-for-chinas-precarious-housing-bubble-to-burst/.

Chen, Cheng. 2021. "Ideology-Building Under Hu Jintao: Reacting to Jiang and Paving the Way for Xi." In *Chinese Ideology*, edited by Shiping Hua. London: Routledge.

Chen, Guangcheng. 2021. "The Supreme Court Rules That If the Law Did Not Stipulates, Then the Judge Can Rule Based on Ideological Considerations." *Radio Free Asia*, March 17, 2021.

Chen, Lei. 2009. "The Historical Development of the Civil Law Tradition in China: A Private Law Perspective." *The Legal History Review* 78 (1) (September). doi:10.2139/ssrn.1479442.

Cohen, G. A. 1979. "The Labor Theory of Value and the Concept of Exploitation." *Philosophy and Public Affairs* 8 (4): 338–60.

Chung, Chris. 2016. "Drawing the U-Shaped Line: China′s Claim in the South China Sea, 1946–1974." *Modern China* 42 (1): 38–72.

Chung, Yen-lin. 2011. "The Witch-Hunting Vanguard: The Central Secretariat's Roles and Activities in the Anti-Rightist Campaign." *The China Quarterly* 206 (206): 391–411.

CSIS. 2021. "How Well-off Is China's Middle Class?" Accessed April 27, 2021. https://chinapower.csis.org/china-middle-class/.

Daxue Consulting. 2021. "Behind the Industry of Counterfeit Products in China and Lawsuit Success Cases." Accessed April 27, 2021. https://daxueconsulting.com/counterfeit-products-in-china/.

DiMatteo Larry A., and Lei Chen, eds. 2017. *Chinese Contract Law: Civil and Common Law Perspectives*. Cambridge: Cambridge University Press.

Dowdle, Michael W. 1999. "Heretical Laments: China and the Fallacies of 'Rule of Law.'" *Cultural Dynamics* 11 (2).

Gill, Chris. 2020. "Insights Into China's New Civil Code." *Asia Times Financial*, May 31, 2020. Accessed May 11, 2021. www.asiatimesfinancial.com/insights-into-china-s-new-civil-code.

Gow, Michael. 2017. "The Core Socialist Values of the Chinese Dream: Towards a Chinese Integral State." *Critical Asian Studies* 49 (1): 92–116.

Guo, Wu. 2021. "Why the Chinese People Are Invisible in US Media." Accessed April 26, 2021. www.thinkchina.sg/why-chinese-people-are-invisible-us-media.

Hamlin, Rebecca. 2021. "Civil Rights." *Britannica*. Accessed May 11, 2021. www.britannica.com/topic/civil-rights.

Howell, Jude. 2019. "NGOs and Civil Society: The Politics of Crafting a Civic Welfare Infrastructure in the Hu-Wen Period." *China Quarterly* 237: 58–81.

Huo Zhengxin. 2020. "China Enters an Era With a Civil Code." *C. J. Observer*, May 29. Accessed April 4, 2021. www.chinajusticeobserver.com/a/china-enters-an-era-with-a-civil-code.

Hua, Shiping. 1998. "The Politics of Gender in the Chinese New Cinema." *Hong Kong Journal of Social Sciences* 12 (Autumn): 53–65.

———. 2019. *Chinese Legal Culture and Constitutional Order*. London: Routledge.

Huang, Youqin, Shenjing He, and Li Gan. 2021. "Introduction to Special Issue: Unpacking the Chinese Dream of Homeownership." *Journal of Housing and the Built Environment* 36: 1–7.

Huntington, Samuel. 1993. *The Third Wave: Democratization in the Late 20th Century*. Oklahoma City: University of Oklahoma Press.

Ikeda, Scott. 2020. "China's New Civil Code Would Be a Historic Expansion of Privacy Rights – Assuming It's Consistently Enforced." *CPO Magazine*, June 11. Accessed May 11, 2021. www.cpomagazine.com/data-protection/chinas-new-civil-code-would-be-a-historic-expansion-of-privacy-rights-assuming-its-consistently-enforced/.

Jiang, Zemin, Interviewed by Mike Wallace, September 3, 2000. Accessed May 1, 2021. www.youtube.com/watch?v=1tNMH2M_jJ0.

Jiao, H. 2006. Wuquanfa (Cao'an) de Hexianxing Fenxi [Constitutional Analysis on the Property Law]. *Legal Science* (3): 39–41.

Kielsgard, Mark D., and Lei Chen. 2014. "The Emergence of Private Property Law in China and Its Impact on Human Rights." *Asian-Pacific Law & Policy Journal* 15 (1).

Lach, Donald F. 1945. "Leibniz and China." *Journal of the History of Ideas* 6 (4): 436–55.

Li, Anthony H. F. 2016. "Centralisation of Power in the Pursuit of Law-based Governance Legal Reform in China Under the Xi Administration." *China Perspectives* 2.

Li, Hua-yu. 2001. "The Political Stalinization of China: The Establishment of One-Party Constitutionalism, 1948–1954." *Journal of Cold War Studies* 3: 28–47.

Ling, Bing. 2020. "The New Contract Law in the Chinese Civil Code." *The Chinese Journal of Comparative Law* 8 (3): 558–634.

Lorenzo, David J. 2021. "Sun Yat-sen and The San Min Chu I Lectures as Ideology." In *Chinese Ideology*, edited by Shiping Hua. London: Routledge.

Lu, Tian. 2020. "First-ever Chinese Civil Code Adopted at National Legislature: No 'IP Section', Yet Still Relevant." *IPKIT*, May 31, 2020. Accessed May 1, 2021. http://ipkitten.blogspot.com/2020/05/first-ever-chinese-civil-code-adopted.html.

MacFarquhar, Roderick. 1999. *The Origins of the Cultural Revolution*, Volume 3 0th Edition. New York: Columbia University Press.

Moody, Peter. 2021. "Some Reflections on Xi Jinping's Political Thought." In *Chinese Ideology*, edited by Shiping Hua. London: Routledge.

Peerenboom, Randall. 2008. *China Modernizes: Threat to the West or Model for the Rest?* New York: Oxford University Press.

Radio France International. Accessed April 5, 2021. www.wenxuecity.com/news/2021/04/15/10486255.html.

Reedsmith. 2021. "The Adoption of the Chinese Civil Code and Its Implications on Contracts Relating to China." Accessed April 28, 2021. www.reedsmith.com/en/perspectives/2020/06/the-adoption-of-the-chinese-civil-code-and-its-implications-on-contracts.

Rödl & Partner. 2021. "China's Civil Code." Accessed April 27, 2021. www.roedl.com/insights/china-civil-code/china-adopts-civil-code.

Schram, Stuart R. 1984. "Economics in Command? Ideology and Policy Since the Third Plenum, 1978–84." *The China Quarterly* 99 (September): 417–61.

Service, Robert. 1997. *A History of Twentieth-Century Russia*, 124–25. Cambridge, MA: Harvard University Press.

Shan, Yuxiao, and Han Wei. 2020. "In Depth: Decoding China's First Civil Code." *Politics & Law*, June 1. Accessed April 17, 2021. www.caixinglobal.com/2020-06-01/in-depth-decoding-chinas-first-civil-code-101561290.html.

So, Alvin Y. 1990. *Social Change and Development: Modernization, Dependency and World-System Theories*. Newbury Park, CA: Sage Publications.

Stanford Encyclopedia of Philosophy. Accessed May 11, 2021. https://plato.stanford.edu/entries/civil-rights/.

Wang, Di. 2020. "Jia, as in Guojia: Building the Chinese Family into a Filial Nationalist Project." *China Law and Society Review* 5 (1): 1–32.

Watson, Burton. 2003. *Han Feizi – Basic Writings*, 2. Columbia University Press.

Wen, Wei. 2018. "China's New General Provisions of Civil Law: Changes and Advancements for the Better." *LAWASIA Journal* (January). Accessed September 19, 2022. https://papers.ssrn.com/sol3/papers.cfm?abstract_id=3171363.

Wong, Yiu-chung. 2021. "Assessing the Era of Jiang Zemin." In *Chinese Ideology*, edited by Shiping Hua. London: Routledge.

World Bank data. 2021. https://data.worldbank.org/indicator/NY.GDP.MKTP.KD.ZG?locations=CN.

Yang, Feng. 2019a. "The Future of China's Personal Data Protection Law: Challenges and Prospects." *Asia Pacific Law Review* (September): 62–82. Published online: August 5.

Yang, Yang. 2019b. "Over 84% Companies in China Are Private." *China Daily*, November 28, 2019.

Yu, Yizhu. 2020. "Cong xibai wenge dao huifu lishixing dingxing, zhongguo jiaokeshu xiugai beihou fasheng le shenmo (From White Wash the Cultural Revolution to Restore the Renouncing it, What Is Going on Behind the Chinese Textbook Revisions)." *Duowei News*, September 7. Accessed May 11, 2021. www.dwnews.com/中国/60210791/从洗白文革到恢复历史定性中国教科书修改背后发生了什么.

Zhai, Keith, Gabriel Crossley, and Yew Lun Tian. 2020. "China Set to Implement Its First Civil Code, as Private Investment Slows." *Reuters*, May 21. www.reuters.com/article/us-china-parliament-civil-code/china-set-to-implement-its-first-civil-code-as-private-investment-slows-idUSKBN22X0TC.

Zhai, Tiantian, and Yen-Chiang Chang. 2019. "The Contribution of China's Civil Law to Sustainable Development: Progress and Prospects." *Sustainability* 11 (294).

Zhang, Laney. 2015. "Chinese Law on Private Ownership of Real Property." *Library of Congress*, March 10. Accessed April 25, 2021. https://blogs.loc.gov/law/2015/03/chinese-law-on-private-ownership-of-real-property/.

Zhang, Xianchu. 2016. "The New Round of Civil Law Codification in China." *University of Bologna Law Review* 1 (1).

Zhao, Suisheng. 1993. "Deng Xiaoping's Southern Tour: Elite Politics in Post-Tiananmen China." *Asian Survey* 33 (8): 739–56.

———. 2016. "Xi Jinping's Maoist Revival." *Journal of Democracy* 27 (3): 83–97.

Zhu, Guobin, Jian Qu, and Han Zhai. 2021. "Paradigm Shift in Chinese Legal Studies." In *Paradigm Shifts in Chinese Studies*, edited by Shiping Hua. London: Palgrave Macmillan.

PART 3

How Is Legality Realized? Institutions in Action

8

CAN XI JINPING STOP THE BUREAUCRATS FROM SEEKING RENTS VIA LEGISLATION?

Chun-Chih Chang and Chien-Min Chao

Introduction

The diffusion of power to various governmental agencies and local authorities has been the main driver behind China's economic success. However, a side effect of this has been the emergence of the corporate state system.[1] Preventing bureaucrats from coalescing with businesses to seek illegitimate interests has been a challenge for Chinese leadership under Xi Jinping.

No sooner had Xi taken the helm to become one of the most powerful leaders in China's history, a "Decision on Some Major Issues Concerning Comprehensively Deepening the Reform" (hereafter referred to as Decision on Comprehensive Reform) was passed by the Third Plenary Session of the Eighteenth Central Committee of the Chinese Communist Party (CCP) in November 2013. A year later, another important resolution was adopted at the Fourth Plenary Session of the Central Committee "to comprehensively push for rule of law" (hereafter Resolution on Comprehensive Rule of Law). Clamping down on officials' pursuit of illicit interests seems to be a priority.

Xi's predecessor Jiang Zemin had already started promoting the "rule of law" as a means to fight against increasingly unruly localism and departmentalism. The policy was stipulated as a "primary guideline" at the Fourth Session of the Eighth National People's Congress (NPC) in 1996. Rule of law was for the first time written into the constitution in 1999. As attention is gradually shifted to the rule of law, progress has been made in the court system slowly. Nevertheless, bureaucrats seeking interests through legislation in what has been known as part of the problem of both localism and departmentalism remains acute (Chen 2010).

Like Jiang Zemin, the main purpose of Xi Jinping's "putting powers into the cage" and to "comprehensively push for the rule of law" is to root out the problems of the "departmentalization of state powers" and the prevalence of interest

DOI: 10.4324/9781003294887-11

seeking by local governments. What is different this time around is that instead of focusing on the enlivening of the judicial system, Xi is taking the fight to the root cause by introducing public opinions into legislation to seal the loophole that bureaucrats find easy to circumvent. The Decision on Comprehensive Reform demands the "strive to perfect the drafting of laws and mechanisms regarding opinion-gathering and ratification" so that the quality of legislation can be enhanced and "local protectionism and departmentalization of interests can be prevented." One problem identified in the Resolution on Comprehensive Rule of Law in strengthening the rule of law in China today that needs to be "resolved with great rigor" is legislation that is controlled by governmental departments without the exposure of public opinions (the other two are selective enforcement of justice, rampancy of corruption and crackdown on legal rights movement), confirming the severity of the issue.

It is indeed advisable to preempt corruption in the lawmaking process by bringing forces from outside the executive-legislative structure into the tightly controlled party-state system. However, how could the people's congresses (PCs), which have been alleged as "rubber stamps," become a venue of interest-swapping in the first place? How have bureaucrats maneuvered the lawmaking process to expand their powers, shirk responsibilities, and even channel interests to themselves? How did Chinese rulers answer the problem of corruption through legislation? As rooting corruption out of the reinforced party-state system has been the main focus of Xi Jinping's great rejuvenation of the Chinese race, it will be interesting to see if the populist approach can help stem the trend toward plutocracy and reenergize the trouble-ridden political system.

This chapter will first examine the shortcomings of state-centered research on China's parliamentary system. Second, we will describe how bureaucrats use the power of writing and amending laws to create an environment conducive to interest seeking. Third, we attempt to evaluate new measures to see whether they are effective and, if not, why. Finally, we conclude by suggesting that although the new methods are useful to some extent, they are not enough to stop corruption.

1. State-Centered Lawmaking Structure

Owing to the predominant role of the CCP in China's political process, scholars have concentrated their work on researching China's PC system by examining the party-state structure itself. Depending on whether the representative organ is functioning, research can further be divided into two schools: a minority view follows the totalitarian model by treating China's PC as nothing more than an instrument of the party state. Given the nature of the Leninist regime, they argue that the lawmaking process is characterized by the ultimate goal of maintaining the authoritarian order (Liebman 2011).

Most mainstream scholars see PCs as part of competitive authoritarianism (Levitsky and Way 2002, 2010) or electoral authoritarianism (Schedler 2006), a future tense, in which China has gradually evolved. Some opt for the term hybrid regimes (Diamond 2002), which have been discussed widely in the field of comparative politics. According to these scholars, pseudodemocratic mechanisms are an important part of the strategy of coalition building in nondemocratic polities for multiple purposes: to continue the reign, stay close to society, and mute dissension (Gandhi 2008; Gandhi, Ben and Milan 2020; Svolik 2012).

The gist of "democracy with Chinese characteristics" is what the Chinese call "democratic centralism" and "consultative collaboration," which offers room for limited pluralism. Over the years, the CCP has been trying to make the PCs more institutionalized and increase its function in information gathering (Chao and Chang 2014; Chang and Chao 2019). Manion (2014a, 2014b, 2015; also see Zhang 2017; Truex 2014, 2016) argues that at the grassroots levels, congressional representation by means of political selection "coexists with the communist party nominating and veto power in the electoral process." Two types of representation can thus be identified: those who are designated by the party and are thus acting as agents of the system who will ferociously defend the collective interests of the party state and the second is those who are more immersed in local interests and are willing to speak up on behalf of the general public.

Some scholars refurbish the party-state logic and argue that the PCs are somehow functioning, albeit restrained compared to Western democracy, not because they have gained autonomy from the grips of the all-encompassing network of the Leninist party state but because they appendix themselves to the power apparatus. In his pioneering work, O'Brien (1994; O'Brien and Luehrmann 1998) suggests that China's representative organs are meeting their duties of lawmaking and oversight at the expense of autonomy. This is because they align with or embed their powers in the most authoritative power center, the party. This strategy of embeddedness sets China's PCs apart from representative organs in other democracies.[2]

A third deviation of this controlled usefulness theorem is relatively new to the field. Scholars note lately that PCs are beefing up their utilities through professionalism and institutionalization. By analyzing the background of members of the nine permanent committees at the National People's Congress's Standing Committee (NPCSC), Chao and Chang conclude that while there is still a long way off before autonomy prevails in China's legislature, professionalism is creeping in as better educated and more experienced bureaucrats are recruited to serve in the assembly (Chao and Chang 2014, 2016; Chang and Chao 2019).

While making inroads into China's opaque political landscape, both schools stress the importance of the party-state machinery in the making of laws in China. This chapter argues that while the approach has successfully embedded its research on the very foundation of the Chinese political system and empowering the henceforth incapacitated Chinese legislature, state-driven utilitarianism is not enough to meet the challenges that China is facing today. Xi Jinping is aware of this predicament, and since assuming the supreme leadership, he has not only tried to deter bureaucrats from accruing illicit interests via legislation but also opened a small window by bringing light into the opaque system.

2. Bureaucratic Interests in China's Lawmaking Process

The market-oriented economic reforms in the post-Mao era were centered around the decentralization of powers to various government agencies and local governments to enliven the ossified centralized command system. Scholars have tried to captivate the new mode of power structure as "fragmented authoritarianism" (Lieberthal and Oksenberg 1988; Liberthal and Lampton 1992).

To these scholars, the growth of local autonomy and the uneven development between regions have given rise to a new type of localism in China, which in turn is reshaping central-local relations in terms of value integration, resource distribution, and policymaking and implementation. As local fiefs grow larger and more powerful, a new cycle of centralization and decentralization is taking shape. In other words, although Mao tried to decentralize powers to the local authorities in an effort to clamp down on the rigidity and ossification that he saw plaguing the bureaucracy at the center, it was based on a strategy known as "a national chess game" (*quanguo yipanqi*) with little regard for individualistic aspirations and values. However, as powers are diffused, the contention for resources and interests by various departments and localities has also been intensified. Embedded in the transition to a market economy that bureaucrats are now, instead of following orders from the above, juggling for advantageous positions and contesting for resources. Andrew Mertha (2009) brings professionalism into the new power equation and coined the term "fragmented authoritarianism 2.0." Policymaking in China is not only a lengthy process involving wheeling and dealing among various sectors at both the center and the local (Wong 2018); the participants have also multiplied to include "policy entrepreneurs," such as private entrepreneurs (Mertha 2009) and NGOs (Froissart 2019).

The aforementioned discussion of interest peddling focuses on the forming and implementing of policies. However, as the demand for the rule of law grows, bureaucrats start to turn their attention to legislation in seeking rents. Compared to the secrecy of rent seeking in the forming of policies in the past, interest peddling via legislation is more complex, as the process is semi-open and -transparent involving actors from the CCP, the administrative and legislative branches, social organizations, domestic and international businesses, and entrepreneurs. The legislative process has opened up opportunities for a host of new players competing for interests (Lu, Liu and Li 2020; Truex 2020).

Scot Tanner was one of the pioneers to bring the fragmented authoritarian model into lawmaking in China (Tanner 1999, 50):

> As a result, power within the lawmaking system, just as in other sectors of the Chinese policy-making system, is fragmented among numerous individuals and organizations. The various lawmaking organizations continue to evolve their own unique packages of power resources which allow them to influence lawmaking in differing degrees, at different stages of the process. The result, in the words of Garbage Can model proponents, is a lawmaking

system with an increasingly "ambiguous decision-making technology," and with multiple arenas in which political struggle can be carried out.

Competition for interests and consensus building seem to be the norms now in China's legislative politics. There are two means through which bureaucratic influences find their way into legislation. The first type of interest peddling is localism. Given its immense size and geographic diversity, most of the laws in China are made by local governments under the authorization of the central government to account for regional differences. It is not unusual that local authorities step outside the boundaries laid down by the central government to create an environment to their own liking in what has been known as a policy of "*shangyou zhengce, xiayou duice,*" i.e., where there is policy, there is a counter policy (Gu and Chao 2018; Wang and Tang 2008). By analyzing the Legislation Law passed by the NPC in 2000, Laura Paler concludes that one of the goals of the act was to consolidate powers by the national assembly in the tripartite juggling for powers against the local people's congress (LPCs) and the State Council (Paler 2005).

The second type of bureaucratic interest peddling comes with departmentalism. Since most of the laws are drafted by various agencies belonging to either the central government or the local governments, this unique privilege has given these departments access to the new game of plutocracy (Lu, Liu, and Li 2020). The problem is so serious as to prompting Cho Young Nam to point out that department protectionism has dominated the lawmaking process in China (Cho 2009, 18–42).

One of the root causes of bureaucratic interest peddling is delegated legislation. According to the Organic Law of Local People's Congresses and Local People's Governments passed in 1979, the provincial PCs (including the five autonomous regions inhabited by the minorities and the four huge municipalities administered directly by the State Council) and PCs of the "larger cities" are entitled to enact their own regulations (Wan 2011). The Legislation Law passed in 2000 further gives special economic zones the privilege to write their own regulations. Generally, delegated legislation comes in various forms. Some delegated legislation is on an experimental basis, while others are complementary to the existing regulations. For example, to let the coastal special economic regions lead the wave of reforming the old Stalinist command system and reconnecting with the West-dominated international economic order, the NPC and the NPCSC on quite a few occasions gave the powers of legislation to the designated coastal areas in Southeast China, such as Guangdong, Fujian, Hainan, Shenzhen, Xiamen, Shantou, and Zhuhai, to set up their own economic zones at the beginning of the economic reforms in the 1980s and 1990s (NPC 2021a). In 2021, the NPCSC again authorized the LPCs in Shanghai and Hainan province to enact regulations for the Pudong New District and Hainan Free Trade Port. However, regulations enacted by local governments often lack strict monitoring, and furthermore, the multiplicity of legislation under authorization has given the delegated parties room for maneuvering.

While departmentalism may come in a variety of shapes, this chapter focuses on the bureaucratic interests in the lawmaking process. Generally, there are three types of interest peddling that are commonly used by bureaucrats.

2.1 Expanding Powers to Hold Onto Vested Interests

Bureaucracy anywhere has the tendency to maximize powers. However, what is different in China today is that it is mostly driven by economic considerations. In the wake of legislating what has been known as the "economic constitution," the Anti-Monopoly Act, the Ministry of Commerce, the State Administration for Industry and Commerce (SAIC), and the National Development and Reform Commission (NDRC) were fiercely engaged in a battle for the right of drafting, and each agency actually came up with a version of its own. The SAIC took the first shot in the drafting in 1999, and it even established an "anti-monopoly bureau" to bolster its resolve. Four years later, the NDRC made public the Provisional Directive to Stop Monopoly in Pricing, followed by the Ministry of Commerce's revelation of its own draft of the anti-monopoly act a year later. The Ministry of Commerce also created its own antimonopoly department. To get an upper hand in the propaganda war, each agency tried to publish its own policy papers.[3]

The reason behind the fight is economics. As all industries, such as the electricity, telecommunications, and railway systems in China, are administered by some government agency (or agencies), it has long been a practice that the agencies and departments look after their own interests by enacting their own rules and regulations. The passage of the Anti-Monopoly Act would take that privilege away from the three agencies and place it in the hands of a single authority. Whoever that authority may be, it will not be appreciated by the other two. It is a winners-take-all game. Therefore, the Ministry of Commerce tried to hold onto the powers of ascertaining, inspecting, and investigating commercially monopolistic behaviors. The SAIC, on the other hand, stressed its jurisdiction over monopoly by international enterprises and its power over enterprises with the potential of being monopolistic in nature. For the NDRC, the strategy was to argue its powers of investigation and punishment of behaviors concerning monopoly in pricing. As a result of the contestation, the State Council created an antimonopoly commission to facilitate interagency coordination. However, the problem of multiauthority over the issue of monopoly remains to date (Wang 2010).

2.2 Channeling Interests Through Legislation

Channeling interests through legislation to a certain government agency, its subsidiaries, or enterprises has been one of the most common practices of departmentalism, and land development has been the main area of concern. A case in point happened in 2010 when the government of Huinan, a city in Anhui Province, passed the Directive Governing the Management of Real Estate, demanding high fees for elevators from real estate developers before a new apartment is sold. As a result of this arbitrary ordinance, huge protests followed (Yang 2010).

The Regulation to Explore and Protect Resources Related to Climate passed by Heilongjiang Province in 2012 is another case. The regulation provides the provincial government power to give permission to explore resources related to climate, infringing the jurisdiction of the Ministry of Land and Resources and National Energy Administration, both agencies of the central government (Tang 2013, 56). A third case surfaced when the State Post Bureau tried to align itself with the exclusive power of mail delivery in the draft Act of Postal Administration, depriving private businesses of the right of service. Facing strong opposition, the proposition was finally dropped (Zhang 2017).

2.3 Evasion of Responsibilities via Legislation

The Regulation on Social Insurance issued by the Labor Department of Taiyuan City, the capital city of Shanxi Province, was rejected by the Taiyuan People's Congress Standing Committee in 2007 on the grounds that the new law was intended to collect fees on social insurance, but there is no mention of protecting the rights of the insured or any oversight mechanism. Commercialism is at play here. After reviewing, Taiyuan's People's Congress decided to send the draft back to the city government so that contents such as rights of the insured and supervision of the fund are added alongside the collection of the fees (China News 2008).

A study by Liu Yaping and Su Jiaoni (2021) on the regulations on the management of small vendors in Guangdong Province found a lengthy quadrilateral power struggle pitting the central government (NPC and the State Council), the local PCs, the local government departments, and different social forces against each other. It is a very tedious and long process without involving interests. Rather, it is a typical case of shirking responsibilities via legislation by various local government departments and yet denying the power being acquired by other agencies. During the legislation, calls were heard asking the local PC standing committee (LPCSC) to take the lead based on public interests and broader perspectives. However, the LPCSC was not powerful enough to take command, and it could only take the role of coordinating amid the juggling of various bureaucratic interests. During the process, social forces were also denied meaningful participation. In the end, in the face of the pressure of the legislative deadline, the LPC could only come up with a compromised version to the pleasure of relevant stakeholders.

It is a commonplace for bureaucracy to enlarge its powers if there is a loophole and rend seeking via legislation has emerged as a new form of this malpractice in China. Since becoming the supreme leader, Xi Jinping has deployed new weaponry to reverse the trend.

3. Legislative Renewal Against Bureaucratic Interests

To seal the loophole in which central and local bureaucracies try to seek rent through legislation, the Decision on Comprehensive Reform demanded change over the legislative organ, vowing to "perfect the legal system, make healthy the drafting, discussion, coordination, and review processes in the legislation so that the quality of laws can be raised." The Resolution on Comprehensive Rule of Law points out three fundamental problems the legal system now faces in China: prevalence of departmentalism at the expense of public opinion, selective justice leading to injustice and corruption, and suppression of legal rights movement by some cadres. The Resolution demanded "double the effort to get the problems resolved."

To counter bureaucratic interests, three new measures have been introduced to the NPC and its standing committee: invigorate the power of the legislation review, revise the legal codes, and offer more transparency, and public opinions are to be included in lawmaking.

First, the NPC has invigorated its power of legislation review. To curb the possibility of bureaucrats enriching themselves, in 2015, Xi Jinping pushed for the revision of the Legislation Law, first passed in 2000. In the future, the revised Law demands that the purpose and scope of delegated legislation must be clearly defined with a maximum validity period of no more than five years. The PCSCs and their permanent committees should adopt a hands-on policy in the lawmaking process by proactively engaging in reviewing the legislation during drafting, rather than waiting until a full draft is provided, and demand change or even stop the work entirely if necessary. Bureaucracies from the center down are asked to strictly follow the laws and regulations laid down by the legislature and the State Council so that chances of interest channeling may be minimized.

To preempt interest seeking, new mechanisms have also been invented. In 2018, in the important Decision on Deepening the Reform of the Party and State Institutions, adopted at the Third Plenary Session of the 19th Central Committee of the CCP, a new Constitution and Law Committee was created by the NPC to replace the old Law Committee established in the 1982 constitution. In addition to the power to review all draft bills before passing, the new committee was given additional power to monitor if the constitution was violated during the lawmaking process. Furthermore, the Legal Affairs Committee (LAC) of the NPCSC has also created an Office for Recording and Reviewing Regulations, tasked with the power of filing review. The office, along with a relevant NPCSC permanent committee, has the power to review all legislation once it is officially approved. The NPCSC can exercise power on its own, or it can also react upon request from government agencies, civil organizations, and even civilians. This filing review covers administrative regulations, local regulations, and judicial interpretations. Since 2017, the filing reviews carried out by the NPCSC have covered a wide range of legislation from environmental protection to food and drug safety, wild life protection, civil codes, Yangze River protection, Population and Family Planning Law, and administrative penalties (Liang 2021). In 2021, the General Office of the NPCSC received 1,921 applications for filing reviews, ranging from administrative regulations to regulations for provinces, autonomous regions, special economic zones, and special administrative regions (NPC 2021b). For those LPCs entitled to write their own regulations, a similar mechanism is also in place.

According to China's Trademark Law, the term "famous trademark" is not allowed to appear on commodities. In 2017, 108 graduate students wrote a letter to the LAC demanding revision of the Measures of Chongqing on Determination and Protection of Famous Trademarks, in which "Chongqing's Famous Trademarks" was reserved for use by vendors. Hence, a comprehensive review of all local regulations alike was activated (Beijing News 2017). The newly accrued powers to review the constitution and the filing review would definitely enhance the authority of the NPC and its Standing Committee.

Second, revising the legal codes already in place is also a means in the fight against departmental protectionism. However, the PCs at all levels will have to take up the challenge and do their job. The Legislation Law was revised to highlight the role of PCs in lawmaking. Article 51 demands that the NPC and its Standing Committee better coordinate and organize so that their role as the pivot in lawmaking might be fully realized. Article 53 stipulates that the NPCSC and its permanent committees become involved in the drafting of laws as early as possible, and for those "laws which have national, comprehensive and fundamental significance," the drafting can be organized by the relevant permanent committees and working institutions of the legislative organ. For laws requiring professionalism, it is allowed to recruit outside experts to participate in the drafting or delegate the power of drafting to academics, research institutions, and social organizations.

The NPC session is notoriously short, lasting only for a couple of weeks each session. New measures were adopted in 2021 to strengthen the connections between the NPCSC and the NPC, including allowing the NPCSC to seek opinions from NPC members in legislating. Relevant information is to be passed on to members of the NPC electronically so that they can be better prepared for the annual gathering. The review process by the NPC is also simplified to allow members more time to participate.

Third, bringing transparency and public opinion into lawmaking has been the most vital reform in recent years with the purpose of changing the culture of legislation. Civil participation in lawmaking is deeply ingrained in the CCP's revolutionary ideology. The tradition is now revived in the PCs with new gadgets added to make connections with the society, including conducting investigative tours, sending draft acts to various governmental and non-governmental organizations for feedback, inviting the draftees, relevant government agencies, scholars, and even the public for consultation (*zishang*), organizing discussion sessions (*lunzheng hui*), holding hearings so that the stakeholders might be able to face off against each other (*tingzheng hui*), and posting draft laws in social and traditional media (Chen 2008, 221–25).

While meeting with a group of Shanghai citizens who had participated in the solicitation of opinions in the drafting of a local regulation in November 2019, Xi Jinping proposed a "whole-process people's democracy" (*quanguocheng renmin minzhu*) as a new foundation in the development of China's political institutions. The new proposal has the following implications for legislation.

First, the rules of procedure of the NPC were amended in 2021 to make its activities more visible to the outside world. It not only requires transparency for congressional agendas and ongoing meetings but also creates a spokesman system while the NPC is in session.

Second, the Legislative Law already requires bills waiting for the review to be publicized in advance and solicit opinions for no shorter than 30 days, and relevant information including reasons for the drafting and outcome of the review carried out by the NPCSC published on the NPCSC gazette and its website. Now, these rules have formally become part of the revised NPC rules of procedure.

Third, over the past few years, the LAC has established ten "grassroots legislative windows" (*lifa lianxizhan*) nationwide to collect public opinions, prompting the LPCs to follow suit. Therefore, a host of new mechanisms borrowing names such as "representative house" and "representative connections" have shot up serving as bases for training LPC deputies, meeting with the public, and acquiring opinions. Some places even go thus far as to evaluate the performance of the LPCs by the public and erect a "duty performance supervisor" to monitor the work of the local assembly.

4. Conclusion

One of the important goals in the drive toward the rule of law advocated by Xi Jinping is to resolve the old issue of self-enrichment by bureaucrats through legislation in what has been addressed as the departmentalization of powers. To that end, this chapter illustrates the reforms carried out by Xi in the lawmaking process, including invigorating the power of legislation review, revising the legal codes, and bringing transparency and public opinions into the lawmaking system to reduce the influences of interest peddling by bureaucrats. Some of these reforms have indeed strengthened the status of the NPC as a legitimate source of power in China's party-state system, while other reforms might only have marginal effects. However, contrary to the assertion by Roxy Truex (2014, 2016, 2020) that reforms in China's PC have given rise to a responsive authoritarianism, this chapter concludes that the legislative reforms undertaken by Xi are deliberate moves by the Chinese leader in the fight against corruption. It is a top-down decision, and hence we should refrain from viewing it as a sound feedback system employed by the party state to regurgitate demands deriving from civil society.

Notes

1 Discourse on Chinese state corporatism could be found in Montinola, Qian, and Weingast (1995), Oi (1992, 1995), and Nan Lin (1995).

2 Xia (2000, 2008) challenges O'Brien's theory and claims that in order to continue its rule, the CCP is unlikely to help institutionalizing people's congress. Xia argues that the PCs could get its powers beefed up only through small scale but constant confrontations against the system. Combining the two opinions, Cho (2002, 2009) points out that cooperation with the CCP is necessary for the PCs to get going at the early stage, but after its

institutional foundation has been stabilized, the PCs have to confront the administrative branch in a limited scope to enlarge its capacities. Cho (2002) remarks this process as an evolution from rubber stamp to iron stamp.

3 In May 2004, the State Administration for Industry and Commerce released a "Report on Behaviors of Restrictive Competition among the Multinational Corporations in China and the Countermeasures." Few months later, the National Development and Reform Commission released a policy paper entitled "Current Economic Situation and Policy Tendencies, 2005."

References

Beijing News. 2017. "Baiming Yanjiusheng Huyu Feizhi Chongqing Zhuming Shangbiao Fagui (More Than One Hundred Graduate Students Appealed to Abolish Chongqing's Famous Trademark Regulation)." Accessed March 21, 2022. www.bjnews.com.cn/news/2017/11/13/464107.html.

Chang, Chun-Chih, and Chien-Min Chao. 2019. "Specialization Without Autonomy: An Informational Approach to the Development of Permanent Committees in China's National People's Congress." *Journal of Contemporary China* 28 (115): 64–80.

Chao, Chien-Min, and Chun-Chih Chang. 2014. "Zhongguo Dalu Quanguo Renda Zhuanmen Weiyuanhui de Zhiduhua Licheng ji Pinggu (Headway on Specialization but Deficiency on Autonomy: Institutionalization of the Permanent Committees in China's National People's Congress)." *Zhengzhi Xuebao* 57: 77–100.

———. 2016. "Education and Training in China's National People's Congress." In *Parliamentarians' Professional Development: The Need for Reform*, edited by Colleen Lewis and Ken Coghill, 171–85. New York: Springer.

Chen, Sixi. 2008. *Renmin Daibiao Dahui Zhidu Gailun (An Introduction to the People's Congress)*. Beijing: Minzhu fazhi chubanshe.

Chen, Titus C. 2010. "Zhongzhu Hongse Tianping: Zhongguo Sifa Gaige de Zhengzhi Luoji Ji Qidui Fazhi de Yingxiang (Reformulating Justice: The Political Logic of the Post-1999 Judicial Reform in China and Its Implications for the Rule of Law)." *Taiwanese Journal of Political Science* 45: 69–105.

China News. 2008. "Taiyuan Tansuo Lifa Zhaobiao (Taiyuan Called for 'Legislative Tenders')." Accessed March 21, 2022. www.chinanews.com.cn/gn/news/2008/03-24/1200395.shtml.

Cho, Young Nam. 2002. "From 'Rubber Stamps' to 'Iron Stamps': The Emergence of Chinese Local People's Congresses as Supervisory Powerhouses." *The China Quarterly* 171: 724–40.

———. 2009. *Local People's Congresses in China: Development and Transition*. New York: Cambridge University Press.

Diamond, Larry. 2002. "Thinking About Hybrid Regimes." *Journal of Democracy* 13 (2): 21–35.

Froissart, Chloé. 2019. "From Outsiders to Insiders: The Rise of China ENGOs as New Experts in the Law-making Process and the Building of a Technocratic Representation." *Journal of Chinese Governance* 4 (3): 207–32.

Gandhi, Jennifer. 2008. *Political Institutions Under Dictatorship*. New York: Cambridge University Press.

Gandhi, Jennifer, Noble Ben, and Svolik Milan. 2020. "Legislatures and Legislative Politics Without Democracy." *Comparative Political Studies* 53 (9): 1359–79.

Gu, Xiao-ting, and Chien-Min Chao. 2018. "Zhongguo Dalu Tudi Chanquan Yizhuan de Liyi Jiegou Wenti: Yi Chongqing Nongcun Jiti Jianshe Yongde Weili (Interest Structure in the Transfer of Collective Farm Land for Commercial Purposes in Rural China: A Case Study of Chongqing)." *Yuanjing Jikan* 19 (2): 41–82.

Levitsky, Steven, and Lucan Way. 2002. "The Rise of Competitive Authoritarianism." *Journal of Democracy* 13 (2): 51–65.

———. 2010. *Competitive Authoritarianism: Hybrid Regimes After the Cold War*. New York: Cambridge University Press.

Liang, Ying. 2021. "Zai Beian Shencha Gongzuo Zhong Fazhan Quanguocheng Renmin Minzhu (Developing Whole-Process People's Democracy in the Work of Filing Review." Accessed March 21, 2022. www.npc.gov.cn/npc/c30834/202112/b62ece379b-304fc7a24c786fa75e9935.shtml.

Liberthal, Kenneth, and David Lampton. 1992. *Bureaucracy, Policy, and Decision Making in Post-Mao China*. Berkeley, CA: University of California Press.

Lieberthal, Kenneth, and Michel Oksenberg. 1988. *Policy Making in China: Leaders, Structures, and Processes*. Princeton, NJ: Princeton University Press.

Liebman, Benjamin L. 2011. "A Return to Populist Legality? Historical Legacies and Legal Reform." In *Mao's Invisible Hand*, edited by Elizabeth Perry and Sebastian Heilmann, 165–200. Cambridge, MA: Harvard University Press.

Lin, Nan. 1995. "Local Market Socialism: Local Corporatism in Action in Rural China." *Theory and Society* 24 (3): 301–54.

Liu, Yaping, and Su Jiaoni. 2021. "Sipin Anquan Difang Lifa yu Bumen Jianguan de Xingdong Luoji ji Yingxiang Yinsu: Yi Guangdongsheng Shipin Xiaozuofang he Xiaotanfan Guanli Tiaoli de Chutai Weili (Local Legislation, Departmental Interest and Food Safety: A Case Study of Provincial Legislation on Small and Medium Sized Food Enterprises)." *Xueshu Yanjiu* 2: 43–53, 177.

Lu, Xiaobo, Mingxing Liu, and Feiyue Li. 2020. "Policy Coalition Building in an Authoritarian Legislature: Evidence from China's National Assemblies (1983–2007)." *Comparative Political Studies* 53 (9): 1380–416.

Manion, Melanie. 2014a. "Authoritarian Parochialism: Local Congressional Representation in China." *The China Quarterly* 218: 311–38.

———. 2014b. "'Good Types' in Authoritarian Elections: The Selectoral Connection in Chinese Local Congresses." *Comparative Political Studies* 47 (7): 1–33.

———. 2015. *Information for Autocrats: Representation in Chinese Local Congresses*. New York: Cambridge University Press.

Mertha, Andrew. 2009. "Fragmented Authoritarianism 2.0: Political Pluralization in the Chinese Policy Process." *The China Quarterly* 200: 995–1012.

Montinola, Gabriella, Yingyi Qian, and Barry R. Weingast. 1995. "Federalism, Chinese Style: The Political Basis for Economic Success in China." *World Politics* 48 (1): 50–81.

NPC. 2021a. "Gaige Kaifang 40 Nian Lai Woguo Lifa Tizhi de Fazhan Bianhua ji Shijian Fenxi (Analysis on Developmental Change and Practice of Legislative System in Our Country During 40 Years of Reform and Open Era." Accessed March 21, 2022. www.npc.gov.cn/npc/wgggkf40nlfcjgs/202108/2924f9ba435c4627942c27821a5ffc5a.shtml.

———. 2021b. "Quanguo Renmin Daibiao Dahui Changwu Weiyuanhui Fazhi Gongzuo Weiyuanhui Guanyu 2021 Nian Beian Shencha Gongzuo Qingkuang de Baogao (A Report on Works of 2021 Filing Review by Legislative Affairs Commission Affiliated to NPCSC)." Accessed March 21, 2022. www.npc.gov.cn/npc/c30834/202112/2606f90a45b1406e9e57ff45b42ceb1c.shtml.

O'Brien, Kevin J. 1994. "Chinese People's Congress and Legislative Embeddedness: Understanding Early Organizational Development." *Comparative Political Studies* 27 (1): 80–109.

O'Brien, Kevin J., and Laura M. Luehrmann. 1998. "Institutionalizing Chinese Legislatures: Trade-offs Between Autonomy and Capacity." *Legislative Studies Quarterly* 23 (1): 91–108.

Oi, Jean C. 1992. "Fiscal Reform and the Economic Foundations of Local State Corporatism in China." *World Politics* 45 (1): 99–126.

———. 1995. "The Role of the Local State in China's Transitional Economy." *The China Quarterly* 144: 1132–49.

Paler, Laura. 2005. "China's Legislation Law and the Making of a More Orderly and Representative Legislative System." *The China Quarterly* 182: 301–18.

Schedler, Andreas, ed. 2006. *Electoral Authoritarianism: The Dynamics of Unfree Competition*. Boulder: Lynne Rienner Publishers.

Svolik, Milan W. 2012. *The Politics of Authoritarian Rule*. New York: Cambridge University Press.

Tang, Jing. 2013. "Difang Lifa Zhong Bumen Liyi zhi Xiaojie Lujing Tanxi (Exploring How to Dispel Departmental Interests in Local Legislation)." *Journal of Social Science of Hunan Normal University* 3: 55–60.

Tanner, Murray Scot. 1999. *The Politics of Lawmaking in Post-Mao China: Institutions, Processes and Democratic Prospects*. Oxford: Clarendon Press.

Truex, Roxy. 2014. "The Returns to Office in a 'Rubber Stamp' Parliament." *American Political Science Review* 108 (2): 235–51.

———. 2016. *Making Autocracy Work: Representation and Responsiveness in Modern China*. New York: Cambridge University Press.

———. 2020. "Authoritarian Gridlock? Understanding Delay in the Chinese Legislative System." *Comparative Political Studies* 53 (9): 1455–92.

Wan, Jigang. 2011. "Dangdai Zhongguo de Shouquan Lifa (Delegated Legislation in Contemporary China)." Accessed March 21, 2022. www.npc.gov.cn/npc/c221/201105/e1e769994cd749ce87aba6029fc2c515.shtml.

Wang, Hsin-hsien. 2010. "Shei Tongzhi? Lun Zhongguo de Zhengce Zhiding Guocheng: Yi 'Fan Longduan Fa' Weili (Who Governs? The Dynamics of Policy-Making in China: The Case of Antitrust Law)." *Zhongguo Dalu Yanjiu* 53 (1): 35–62.

Wang, Meiwu, and Liang Tang. 2008. "Junheng yu Hexie: Dui Difang Lifa de Liyi Jiedu (Balance and Harmony: Interpreting the Meaning of Interest in Local Legislation)." *Jiangxi Guangbo Dianshi Daxue Xuebao* 4: 19–21.

Wong, Audrye. 2018. "More Than Peripheral: How Provinces Influence China's Foreign Policy." *The China Quarterly* 235: 735–57.

Xia, Ming. 2000. "Political Contestation and the Emergence of Provincial People's Congresses as Power Players in Chinese Politics: A Network Explanation." *Journal of Contemporary China* 9 (24): 185–214.

———. 2008. *The People's Congresses and Governance in China: Toward a Network Mode of Governance*. New York: Routledge.

Yang, Yuhua. 2010. "Lifa Quan Heyi Chengwei Bumen Liyi Baohusan (How Could the Legislative Authority Provide Protection for Departmental Interests)." Accessed March 21, 2022. http://zqb.cyol.com/content/2010-11/05/content_3438296.htm.

Zhang, Changdong. 2017. "Reexamining the Electoral Connection in Authoritarian China: The Local People's Congress and Its Private Entrepreneur Deputies." *China Review* 17 (1): 1–27.

Zhang, Rui. 2017. "Woguo Lifa zhong de Bumen Liyi Tanjiu (Exploring Departmental Interests in Legislation of Our Country)." *Shanxi Shengwei Dangjiao Xuebao* 40 (6): 93–98.

9

POLITICS, LAW, AND POLICING IN REFORM ERA CHINA

Suzanne E. Scoggins

Introduction

How has the process of legal institutionalization affected policing in China? At a teahouse one evening in Beijing, I spoke with a senior city police leader about his experience with the legal developments of the Reform Era.[1] At the time of our meeting, officer Liu was nearing retirement and had accumulated several decades of experience as both an officer and a leader in the Beijing municipal police force. "[In the 1980s], the police had a lot of power because there were no real laws," explained officer Liu when I asked about the changes to policing he had observed over the course of his career.

> Police could do whatever they wanted, but this was bad for the country. Now, the law is more important. . . . People are afraid of the law, not the police. They know they must adhere to the law, so they may treat the police with less respect because they know they should be judged by the law, not an individual. . . . This means sometimes it takes several officers to do the work [such as performing an arrest], but that doesn't matter. Overall, this is a type of progress.

Officer Liu's observations illustrate the development of legal norms for policing over time in China. At the start of the Reform Era, police leaders sought to rebuild an organization that was nearly decimated by the chaos of the Cultural Revolution. As the scaffolds of law and order went up, policing in the early Reform Era was often haphazard and loosely enforced since rules were poorly defined and supervised. In contrast, policing in the present day operates under an increasingly complex set of legal norms and directives, while the police themselves are more

DOI: 10.4324/9781003294887-12

carefully monitored. Such routinization was the goal of the 1995 Police Law and subsequent reform efforts, which focused on the codification of laws and professionalization standards. These reforms come with constraints on individual policing power on the ground, as illustrated by officer Liu's response, and demonstrate the enormity of the Ministry's efforts to reshape the relationship between police and legal directives over time.

Simultaneously, the political role of the police has continued to develop. Jean-Paul Brodeur classifies policing activities into two categories: low policing efforts such as the handling of murders, thefts, and traffic violations and high policing efforts that protect the political system such as protest control, surveillance, and anti-terrorism efforts (Brodeur 1983, 2010). Police in China were first thrust into political duties when they became agents of the mass line under Mao, and campaign-style policing has continued throughout the Reform Era. With the rise of the stability maintenance system, the police organs have also become frontline enforcers of social stability, a near-paramount state goal. Moreover, police are the ground-level agents of the party state during times of crisis such as the Covid-19 pandemic.

One way to understand the relationship of the police to politics and law is to analyze the language that guides police behavior and law enforcement on the ground. Police reform documents are an essential source for identifying changes to language over time. Reform documents also provide the closest possible articulation of Ministry requirements and ambitions. In this chapter, I use text analysis to parse 153 police reform documents posted online between 1993 and 2021 to understand how legal and political language is used over time. The results demonstrate subtle shifts in language as well as numeric trends. While a disconnect may exist between the official language and actual implementation, text analysis of reform documents unlocks valuable insight into how the Ministry uses legal and political language during times of crisis, transition, reform, and uncertainty.

Before we can understand the current shifts in language, however, we must first identify the foundational underpinnings and circumstances under which the legal and political roles of policing developed in China. The following section outlines the basic contours of legality and policing in the Mao Era, which was marked by the rise of political policing and culminated in the disruption of the Cultural Revolution. This period set the stage for the current institutionalization of legal norms in policing by providing a road map for what police leaders should avoid as well as what they might keep. I then discuss the data collection process and examine the ways in which the language of law and politics are presented in the 1990s, through the rise of the stability maintenance system, and during the most recent changes to policing under Xi Jinping. By looking closely at the language of legality and comparing it to political language in the same documents, it is possible to see how police leaders increase their usage of legal language to bolster credibility during times of uncertainty such as leadership transitions or crises like the Covid-19 pandemic.

1. Law and Policing in the Era of Mao

As with most facets of Chinese politics, any attempt to understand the contours of legal and political language must first begin with a discussion of the Mao period. When the communist forces emerged victorious in 1949, they inherited both the officers and bureaucracy of the Republican era. Modern policing has a relatively short history in China, and the Republican government officials sought to take the fledging police ministry established during the late Qing Dynasty and expand its powers to create a more diversified and hierarchical system (Reynolds 1995). Inspired by police professionalization efforts in countries such as England, France, Germany, and the US, Republican leaders were also eager to develop police forces that were independent of local elites (Wakeman 1988). These goals were ambitious, and implementation often fell short. Efforts were concentrated in the largest cities, leaving the countryside and many smaller cities untouched. Even in areas that saw greater police development, understaffed local stations faced considerable challenges policing a wide range of crime and disorder, particularly in diverse metropolises such as Shanghai (Wakeman 1995).

Police leaders under Mao inherited this system and all the associated problems of urban crime, limited person power, and local level corruption. Simultaneously, they were instructed to expand the organization's focus beyond traditional, low policing functions to assume political duties as frontline agents of the mass line (Dutton 2005). A new Ministry of Public Security was formed in October 1949 and charged with strengthening the ideological education work of the forces and combatting political threats to the Communist Party. Sometimes, this meant policing the police themselves, some of whom were deemed loyal to the cause of the departed nationalists.

Throughout this period, formal laws played a secondary role at best. Mao disdained bureaucracy and preferred flexibility for handling political and legal matters. Legal enforcement thus developed an informal and distinctly Maoist approach in which Communist Party dictates were largely handed down to the police in the form of slogans (Dutton 2000). While the new Communist government did enact formal statutes and laws, "justice" was often carried out by the police, ad hoc people's tribunals, and mass trials through national political campaigns (Leng 1977, 357).

Such political functions of the police expanded rapidly alongside more traditional policing concerns. In March 1950, the Campaign to Suppress Counter-Revolutionaries saw the police joining forces with newly established work unit security committees to unearth counter-revolutionaries and other political opposition. By 1957, counter-revolutionary crime made up almost half of all reported crime (Bakken 1993), with officers around the country chasing after spies, landlords, nationalists, and political assassins, in addition to the more typical criminal suspects. Local forces also continued to struggle with low per capita force numbers and often leaned on work units and neighborhood committees as well as the household registration system to help keep tabs on the local population.

The Cultural Revolution devastated any sense of normalcy and order that had been established for police in the early Mao years. Turmoil hit in 1966 when both the Beijing local police and the Ministry of Public Security were targeted by a leadership purge that created a vacuum at the top. A new Ministry of Public Security Cultural Revolution Group was then installed with the intent of carrying out revolutionary goals, and the political role of the police ballooned. Individual officers were now charged with supporting the revolutionary efforts of the Red Guards, even when those actions turned violent. Police themselves were also targeted, and many responded by leaving the force. Even the resident-staffed public security committees disbanded during this time due to safety concerns (Dai and Huang 1993, 140). A small plaque at the Beijing Police Museum sums up the effects of this period succinctly: "From 1966 to 1976, in this special historical period, the Beijing Municipal Public Security Bureau was severely damaged. The public security work almost stopped completely."[2]

2. Law and Policing in the Wake of the Cultural Revolution

Police leaders of the early Reform Era were charged with reconstructing the institution in the wake of the Cultural Revolution's "lawless era" (Wong 2004). Just as in 1949, the Reform Era incarnation of China's police bureaucracy was faced with the momentous task of expansion and adaptation. But this time, norms of professionalization, specialization, and adherence to the rule of law were emphasized rather than the communist party slogans and informal rules of years past (Dutton 2000). Law was thus the primary vehicle for reshaping the police organs to serve reform-era state needs under Deng Xiaoping's leadership.

The Criminal Law and the Criminal Procedure Law of 1980 guided the early years of this transition. Both laws established formal rules that set forth a path for the institutionalization of the policing system to enforce behavioral norms for police and provide some legal protection to individual civilians (Tanner 1999). Subsequent reforms were enacted in the 1980s, but the 1995 Police Law was the next most significant effort to institutionalize policing (Ma 1997). With its eight chapters and 53 provisions, the Police Law sought to define the duties, powers, and disciplinary procedures for the police in addition to articulating professionalization standards and establishing a citizen complaint mechanism.

The political functions of the police did not, however, recede into the background. New hard strike campaigns flourished in the early reform period, cementing rather than banishing the political role of the police. Institutional memory played a role in the revival of the campaign (Dutton 2000), but Reform Era campaigns were also a response to a potentially destabilizing crime situation (Tanner 2000). Developing cities and an increasingly mobile population fueled the rise of both traditional crime and relatively new problems such as human trafficking, drug smuggling, and arms trading (Ma 1997). Campaigns provided government and police leaders with additional flexibility for addressing certain types of crime, but assessments of the efficacy of these campaigns for reducing crime are mixed at best (Bakken 1993; Dutton and Lee 1993; Tanner 2005).

The process of legal institutionalization in the early Reform Era thus developed out of the police bureaucracy's historical past. Police leaders were not operating in a vacuum. Previous institutional structures were revived and old political playbooks resurfaced, even as frontline agents faced new threats under an entirely different economic system. Like other political reforms in this period, changes were relatively gradual and spread out, as a new mission was forged to put law—rather than individuals—front and center, while simultaneously serving the state's political goals.

3. Methodology

Legal institutionalization of policing did not end with the 1995 Police Law. The process has continued to evolve as political and police leaders harness laws and legal processes as tools for implementing political and social goals. This chapter seeks to understand the contours of that process through an analysis of language. Specifically, I look at the evolution of legal language in comparison to political language to understand how leaders at the Ministry of Public Security conceptualize legality as well as how they seek to communicate legal-related norms.

To parse the language of legal institutionalization, I analyze police reform-related documents posted on the Ministry of Public Security and other government websites. The documents include a range of official public security orders, meeting reports, press releases, and other announcements or notices, as well as a handful of public relations press materials that pertain to police reform.[3] In total, the corpus contains 153 documents ranging in date from 1993 to 2021. Because the number of documents is low, all items were manually collected. I first began collecting documents in 2017, and some of the links that were available in earlier years were subsequently taken offline. Moreover, at the time of research and writing, the Ministry's website was difficult to access. I used cached search results and/or the main government website (www.gov.cn) to obtain Ministry orders after February 2019. As a result, some documents between 2019 and 2021 may be missing.

As is often the case, there are research tradeoffs to looking at reform documents such as the ones included in this study. These documents were made available online, which makes them convenient to access for researchers and denotes a certain level of importance for each document. The Ministry does not release any information about why these documents were selected for inclusion on their website, but we can assume the documents were vetted and deemed important at the time of their posting. Because the documents are public, however, they also raise questions about the content of other, internal police materials that are not made available. The content of internal documents may be substantively different from the content of the corpus, and it is not possible to determine the nature of those differences. Finally, the number of documents per year is not evenly distributed.

Early years typically have fewer documents, as do a few later years such as 2014. The resulting corpus is thus an important but imperfect source for tracing the language of developments in legal and political language.

To assess trends over time, I isolated a set of keywords in a multi-step process. First, I compiled an initial list by manually inspecting the reform documents and pulling out key terms. This process was informed by my past research on policing in China.[4] Key phrases of interest for this phase of the identification process include terms such as rule of law (法律规定) and rule by law (依法治国). I also identified more generic terms such as law (法律) and legal institutions (法制).

In the second phase of the identification process, I utilized Wingo's deep learning word similarity model. Wingo's model uses neural networks and a large corpus of Chinese language documents related to government and economics to identify and sort similar words according to semantics and syntax.[5] Wingo's model returns the top 30 most similar words, but there are some limitations. Wingo is a Chinese-based company and restrictions on political language may be in place. While terms such as rule of law were searchable, for example, other terms such as social management (社会管理) and social governance (社会治理) are not. To compensate, I conducted additional manual searches to identify the language of interest. In total, 42 terms related to law or politics were identified either manually or with the assistance of the word similarity model.

To plot language changes over time, I used Python to preprocess the text and count the frequency of key terms. Chinese is a character language in which words are not separated by spaces, I therefore utilize the jieba package to segment unbroken strings of characters into words so that they may be properly counted (Qin et al. 2016).[6] I also preprocessed the text by removing all blank spaces, numbers, non-Chinese characters, and common "stopwords," which are frequently used function words that carry little meaning on their own.[7] Removing stopwords is a common step in text analysis, and I relied on pre-existing dictionaries of Chinese stopwords from the Harbin Institute of Technology and Baidu. Once the text was preprocessed, I was then able to analyze individual terms and compare trends in language across time.

In the following sections, I group the resulting keywords according to two categories: legal language and political language. Comparing trends in the words both individually and as grouped sets allows us to see how language is used to convey the priorities and goals of the Ministry during key political years. The issue is not only one of semantics. In police reform documents, the Ministry is interpreting the intent of higher government levels and communicating those decisions to others within the police bureaucracy as well as people outside the organization, since these documents are public. Moreover, documents such as Ministry orders—which are often but not always included in the posted documents online—help lower levels determine how to prioritize limited police resources. Most critically for the purposes of this study, analysis of language can help outsiders understand how legal and political language is used during times of transition, such as major reform efforts or leadership changes.

4. Tracing Legal Language Over Time

The 1995 Police Law remains the foundation for the process of institutionalizing the legality of policing in China. Subsequent reform efforts have built off this law, and another major round of reforms was introduced in early 2015 under President Xi Jinping. Although the date range of the police reform documents analyzed here is not quite broad enough to fully capture the before and after language of legalization for the 1995 law, we know that many of the reforms under the law took years to implement (Scoggins 2021a, 70). Beyond specific police reform efforts, we may also see some increase in legal language around national developments, such as leadership transitions, the 2006 "Resolution on Building a Harmonious Society" at the Sixth Plenum of the National Party Congress, the 2014 arrest of security czar Zhou Yongkang, or the 2020 start of the Covid-19 pandemic.

To see how the language of legality varies across time, I track frequency counts for 22 base terms identified manually and with the assistance of Wingo's word similarity model. The terms and their English translations are presented in Table 9.1. There are also additional words identified by the Wingo similarity model that are not included in this list either because they did not appear in the documents or because they were not relevant to the study.

How do these words track over time? Many of the words appeared only a handful of times across years, but others were more prevalent. Figure 9.1 shows the

TABLE 9.1 Terms Associated With Legal Institutionalization

Chinese	*English Translation*
法律	Law
法制	Legal System/Legality
法治	Rule of Law
法纪	Law
法规	Law and Regulations
依法治国	Rule by Law
依法行政	Administration by Law
依法决策	Decision According to Law
民主法治	Democratic Rule of Law
法制教育	Legal Education
立法	Legislation
决策程序	Decision-Making Process
行政监督	Administrative Supervision
规矩	Rule
宪法	Constitution
政治规矩	Political Rules
刑法	Criminal Law
行政诉讼法	Administrative Procedure Law
政府规章	Government Regulations
法庭	Court
法院	Court
检察院	Procuratorate

Source: Created by author.

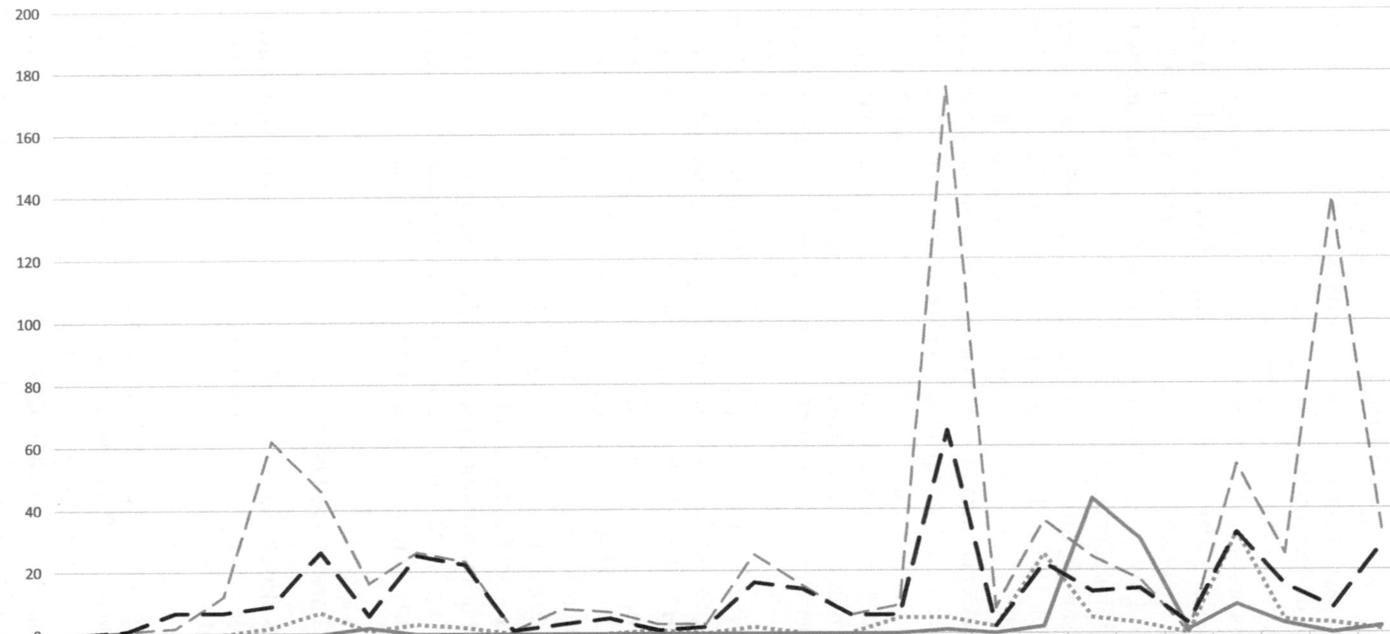

	1993	1995	1996	1997	1998	1999	2000	2001	2002	2003	2004	2005	2006	2007	2008	2009	2010	2011	2012	2013	2014	2015	2016	2017	2018	2019	2020	2021
法律	0	1	2	12	62	46	16	26	23	1	8	7	3	3	25	15	6	9	175	8	36	24	17	0	54	25	139	33
法制	0	0	0	0	2	7	1	3	2	0	0	0	1	0	2	0	0	5	5	2	25	5	3	0	32	4	3	1
法治	0	0	0	0	0	0	2	0	0	0	0	0	0	0	0	0	0	0	1	0	2	43	30	1	9	3	0	2
法规	0	1	7	7	9	26	6	25	22	1	3	5	1	2	16	14	6	6	65	2	22	13	14	3	32	15	8	28

法律 法制 法治 法规

FIGURE 9.1 Frequency Counts of Legal Language in Police Reform Documents

Source: Created by author.

trends with the specific yearly frequency counts for the four most common terms. Interestingly, the Hu Jintao era was marked by slightly less, not more, language of legality. This trend is reasonably consistent across years but may be influenced by the availability or length of documents in those years.

Law (法律) is consistently the most common word used across the years, followed by the slightly less prevalent law and regulations (法规). Interestingly, both terms rise and fall in the same years. Since the intent of the documents is to focus on police reform and developments, this is not necessarily surprising. Legal System (法制) and Rule of Law (法治) also appear infrequently across time with greater upticks in the Xi Jinping period.

The temporal dimension is particularly interesting. We see spikes in the years that follow the 1995 Police Law as these ambitious goals were gradually rolled out and enforced. There is also a heavy spike in the year that Xi Jinping takes office, even though the police reforms under his administration were not introduced until 2015. In that year, we see a small bump for law and regulations but not the other most-frequent terms. We also see a spike in the word law (法律) in 2020, the year the Covid-19 pandemic began. Overall, we see a rise in legal language throughout the Xi Jinping era that holds reasonably steady across the years.

There are several other trends of note for terms that appear less frequently and thus are not presented in Figure 9.1. Administration by law (依法行政) and decision according to law (依法决策), for example, do not appear until 2015, the year that the Ministry announced police reforms. Similarly, rule by law (依法治国) does not appear until 2015, after which it is used again in 2016 and 2018 but in no further years. Moreover, constitution (宪法) makes an appearance in the early years (1997, 1999, and 2000) but does not appear again until 2015, after which it regularly surfaces in police documents. Understanding these terms and when they vary is important for analyzing the trends of legal institutionalization. Overall, we see a rise over time after a notable dip in all terms between 2003 and 2011. The only year in which none of the documents saw a single mention of a term in the legal language category was 1993, which tracks with our understanding of legality and policing in the early Reform Era prior to the 1995 Police Law.

5. Tracing Political Language Over Time

Police reform documents also provide insight into shifts in political language over time. The police continue to serve as the ground-level agents of the party state, and as such, the political role of policing has grown beyond the campaigns of the early Reform Era. In no area is this more apparent than in the rise of the stability maintenance system. In the wake of the 1989 protests that culminated in the crackdown on Tiananmen Square, CCP and police leaders were left with a dilemma about how to control social unrest. With regime stability at stake, resources were marshaled and a more unified approach to dealing with protest and dissent was gradually formulated and implemented. In 2005, President Hu Jintao called on provincial and Ministry level cadres to build a "socialist harmonious society," and by the end of the National Party Congress in 2006, the concept of stability maintenance had achieved national prominence. For nearly two decades, stability maintenance has remained a critical focus of the public security organs.

Stability maintenance of course spans far beyond the police,[8] but police are the frontline agents for enforcement, which includes responding to protests and managing dissidents.[9] Together, these forces are called upon to implement party-state goals of stability. Moreover, when other political and social threats such as the Covid-19 pandemic arise, the police are summoned to enforce new state policies. Since 2020, police have assumed the duties of enforcing mask mandates, assisting in inspections, and enforcing restrictions on social gatherings and lockdown requirements to help the state achieve its Zero Covid goals. Such mandates span well beyond traditional duties of policing and highlight the integral, political role police play as ground-level enforcers for the party state.

In China, the realms of politics and law are closely linked, making the selection of keywords more challenging. Starting with politics and law (政法) and law and discipline (法纪) as reference terms for the Wingo similarity model, I looked for keywords that have overt associations with the party, political slogans of the past and present, and any mention of common terms from the Mao era as well as references to socialism or socialist values. I also included slogans and terms that relate to the stability maintenance system such as harmonious (和谐), stability maintenance (维稳), and social stability (社会稳定).[10] As with the language related to legality, many of the suggested terms did not appear in the corpus. Table 9.2 lists the 20 keywords that are used for the analysis.

TABLE 9.2 Words Associated With Political Language

Chinese	*English Translation*
执法为民	Law Enforcement for the People
党纪	Party Discipline
政纪	Political Discipline
政治纪律	Political Discipline
党规	Party Rules
党的纪律	Party Discipline
社会主义核心价值观	Core Socialist Values
社会主义	Socialism
人民服务	Serve the People
党政	Party Policy
同志	Comrade
中国梦	China Dream
同胞	Compatriot
群众路线	Mass Line
群众	Masses
宣传 (noun)	Propaganda
严打	Strike-Hard Campaign
和谐	Harmonious
维稳	Stability Maintenance
社会稳定	Social Stability

Source: Created by Author.

	1993	1995	1996	1997	1998	1999	2000	2001	2002	2003	2004	2005	2006	2007	2008	2009	2010	2011	2012	2013	2014	2015	2016	2017	2018	2019	2020	2021
社会主义	0	0	0	1	2	0	0	0	0	0	0	0	0	0	0	0	0	0	2	0	0	9	4	0	12	0	2	6
同志	0	0	0	0	0	0	1	0	0	0	0	0	0	0	0	0	0	0	0	0	2	15	21	25	6	0	0	13
群众	0	0	0	0	8	25	14	0	1	5	0	0	0	1	2	2	3	7	12	0	3	81	71	39	16	7	4	24
社会稳定	0	0	0	1	0	1	0	0	0	1	0	0	0	0	0	0	0	0	0	0	0	5	4	2	5	0	0	1

FIGURE 9.2 Frequency Counts of Political Language in Police Reform Documents

Source: Created by author.

Figure 9.2 presents frequency counts for the top four politically focused terms. As the graph shows, political language appears somewhat more frequently in earlier years before a dip in the early Hu Jintao period, and substantial rises in 2009 and beyond. References to the masses (群众) appear with regularity across documents but are most frequent in the earlier and later years, with a spike following the 2015 reforms under Xi Jinping's leadership. Meanwhile, comrade (同志) barely surfaces in the documents prior to 2014. The term propaganda (宣传) (not shown) also appears with a fair degree of regularity, although this word is increasing along with other terms related to public relations and serving the people and tracks closely with the Ministry's public outreach efforts during this time.[11] Both socialism (社会主义) and social stability (社会稳定) appear less frequently in the documents until the 2015 reforms, at which point they become more frequent.

Comparing all terms together, we see substantial increases around the 2015 reforms until 2017, after which political language for the most frequent terms returns to the level of prior years. There is also a noticeable dip in 2020, the first pandemic year, for all five terms. Political language for these words is also low in 2014, the year of Zhou Yongkang's arrest, but this may be related to the lower number of documents in that year. The following section provides a more detailed analysis of these trends by combining all political terms together and comparing the variation over time with legal language.

Overall, frequency counts for the 20 political language terms are lower than for the legal language category. This may be because some types of political language are muted in the documents. Xi Jinping's slogan, China Dream (中国梦), appears only a few times beginning in 2018, but Harmonious Society (和谐社会) does not appear at all. The word harmonious (和谐) is used, but oddly, does not appear during the Hu Jintao years. Instead, it surfaces in 2015 and continues with some regularity in the years thereafter. Of greatest interest is the absence of robust discussions about stability maintenance (维稳), which appears only three times across documents despite its outsized importance for policing. In contrast, the term social stability (社会稳定) appears with more regularity, as do specific references to detention centers and other police-related facets of the stability maintenance system that are more operational in nature and thus not included here as political language. Finally, there are only three references to the Covid-19 pandemic (epidemic, 疫情) in the documents, all in 2021.

6. Parsing the Political and the Legal

While it is helpful to view individual terms related to legal and political language across the documents, broader comparisons are perhaps the most revealing. Figure 9.3 presents the results of all the combined legal words in comparison to the combined political words over time. As we already knew from the frequency counts in the individual analyses of political and legal terms, words related to legal matters are more prevalent overall and both categories see increases after Xi Jinping takes office. Of greatest interest, however, are the spikes in legal language

	1993	1995	1996	1997	1998	1999	2000	2001	2002	2003	2004	2005	2006	2007	2008	2009	2010	2011	2012	2013	2014	2015	2016	2017	2018	2019	2020	2021
Legal Terms	0	2	9	21	220	92	34	59	48	3	13	12	5	5	93	29	13	24	459	43	94	117	77	5	142	50	403	98
Political Terms	2	0	0	2	11	28	18	1	8	7	0	0	1	1	3	19	3	16	18	0	11	131	116	72	54	11	6	57

FIGURE 9.3 Comparison Chart of Legal and Political Terms Over Time

Source: Created by author.

in 1998, 2008, 2012, 2015, 2018, and 2020. Clearly, political and legal terms are not always in step.

Almost every spike in the legal language corresponds with a year marked by political uncertainty. The biggest contrast is in 2012, the year Xi Jinping secured power and Zhou Yongkang retired amid abuse of power rumors.[12] In this year, we see the largest rise in legal language across years but very little change from previous years in political language. The same phenomenon happens again in 2020, which is the year the pandemic began. Interestingly, in this year, we also see a slight drop in political language from 2019, which was already quite low in comparison to previous years. In 2008, the year of the Beijing Olympics, we also see lower levels of political language and a bump in legal language. Potential explanations for the sudden rises in legal language in 1998 and 2018 are perhaps less clear, but in the summer of 1998, severe flooding in 24 provinces killed approximately 300 people and displaced another 220 million.[13] Police were a significant part of the front-line response. 2018 was the year the Chinese constitution was amended to abolish presidential term limits, paving the way for Xi to keep the presidency indefinitely. Interestingly, political language dips in this year as legal language spikes, but the overall number of political terms is still relatively high.

The data thus show that police leaders dial legal language up and political language down during times of greater uncertainty, such as Xi's leadership transitions, the emergence of the pandemic, or China's first opportunity to hold the Olympic games. Moreover, 2008 was a significant year not just because it was an opportunity for China to shine on an international stage but also because the country faced a series of high-profile and violent protests from Tibetans, Uyghurs, and non-political groups (Scoggins 2021a, 131–32). Because these documents are public facing, increased reliance on legal language during uncertain times may be a strategic move. It is important to note, however, that we do not observe significant differences when Hu Jintao assumed power in 2002/2003.

Spikes in legal language stand in stark contrast to the way legal and political language are presented in 2015. In this year of police reform, we instead observe a considerable rise in both legal and political language, with political language even overtaking legal language for one of the only times across all years. 2015 was a year unmarked by other significant political moments of uncertainty; therefore, legal and political language could be used in tandem to marshal resources and legitimacy for Xi's ambitious set of reforms. In other years, the ebbs and flows of legal and political language are similarly in step with one another, such as the drops in 2013 and 2019. The only remaining question is 2021. It is not immediately clear why we see a drop in legal language and a rise in political language for this year.

7. The Legal Is Political

Police reform documents can tell us much about how and when language is used to convey messages. They also raise questions about how other government entities use legal and political language. Perhaps, police leaders at the Ministry are in a unique position because of the frontline role of the police in enforcing stability and carrying out Party goals, but other agencies may still be using language in similar ways by leaning on legal language during times of political uncertainty. Looking at central government documents to see if similar patterns hold would be illuminating, as would a finer grain analysis of Ministry of Public Security documents to see what type of language is used around political and legal terms. Specific links to major political events, however, are difficult or impossible to establish, since the broader political context of the government documents is often left unsaid. The shadow of Covid-19 most certainly hangs over every document in 2020 and 2021, for example, yet the pandemic is only mentioned three times.

Throughout the research for this chapter, one phrase loomed large: *zhengfa* (politics and law, 政法). Although I used the term to identify semantically similar words, it was impossible to lump *zhengfa* into either the political or legal category because it is—quite simply—a combination of both. Many democracies aspire to separate politics and law, but in China, the two are inextricably and unapologetically linked. The term *zhengfa* appears 88 times in the document, and one way to categorize it is to see how it tracks alongside the combined political and legal terms. Use of *zhengfa* spikes in 2012 (24 mentions), 2018 (15 mentions), and 2008 (5 mentions), which tracks closely with increases in legal language. It also rises (six mentions) in 2015, the reform year, alongside both legal and political terms. Beyond these years, however, the trends are harder to parse because the numbers are so small. There is another bump (eight mentions) in 2014, a year that was largely insignificant for legal and political language.[14]

Ultimately, law is a function of politics in China, a useful tool for pursuing means to a political end. While untangling legal and political language is illuminating, the two do not exist in a vacuum. We must therefore not lose sight of legal language's utility for China's party state because when political uncertainty arises, legal language can become a political instrument. Perhaps ultimately it is the order of *zhengfa* that matters most. *Zheng*—politics—comes first.

Notes

1 Interview with author, 2012. Officer Liu's name has been changed and his specific position is not identified to preserve anonymity. For more on interviewing police in China, see Scoggins (2014).
2 Author's observation, July 2018.
3 Author's note: The list of the documents is too long for a printed appendix but will be made available online for interested readers at www.sescoggins.com.
4 See, for example, Scoggins (2021a).
5 www.wingodata.com.
6 Some words such as rule of law get cut into two words by jieba. In such cases, I edit the cutting process to ensure important words are kept together.
7 Stopwords are useful when speaking or writing a sentence but have little value for text analysis. Some examples of common stopwords include I (wo 我), and (he 和), that (nage 那个), have (you 有), and so on.

8 What makes stability maintenance so unique is how many areas it touches. Weiwen is not just a platform for social control but also a crucial element of China's larger development model (Yang 2017). It is also a core part of cadre evaluation, and cadres may be fired if they fail to maintain public order, regardless of whether they perform well in other areas. This type of unified coordination can be extraordinarily effective (Scoggins 2021a).
9 Larger-scale incidents are handled by the People's Armed Police.
10 The documents also contain references to detention centers that are not included.
11 See Scoggins (2021b) for a discussion of the Ministry of Public Security's propaganda campaigns.
12 Author interview with central ministry official, 2012.
13 Jun Mai. 2016. "Why China's Massive Floods This Year Are Different From 1998's." *South China Morning Post*. 6 July, www.scmp.com/news/china/society/article/1986125/why-chinas-massive-floods-year-are-different-1998s-catastrophic.
14 2014 is the year that Zhou Yongkang was arrested, but a broader study with more documents would be needed to assess this potential link.

References

Bakken, Børge. 1993. "Crime, Juvenile Delinquency and Deterrence Policy in China." *The Australian Journal of Chinese Affairs* 30: 29–58.

Brodeur, Jean-Paul. 1983. "High Policing and Low Policing: Remarks About the Policing of Political Activities." *Social Problems* 30 (5): 507–20.

———. 2010. *The Policing Web*. New York: Oxford University Press.

Dai, Yi Sheng, and Zu-Yuan Huang. 1993. "Organization and Functions of Public Security Agencies of the People's Republic of China." *EuroCriminology* 5: 137–43.

Dutton, Michael. 2000. "The End of the (Mass) Line? Chinese Policing in the Era of the Contract." *Social Justice* 27 (2): 61–105.

———. 2005. *Policing Chinese Politics: A History*. Durham, NC: Duke University Press.

Dutton, Michael, and Lee Tianfu. 1993. "Missing the Target? Policing Strategies in the Period of Economic Reform." *Crime & Delinquency* 39 (3): 316–36.

Leng, Shao-Chuan. 1977. "The Role of Law in the People's Republic of China as Reflecting Mao Tse-Tung's Influence." *Journal of Criminal Law and Criminology* 68 (3): 356–73.

Ma, Yue. 1997. "The Police Law 1995: Organization, Functions, Powers and Accountability of the Chinese Police." *Policing: An International Journal of Police Strategies & Management* 20 (1): 113–35.

Qin, Wenfeng et al. 2016. Package "Jieba." https://github.com/fxsjy/jieba.

Reynolds, Douglas R. 1995. *China, 1895–1912: State-Sponsored Reforms and China's Late-Qing Revolution*. New York: ME Shape.

Scoggins, Suzanne E. 2014. "Navigating Fieldwork as an Outsider: Observations From Interviewing Police Officers in China." *PS: Political Science & Politics* 47 (2): 394–97.

———. 2021a. *Policing China: Street-Level Cops in the Shadow of Protest*. Ithaca: Cornell University Press.

———. 2021b. "Propaganda and the Police: The Softer Side of State Control in China." *Europe-Asia Studies* 73 (1): 200–20.

Tanner, Harold M. 1999. *Strike Hard! Anti-Crime Campaigns and Chinese Criminal Justice, 1979–1985*. Cornell, NY: Cornell University East Asia Program.

Tanner, Murray Scot. 2000. "State Coercion and the Balance of Awe: The 1983–1986 'Stern Blows' Anti-Crime Campaign." *The China Journal* 44: 93–125.

———. 2005. "Campaign-Style Policing in China and Its Critics." In *Crime Punishment, and Policing in China*, ed. Borge Bakken, 171–88. Lanham, MD: Rowman & Littlefield.

Wakeman Jr, Frederic. 1995. *Policing Shanghai, 1927–1937*. Berkeley, CA: University of California Press.

———. 1988. "Policing Modern Shanghai." *The China Quarterly* 115: 408–40.

Wong, Kam C. 2004. "Govern Police by Law (yifa zhijing) in China." *Australian & New Zealand Journal of Criminology* 37 (1): 90–106.

Yang, Dali L. 2017. "China's Troubled Quest for Order: Leadership, Organization and the Contradictions of the Stability Maintenance Regime." *Journal of Contemporary China* 26 (103): 35–53.

10

LEGALITY AND THE HONG KONG PROTESTS

Stephan Ortmann

Introduction

Hong Kong was once known as the beacon of liberty in China, but this changed fundamentally in 2020 when the Chinese government implemented a National Security Law (NSL) that poses serious challenges to legality in the territory. The law came in response to months of sometimes violent protests which had demanded the withdrawal of an extradition bill that would have threatened the rule of law and potentially the widely cherished political liberties. While protesters had demanded genuine universal suffrage that would have strengthened Hong Kong's liberal political system, electoral changes in 2021 furthermore transformed the political system from the previous liberal authoritarian regime into an illiberal one. These developments were driven, as Davis (2022, 100) rightly points out, by a regime that is "(h)ostile to liberal constitutionalism and the values that it represents." As a result, Hong Kong's legality has been significantly altered with consequences for anything from the courts to civil society to business. The full extent of the implications is yet to emerge, but it is already clear that there is a fundamental regime transformation that has imperiled the rule of law because the independence of the judiciary is no longer guaranteed. While the Chinese government may want to establish an illiberal form of rule of law, which only uses harsh laws against dissidents (Rezvani 2022), the newly created institutions have initiated a process for the complete erosion of the liberal constitutional order.

This chapter will first lay out the form of legality that existed in Hong Kong in the past as it developed under British colonial rule and later under Chinese rule from 1997. This will show that Hong Kong had most of the characteristics of a liberal constitutional regime and that those principles were fundamental to the development of the colony. It has also ensured Hong Kong's advantage within China, which despite the high costs of doing business, has been an important link

DOI: 10.4324/9781003294887-13

between developed economies and China. However, the economic transformation in China has created the idea that Hong Kong's significance has declined and also that the socialist rule of law might be superior to the British legal tradition in Hong Kong. Moreover, with the rise of Xi Jinping, the Chinese government has formally rejected the idea of separation of powers and abandoned the process of separating state and party and creating a rule of law regime (Ma 2021). Instead, power has been centralized in the Communist Party, which rules in a top-down manner and is not subject to any legal constraints. The courts are instead considered tools of the Party. These developments of course had a fundamental consequence for Hong Kong. Massive protests in 2019 and 2020 to protect the rule of law eventually legitimated the transition to an illiberal regime and led to the erosion of the rule of law, the decline of the liberal society, and the downgrading of the electoral system.

1. Legality in Hong Kong

Developed under British colonial rule, Hong Kong has adopted a common law system that is practiced not only in the UK but also in many of its former dependencies and colonies. The principles of equality under the rule of law and judicial independence were from the beginning very attractive to many immigrants who settled in Hong Kong and set up their business. It was very different from the Chinese system in which one's position in the social hierarchy defined privileges and duties (Sommer 2000). It contributed to the ideas of Chinese revolutionaries, such as Sun Yat-sen, who were deeply impressed by these progressive ideas. Among other ideas, Sun proposed to adopt a liberal constitution and separation of powers in the new Chinese republic in his *Three Principles of the People (三民主義)* of 1905 although he also concluded that Western institutions, although superior, could not be copied to the Chinese context. While the British colonial regime was clearly not democratic in the sense of an elected government, it did include both a law-making legislature and an independent judiciary, which were primarily established by the British government to maintain control over the governor. As the primary check by the British government on its governor, the courts had a very important function during colonial rule. Even though judicial independence had not been enshrined in the Letters' Patent, there was hardly any interference in the judiciary with the Supreme Court the most respected institution in the early colonial period (Munn 2001). The Privy Council in London served as the court of final appeal and ensured that the laws were properly implemented.

The handover from British to Chinese rule in 1997 changed the significance of the judiciary because the courts were no longer needed to maintain a check on executive power. Instead, the central government controlled the executive directly through the Basic Law which states that the chief executive is accountable to the central government. As such, the courts became a potential obstacle to the central government because of the possibility of unfavorable decisions. This was already apparent in the discussion over the role of the Court of Final Appeal and its role in the interpretation of the Basic Law, which had taken place before the handover (Lo 2000). The politicization of the process occurred first in the case of the right of abode of permanent residents in 1999. The Chief Executive had appealed to the National People's Congress Standing Committee for a constitutional interpretation, although such a right did not exist in the Basic Law. The NPCSC ruled that the Court of Final Appeal should have referred the case to the central government, which decided that children born in the mainland of permanent residents did in fact not have the right of abode. The chief executive had initiated this process because of the great concern about a wave of migrants, which also deeply worried many Hong Kongers. This meant that there was little public opposition to the NPCSC's interpretation. However, the case showed that the courts could be overruled in political cases (Tai 2010).

The transfer of power had occurred under a "one country, two systems" framework granting the future special administrative region a "high degree of autonomy." The Chinese and British authorities signed the Sino-British Joint Declaration in 1984 which stated that the region "will be vested with executive, legislative and independent judicial power, including that of final adjudication. The laws currently in force in Hong Kong will remain basically unchanged." This suggested that the previous form of legality would continue to exist in order to assuage investors who might be worried about the change (Davis 2020). A Basic Law, often labeled a "mini-constitution," was established in 1990 after consultations within the colony. Only two pan-democratic members had joined the process led by Leung Chun-ying, who would serve as the chief executive from 2012 to 2017. However, before the conclusion of the process, the Chinese government under Deng Xiaoping decided to violently crack down on pro-democracy protesters in Beijing on June 4, 1989. Not only did hundreds or even thousands die, but the government later also arrested and jailed many of the activists who had fled. The images of the events not only reverberated around the world but also had a deep and lasting impact on Hong Kong. Trust in the central government had eroded. While many people sought to leave the British colony, others sought to hold the Chinese government to its promise of a "high degree of autonomy" which was enshrined in Article 1 of the Basic Law. In essence, the idea was that the liberal system in Hong Kong would remain unchanged for at least 50 years. This included many freedoms such as those of speech, assembly, and the press, as well as an independent judiciary. In addition, Hong Kongers also prided themselves in their neutral civil service and police force (Hui 2020). There was even a promise of eventual universal suffrage. However, the Basic Law also included Article 23, which required the local government to pass a law that could potentially minimize many of these liberties in the name of national security. This section had been strengthened following the Tiananmen crackdown because the Chinese government was concerned about the massive support for the democracy movement in Hong Kong.

Even today, the Hong Kong government prides itself in the rule of law. The Department of Justice declares on its website: "The legal system of the Hong

Kong Special Administrative Region (HKSAR) is based on the principles of the rule of law and the independence of the judiciary" (Department of Justice 2021). Elsewhere the government asserts that "if Hong Kong people have a defining ideology, it is the rule of law"(Information Services Department 2002). It also states that Hong Kong's legal system is different from China's as adopted under the "One Country, Two Systems" principle and calls the Basic Law a constitutional framework although it is "enacted by the National People's Congress of the People's Republic of China (PRC) in accordance with Article 31 of the Constitution of the PRC." The relationship with the central government, however, has left room for legal uncertainty in the overall framework as the legal system in Hong Kong has clashed with the socialist legal tradition in China where the courts are subordinate to the party state. This conflict has marked the development of the rule of law since the handover.

2. The Struggle to Preserve the Rule of Law

While the independent judiciary was only seen as a tool by the Chinese government to cater to the business sector, many in Hong Kong actually saw it as a guarantee to maintain the autonomy of the state. A key problem from the beginning was the definition of the "high degree" of autonomy and the discussion evolved around the need to protect as much as feasible. The vague promise of universal suffrage in the Basic Law was seen by pro-democracy activists as an important pathway toward ensuring autonomy. If the local government was able to elect its own leaders, they would be in a better position in defending the autonomy. However, this did not resolve questions about the limits of autonomy which were left open. The Chinese government maintained significant power under the Basic Law in terms of interpretation and amendment. A growing number of interventions subsequently shifted the balance of power further in the direction of the Central Government (Horlemann 2003).

At the heart of Hong Kong's protest movement since 1997 has been the concern over the ability to preserve the liberal aspects of the territory including various freedoms and the rule of law. The first threat came in 2003 when the government decided it was time to table Article 23 legislation. Not surprisingly, the proposed law was very vague and many saw it as a threat to the cherished liberties and the rule of law (Ma 2005). In mainland China, a similar law is often used to repress political opposition. Hence, an estimated 500,000 people went onto the streets on July 1 in a protest march organized by the Civil Human Rights Front, the largest civil society alliance in the territory's history. The protest was eventually successful in suspending the law. One year later, Tung Chee Hwa, the first chief executive of the territory, resigned as well (Holliday, Ma, and Yep 2004).

In the aftermath, there was a period of indirect measures to integrate Hong Kong more into China and provide economic benefits through the Closer Economic Partnership Arrangement (CEPA), which reduced many trade barriers, as China believed the massive opposition to the government was primarily a sign of economic discontent. However, the next major movement was not about economic concerns but rather the attempt to introduce national education into the school curriculum in Hong Kong in 2012. In particular, the new subject appeared to propagate the need to unquestionably support China's illiberal political system. A leaked textbook had praised the Communist Party regime as progressive and selfless while criticizing the system of the US (Lin and Lin 2017). This indicated that the main goal was to foster greater support for the party state, which in the Chinese understanding is equated with the nation. Driven by secondary school children, a ten-day siege took place. According to the organizer, more than 90,000 people participated in a protest movement against the changes. The large-scale protest did, however, lead to some success as the government formally withdrew the proposal.

In 2014, a white paper on "one-country, two systems" declared that the Chinese government had "comprehensive jurisdiction" over Hong Kong, which raised concerns about local autonomy. It also included the requirement that judges would have to "swear to uphold the Basic Law and swear allegiance to the HKSAR of the PRC." Moreover, their duty was to "correctly" understand the Basic Law, which suggested that judges need to follow the National People's Congress Standing Committee's interpretation and thus were subject to political control. As the text is vague about which people are included as administrators who need to be patriotic, concern was raised that this could include judges which led to a protest of around 1,800 lawyers (Lau, Chiu, and Yap 2014). The document had, however, also stressed that the HKSAR was "vested with executive, legislative and independent judicial power, including that of final adjudication." This seemed to reinforce the separation of powers that underlies the Hong Kong system. However, in 2020, Chief Executive Carrie Lam suggested that this was in fact not the case. Her intention was to justify the growing centralization of power in the executive (Cheung 2020). As Davis (2020) argues, this can be seen as an attack on judicial review and thus the principle of the rule of law.

In addition to the concerns about the judiciary raised by the document, there was also the ambiguous requirement that "loving the country is the basic political requirement for Hong Kong's administrators." This essentially meant that there were Hong Kongers who were considered unpatriotic. Although unspecified, it was clear that this meant the central government would be able to define who can become an "administrator" including the chief executive. Naturally, this entailed that some people would be excluded from the selection process. As the Chinese government equates the country with its own rule, loving the country entails unconditional support for the Communist Party and its policies. This of course means that in the end, there is not really any choice between different options but rather an affirmation of the party that rules China. A democratic solution within an authoritarian regime thus became an inherent contradiction that could not be overcome.

It came as no surprise that the proposal for universal suffrage in 2014 had a serious shortcoming which was that the candidate selection would be done by a committee whose majority is dominated by pro-Chinese elites. A pro-democratic candidate running for office, as had been the case in the past, would become impossible. Activists therefore launched a movement of civil disobedience that demanded "real universal suffrage" known as Occupy Central with Love and Peace. When protesters defended themselves with umbrellas against teargas, the protest became known as the Umbrella Movement, which lasted for 79 days (Ortmann 2015). Davis (2020, 170) sees the movement as "ultimately in defense of Hong Kong's rule-of-law tradition." The lack of sovereignty, however, made it impossible to achieve the primary goal of the protesters that had been genuine universal suffrage (Ortmann 2016).

It is no coincidence that the rise in political activism in Hong Kong took place when previous moderate reforms in mainland China were rolled back under Xi Jinping who centralized power further under his personal leadership, deepened the state's role in society, strengthened controls over ideas and financial flows, and publicly asserted Chinese power (Economy 2018). His approach has been to strengthen party institutions rather than creating a stronger and more independent judiciary for instance in his fight against corruption. Televised confessions have returned. The government has tightened limits for non-governmental organizations and arrested human rights activists, women's rights activists, and other societal actors independent of the government. The growing power centralization has also increasingly affected Hong Kong. The disappearance and arrest of booksellers from a small bookshop in Causeway Bay in 2016 was an example of how the central government sought to strengthen control over politics in the SAR. The televised confessions showed that Hong Kongers were not immune to the mainland's legal methods. Rather than closing the gap between the two legal systems, it seemed to widen prior to the introduction of the NSL, which would bring Hong Kong more in line with China's legal practices.

3. The Anti-Extradition Bill Movement of 2019–20

In 2019, the government introduced the so-called Fugitive Offenders and Mutual Legal Assistance in Criminal Matters Legislation (Amendment) Bill, which is also known as the extradition bill because it would have enabled suspects to be extradited to mainland China. The government claimed the law was needed because a Hong Konger, who had killed his girlfriend in Taiwan, could not be extradited for trial there. Fears about the implications of the bill, however, led to serious criticism within Hong Kong and abroad. The Hong Kong Bar Association asserted that the lack of such an agreement was due to the serious differences in the two criminal justice systems where there are serious concerns over the protection of fundamental rights of suspects in mainland China (Citizen News Op-ed 2019). Judges, who usually do not comment on political issues, also voiced their concerns. Three judges asserted that extraditions in a common law system were based on the assumption of a fair trial and punishments that are proportionate to the crime, both of which is not the case in China (Torode and Pomfret 2019).

Meanwhile, a protest movement gathered pace in 2019. The first action was a sit-in at the government headquarters on March 15 and eventually resulted in the largest post-1997 protest on June 9 which organizers claim was attended by over a million people. Although the size of the crowd is hard to verify, the massive number of people resulted in an extremely slow progress with people waiting all afternoon to leave the starting point in Victoria Park. The protest did not dissuade the government from proceeding and on June 12 a second reading of the bill was planned. As the bill could have been approved on that day, protesters grew anxious and blockaded the space around the Legislative Council. As they pushed toward the legislature to ensure the reading could not proceed, the police sought to clear them with teargas and pepper spray. The police failed to distinguish between radical and peaceful protesters, which led to great anger among many participants. When the police called the event a riot, it opened the possibility for serious punishment of any of the protesters, even those who were peaceful. Meanwhile, Carrie Lam decided to suspend the bill but refused to withdraw it. In response, an even larger crowd of people marched the following Sunday with additional demands. Protesters now wanted the government to rescind the riot declaration and the release of those who had been arrested. Moreover, they demanded an inquiry into the police violence during that first incident. All of these demands were of a legal matter but the government refused to make any additional concessions. Eventually, protesters decided collectively to add the call for genuine universal suffrage to the official demands, which was then called the five demands (Holbig 2020).

The government's obstinacy repeatedly entailed that protesters needed to escalate the situation in an attempt to force concessions. Perhaps, the most consequential decision was the storming of the Legislative Council on July 1, the day of the handover that had become an annual day for protests. In the evening, a group of young protesters took control of the legislative chamber and demanded to be listened to. Graffiti and imagery in the chamber illustrated the growing demand for autonomy or even full independence since the protesters believed that the Chinese government was the main obstacle for preserving Hong Kong's "core values" including the rule of law. After that, some protesters increasingly broke the law to force the government to listen to the movement's demands. The Chinese government was also targeted with graffiti on the sign of the Liaison Office on July 29. Later that day, a violent mob attacked train passengers in the Yuen Long MTR station, many of whom had been protesters. Anger about the violence and police inaction resulted in further escalation of the movement (Lee et al. 2019). Moreover, in China, the government switched from censoring the protests to vilifying them (Holbig 2020).

When Carrie Lam finally withdrew the bill on September 4, 2019, the main focus had already become the police response which protesters considered excessive. Over time, more and more teargas, pepper spray, and other forms of crowd control had been used all across the territory. Occasionally, people were hit by teargas without any warning. An incident in Prince Edward station on August 31, which was captured on camera, showed unarmed protesters kneeling in front of a police officer who was spraying them with pepper spray. The police also decided to deploy high-powered water cannons to disperse protesters. Colored dye was added in order to better capture the elusive protesters, but it only had a minimal impact. In one incident, a mosque was hit by the colored dye in an attempt to blame the protests for damage to the building. Unfortunately, witnesses had seen that the building was targeted on purpose. The police increased its force as protesters moved from merely blocking the road and throwing items to starting fires on the road and in MTR station entrances while vandalizing shops regarded as supportive of the regime and police. The anger was about the failure to allow an independent investigation into police violence and restore a sense of justice in the society. However, Carrie Lam refused a Commission of Inquiry because it could harm the morale of the police force, which regarded itself as a victim of violence rather than a perpetrator, and despite even calls from pro-establishment forces, no attempt to investigate either the police or the whole movement was conducted in 2019. Finally, in 2020, a report by the Independent Police Complaints Council eventually found "room for improvement" although it largely exonerated the police force.

Rather than choosing reconciliation, the Chinese government sought to use force to quell the protests by implementing numerous institutional reforms that would threaten the autonomy of the territory and its independent legal system. While people could do little to resist the changes dictated by the central government, there was a growing exodus to other countries. The UK allowed the right of abode to Hong Kong's estimated 5.4 million holders of the British Nationals (Overseas) or BNO passport, which was a significant change from its policy after 1989, when the British government had denied this in spite of protests. In 2021, it was reported that the city had lost 1.2% of its population with 89,200 residents moving to other places. This was the largest population decline since records were kept in 1961 (Gu 2021). More people are also still planning or considering to leave the city. Even among those who have decided to stay or cannot leave, the repression has not changed their opinion in regard to the movement (Ting 2020; Kobayashi, Song, and Chan 2021). While there are currently almost no protests due to very stringent restrictions justified by the Covid-19 pandemic, there is also very little support for the government and its policies.

4. The Decline of the Rule of Law

The authoritarian leaders in China have become increasingly uncomfortable with the independent judiciary in Hong Kong, which can make decisions that run counter to the interests of the Chinese government. The threat to the system has become stronger since the rise of Xi Jinping to power who has firmly asserted that the judiciary in mainland China has to be under the control of the Party. Despite the differences in the legal system in Hong Kong, there has been growing pressure on the special administrative region to limit the independence of the judiciary. There have even been calls to enact judicial reforms such as requiring judges to undergo "patriot education" in the mainland, creating a new committee that reviews sentences the Chinese government considers too lenient, and remolding the Judicial Officers Recommendation Commission that makes recommendations about judicial appointments and thus is critical to the selection of judges (Lo 2021).

In this section, I want to provide some examples of how recent developments have eroded the rule of law in Hong Kong. The greatest threat obviously is the NSL enacted in 2020, which has been dubbed by Hui as the "regime-security law" (2020, 124) because it is meant to strengthen the party state's control over Hong Kong. As John Lowe (2021, 629) has stated, the law removed "the firewall between Hong Kong's judiciary and Mainland China's rule by law." The following will detail some of the most important steps in the process.

In response to the protest movement, the government enacted the NSL on June 30, 2020, which significantly redefines legality in Hong Kong. The law was directly inserted into the Basic Law thus avoiding the need for the legal process stated in Article 23. The government has already announced that it will in addition pass another NSL to also fulfill that requirement. This, however, does not negate the fact that the law was introduced through the Chinese government's interpretative power, which reinforced the limits of autonomy of the SAR. The law itself has a very wide scope and includes secession, subversion, terrorism, and collusion with foreign powers, and people convicted of such crimes face life sentences. Critics like Amnesty International have pointed out that the law is "dangerously vague and broad" and its application since has shown that it will be used liberally against any number of offenses and also as possible threats to silence dissent. It is thus more in line with similar rules in mainland China, which is known for very strong limits on political freedoms.

Within a very short period of time, new supralegal institutions have been created to enforce the law. First, an Office for Safeguarding National Security of the Central People's Government in Hong Kong Special Administrative Region has been established, which is beyond the legal constraints in the territory and thus acts outside of the jurisdiction of the legal system. Moreover, the Hong Kong government has set up a Committee for Safeguarding National Security of the Hong Kong Special Administrative Region, which also stands outside of the normal checks on power because other institutions cannot interfere with its work nor is it subject to any judicial review. To enforce the law, a special unit has been set up in the police force that is responsible for implementing the NSL. It is allowed to monitor the communication of all people and conduct other covert surveillance without the need for approval from a panel of judges. It can even prevent suspects from leaving the territory and gain access to online information without the need for a warrant. As such, it provides new wide-ranging powers under the justification of national security. This new massive national security apparatus has greatly narrowed the space for political dissent.

While supporters of the law asserted that it was not different from similar laws in the West, the application of the law proved otherwise. Already on July 1, 2020, ten people were apprehended under the new law. By June 2021, at least 128 people had been arrested and more than half had been charged under the law. On May 6, five suspected members of a student group called Returning Valiant were detained and the police seized Hong Kong independence flags and an air gun. Although some of them were secondary school students, a source told the *South China Morning Post* that "Their comments left on social media could constitute the offence of subversion under the national security law" (cited in SCMP Reporter 2021). On June 23, the first case of a protester arrested under the NSL went to court without a jury. A three-judge panel found Tong Ying-kit guilty of inciting secession and terrorism and sentenced him to nine years in jail. It was found that the slogan "Liberate Hong Kong, Revolution of our Time" could incite people to commit secession. Such cases have inevitably created widespread fear among democracy activists and its supporters because any call for democracy could be interpreted similarly.

One of the most problematic articles of the NSL is Article 14, which places the law outside of judicial review and has thus been called the "NSL Ouster Clause" (Lam 2021). This is a potential threat to judicial independence because it elevates the newly created institutions above the law and reduces any possible oversight over them. Hingchun Lam (2021) argues that the ouster clause would not be effective due to "long established principles of the *ultra vires* doctrine and the rule of law." However, this presupposes the continuation of an effective rule of law which will be difficult in the current context. Judges in Hong Kong are unlikely willing to question the Chinese authorities in regard to national security cases because this could harm their own careers. This is reinforced by the fact that special judges are selected by the chief executive for such cases, which further constraints any possibility of judicial review and thus fundamentally upends the liberal principles of legality in Hong Kong.

5. The Decline of the Liberal Society

Once Hong Kong was known for its liberal constitutional regime that allowed more freedom than anywhere in China. This came to an end in 2020 when the NSL and other laws were used to start a frontal assault on this legacy. Immediately after passing the law, a number of protesters were arrested under the new law. Seven months later, already over 100 people had been put in jail (Wong and Kellogg 2021). Prominent slogans and the protest anthem of the 2019 movement were declared violations under the new law despite their ambiguity. The Hong Kong government has used the law and other procedures to threaten or undermine various pro-democratic organizations from the media to civil society and even various businesses that have shown their support for the cause, generally known as the "yellow circle" which represents the color of the pro-democracy movement.

Many civil society organizations have been forced to dissolve. Already by September 2021, 49 different organizations had either ceased operation or been disbanded. One victim was the Civil Human Rights Front which chose to dissolve under pressure on August 15, 2021. It had been the main organizer of protest marches since 2003. In 2019, it had also played a key role in organizing peaceful demonstrations. Leading members of the alliance left the group when rumors surfaced that it was under investigation for violations of the NSL. It was no surprise that the government also went against the Alliance in Support of Patriotic Democratic Movements of China which had regularly organized the Tiananmen vigil. It has become a national security concern similar to mainland China where any mention of the violent crackdown on June 4, 1989, is immediately censored. Moreover, the organization regularly called for an end to one-party rule. It therefore disbanded on September 25, 2021, which did not prevent the government from starting legal procedures under the NSL anyway. Through an unusual executive order by Chief Executive Carrie Lam, the group was eventually struck from the companies' registry on October 26. Another prominent group that decided to dissolve was on September 11, 2021, the Hong Kong Professional Teachers Union, one of the oldest professional unions and civil society groups founded in the 1970s. It was not directly linked to the NSL but following criticism in the Chinese press, the government cut its ties to the union making it impossible for it to provide important services for its 90,000 members such as teacher training.

The pro-democratic media became a natural target of the new repressive regime. In June 2021, *Apple Daily* newspaper was forced to close down after it was accused of violating the NSL in some of its articles. The chief editor and five other executives were subsequently detained while the assets of the company were frozen making it impossible to pay its employees and suppliers. This left it with little choice but to close down even before anyone had been convicted of a crime. In December 2021, the government also went against *Stand News*, a major online news portal that leaned pro-democratic. Seven current and former editors were arrested under the NSL and its assets were also frozen. This meant that it also had to close down. A few days later, *Citizen News*, another news website, shut down due to concerns that it could be targeted as well. Eventually, even US-government-funded *Radio Free Asia* ended its Cantonese service amid concerns it could be targeted under the law as well.

In addition to the news, pro-democratic businesses that have officially taken a political stance have also been targeted. Under the claim of normal law enforcement, many of them have been singled out for violations. One case in point is the Thai supermarket chain AbouThai, which was targeted for lack of localized labels on imported goods, a habit prevalent in other similar chains such as PrizeMart. While the Customs Office rejected any political motivation, many Hongkongers supported the chain which led to very long queues (Chow 2021). Another case is the Chickeeduck group, which announced that it would leave in the second half of 2022 following "disturbances from unknown evil sources." The store had once proudly displayed protest artworks and messages. In June 2020, the Tsuen Wan branch was forced to remove a Lady Liberty statue after it had been pressured by the shopping mall owner. In May 2021, another branch in Tsuen Wan was surrounded by National Security police, and the CEO was questioned (Chau 11/18/2021).

The change in the legality has been especially problematic for universities as academic freedom declined. As many administrators in the universities have already been replaced with regime conformists, it may not be surprising that the free expression of opinions on campus has narrowed significantly. The most obvious expression of that has been the censorship of the June 4th massacre in 1989 which used to be remembered annually with a candlelight vigil and which forms a core collective memory of Hongkongers about their relationship with the Chinese state. Under the pretense of legal procedures, the University of Hong Kong (HKU) objected to an artwork by a Danish artist which had been in front of the university canteen since 1998. The Pillar of Shame not only represented the memory of the fateful night on June 4 but also was a place that activists visited annually to clean the statue prior to the candlelight vigil. The university asserted that the statute had posed a legal risk. The artist sought to rescue his statue but was concerned about the possibility of becoming subject to the NSL. Eventually, the statue was removed in an overnight operation during the Christmas period of 2021. A few days later, the Chinese University of Hong Kong and Lingnan University both also removed their memorials of the crackdown. A month later, HKU covered up the last reminder. Due to the fear of legal consequences, these acts can be seen as part of a so-called state-enforced amnesia of the historical event, which is common in Mainland China (Lim 2014). It indicated another step in the disappearance of Hong Kong's liberal nature as it raised serious concerns about academic freedom. Meanwhile, university administrators have also sought to take out student unions that have played a key role in political activism, which was also done under the claim of legality. Finally, prominent scholars such as Sing Ming (The Hong Kong University of Science and Technology) and Brian Fong (The Education University of Hong Kong) have left their positions after having been criticized in the pro-Beijing press.

In the legal sector, the Bar Association has been attacked when its head, Paul Harris, made suggestions to modify the NSL and when he criticized the harsh sentencing of members of the democratic movement. The Liaison Office accused him, for instance, of "spreading distorted opinion" and then indicated that he should be replaced lest the organization were to face serious consequences (Chau 04/29/2021). In 2022, a new chairman, Victor Dawes, was subsequently elected who declared that the "rule of law" was not dead and that the association would continue to speak up on issues related to it. However, he also said that the association should not discuss political issues without making clear how the two could be separated (Ho 2022). After being questioned by the National Security police, Harris left the city in early 2022. The Law Society also elected a new chairman, Chan Chak-min, who similarly declared that the organization would remain politically neutral although he also asserted that the vague NSL was "mild when compared to Western countries" (Ng 2021). This indicated that leaders politically loyal to the Chinese government had been put in leadership positions of these two organizations.

As the attacks on the civil society and pro-democratic individuals continue, it is unclear how far the ongoing crackdown will go. However, many of those that remain active have chosen to engage in self-censorship. Scholars are changing their research focuses and altering their course contents. Assurances that the NSL will only apply to those advocating independence or other radical stances are quickly overshadowed by frequent news reports of additional investigations under the law.

6. The 2021 Electoral Reform

In 2019, the District Council election led to a landslide victory for pan-democrats. This was an unexpected outcome for the Chinese government which had believed that the violence of the protesters would harm the opposition camp. Quite to the contrary, the majority of politically mobilized Hong Kongers were supportive of the movement and saw the election as a way to express their desire for change. For that reason, there was a record turnout which made attempts by the Chinese government to mobilize its own supporters much more difficult. Following this success, the pan-democratic camp organized an unofficial primary election to improve its chances in the upcoming Legislative Council election. This was perceived as a real threat by the pro-Beijing camp. The Secretary for Constitutional and Mainland Affairs Erick Tsang warned that the election could violate the NSL and in 2021, the pan-democrats, who had participated in the primary, were subsequently arrested. This highlights Beijing's strong concern about participatory democracy. Meanwhile, the government proceeded in using new oaths to remove district councilors from their positions. Some were disqualified while others resigned voluntarily. By October 2021, 33 district councilors had been ousted on the assertion that their oath was "invalid." The government stated that this was the case "based on the principles laid down by the Interpretation and the relevant legal provisions" (Kwan 2021); 200 others resigned because of rumors that they would have to repay salaries after being disqualified.

The electoral reorganization in 2021 reversed a trend of making elections more representative of the population. The directly elected seats were reduced and a third form of constituency, the Election Committee constituency, which had been abolished with the 2004 election, was reintroduced. Not only that but also the proportion and thus influence of directly elected legislators was reduced significantly. They now only make up 20 seats of the 90 legislators, while the Election Committee is 40 seats and Functional Constituencies make up 30. As such, directly elected seats are in the minority. On top of that, a selection process was put into place which limits the potential candidates to only those approved by the Election Committee. This has been dubbed as a "patriots only" election and has allowed the disqualification of any candidate seen as not supportive of the Chinese government. Anticipating anger over the electoral changes, government officials suggested that calling for a boycott could breach the NSL. Four people were even arrested for supposedly inciting a boycott by sharing a Facebook post. They were apprehended under an amended Election Ordinance which now made such appeals a crime. Nevertheless, the Legislative Council election on December 19 drew a record low voter turnout of 30.2% of the electorate and resulted in a legislature that was almost completely controlled by the pro-establishment camp (Davis 2022).

The use of the law to not only reduce the democratic representativeness of the legislature but also stifle debate prior to the election clearly marked an end to the partially liberal electoral system in place before. The government hoped that the newly constituted legislature would make policy-making easier since there would be less resistance. As such, the changes meant there would be fewer checks on the government. Meanwhile, the government has strongly defended the executive aggrandizement from both local and international criticism while even suggesting that such criticism could be against the law.

7. Conclusion

This chapter has shown that the changes in Hong Kong's autonomy under the vague concept of "one country, two systems" have entailed a significant shift in the understanding of legality from the rule of law established under British colonial rule to an increasing erosion of these principles in exchange for a more instrumental use of law in the service of the authoritarian regime. While for the British empire, the rule of law was a way to control the governor, the Chinese government has seen it as an obstacle to its power. As a pro-democracy movement in Hong Kong sought to prevent the erosion of the rule of law and demanded greater political participation, the Chinese government has increasingly felt threatened by the attempt to assert greater autonomy and has used its power of interpretation and amendment to hollow out the rule of law which culminated in the passing of the NSL in 2020 and an institutional apparatus that is outside of judicial oversight.

The Covid-19 situation has further eroded China's trust in Hong Kong's system. A rapid increase of cases in early 2022 led to the unprecedented step by Xi Jinping to publicly chide the local government. He stated that the "overriding task" was to control the virus, thus reducing the state's authority. In response, Carrie Lam postponed the chief executive election from March to May. She has also announced territory-wide testing of all 7.5 million residents. Still, the differences in the two systems which makes it impossible to apply similar enforcement mechanisms in Hong Kong, have raised questions in China about whether local officials were sufficiently loyal (Wang and Ramzy 2022). There have even been concerns about whether a debate on the strategy of how to deal with the virus is legitimate as pro-Beijing politician Junius Ho suggested that any discussion about living with the virus might violate the NSL. While the government has rejected this suggestion, the comments suggest that legality is increasingly driven by political concerns and the principle of the rule of law could soon become only a faint memory in the history of the territory. This, however, would come at a very high price for Hong Kong, which has long benefited from the rule of law. As a consequence, many businesses that value predictability and legal certainty will likely move to Singapore or other nearby locations.

References

Chau, Candice. 2021. "'Daily Torture': Pro-democracy Retail Chain Chickeeduck to Exit Hong Kong in 2022 Citing Pressure, Threats." *Hong Kong Free Press*, November 18, 2021. https://hongkongfp.com/2021/11/18/daily-torture-pro-democracy-retail-chain-chickeeduck-to-exit-hong-kong-in-2022-citing-pressure-threats/.

———. 2021. "'Not What I Said': Hong Kong Bar Assoc. Chief Paul Harris Clarifies Security Law Comments." *Hong Kong Free Press*, April 29, 2021. https://hongkongfp.com/2021/04/29/not-what-i-said-hong-kong-bar-assoc-chief-paul-harris-clarifies-security-law-comments/.

Cheung, Gary. 2020. "Why Escalating Row Over Whether Hong Kong Has 'Separation of Powers' in Its Political System Is Not Just a Fight Over Words." *South China Morning Post*, September 3, 2020.

Chow, Carine. 2021. "Queues Grow in Support of AbouThai." *The Standard*, April 12, 2021.

Citizen News Op-ed. 2019. "Observations of the Hong Kong Bar Association on the Fugitive Offenders and Mutual Legal Assistance in Criminal Matters Legislation (Amendment) Bill 2019." *Citizen News*, April 2, 2019. www.hkcnews.com/article/19529/bar_association-fugitives_bill-19529/observations-of-the-hong-kong-bar-association-on-the-fugitive-offenders-and-mutual-legal-assistance-in-criminal-matters-legislation-amendment-bill-2019.

Davis, Michael C. 2020. "The Clash of Legal Cultures: Hong Kong Efforts to Maintain the Liberal Rule of Law vs. Beijing's Hardline Authoritarian Legality." In *Authoritarian Legality in Asia: Formation, Development and Transition*, edited by Weitseng Chen and Hualing Fu, 169–86. Cambridge: Cambridge University Press.

———. 2022. "Hong Kong: How Beijing Perfected Repression." *Journal of Democracy* 33 (1): 100–15.

Department of Justice. 2021. "Our Legal System." *Hong Kong Government Website*, November 5, 2021. www.doj.gov.hk/en/our_legal_system/index.html.

Economy, Elizabeth. 2018. *The Third Revolution: Xi Jinping and the New Chinese State*. New York: Oxford University Press.

Gu, Vanessa. 2021. "Almost 90,000 People Left Hong Kong in the Past Year. It Marks the City's Biggest Population Decrease in 60 Years." *Insider*, August 13, 2021. www.insider.com/hong-kong-exodus-people-leaving-political-turmoil-2021-8.

Ho, Kelly. 2022. "Hong Kong Bar Association Should Not Discuss Politics, New Chairman Says." *Hong Kong Free Press*, January 21, 2022. https://hongkongfp.com/2022/01/21/hong-kong-bar-association-should-not-discuss-politics-new-chairman-says/.

Holbig, Heike. 2020. "Be Water, My Friend: Hong Kong's 2019 Anti-extradition Protests." *International Journal of Sociology* 50 (4): 325–37.

Holliday, Ian, Ma Ngok, and Ray Yep. 2004. "After 1997: The Dialectics of Hong Kong Dependence." *Journal of Contemporary Asia* 34 (2): 254–70.

Horlemann, Ralf. 2003. *Hong Kong's Transition to Chinese Rule: The Limits of Autonomy*. London: Routledge.

Hui, Victoria Tin-bor. 2020. "Crackdown: Hong Kong Faces Tiananmen 2.0." *Journal of Democracy* 31 (4): 122–37.

Information Services Department. 2002. *HKSAR The First Five Years 1997–2002*. Hong Kong: Government Printer.

Kobayashi, Tetsuro, Jaehyun Song, and Polly Chan. 2021. "Does Repression Undermine Opposition Demands? The Case of the Hong Kong National Security Law." *Japanese Journal of Political Science* 22 (4): 268–86.

Kwan, Rhoda. 2021. "16 More Hong Kong District Councillors Ousted Over 'Invalid' Oaths of Loyalty to Gov't, Bringing Total to 33." *Hong Kong Free Press*, October 8, 2021. https://hongkongfp.com/2021/10/08/16-more-hong-kong-district-councillors-ousted-over-invalid-oaths-of-loyalty-to-govt-bringing-total-to-33/.

Lam, Hingchau. 2021. "The Ouster Clause in the Hong Kong National Security Law: Its Effectiveness in the Common Law and its Implications for the Rule of Law." *Crime, Law and Social Change* 76 (5): 543–61.

Lau, Stuart, Austin Chiu, and Brian Yap. 2014. "Hong Kong Lawyers March to Defend Judiciary in Wake of Beijing's White Paper." *South China Morning Post*, June 27, 2014.

Lee, Francis L. F., Samson Yuen, Gary Tang, and Edmund W. Cheng. 2019. "Hong Kong's Summer of Uprising." *China Review* 19 (4): 1–32.

Lin, Fen, and Sixian Lin. 2017. "Why Framing National Identity Fails: A Case Study of the Anti-Moral and National Education Movement in Hong Kong." SSRN 3032869.

Lim, Louisa. 2014. *The People's Republic of Amnesia: Tiananmen Revisited*. New York: Oxford University Press.

Lo, Shiu-hing. 2000. "The Politics of the Debate Over the Court of Final Appeal in Hong Kong." *The China Quarterly* 161: 221–39.

Lo, Sonny. 2021. "Hong Kong in 2020: National Security Law and Truncated Autonomy." *Asian Survey* 61 (1): 34–42.

Lowe, John. 2021. "The Affective Cultural Commons of Hong Kong's Pro-Democracy Movement and Figurations of the Anonymous Protestor." *Continuum*: 1–20.

Ma, Josephine. 2021. "Party-State Relations Under China's Communist Party: Separation of Powers, Control Over Government and Reforms." *South China Morning Post*, May 17, 2021.

Ma, Ngok. 2005. "Civil Society in Self-Defense: The Struggle Against National Security Legislation in Hong Kong." *Journal of Contemporary China* 14 (44): 465–82.

Munn, Christopher. 2001. "The Rule of Law and Criminal Justice in the Nineteenth Century." In *Judicial Independence and the Rule of Law in Hong Kong*, edited by Steve Tsang, 19–47. London: Palgrave Macmillan.

Ng Kang-chung. 2021. "Hong Kong's National Security Legislation 'Mild Compared to the West', Says New Head of City's Law Society, as He Reiterates Confidence in Legal System." *South China Morning Post*, September 20, 2021.

Ortmann, Stephan. 2015. "The Umbrella Movement and Hong Kong's Protracted Democratization Process." *Asian Affairs* 46 (1): 32–50.

———. 2016. "The Lack of Sovereignty, the Umbrella Movement, and Democratisation in Hong Kong." *Asia Pacific Law Review* 24 (2): 108–22.

Rezvani, David A. 2022. "National Security: How Stifling Political Dissent Became Part of Hong Kong's Rule of Law." *South China Morning Post*, February 20, 2022.

SCMP Reporter. 2021. "National Security Law: Hong Kong Police Arrest Five for Alleged Acts of Subversion on Social Media, Sources Say." *South China Morning Post*, May 6, 2021.

Sommer, Matthew Harvey. 2000. *Sex, Law, and Society in Late Imperial China*. Stanford: Stanford University Press.

Tai, Benny Y. T. 2010. "Judicial Autonomy in Hong Kong." *China Information* 24 (3): 295–315.

Ting, Tin-yuet. 2020. "From 'Be Water' to 'Be Fire': Nascent Smart Mob and Networked Protests in Hong Kong." *Social Movement Studies* 19 (3): 362–68.

Torode, Greg, and James Pomfret. 2019. "Exclusive: Hong Kong Judges See Risks in Proposed Extradition Changes." *Reuters*, May 29, 2019.

Wang, Vivien, and Austin Ramzy. 2022. "Hong Kong Can't Live with the Virus. It Can't Stop It, Either." *The New York Times*, February 16, 2022.

Wong, Lydia, and Thomas E. Kellogg. 2021. "Hong Kong's National Security Law: A Human Rights and Rule of Law Analysis." *Center for Asian Law, Georgetown Law,* February. https://www.law.georgetown.edu/law-asia/wp-content/uploads/sites/31/2021/02/GT-HK-Report-Accessible.pdf.

11

POLICING THE POLICE, PARTY, AND STATE

Corruption and Anti-Corruption in China

Andrew Wedeman

Introduction

In the spring of 2019, the Chinese Communist Party (CCP) launched a new drive against organized crime. Organized crime was not a new problem, and there had been periodic crackdowns on criminal gangs in the past. The new drive, however, soon morphed into an attack on the police officers and officials who provided organized crime syndicates the "protective umbrellas" (保护伞), collusive screens which hid the nefarious activities of the gangs from law enforcement. Over the next several years, the drive grew into a broader crackdown on official malfeasance in the public security, procuratorial, and judicial systems and merged with the larger drive against official corruption launched after Xi Jinping assumed power in 2012.

Like criminals and corrupt police, corrupt officials had built "offensive and defensive alliances" (攻守同盟) and formed "cliques" (团团伙伙) to shield themselves from unwanted scrutiny by investigators from the anti-corruption agencies. They were also able to take advantage of imperfections in institutional monitoring capabilities and the resulting "blind spots" to surreptitiously usurp their authority for personal gain (i.e., engage in corruption). In key respects, corrupt officials and anti-corruption investigators play a "cat-and-mouse" game in which the corrupt "mice" try to stay hidden in the shadows while the anti-corruption "cat" roams about in an institutional "room" rendered dim by inadequate monitoring and obstructed by the informational barricades thrown up by the corrupt mice. Anti-corruption work thus entails not only trying to uncover things that some police officers and officials wish would remain unseen but also breaking through the screens they throw up to obscure prying eyes. Anti-corruption work is rendered even more difficult because not only are police and officials susceptible

DOI: 10.4324/9781003294887-14

to corruption but so are the investigators and prosecutors tasked with fighting corruption. In this chapter, I delineate the structural factors that facilitate corruption and the institutional structures the Chinese regime has set up to control corruption.

When he came to power in 2012, Xi promised that he would "hunt tigers" (打虎)—corrupt high-level officials—as well as "swatting flies" (拍蝇)—corrupt rank-and-file officials and state agents.[1] Xi launched a three-prong attack. First, he "swamped the zone" by ordering the anti-corruption agencies to throw all their forces into a frontal assault on corrupt officials. Second, he and Wang Qishan, the Secretary of the party's internal anti-corruption agency, the Central Discipline Inspection Commission (中国共产党中央纪律检查委员会) (CDIC), ordered a reorganization of the regime's anti-corruption agencies and the merger of party, state, and judicial units into a new unified National Supervisory Commission (中华人民共和国国家监察委员会). The merger was not only designed to consolidate and streamline the anti-corruption effort, but it also sought to wrest control of the anti-corruption system from local party committees, some of which had suborned local anti-corruption agencies, and bring the anti-corruption agencies more tightly under central control. Finally, they ordered a "flanking attack" by Central Inspection Teams (中央巡视组) dispatched by the CDIC and later the National Supervisory Commission to "police the police" by scrutinizing the work of other agencies' organic disciplinary units.

Although the immediate goal of Xi's three-prong attack was to take down corrupt officials, on a broader level, its goal was to re-assert the power of the central leadership and, from the perspective of this volume, the law. If individual officials flaunt the dictates of the regime leadership and use their authority to seek private gains, then laws and regulations are little more than words on paper.

In addition to delineating how the structure of the Chinese party state and its anti-corruption agencies facilitate corruption, I examine the extent of corruption within the regime's police and anti-corruption agencies. Corruption in these agencies compounds the problem of corruption in the regime's line agencies. Quite simply, if a regime's anti-corruption agents are corrupt, then the leadership cannot rely on them to root out corruption among its other agents and thereby establish the primacy of the leadership and the law. As documented in the final section of this chapter, there is evidence of extensive high-level corruption within the law enforcement and supervisory-disciplinary agencies. As a result, Xi has found himself having to fight a two-front battle with corruption.

1. The Structural Challenge

Although at some basic level corruption grows out of human greed, it is nurtured by institutional factors that create the monitoring and supervisory slack that enables officials to not only think they can get away with usurping the authority delegated to them but also actually allow them to evade detection and punishment. Complex organizations such as the Chinese party state consist of hierarchies in which a "principal" engages a set of "agents" to act on its behalf. Although some agents may faithfully carry out the tasks assigned to them, others may:

> Slack off, not perform their assigned tasks or perform them in a desultory manner; Unintentionally failed to correctly carry out their assigned tasks; or Consciously and willingly use the resources and authority delegated to them by the principal to pursue their own interests, including interests that are at cross-purposes to the desires of the principal.

Once a principal has assigned an agent a task, the principal then needs to determine if the agent has carried out the assigned task and has carried it out correctly. The challenge for the principal of a large and complex organization is that the principal acting on its own can never constantly and closely monitor all its agents. Nor can the principal assume that rigorous selection and training will screen out all the incompetents and "bad apples" and ensure that all of its agents are honest, upright, and incorruptible.

Agency problems multiply as institutions grow in size and complexity. A single principal or even a compact inner leadership can obviously not closely monitor a state and its ancillary public agencies like China's which have a total staff of upward of 18 million civil servants, police officers, and other public functionaries spread out across 3.7 million square miles. The Chinese state is thus organized into a set of hierarchies that extend vertically downward through the central agencies and horizontally across the provinces and then downward from there to the grassroots. In theory, the Chinese state is a "unitary" state in which the central government has a monopoly on sovereign power. The state in fact consists of a complex latticework in which "reaching down" from Beijing to the street entails moving down through a five-layered hierarchy. In this hierarchy, the leadership (aka regime-principal) selects first-order agents at the ministerial and provincial levels. These first-order agents then act as agents-cum-principals who select second-order agents at the municipal/prefectural and bureau levels. These second-order agents then act as second-order principal-cum-agent who select third-order agents at the county/district and departmental levels. These third-order agents then act as third-order principal-cum-agents to select fourth-order agents at the township/sub-district and section levels. Below these fourth-order agents are the host of rank-and-file officials, functionaries, public agents, and, police officers who are ultimately responsible for implementing the "will" of the leadership in distant Beijing.

By the same token, information and intelligence on local conditions and the activities—compliant and malfeasant—of the regime street-level agents have to transit up this multilayer hierarchy before it reaches the eyes and ears of the regime principal. Information asymmetries embedded in the hierarchy of principal-agent and principal-cum-agent-agent dyads can distort and contaminate information as it transits upward. As a result, the regime principal is apt to have an imperfect picture of conditions at the grassroots and the reliability of its agents.

In China, the regime principal must monitor and direct two parallel hierarchies—the state apparatus and the party apparatus. Hypothetically, the two are separate institutions, and the party agencies direct and monitor the state agencies. In reality, party and state overlap. Leading party cadres often hold concurrent state positions. Thus, for instance, the party secretary of a county might also be a county magistrate or have served as a magistrate before being named party secretary. The intertwining of the party and state creates further monitoring challenges for the regime principal because party cadres and state officials may collude together to keep the regime principal in the dark and hide their malfeasance or the malfeasance of their colleagues and subordinates. Perhaps more critically, party secretaries not only tend to dominate parallel state agencies, but they often exert leverage over the disciplinary and supervisory agencies China's regime principal has tasked with policing the party and state hierarchies.

2. Institutional Countermeasures

Complex institutions inevitably create "slack" which self-interested agents can take advantage of to either neglect their assigned duties or actually usurp their delegated fiduciary authority for personal gain (i.e., engage in corruption) or otherwise abuse their delegated authority. In order to combat malfeasance and indiscipline, a regime principal can—and usually does—set up a system of units embedded in its vertical and horizontal agencies that are tasked with monitoring and supervising the personnel assigned to their host agency. A regime principal can then supplement these internal monitors with external agencies tasked with monitoring and supervising other agencies

China has set up a series of such agencies. The paramount disciplinary-supervisory agency is the Central Committee's Politics and Law Committee (中共中央政法委员会) which oversees the state's public security agencies, the party disciplinary committees, the Procuratorate, the courts, and the prison system. Politics and law committees are attached to the various regional party committees from the provincial level down to the county level. The party's Central Discipline Inspection Commission acts as the party's internal police force and is tasked with enforcing discipline for all party members, including those employed by the state and those working outside the state, as well as party members who are students, farmers, ordinary workers, and retirees (see Gong 2008, 2010; Guo 2012, 2013; Ling 2017; Yeo 2014). Like the politics and law committee system, discipline inspection committees exist at all levels of the party apparatus down to the county level. Established in 1988, the state Ministry for Supervision was tasked with disciplining state officials. Because many state officials are also party members, the Discipline Inspection Commission and the Ministry for Supervision had overlapping jurisdictions. In 1993, they were operationally merged. The Procuratorate and its Anti-corruption Bureau are responsible for the prosecution of those accused of transgressing the law. The Peoples Courts try those indicted for violations of law. The Ministry of Justice's Prison Bureau, finally, incarcerates those convicted of criminal violations of the law.

In 2018, the CDIC, the Ministry for Supervision, and the Anti-corruption Bureau of the Procuratorate were merged to form the National Supervisory Commission (see Li and Wang 2019; Zhou 2018). The commission is a party-cum-state-cum-judicial body in which the party retains the upper hand. The commission conducts investigations of party members; state officials; and other public employees, including doctors, teachers, and employees of state-owned companies. After conducting an investigation the commission may close the case, impose party and/or administrative sanctions (warnings, demotions, and dismissal from office), or expel the accused from the party, dismiss them from public office, and remand the case to the Procuratorate for criminal prosecution. The merger was intended to streamline the investigation-prosecution process by integrating the Procuratorate Anti-corruption Bureau into the previously merged party discipline inspection and state supervisory agencies and thereby facilitate the movement of a case from the disciplinary-supervisory system which lacks judicial authority to the Procuratorate which is a judicial agency and is authorized to conduct criminal investigations and prosecute suspects in the courts.

The merger also sought to loosen the grip of parallel party committees on the supervisory and disciplinary agencies. Party committees and their leadership are generally the most powerful actors in a locality or bureaucratic area because they can pigeonhole and block uncooperative investigators and promote cooperative ones. In the past, party secretaries often exercised *de facto* veto power over investigations. They were thus able to shield their friends, cronies, and henchmen—and themselves of course—from unwanted scrutiny. By linking the supervisory and disciplinary agencies more closely to the CDIC which is elected by the National Party Congress is hence on a par with the party Central Committee, the 2017–2018 reorganization sought to bind the various supervisory and disciplinary agencies to the center and disentangle them from the party and state agencies, including the public security system, which they are tasked with policing.

As is the case with the regime principal and its other agents, the regime principal faces the same principal-agent problems with its supervisory and disciplinary agents. Both the disciplinary and supervisory systems are multi-layered hierarchies of principal-agent and principal-cum-agent-agent dyads. These systems are thus subject to the same information asymmetries that make it difficult for the regime-principal to ensure that its will is carried out at the progressively lower rungs of the disciplinary-supervisory hierarchy and detect slacking off and malfeasance.

Corruption within the supervisory and disciplinary agencies can, obviously, compound the difficulty of controlling corruption. Quite simply, if the anti-corruption agencies suffer from corruption, that will exacerbate the problem of trying to attack corruption elsewhere. In fact, the regime principal must worry that corrupt agents in the supervisory and disciplinary agencies will use the authority delegated to them not to attack corruption but rather to line their own pockets by extorting protection money from corrupt officials or by working in league with them in return for a "cut" of their dirty monies.

Chinese regime principals, going back to before the communist takeover in 1949, have sought to bypass the problem of corruption in the regular multi-layered hierarchy of supervisory-disciplinary agencies by deploying additional extra-agency agents tasked with bypassing regular channels. As far back as the Qin Dynasty (221–209 BCE), imperial governments relied on what became known as the "Censorate." In theory, the Censorate was independent of the regular bureaucracy and responsible for investigating officials. Censors could impeach those they found to be corrupt, incompetent, or disloyal. Censors were supposed to travel incognito and unannounced to localities and offices (see Hucker 1951, 1966; Walker 1947; Herson 1957). The Ming dynasty also set up provincial surveillance commissions headed by officials holding bureaucratic ranks equal to those of the provincial governor and tasked them with detecting and punishing malfeasant officials (see Hucker 1998; Rowe 2010).

During the 1990s, the party adopted a series of regulations authorizing the CDIC to dispatch Central Inspection Teams (中央巡视组) to audit state and party institutions. Xi and Wang Qishan ordered repeated waves of inspections beginning in 2013 (see *China Daily* 2017). The teams were formed under the Central Committee's Inspection Work Leading Group, which was housed in the offices of the CDIC and reported to the Secretary of the CDIC. The teams did not conduct investigations themselves but rather inspected the disciplinary and supervisory work of the targeted localities and agencies. In addition to searching for evidence of corruption, the teams were tasked with detecting extravagance, waste, collusion, illegal bidding, personnel problems, buying and selling offices, formalism, irregularities in land requisition and demolition, falsification of official records, bribery, lazy politics (i.e., sloth), and "naked officials" (officials whose families were living abroad) (*Caixin* 2014). The provincial discipline inspection committees and later the provincial supervisory committees also dispatched inspection teams to audit the work of lower-level disciplinary and supervisory units (Wang 2022).

Between 2013 and 2022, the CDIC and its successor the National Supervisory Commission conducted 19 rounds of inspections during which teams conducted 551 inspections of 354 provincial-level governments, ministries, state agencies, state-owned companies, and party organizations with some receiving repeated inspections.[2] Provincial discipline inspection committees conducted some 2,900 inspections between 2012 and 2017. Among the policing, disciplinary, and supervisory agencies, the Ministry for Public Security, the Ministry for Justice, the Supreme People's Procuratorate, and the Supreme People's Court were inspected twice. The National Supervisory Commission was itself inspected in March 2022.

3. Corruption in the Senior Police, Supervisory, and Disciplinary Ranks

In China, as in most countries, police corruption and abuse have been a persistent problem, but police and disciplinary personnel have accounted for a relatively small fraction of those charged with corruption (see Figure 11.1) (see Wong 1998). Despite repeated campaigns against organized crime have also failed to eradicate criminal syndicates or smash criminal gangs (see Broadhurst 2012, 2013; Chen 2009; Lo 2016; Wang 2017; Xia 2008). In 2009, the police-organized crime nexus became the target of a massive campaign to "sweep the black" ordered by Chongqing Party Secretary Bo Xilai (see Ho 2012; Wang 2013). In all over 20 law-enforcement officials, including Wen Qiang, Director of the Chongqing Justice Bureau and former Director of the Chongqing Public Security Bureau; Zhang Tao, the Vice President of the Chongqing High Court; and Peng Changjian, Deputy Director of the Chongqing Public Security Bureau, were charged (see Table 11.1). Wen was executed. Chang and Peng received suspended death sentences (see Wedeman 2013).[3]

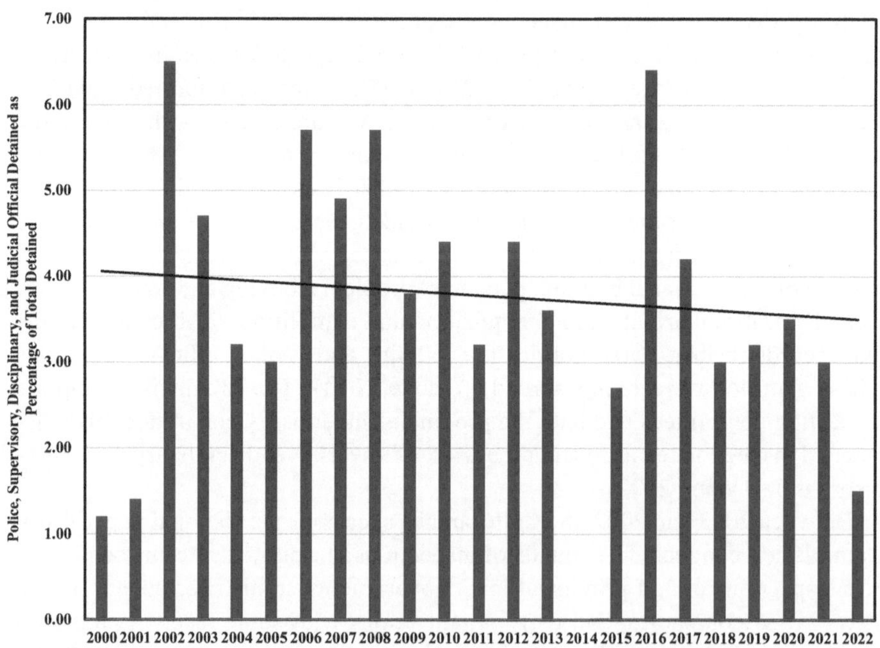

FIGURE 11.1 Police, Disciplinary, Supervisory, and Judicial Corruption

Source: Figure created by author using data drawn from a database of individual corruption cases coded and maintained by the author. The database currently documents approximately 38,000 cases dating from the early 2000s to the present. Data are drawn from a wide variety of Chinese and English language sources. The major sources are Caixin (www.caixinglobal.com/), South China Morning Post (www.scmp.com), China Daily (www.chinadaily.com.cn/), China Court (www.Chinacourt.org), the website of the Central Discipline Inspection Commission (www.ccdi.gov.cn/), The Paper (www.thepaper.cn/list_25490), and China Judgements Online (https://wenshu.court.gov.cn/).

TABLE 11.1 Chongqing Anti-Organized Crime Campaign, 2009–2010 Officials Convicted

Name	*Position*	*Charge*	*Sentence*
Chen Guangming	Police Captain	Bribery and protecting a syndicate	
Chen Honggang	Chief Chongqing Municipal Traffic Police	Accepting bribes	20 years
Chen Hongqiang	Deputy Captain Crime Squad of Chongqing Public Security Bureau	Accepting bribes	
Chen Tao	Deputy Director Chongqing Municipal Public Security Police Division	Bribery and protecting a syndicate	19 years
Gan Yong	Police Officer	Bribery and protecting a syndicate	12 years
Guo Sheng	Police Officer	Bribery and protecting a syndicate	13 years
Huang Daiqiang	Deputy Director Criminal Police Division Chongqing Municipal Police Bureau	Bribery and protecting a syndicate	20 years
Li Hanbin	Chief Chongqing Municipal Bureau of Justice	Accepting bribes	16 years
Liu Hanbain	Police officer	Bribery and protecting a syndicate	
Luo Li	Deputy Chief Anti-Narcotics Brigade Chongqing Municipal Public Security Bureau	Bribery and protecting a syndicate	Death
Mao Jianping	Deputy Chief Chongqing Municipal Procuratorate	Bribery and protecting a syndicate	
Peng Changjian	Deputy Chief Municipal Public Security Bureau		Life in prison
Su Yang	Police officer	Bribery and protecting a syndicate	3 years 6 months

(*Continued*)

TABLE 11.1 (Continued)

Name	*Position*	*Charge*	*Sentence*
Wen Qiang	Director Chongqing Municipal Judicial Bureau, former Deputy Director Chongqing Public Security Bureau	Accepting bribes	Death
Wu Xiaoqing	Director Enforcement Bureau Chongqing Municipal Higher People's Court	Accepting bribes	Committed suicide
Xie Dejiu	Director Beibei District Public Security Bureau	Accepting bribes	
Xie Gang	Deputy Head Economic Crime Unit, Chongqing Police	Bribery and protecting a syndicate	20 years
Yue Cun	Police Officer Nan'an District	Protecting a criminal syndicate	Death
Zhang Tao	Vice President Chongqing Municipal High Court	Accepting bribes	Suspended Death
Zhao Liming	Deputy Director Public Transportation Security Police Division Chongqing Municipal Police	Bribery and protecting a syndicate	17 years 6 months

Source: See Figure 11.1.

In the wake of the Chongqing anti-organized crime drive, the regime seemed to back off its attack on organized crime and dirty law enforcement officers linked to criminal gangs. In 2018, Xi ordered a new drive (Organized Crime and Corruption Reporting Project 2019, *The Economist* 2019). Over the next three years, according to Guo Shengkun, Secretary of the Central Politics and Law Committee, the authorities smashed over 3,600 mafia-style criminal syndicates and some 11,600 criminal gangs and arrested 242,000 suspects. Guo claimed that the supervisory authorities had investigated 115,813 officials for possible involvement in criminal gangs of which 80,649 received administrative punishments and 10,342 were remanded to the Procuratorate for further investigation (Yang 2021). Indictments for protecting criminal syndicates—or acting as a "protective umbrella" in the parlance of the mainland Chinese-language media—show a clear uptick during 2019 and 2020 (see Figure 11.2).

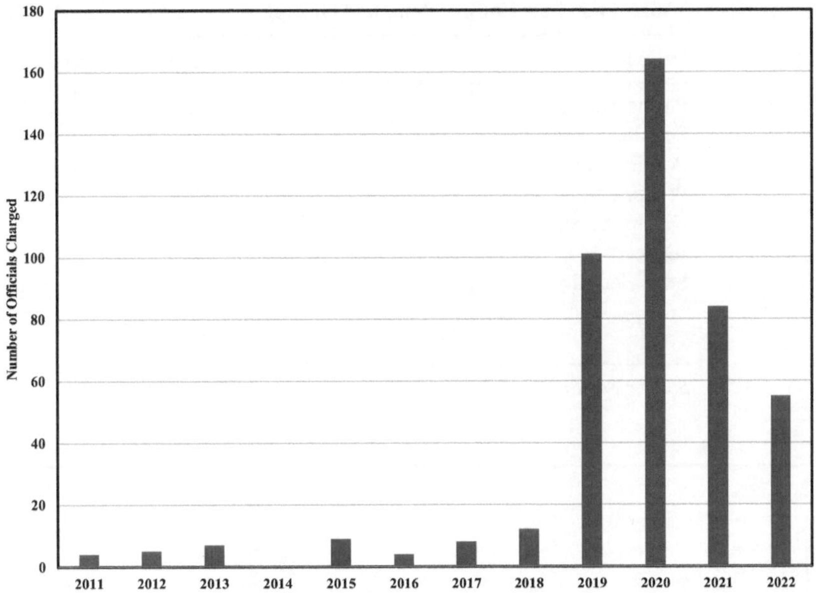

FIGURE 11.2 Protecting Criminal Syndicates

Source: See *Figure 11.1.*

While the drive against criminal syndicates and their police protectors revealed the existence of extensive street-level police corruption, from its inception, Xi's wider drive against corruption revealed serious corruption at higher levels in the security apparatus. It also revealed that corruption was not limited to the police. On the contrary, as the "tiger hunt" unfolded, investigators uncovered evidence of high-level corruption involving officials in the disciplinary, supervisory, and judicial systems.

Of the 301 officials and party cadres holding ranks at or above the vice-ministerial and vice-gubernatorial levels investigated, detained, and/or convicted on corruption-related charges between 2012 and April 2022, nearly one in six (17%) worked in either law enforcement or anti-corruption work (see Table 11.2 and Figure 11.3).[4] Early on, the primary target of the tiger hunt seemed to be Politburo Standing Committee Member Zhou Yongkang. Zhou, who had been Secretary of the Central Politics and Law Committee. Zhou was said to have been the man behind Chongqing Party Secretary Bo Xilai, who was caught up in a scandal involving the alleged murder of an English businessman by his wife Gu Kailai. Bo, it was argued, was taken down not so much for the murder or due to evidence that Gu was acting as a go-between for businesses seeking to influence Bo, but rather because he was part of an effort to either block Xi Jinping's selection as General Secretary or, according to unsubstantiated rumors, either assassinate Xi or overthrow him in a coup. Bo was, it was claimed, actually the front

TABLE 11.2 Law Enforcement, and Disciplinary Tigers

System	*Tigers*
Public Security	22
Peoples Court	12
Politics and Law	9
Procuratorate	3
Discipline Supervisory	3
Justice	2
State Security	1
Total	52

Source: *See Figure 11.1.*

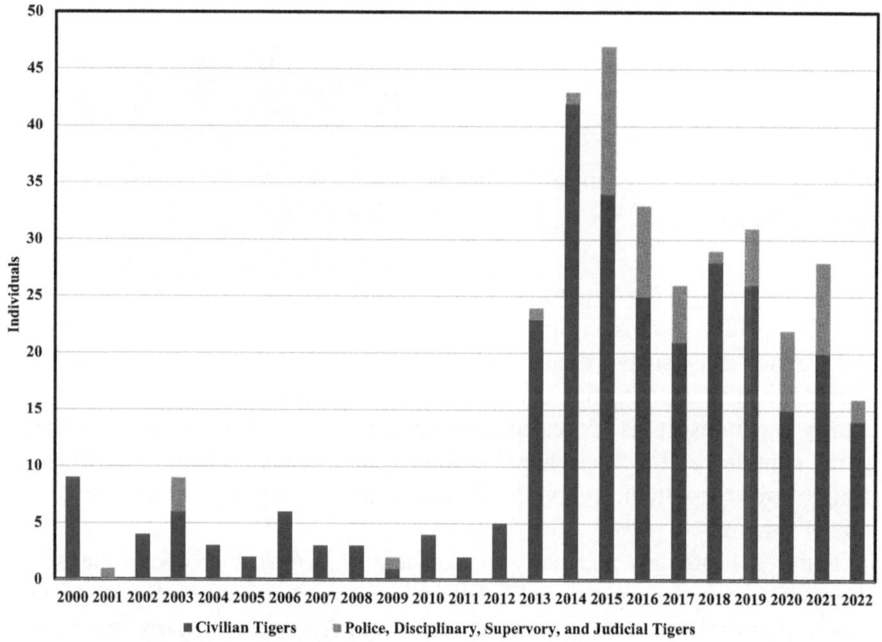

FIGURE 11.3 Senior Officials (Tigers) Detained

Source: See *Figure 11.1.*

man for a larger faction led by Zhou. Although due to retire at the upcoming 18th Party Congress, Zhou was a powerful man and was said to have a vast network of henchmen built during his service as General Manager of the Chinese National Petroleum Corporation (CNPC) (1996–1998); Minister for Land and Resources (1998–1999); Party Secretary of Sichuan Province (1999–2002); Minister for Public Security (2002–2007); Secretary of the Central Politics and Law Committee (2007–2012); and a member of the Politburo (2002–2007) and its Standing Committee (2007–2012).

Zhou was put under investigation in August 2014. Over the next several years, a series of senior officials in the Ministry for Public Security were detained. In December 2014, Li Dongsheng, a Vice Minister for Public Security, was detained.[5] Li was followed by Ma Jian, another Vice Minister for Public Security, in January 2015.[6] That same year, Yang Huanning, Vice Minister for Public Security and a former subordinate of Zhou, was demoted and transferred to the Work Safety Administration. The following year, Zhang Yue, who had served in the Ministry for Public Security under Zhou from 2003 to 2007 when he was transferred to Hebei province to head the provincial Public Security Bureau and serve as Secretary of the provincial Politics and Law Committee, was detained. In 2017, Chen Zhimin, yet another Vice Minister for Public Security with ties to Zhou, was sacked. Most of the senior officials with ties to Zhou who were taken down worked, however, outside of the public security apparatus and were tied to him through their service as subordinates during Zhou's time at CNPC and in Sichuan.

The focus on Zhou Yongkang notwithstanding, the weight of the attack on corruption in law enforcement early on seemed to fall on the Peoples Armed Police (PAP). In 2015, the CDIC remanded five senior PAP officers to the Procuratorate after concluding they were involved in corruption. A sixth, Major General Yin Zhishan, the commander of the Security Guards Bureau, the unit responsible for the security of the senior party and state leadership, was demoted without being specifically charged with corruption. In 2016, three more senior PAP officers were sidelined. Because most of the PAP cases were referred to the Military Procuratorate, few details are available on the offenses the CDIC suspected these officers of committing.[7]

As the crackdown unfolded between 2015 and 2017, current and former secretaries of the Hebei, Henan, and Liaoning political and law committees fell.[8] Senior judges in Guangxi, Jiangsu, and Yunnan, along with Li Xiaoming, Vice President of the Supreme People's Court, were accused of corruption. The directors of the Tianjin and Nei Menggu Public Security Bureaus were detained, as were Chen Xu, head of the Shanghai Procuratorate, and Zhang Huawei, an inspector for the CDIC.[9] Wu Aiying, the Minister for Justice, who some said had ties to Zhou Yongkang, stepped down and was then expelled from the National People's Congress in 2017.

As noted earlier, when Xi and Wang moved against Zhou Yongkang most of those linked to him worked outside the public security apparatus. There were rumors, however, that Zhou, Bo Xilai, and others were involved in a coup plot. The purported plan, however, seems implausible since it involved using PAP units stationed in Chongqing and military units based in Kunming. Kunming is 2,600 km from Beijing, the seat of political power in China, while Chongqing is 1,763 km from the capital—distances that would make the odds of a successful lightning seizure of power seem extremely remote (Google Maps 2022).

Talk of what might have been a somewhat more realistic attempt to assassinate Xi surfaced amidst a new series of arrests of senior officials in the public security apparatus that began in October 2018 with the detention of Meng Hongwei. Meng, who was a Vice Minister for Public Security, was arrested when he returned to China from Europe where he was serving as President of Interpol at the time. According to various sources, the investigation into Meng, who had served under Zhou Yongkang when Zhou was Minister for Public Security, led investigators to suspect Sun Lijun, another Vice Minister for Public Security. Sun, in turn, had ties to Meng Jianzhu, former Secretary of the Party Central Politics and Law Commission (2012–2017), having served as Meng's secretary when Meng was Minister for Public Security.

According to Willy Wo-lop Lam, Sun was part of a plot led by Luo Wenjin, Director of the General Criminal Investigation Brigade of the Jiangsu Provincial Public Security Bureau, that involved:

Wang Like, a member of the Standing Committee of the Jiangsu Provincial Party Committee and Secretary of the Jiangsu Party Politics and Law Committee;
Deng Huilin, Deputy Mayor of Chongqing;
Gong Dao'an, Deputy Mayor of Shanghai and Director of the Shanghai Public Security Bureau;
Yan Ming, Chair of the Proposals Committee of the Jiangsu Provincial People's Political Consultative Conference and former Deputy Party Secretary and Deputy Procurator of the Jiangsu Provincial Procuratorate; and
Lai Xiaomin, Chair of the China Huarong Asset Management Corporation.[10]

The plotters allegedly planned to assassinate Xi Jinping during a visit to Nanjing in 2017 (Lam 2021, 2022).

In the following months, additional members of the public security apparatus were linked to the plotters. In October 2021, Chen Yizhong, retired Deputy Director of the Jiangsu Provincial Public Security Bureau and a former subordinate of Wang Like, who was himself a former subordinate of Wang Lijun, the former Director of the Chongqing Public Security Bureau whose unsuccessful attempt to flee to the US Consulate in Chengdu in 2012 exposed the Bo Xilai case, was detained. The following month, Shen Haiqing, Deputy Mayor of Panjin City and Party Secretary and Director of the Panjin Municipal Public Security Bureau, was detained. In February 2021, Tan Xiaorong, Deputy Secretary of the Chongqing Municipal Party Politics and Law Commission, who had ties to Deng Huilin, was detained. In April 2022, Yao Changxu, Inspector for the Chongqing Public Security Bureau, was detained. Gong Dao'an was linked to Zhang Jian, Party Secretary and Director of the Technical Investigation Bureau (Number 12 Bureau) of the Ministry for Public Security, who was at the center of a 2010 case that allegedly involved an attempt to blackmail He Jintao, the son of former Politburo member He Guoqiang. Gong was also said to have served with Xiao Tianfu, Deputy Mayor of Xianning City and Director of the Xianning Municipal Public Security Bureau, Hubei, who was detained in January 2022. Zeng Xin, a member of the Standing Committee of the Guangxi Regional Party Politics and Law Committee, was also said to have been part of the Sun-Gong group.

The plot thickened further. In July 2020, Fu Zhenghua, the Minister for Justice and a former Vice Minister for Public Security, was detained. Fu had served under Zhou Yongkang when Zhou was Minister for Public Security but was rumored to have "sold out" to Xi Jinping after Zhou ordered Fu to withhold news of the death of Ling Jihua's son Ling Gu in a March 2012 car crash from Hu Jintao, Premier Wen Jiabao, and Xi Jinping. In April 2022, Fu was expelled from the party and branded a "political swindler" with "extremely inflated and despicable political ambitions" who had made "insidious comments about the party's major politics and directions" and "had for a long time made friends with a number of political liars." Fu was then linked to Sun Lijun's "political gang" and Meng Qingfeng, a Vice Minister for Public Security who was detained in 2020. Liu Xinyun, Vice Governor of Shanxi and Director of the Shanxi Provincial Public Security Department, was also said to be part of Sun's gang, as was Zeng Xin, a member of the Standing Committee of the Guangxi Regional Party Politics and Law Committee. Concurrently, Liu Yanping, who retired in 2014 after serving as a Vice Minister of Public Security and Director of the Guards Bureau, was detained in March 2021. Liu had served with Li Dongsheng, Meng Hongwei, and Fu Zhenghua and was accused of being part of the "Sun Gang."

There was also evidence of high-level corruption in the law enforcement and disciplinary system beyond the Sun Gang. Between 2019 and 2021, 13 other senior law enforcement and judicial officials were detained. With the exception of Gan Rongkun, Secretary of the Henan Provincial Party Politics and Law Committee, none of these appeared to have been connected to each other or the members of the alleged Sun Gang.[11] Six of those detained were provincial high court justices in Anhui, Hainan, Hebei, Jilin, Shandong, and Yunnan; two were secretaries of provincial politics and law committees in Henan and Jiangxi; two were senior prosecutors in Jilin and Qinghai; one was a senior official of the Supreme Court; one was a vice governor and director of the Liaoning Public Security Bureau; and one was an inspector for the CDIC.

As a percentage of all detentions, officials in the police, disciplinary, supervisory, and judicial systems increased nearly fourfold between 2017 and 2021, and the number of officials holding leading positions at the prefecture, city, and bureau levels shot up from 7 in 2020 to 63 in 2021, a ninefold increase (see Figure 11.4).

It is, of course, difficult to sort out how much of the allegations about a plot to assassinate Xi or the existence of a "gang" of current and former senior public security officials is fact and how much of the preceding is fiction. At bottom, however, the fact stands that a large number of senior public security officials whose careers have overlapped and many of who rose to senior posts during the years when Zhou Yongkang was Minister for Public Security and Secretary of the Central Politics and Law Committee, were accused of corruption. Even discounting the wilder rumors about nefarious plots and scheming, the data make clear that there has been a sharp intensification of the attack on corruption in the police, disciplinary, supervisory, and judicial sectors. The necessity for such an intensification suggests, in turn, that the regime's policing agencies, both those

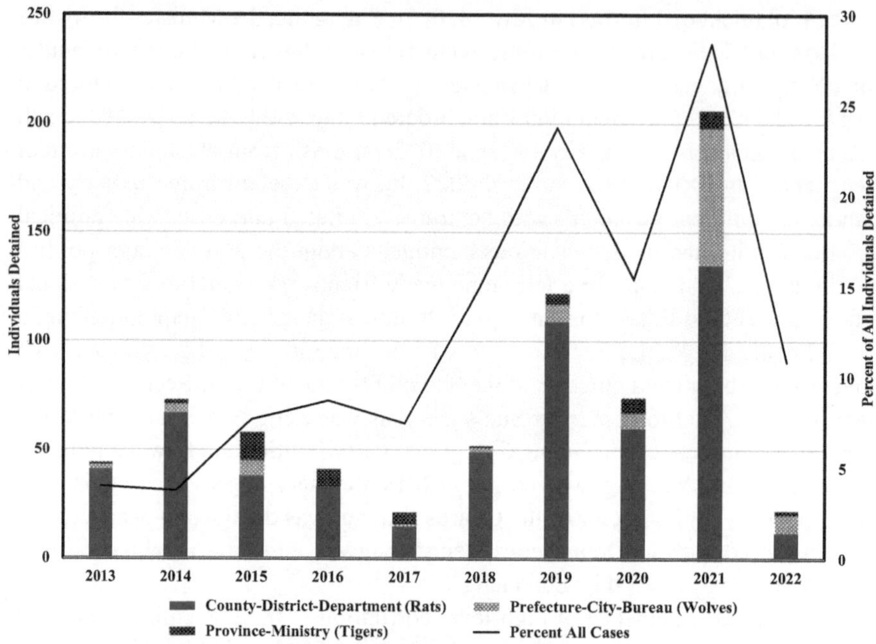

FIGURE 11.4 Police, Disciplinary, Supervisory, and Judicial Officials Detained

Source: See *Figure 11.1*.

Note: Following the Chinese media's tiger and fly labels for rank-and-file and top-rank officials, I have tagged leading officials at the county-district-department levels "rats" and those at the prefecture-city-bureau level "wolves."

tasked with policing China's citizenry, and, more importantly, the anti-corruption agencies tasked with policing the police and other corrupt officials are prone to corruption like other parts of the party state.

4. Conclusion

The law is only meaningful if it is obeyed and, if it is not obeyed, transgressors are brought to task, and those responsible for enforcing the law act properly and eschew corruption. Since the beginning of the reform period in the late 1970s, the party has worked to build up and improve China's legal system. At the end of the Maoist era, the party faced major gaps in the law (e.g., the absence of a promulgated criminal code) and a court system that was largely populated by former military officers who had little if any legal training and enforced the law according to their "sense" of justice and—of course—the prevailing political winds. The police were perhaps in better shape but operated without clear procedural rules and guidelines. Over the past four decades, the regime has filled in most of the gaps in the law, improved the training of judges, and professionalized the police.

The regime also re-established judicial and party agencies that had been set up in the 1950s to act as watchdogs but had been "pulverized" during the Cultural Revolution. Within the party, it set up a hierarchy of discipline inspection committees tasked with investigating malfeasance by party members, including those working as state officials and functionaries. The regime also rebuilt the Procuratorate, a judicial body charged with investigating and prosecuting cases involving criminal violations of China's anti-corruption statutes. In 1988, it formed the Ministry of Supervision that was to investigate violations of administrative regulations by state officials. The Ministry of State Supervision was soon folded into the discipline inspection system due to overlaps in their jurisdictions. After Xi Jinping ordered a new crackdown on corruption in 2013, the CDIC stepped up its use of on-the-spot inspections by teams dispatched from Beijing. In 2017–2018, the leadership formally merged the CDIC, the Ministry of Supervision, and the Anti-corruption bureau of the Procuratorate to form the National Supervisory Commission and put the commission in control over discipline inspection committees at all levels of government.

On paper, the result is a robust system that parallels both the party and state apparatus. But like any large, complex institution, the supervisory system is vulnerable to principal-agent problems that create room for misunderstanding, incompetence, and—of course—corruption. Xi Jinping's crackdown on corruption has, however, revealed that not only are the law enforcement agencies not corruption free, in some localities, the police are actively in league with criminal syndicates and criminal gangs. More critically, the crackdown has also uncovered evidence of corruption at the top of the police and judicial agencies and within the the supervisory agencies the regime set up to police the police and officials. Given the structural challenges and evidence of corruption in the anti-corruption agencies, it is perhaps not surprising; therefore, in the first quarter of 2022, nearly a decade after Xi vowed to smash corruption, the investigators detained yet another 17 senior officials.

APPENDIX

Senior Police, Supervisory, and Disciplinary Officials Detained or Disciplined 2013–2022

Year	*Name and position*	*Organization*
2013	Zhou Yongkang (周永康), Member of the Politburo and Secretary of the Central Politics and Law Committee, former Minister for Public Security (accepting bribes, life in prison)	Politics and Law
2013	Li Dongsheng (李东生), Vice Minister of Public Security (accepting bribes, 15 years imprisonment)	Public Security
2014	Wu Changshun (武长顺), Vice Chairman of the Tianjin Municipal CPPCC and Director of the Tianjin Public Security Bureau (accepting bribes, suspended death sentence)	Public Security
2015	Major General Cai Guangliao (蔡广辽), Major General of the People's Armed Police and Deputy Secretary of the Guangdong Provincial Public Security Bureau (accepting bribes, 8 years imprisonment)	PAP
2015	Major General Liu Zhanqi (刘占琪), commander of the Traffic Police Division of the Peoples Armed Police (corruption, remanded to procuratorate)	PAP
2015	Major General Miao Guirong (缪贵荣), Chief Engineer of the Peoples Armed Police Communication Command Department (corruption, remanded to procuratorate)	PAP
2015	Major General Wang Xin (王信), Political Commissar Peoples Armed Police (corruption, investigated)	PAP

Year	*Name and position*	*Organization*
2015	Major General Qu Mutian (瞿木田), Deputy Commander of the Traffic Headquarters, People's Armed Police (corruption, remanded to the procuratorate)	PAP
2015	Major General Yin Zhishan (尹志山), Deputy Director of the Ministry of Public Security Guards Bureau (unknown, demoted)	PAP
2015	Ma Jian (Public Security 2015) (马建), Vice Minister of the Ministry of State Security (accepting bribes, life in prison)	Public Security
2015	Qiu Jin (邱进), Vice Minister for State Security (unknown, dismissed from office?)	State Security
2015	Zhao Liping (赵黎平), retired Director of the Nei Menggu Regional Public Security Bureau and Vice Chair of the Nei Menggu Regional People's Political Consultative Conference (accepting bribes and murder, death)	Public Security
2015	Yang Zhaomin (杨照民), Judge and Executive Secretary of the Yunnan Provincial High Court (accepting bribes, 13 years imprisonment)	People's Court
2015	Xi Xiaoming (奚晓明), Vice President of the Supreme People Court (accepting bribes, life in prison)	People's Court
2015	Yang Huanning (杨焕宁), Vice Minister for Public Security (disciplinary, demoted)	Public Security
2015	Lan Haining (兰海宁), Vice President of the Guangxi Regional High People's Court (accepting improper gifts, expelled from party and demoted)	People's Court
2016	Lieutenant General Wang Jianping (王建平), former commander of the People's Armed Police (accepting bribes, investigated)	PAP
2016	Lieutenant General Niu Zhizhong (牛志忠), Deputy Commander of the People's Armed Police and Alternate Member of the CCP Central Committee (corruption? expelled from the Party)	PAP
2016	Lieutenant General Dai Sujun (戴肃军), Deputy Commander of the Peoples Armed Police (unknown, dismissed from office?)	PAP
2016	Cao Weiping (曹卫平), Vice President of the Henan Provincial High Court (accepting bribes, 8 years imprisonment)	People's Court
2016	Su Hongzhang (苏宏章), Party Secretary of the Politics and Law Committee of the Liaoning Standing Committee (vote buying, 14 years in prison)	Politics and Law

(*Continued*)

(Continued)

Year	*Name and position*	*Organization*
2016	Zhang Yue (张越), Secretary of the Hebei Provincial Politics and Law Committee (accepting bribes, 15 years imprison)	Politics and Law
2016	Li Feng (李峰), Vice Chair of the Liaoning Provincial People's Congress and Secretary of the Liaoning Provincial Party Politics and Law Committee (accepting bribes and protecting a criminal syndicate, demoted)	Politics and Law
2016	Wu Tianjun (吴天君), Secretary of the Henan Provincial Politics and Law Committee (accepting bribes, 11 years imprisonment)	Politics and Law
2017	Chen Xu (陈旭), Director of the Shanghai People's Procuratorate (accepting bribe, life in prison)	Procuratorate
2017	Zhang Huawei (张化为), Inspector Central Discipline Inspection Commission (accepting bribes, 12 years imprisonment)	Discipline Inspection
2017	Chen Zhimin (陈智敏), Vice Minister for Public Security (unknown, dismissed from office)	Public Security
2017	Xu Qianfei (许前飞), President and Party Secretary of the Jiangsu Provincial High Court (investigated)	People's Court
2017	Wu Aiying (吴爱英) (f), former Minister of Justice (disciplinary, expelled from the party)	Justice
2018	Meng Hongwei (孟宏伟), Vice Minister for Public Security and President of Interpol (accepting bribes, 13 years 6 months imprisonment)	Public Security
2019	Zhang Jiahui (张家慧) (f), Vice President of the Hainan Provincial High Court (accepting bribes, 18 years imprisonment)	People's Court
2019	Yang Keqin (杨克勤), Party Secretary and Chief Procurator of the Jilin Provincial Procuratorate (accepting bribes, 13 years imprisonment)	Procuratorate
2019	Zhang Jian (张坚), Chief Justice of the Anhui Provincial High Court (accepting bribes and protecting a criminal syndicate, 15 years imprisonment)	People's Court
2019	Li Yong (李勇), Deputy Party Secretary and Vice President of the Shandong Provincial High Court (accepting bribes, 12 years 6 months imprisonment)	People's Court
2019	Zhao Shijie (赵仕杰), President of the Yunnan Provincial High Court (abuse of authority, probation)	People's Court

Year	*Name and position*	*Organization*
2020	Lu Hongmin (吕洪民), Vice President of the Jilin Provincial High Court, Changhun City, Jilin (accepting bribes, 10 years imprisonment)	People's Court
2020	Sun Lijun (孙力军), Vice Minister for Public Security (accepting bribes, suspended death)	Public Security
2020	Meng Qingfeng (孟庆丰), Vice Minister for Public Security, Beijing (dismissed from office?)	Public Security
2020	Gong Dao'an (龚道安), Deputy Mayor of Shanghai and Director of the Shanghai Public Security Bureau (Accepting bribes, life)	Public Security
2020	Dong Hong (董宏), Leader of Number 5 Group of the Investigation Office of the Central Discipline Inspection Commission (accepting bribes, suspended death)	Discipline Inspection
2020	Wang Like (王立科), member of the Standing Committee of the Jiangsu Provincial Party Committee and Secretary of the Jiangsu Party Politics and Law Commission (accepting bribes and protecting a criminal syndicate, arrested)	Politics and Law
2021	Fu Zhenghua (傅政华), Minister of Justice and former Vice Minister for Public Security (accepting bribes, suspended death)	Public Security and Justice
2021	Pan Jiahua (潘家华), Secretary of the Discipline Inspection Group of the Central Discipline Inspection Commission for the State Tobacco Monopoly Administrative (accepting bribes, indicted)	Discipline Inspection
2021	Meng Yongshan (蒙永山), Procurator of the Qinghai Provincial Procuratorate, Xining City, Qinghai (accepting bribes, 11 years imprisonment)	Procuratorate
2021	Gan Rongkun (甘荣坤), member of the Standing Committee of the Henan Provincial Party Committee and Secretary of the Henan Provincial Party Politics and Law Committee (accepting bribes, indicted)	Politics and Law
2021	Meng Xiang (孟祥), member of the Supreme People's Court Judicial Committee, and Director of the Executive Committee of the Supreme People's Court, Beijing (accepting bribes, arrested)	People's Court
2021	Zhao Zengguo (赵增国), Vice President of the Hebei Provincial High Court, Shijiazhuang City, Hebei (accepting bribes and embezzlement, remanded)	People's Court

(*Continued*)

(Continued)

Year	*Name and position*	*Organization*
2021	Zeng Xin (曾欣), member of the Standing Committee of the Guangxi Regional Party Politics and Law Committee, Nanning City, Guangxi (unknown, rumored)	Politics and Law
2021	Zhang Hongxing (张鸿星), Vice Governor Jiangxi, member of the Standing Committee of the Jiangxi Provincial Party Committee, and Secretary of the Jiangxi Provincial Party Politics and Law Committee (unknown, rumored)	Politics and Law
2022	Liu Yanping (刘严平), Vice Minister of Public Security, former Director of the Guards Bureau (discipine, under investigation)	Public Security
2022	Wang Dawei (王大伟), Vice Governor of Liaoning and Director of the Liaoning Provincial Public Security Bureau (discipline, under investigation)	Public Security

Source: Author's database.

Notes

1 Many of those serving at the village and neighborhood levels are not actually civil servants and do not receive salaries or benefits from the state. In the past, however, they were treated as if they were *de facto* public servants. In 2020, changes in the law formally designed them "public agents" (公职人员). See Wang and Mou 2021.

2 Between 2017 and 2022, central inspection teams visited Anhui, Chongqing, Gansu, Guangxi, Hubei, Jiangxi, Jilin, Nei Menggu, Shaanxi, and Yunnan four times; Beijing, Henan, Hunan, Liaoning, Qinghai, Shandong, Tianjin, Xinjiang, and Xizang, three times; Fujian, Guangdong, Guizhou, Hainan, Hebei, Heilongjiang, and Jiangsu, Ningxia, Shanghai, Shanxi, and Zhejiang twice; and Sichuan once.

3 A suspended death provides for a two-year reprieve after which, if a convict has served good time and cooperated with authorities, the sentence is commuted to life in prison, a term that allows for medical parole for ill and elderly convicts.

4 See the Appendix at the end of this chapter for a full list of the "tigers" in the law enforcement and disciplinary sectors.

5 Li had been a senior producer at Chinese Central Television (CCTV) prior to being transferred to the Ministry for Public Security in 2009. Li was rumored to have introduced Zhou to Jia Jiayu, a CCTV reporter and producer, who became Zhou's second wife after Zhou's first wife was killed in a car accident.

6 Ma was linked by various sources to not only Zhou, but also Ling Jihua, who was widely seen as retired General Secretary Hu Jintao's right hand and a candidate for election to the Politburo at the 18th Party Congress before his son was killed in an early morning car accident involving an expensive Ferrari; and Zeng Qinghong, retired Politburo Standing Committee member, Secretary of the Central Committee's Organizational Department, and a close ally of retired party Secretary General Jiang Zemin In addition to being associated with Zhou Yongkang, Ma allegedly had ties to Guo Wengui, a billionaire real estate developer who fled to the US as investigators closed in him with a host of questions about his financial dealing and times to a range of potentially criminal schemes.

7 Criminal investigations and trials are conducted by the military and only rarely do details about the charges against PLA and PAP officers or the disposition of their case surface in the media.

8 In both Liaoning and Henan, two current and former secretaries were removed.
9 Zhao Liping, retired director of the Nei Menggu Public Security, was convicted of accepting Y23,5800 in bribes and murdering his mistress when she threatened to expose him. Zhao was executed in 2017.
10 In January 2021, Lai was executed after being convicted of accepting Y1,79 billion in bribes between 2008 and 2018.
11 A source suggested the Gan had connections to Lai Xiaomin because both are native of Jiangxi and both attended the Jiangxi University of Finance and Economics. As such, the connection seems circumstantial rather than substantial.

References

Broadhurst, Roderic. 2012. "Black Societies and Triad-Like Organized Crime in China." In *Routledge Handbook of Transnational Organized Crime*, edited by Fella Allum and Stan Gilmou, 157–76. New York: Routledge.

———. 2013. "The Suppression of Black Societies in China." *Trends in Organized Crime* 16: 95–113.

Caixin. 2014. "Caixin Explains: Central Committee Discipline Inspection Teams." *Caixin*, July 29, 2014. www.caixinglobal.com/2014-07-29/caixin-explains-central-committee-discipline-inspection-teams-101013177.html.

Chen, An. 2009. "Secret Societies and Organized Crime in Contemporary China." *Modern Asian Studies* 39 (1): 77–97.

China Daily. 2017. "Facts and Figures on CCP Discipline Inspection Work." *China Daily*, October 3, 2017.

The Economist. 2019. "China is Waging a Nationwide Campaign Against Gang Crime." *The Economist*, March 3, 2019. Accessed April 8, 2022. www.economist.com/china/2019/02/28/china-is-waging-a-nationwide-campaign-against-gang-crime.

Gong, Ting. 2008. "The Party Discipline Inspection in China: It Evolving Trajectory and Embedded Dilemmas." *Crime, Law and Social Change* 49 (2): 130–52.

Gong, Ting. 2010. "The Institutionalization of Party Discipline In China: Dynamics and Dilemmas." In *Preventing Corruption in Asia: Institutional Design and Policy Capacity*, edited by Ting Gong and Stephen K. Ma, 86–102. New York: Routledge.

Google Maps. Accessed April 13, 2022. www.google.com/maps/dir/Kunming,+Yunnan,+China/Beijing,+China/@30.0303379,101.0016299,4.45z/data=!4m14!4m13!1m5!1m1!1s0x36d083c31227d3cb:0xccb1f3a4984f0a36!2m2!1d102.83322!2d24.8796599!1m5!1m1!1s0x35f05296e7142cb9:0xb9625620af0fa98a!2m2!-1d116.407395!2d39.904211!3e0 and www.google.com/search?q=distance+chongqing+to+beijing&rlz=1C1GCEU_enUS822US822&oq=distance+chongqing+to+beijing&aqs=chrome.69i57j0i22i30j0i39014.10545j0j7&sourceid=chrome&ie=UTF-8.

Guo, Yong. 2012. "The Evolvement of the Chinese Communist Party Discipline Inspection Commission in the Reform Era." *China Review*: 1–13.

———. 2013. "Controlling Corruption in the Party: China Central Discipline Inspection Commission." *China Quarterly* 219: 567–624.

Herson, Lawrence J. R. 1957. "China's Imperial Bureaucracy: Its Direction and Control." *Public Administration Review* 17 (1): 44–53.

Ho, Norman. 2012. "Organized China in China: The Chongqing Crackdown." In *Law Policy for China's Market Socialism*, 202–2014, edited by John Garrick. New York: Routledge.

Hucker, Charles O. 1951. "The Traditional Chinese Censorate and The New Peking Regime." *American Political Science Review* 45 (4): 1041–57.

———. 1966. *The Censorial System of Ming China*. Stanford, CA: Stanford University Press.

———. 1998. “Ming Government.” In *Cambridge History of China, Volume 8 the Ming Dynasty*, edited by Denis C. Twitchett and Frederick W. Mote, 9–105. New York: Cambridge University Press.

Lam, Willy Wo-Lap Lam. 2021. “Xi Facing Opposition on Different Fronts in Run-Up to Key Party Plenum.” *China Brief*, September 23, 2021. Accessed April 13, 2022. https://jamestown.org/program/xi-facing-opposition-on-different-fronts-in-run-up-to-key-party-plenum/.

———. 2022. “As Rival Factions Gain Traction, Xi Seeks to Secure Support From the Military.” *The Jamestown Foundation*, January 1, 2022. Accessed April 13, 2022. https://jamestown.org/program/as-rival-factions-gain-traction-xi-seeks-to-secure-support-from-the-military/.

Li, Li, and Wang Peng. 2019. “From Institutional Interaction to Institutional Integration: The National Supervisory Commission and China New Anti-corruption Model.” *China Quarterly* 240: 967–89.

Ling, Li. 2017. “The Rise of the Discipline and Inspection Commission 1927–2012: Anti-corruption Investigation and Decision-Making in the Chinese Communist Party.” *Modern China* 42 (5): 447–82.

Lo, Shiu Hing. 2016. *The Politics of Controlling Organized Crime in Greater China*. New York: Routledge.

Organized Crime and Corruption Reporting Project. 2019. “Crime Crackdown Campaign a Success, Says China.” February 2, 2019. Accessed April 8, 2022 www.occrp.org/en/daily/9192-crime-crackdown-campaign-a-success-says-china.

Rowe, William T. 2010. *China's Last Empire: The Great Qing*. Cambridge, MA: Harvard University Press.

Walker, Richard L. 1947. “The Control System of the Chinese Government.” *The Far Eastern Quarterly* 7 (1): 2–21.

Wang, Erik H. 2022. *Frightened Bureaucrats: The Problem of China's Anti-corruption Campaign*. Unpublished manuscript.

Wang, Juan, and Yu Mou. 2021. “The Paradigm Shift in the Disciplining of Village Cadres in China: From Mao to Xi.” *China Quarterly* 248 (S1): 181–199.

Wang, Peng. 2013. “The Rise of the Red Mafia in China: A Case Study of Organized Crime and Corruption in Chongqing.” *Trends in Organized Crime* 16 (1): 49–73.

———. 2017. The Chinese Mafia: Organized Crime, Corruption, and Extra-Legal Protection. New York: Oxford University Press.

Wedeman, Andrew. 2013. “The Challenge of Commercial Bribery and Organized Crime in Mainland China.” *Journal of Contemporary China* 22 (79): 18–34.

Wong, Kam C. 1998. “A Reflection on Police Abuse of Power in the People's Republic of China.” *Police Quarterly* 1 (2): 77–112.

Xia, Ming. 2008. “Organizational Formations of Organized Crime in China: Perspectives From the State, Market, and Networks.” *Journal of Contemporary China* 17 (54): 1–22.

Yang, Zekun. 2022. “Gang Crime Crackdown Successful.” *China Daily*, March 31, 2021. Accessed April 8, 2022. www.chinadaily.com.cn/a/202103/31/WS6063c908a31024ad0bab2a6f.html.

Yeo, Yukyung. 2014. “Complementing the Local Discipline Inspection Commissions of the CCP: Empowerment of Central Discipline Inspection Commission.” *China Quarterly* (219): 597–624.

Zhou, Na. 2018. “The National Supervisory Commission from Xi Jinping's Anti-Corruption Campaign.” *East Asian Policy* 10 (4): 79–80.

12

LEGALITY OF REPRIMAND AND CONTEST OF PUBLIC TRUST AMID THE PANDEMIC

The Case of the Inadvertent Whistleblower Li Wenliang

Bin Liang

Introduction

Major public emergencies and crises often present significant challenges to a regime beyond natural disasters. As people tie their evaluation of a government to its capability to handle these crises, how the authorities face and manage such crises carries a significant impact on citizens' political trust, especially in nations such as China where citizens lack effective avenues to voice their concerns (Ma and Christensen 2019; Wu, Yang, and Chen 2017). The Covid-19 pandemic, first broke out in Wuhan, China, in December 2019, presented such a major public health crisis.

This study examines the experience of Li Wenliang, a Chinese doctor at Wuhan Central Hospital (WCH) who tried to warn his fellow colleagues about a possible outbreak of an unknown virus in December 2019. Nevertheless, he was summoned by the local police and reprimanded for publicizing untrue statements. Li subsequently contracted the virus at work and passed away. What was unexpected, to both Li himself and the Chinese authorities, was the strong public outrage after Li's reprimand and death were publicized. The masses embraced Li as a whistleblower who sacrificed his own life for the public, strongly questioned the legitimacy of the police reprimand, and criticized China's tight information control and surveillance. Facing the public pressure, the central government intervened promptly, forced the local police to rescind its reprimand, and labeled Li as an official martyr (烈士).

This study focuses on two major issues in Li's case. First, I focus on the legality of the police reprimand meted out against Li. Although the central government rejected the reprimand after conducting its own investigation, the rationales were not detailed in its official report (see the following discussion). Scholars, in post

DOI: 10.4324/9781003294887-15

hoc analysis, questioned the legality of the reprimand due to its lack of legal basis. However, it would be very unlikely, if not impossible, to ask lay people including the highly educated such as Li to challenge the legality of daily operations of the powerful Chinese police. Second, there is little doubt that the unexpected public trust challenge generated in Li's case played a determinant role in reversing the police sanction against Li. Thus, I focus on trust issues at different levels in this case and show how complex and interactive relations of multiple groups of players collectively helped contest the legality of Li's sanction.

My analysis relies on open source information, besides academic publications. To generate relevant reports and articles in Chinese, two major Chinese search engines were utilized, including the most popular Chinese search engine, baidu.com (百度), and an academic search engine, the China Knowledge Resource Integrated Database (www.cnki.net/, 中国知网). In terms of the sources, Baidu search results mainly consisted of the following types of documents: 1) reports from official agencies; 2) newspaper reports and articles; 3) articles published on popular or lesser known websites; 4) individual blogs; and 5) entries from discussion forums (e.g., tianya.cn 天涯社区). In comparison, the English search results are primarily from Western mainstream media. Multiple data sources are cross-checked to ensure the accuracy of the facts discussed later.

In the remainder of this chapter, I first review Li's case in detail and document the chain of events, and discuss the legality of the police reprimand against Li. Next, I turn to issues of public trust, briefly review the relevant literature, and provide a detailed analysis of trust issues at three different levels in Li's case. Lastly, in the conclusion section, I draw some important lessons from this study.

1. Reprimand of Li Wenliang, the Inadvertent Whistleblower

Li would likely have remained an unknown doctor but for the pandemic. Born in Beizhen (北镇) city in Liaoning province in 1985, Li studied clinical medicine at Wuhan University. After graduation, he worked in Xiamen for three years before he took a position as an ophthalmologist at WCH in 2014. The outbreak of the pandemic changed Li's fate. With cases being reported and diagnosed in December 2019, Li circulated several messages via the Chinese messaging app WeChat on December 30 and warned his fellow medical school alumni of a possible "SARS-like" epidemic. Specifically, at 17:43 local time, Li texted "There are seven confirmed cases of SARS at Huanan Seafood Market," posted a picture of a diagnosis report and a video of CT scan results, and added, "They are being isolated in the emergency department of our hospital's Houhu (后湖) Hospital District." At 18:42, someone from the WeChat group warned, "Be careful, or else our chat group might be shut down." Li texted back "The latest news is, it has been confirmed that they are coronavirus infections, but the exact virus is being subtyped," "Don't circulate the information outside of this group; tell your family and loved ones to take precautions," and another long message describing coronaviruses in different years.[1] The report Li cited was originated from Ai Fen (艾芬), director of the emergency department at WCH, who became alarmed after receiving laboratory results of a patient. Clearly, Li's circulation meant to be private and aimed to protect fellow colleagues and their family members.

The warning of his colleague seemed to have foreseen the forthcoming discipline, as Li's messages quickly spread to the public. On December 31, officials at WCH had a talk with Li and blamed him for leaking the information, and Li had to write a self-critique (认识材料) afterward. On January 3, 2020, police from the Zhong Nan Lu division of the Wuchang Municipal Public Security Bureau (武昌分局中南路派出所) of the Wuhan Public Security (WPS) summoned Li to the police station, issued a formal written reprimand (the so-called "reprimand letter," 训诫书), and censured him for publishing untrue statements about SARS cases that disturbed public order. Reportedly, Li was one of eight people who were criticized and disciplined for "spreading rumors."

Li was subdued but continued his work. On January 8, Li contracted the coronavirus while treating an infected patient and developed symptoms of coughing and fever on January 10. On January 12, he was admitted to WCH, quarantined and treated, and then tested positive on January 31. His condition deteriorated in early February and Li passed away on February 7 at the age of 33. Li's parents were also infected with the virus but fully recovered. Li is survived by a son and his wife, who was pregnant during Li's ordeal. Their second son was born on June 12, 2020.

Li's popularity continued to grow as his noncompliant experience and the discipline he received were publicized. During his struggle with the virus in the hospital, he communicated with family members and friends via social media and held interviews with the media. In his interviews, Li shared that he did not believe what he circulated was a rumor, as it meant to call for precaution (Liu 2020). He mentioned that "If the officials had disclosed information about the epidemic earlier, I think it would have been a lot better," "There should be more openness and transparency," and "I think a healthy society should not have just one voice" (Green 2020). It is during this process that he transformed into a public figure and was labeled a "whistleblower."

With public support growing for Li, a series of revisions was taken by the Chinese authorities. As early as January 28, an article was published on the official WeChat account of the Chinese Supreme People's Court (SPC) that addressed issues related to the alleged eight Wuhan "rumor mongers" (see the full article cited in Tang 2020). The article pointed out that what the rumor mongers spread was *not* entirely false, and "it might have been a fortunate thing if the public had believed the 'rumors' then and started to wear masks and carry out sanitization measures, and avoid wild animal markets." It further clarified what kinds of rumors should be (legally) punished and called for information transparency and more tolerance for disinformation. On February 7 (the day when Li passed away), the National Supervisory Commission (国家监察委员会, NSC), the country's highest anti-corruption agency, announced its decision to investigate Li's death, and the Wuhan municipal government and the National Health Commission (国家卫生健康委员会) issued condolences to Li's family. The NSC released its investigation report on March 19, concluded that the WPS's reprimand was inappropriate, and encouraged an official revocation (NSC Investigation Team 2020a).[2] On the same night, the WPS rescinded its reprimand against Li, made an apology to Li's family, and sanctioned two officers (including one deputy chief) from the police station where Li was summoned. Besides financial compensation and support estimated at millions of yuan,[3] Li received a number of prestigious honors posthumously. For instance, on April 2, 2020, Li and 13 other front-line workers who died in the fight against Covid-19 were declared "official martyrs," the highest title of honor given to those who sacrificed their lives for the nation; on April 20, he was awarded the "May 4th Chinese Youth Medal."

2. Legality of Li's Reprimand

Once the case broke out, the legitimacy of Li's reprimand was heatedly debated. The reprimand letter is widely available online (see, e.g., Luo 2020). The letter was typed on a piece of letterhead paper: the first part of the letter filled Li's name, sex, date of birth, ID number, address, and workplace; the next underlined section summarized Li's "illegal behavior" (违法行为) as "(Li) circulated untrue statements about seven confirmed SARS cases from the Huanan Fruit and Seafood Market in a WeChat group on December 30, 2019." The section immediately below typed,

> Per law, (We) now give you a warning and reprimand because of your illegal behavior regarding the untrue statements circulated online. Your behavior seriously disturbed public order. Your behavior went beyond the legal limits, violating relevant regulations in the Law of the People's Republic of China on Penalties for Administration of Public Security (中华人民共和国治安管理处罚法, the *Administrative Penalty Laws*), thus an illegal behavior!

In the next section, two specific questions followed: one asked Li to "listen to the reprimand by the police, and stop (his) illegal behavior. Can you do it?"; the other warned that "If you continue (your) illegal behavior, you will receive legal punishment! Do you understand?" Li answered, in his own handwriting, "Yes (能)" and "Understood (明白)" and stamped them with his own fingerprints. The last section of the letter showed Li's signature (again, with his fingerprint) and the date, the names of the two offices in charge, and the seal of the Wuchang Municipal Public Security Bureau of the WPS on top of the date (in which the year was filled as 2029 by mistake).

Regarding the legitimacy of the reprimand, the NSC investigation report released on March 19 used very general terms indeed: the last paragraph of the report merely stated that

> because the reprimand letter issued by the Zhong Nan Lu division is not appropriate and the law enforcement is improper, the investigation team has already advised that the supervisory bodies of Wuhan city, Hubei province correct the matter and encourage the police to rescind the reprimand and hold involved personnel accountable, and publicize decisions accordingly.
> *(NSC Investigation Team 2020a)*

Though the report went over in detail the chain of events in Li's case, it did not discuss specifically *why* and *how* the reprimand was inappropriate.

The gap was filled by scholarly discussions. First, it is pointed out that the reprimand lacked proper legal basis. For instance, Li and Jin (2020) focused on the term "reprimand" and found that the way "reprimand" was stipulated in all existing laws and regulations *did not* apply and *could not* be applied to Li's case. For instance, Article 9 of the Regulations of the People's Republic of China on Administrative Penalties for Public Security (治安管理处罚条例) (the *Regulations*), adopted in 1986, stipulated that

> Acts violating the administration of public security committed by a person between fourteen and eighteen years of age shall be given relatively light penalties; acts violating the administration of public security committed by a person under fourteen shall be exempted from penalties, but a *reprimand* may be given and his guardian shall be instructed to subject the offender to strict discipline.

The *Regulations* was replaced by the *Administrative Penalty Laws* in 2006. However, the *Administrative Penalty Laws* no longer carries rules on "reprimand" per se, thus providing no legal basis for its practice. Note that the targets of police's reprimand in the *Regulations* were juveniles only. This power of reprimand is apparently transferred to the Law of the People's Republic of China on Prevention of Juvenile Delinquency (预防未成年人犯罪法), first adopted in 1999 (see Articles 37, 49, and 50) and last amended in 2020 (Articles 41 and 61). Nevertheless, the reprimand thus stipulated still cannot be applied to Li, an adult. In the same vein, Li and Jin (2020) pointed out that police reprimand power stipulated in other existing laws and regulations such as the Community Correction Law (社区矫正法, Article 28), the Letters and Visits Regulations (信访条例, Article 47), the Regulations on Administration of Security Services (保安服务管理条例, Article 45), the Detention Facility Regulations (拘留所条例, Article 23), and Public Security Organs' Management of Compulsory Isolation and Drug Treatment Centers (公安机关强制隔离戒毒所管理, Article 36) could not be applied to Li either due to the limited scopes and specific targets of these laws and regulations. Further, scholars made it clear that it was improper for the police to cite the *Administrative Penalty Laws* specifically in Li's reprimand letter. Though not mentioned in the letter, the clause that would have suited Li's case is Article 25 which regulates people who "intentionally disturb public order by spreading rumors, making false reports of dangerous situations or epidemic situations, raising false alarms or by other means." The available penalties stipulated in Article 25, however, include detention (no more than 10 days) and/or a fine (no more than 500 yuan) only, but not reprimand (Li and Jin 2020). Luo (2020) further argued that the use of the letterhead paper itself for reprimand purposes by the Wuhan police lacked proper legal basis and authorization.

Second, even if Article 25 of the *Administrative Penalty Laws* contained "reprimand" as a possible penalty, scholars argued that it would not have been properly applied to Li's case because Li did not have the intention (mens rea) to "spread rumors or disturb public order," and his behavior (actus reus) was not spreading "rumors or untrue statements" and carried no impact of "disturbing public disorder" (Yang 2020). In fact, as mentioned earlier, the SPC's open letter issued on January 28 suggested that it would have been fortunate if people heeded Li's warning and took precautions early. The claim that Li's behavior disturbed public order was thus not supported by facts substantively, and procedurally, the conclusion was drawn hastily without conducting proper investigations such as conferring with proper authorities and professional experts. Ironically, the decision was imposed by the police on a medical doctor who was discussing the nature of a new virus with colleagues (Yang 2020). Third, scholars noticed the impact of the reprimand on Li, including damage to his reputation (e.g., being summoned and sanctioned by police still carries a strong negative impact on the affected individual in Chinese society), infringement of his freedom of speech right, and potential negative impact on his work (Yang 2020).

Last but not least, after concluding that the police reprimand in Li's case lacked legitimacy, scholars proposed to revise laws and regulations (e.g., the *Administrative Penalty Laws*) accordingly. Despite its misuse in Li's case, the consensus is seemingly to keep and legitimize the reprimand power (e.g., explicitly adding it as one form of punishment in laws and regulations, Li and Jin 2020). Although scholars argued that the spirit of key legal principles such as "Everything which is not forbidden is allowed (for individual citizens); everything which is not allowed is forbidden (for governmental branches)" (see, e.g., Laws 2017, 368) and "nulla poena sine lege (no penalty without law)" should be observed (Li and Jin 2020; Yang 2020), their reform proposals rarely discussed how to *check and curb* the reprimand power in practice. Rather, most scholars debated on the legal nature of the reprimand and expressed concerns about the lack of proper legal remedies once a wrongful reprimand is meted out such as what had happened in Li's case (e.g., Wang 2021; Zhou and Li 2021). In particular, Yi (2020) questioned if police possessed too much power in exercising reprimands which might lead to its abuse in daily practice, and called for setting up a hearing system (which would allow the reprimanded subject to voice his or her opinions before a decision is made) and post hoc compensation in case of wrongful decisions (126–27). A real question, not addressed by Chinese scholars, is how lay people including the highly educated such as Li would have the legal consciousness, resources, and willingness to challenge police discretion when police exercise broad power in China, either stipulated or unstipulated by laws and regulations. One real concern is that the formalization of powers such as the power to reprimand, as suggested, may actually defeat the purpose of "limiting governmental powers and protecting citizens' rights and freedoms." To date, no formal actions have been taken to reform the reprimand power by the Chinese legislature.

3. Public Trust and Its Unique Features in China

What was not expected, from both Li himself and the Chinese authorities, was the strong backlash from the public against Li's reprimand, thus representing a round of public trust crisis (Li and Jin 2020; Yi 2020). A rich body of Western literature has shown that political trust is a multi-level concept (for a review, see Citrin and Stoker 2018; Levi and Stoker 2000). Dalton (1999), for instance, classifies political trust into five categories based on the trust subject, including trust for political community, regime principles, regime performance, regime institutions, and political actors. Compared to other subjects, more studies have been devoted to institutional trust and tried to explain varying institutional trust levels with institutional and cultural theories (e.g., Mishler and Rose 1997, 2001; Wong, Wan, and Hsiao 2011). While institutional explanations hold that trust in institutions is based on people's evaluations of institutional performance, cultural theories suggest that institutional trust has its origins in political culture, and values and attitudes of the people, thus exogenous to political institutions.

Studies of political trust in China displayed a number of unique features. First, in contrast to the declining trust level among Western democratic nations (e.g., Citrin and Stoker 2018), China continued to display a high level of institutional trust (e.g., Wang 2005; Yang and Tang 2010), albeit more recent studies showed some signs of declining (Wang and You 2016; Wu, Li, and Song 2020; Zhao and Hu 2017). Scholars attributed such high levels of political trust in China to different institutional and cultural factors. Institutionally, China's strong economic performance in the last four decades was credited (Wang 2005; Yang and Tang 2010), although rising inequality and corruption, byproducts of China's economic development, also generated distrust toward the central and local governments (Chen 2017; Lei 2020; Yang and Xin 2020; Zhu, Lu, and Shi 2013). Culturally, scholars examined the impact of traditional Chinese culture and values on institutional trust such as people's orientations toward power and authority (e.g., paternalism, authoritarianism) and conflict (e.g., harmony) (Shi 2001; Yang and Tang 2010).

Second, studies consistently found a higher trust level in China's central government than the local governments, the so-called "hierarchical trust" (Li 2004, 2016; Zhong 2014). Again, scholars attributed China's hierarchical trust to different factors such as China's culture, its control over the media, and its political strategies (Li 2013, 2016; Liu and Raine 2016; Wu and Wilkes 2018). Third, given China's size, the divide between the rural and the urban caught scholars' attention. Researchers identified both common and distinctive factors that affected public trust in urban and rural China (Lo et al. 2016; Zhao and Hu 2017; Zhong 2014). Indeed, China has adopted different strategies to manage rural and urban issues. For instance, village elections in rural China aimed, among other purposes, to boost villagers' trust in the authorities and produced some positive effects (Heberer and Schubert 2011; Manion 2006; Tao et al. 2011).

Last but not least, the media effect on political trust received scholarly attention given China's information control. The effect of media control and official propaganda, however, is less clear, depending upon factors such as the timing of the reporting, the subject matter being reported, and the type and nature of the media (e.g., traditional media vs. social media). The arrival of the digital age and the use of social media have transformed information dissemination in China. In response, the Chinese government adapted to the challenges, built its censorship and surveillance, and took advantage of the new technology to engage the public via strategies such as agenda setting and issue framing (King, Pan, and Roberts 2013, 2017; Lorentzen 2014).

One unsettled issue in this field is the relationship between political trust and social (generalized interpersonal) trust (Braithwaite 1998; Levi and Stoker 2000). Building upon Putnam's conceptual framework (1995) that defined social trust as a form of social capital, scholars explored the "spill over" effect of interpersonal trust on institutional trust (e.g., Keele 2007; Mishler and Rose 2001; You 2012). In the context of China, survey studies found a positive correlation between interpersonal and institutional trust, but the causal order was more complexed: while some (Liu and Raine 2016; Wang and You 2016) found that interpersonal trust could foster institutional trust, others (Ma and Christensen 2019; Steinhardt 2012; Tao et al. 2014) found vice versa. Further, scholars argued that it is necessary to distinguish varying levels of social trust in China (beyond a simple measure of 'trust of most people or strangers' typically adopted in survey studies) as traditional Chinese culture treated members of one's own group (in-groups) very differently from members of out-groups (Feng et al. 2016; Yang and Tang 2010). Such fine distinctions, however, are difficult to operate in survey studies as issues of trust are highly contextualized and often subject to change.

4. Contest of Public Trust in Li's Case

Li's case, incidentally, turned out to be a good study of trust, as trust issues at different levels involving different players played a prominent role. I argue that three levels of trust issues are evident in this case as follows. The first is interpersonal trust within Li's inner circle, mostly from his family, friends, and colleagues. Li had received broad support from his inner circles: he was not only loved by his family and friends but also endorsed by his colleagues.

His professional networks such as his WeChat groups functioned well to build alliances and group solidarity during the Covid-19 pandemic. Again, Li had no plan to be a public voice and a hero to start with. His initial warning was built upon trust within his intimate circles, reaching out to colleagues, friends, and their family members. Possibly foreseeing unwelcomed consequences, he called "not to circulate his warning." Nevertheless, his messages spread to the public and he was disciplined because his voice was different from the official voice,[4] and viewed as likely to generate panic and disrupt social order. Catering to the greater interest of society, Li's voice was labeled "rumor" and silenced by the local authorities.

The second level of trust is the social trust bonded between Li and the general public. The temporary submission of Li did not stop the deadly virus from spreading, and Li's experience landed him enormous trust and support from the public. The discipline he received and his death sparked public outrage, and countless citizens voiced their gratitude for Li and criticized the sanctions by the WPS and WCH administrators. Though there lacked details on how he was transformed, Li had become a public voice and a symbol of speaking up, the "whistleblower." His messages such as demanding more openness and transparency and tolerance of different voices echoed strongly both inside and outside China. Even after his death, his Sina Weibo account lived on with millions of followers[5] and was labeled the virtual "wailing wall" (哭墙) of China. Millions of people visited his blog and left comments after his last message dated February 1, 2020, when he wrote: "Today the test turns out to be positive. All finalized, [and] confirmed (今天核算检测结果阳性, 尘埃落定, 终于确诊了)." Visitors to his blog spoke to him about everything, and some called his site the "tree hollow" (树洞),[6] and more called him a brother, uncle, doctor, hero, comrade, martyr, and friend (Su 2020). Zhou and Zhong's study (2021) of visitors' comments suggests that the practice of public mourning and affective expression reconfigured both the relationship between the mourners and Li and the relationship among the mourners. Li's blog has become a unique place for affective publics with a distinct practice of collective memory (see also Cao, Zeng, and Evans 2021). One incident attested to its significance to Li's followers: on the night of June 19, 2020, some comments on his blog disappeared temporarily but were restored promptly after netizens brought the issue to the attention of Weibo tech support and pressed for restoration. Weibo explained that it happened due to a system error (Phoenix New Media 2020). Li's followers, nevertheless, warned Weibo not to delete their "memories," showing their determination to defend the wailing wall. One commentator wrote:

> A healthy society should not have just one voice; a healthy society should not have just one expression. Countless citizens share their daily thoughts under doctor Li Wenliang's historical posting. Even if it is called the wailing wall, what's wrong with it?!"
>
> *(cited in Xiao Siyao 2020)*

People embraced Li for a number of reasons. First, Li represented front-line medical workers who devoted themselves to the fight against the pandemic. In one interview, Li told the press that "After I recover, I still want to return to the front line," and "The epidemic is still spreading, and I don't want to be a deserter" (Buckley 2020). Second, he had inadvertently become the whistleblower who dared speak up with an independent voice despite the reprimand against him. His death gained him more public support. To his followers, he sacrificed his own life to save the world. One of Li's most popular Weibo postings was one that he addressed the rumor about the doom's day (December 21) in 2012. He wrote "Friends, maybe you won't be able to reach me tomorrow, because I'm off to save the earth. If the sun rises as normal on the 22, it means that I succeeded. Don't thank me, [because] it should be done! I'm here." Likely Li wrote this message to express a sense of humor, but his followers cited it as a tribute to his heroic effort to save the world (Su 2021). Third, yet too many, Li's "normal guy" persona and sense of duty transformed him into a household hero (Bociurkiw 2020). People commented on his daily lives, such as his favorite TV series and food, and his excitement after learning that he can have a second child.[7] One netizen wrote:

> Why are we so sad? Because Li Wenliang is ourselves! We would give in when facing the authorities, fear that the police will knock on our door, don't want to be a hero, but always want to protect those people nearby! . . . He is not a hero, but he is real. He is one of the numerous living beings, not great but a quiet and kind commoner. Therefore, when he cannot escape his fate, we are so sad!
>
> *(cited in First Director 2020).*

Despite his ascendance as a public figure and his calls for more transparency and tolerance of different voices, Li, being a pro-government Chinese Communist Party (CCP) member, remained a calm and positive character and never took a proactive and extreme approach in his "protest." His low-key character and mild approach to gradually improving one's life fit well into the government's propaganda and scheme. In addition, Li and his family deliberately shied away from overexposure and appraisal by the Western media. For instance, Li's wife wrote on her Weibo account in May 2020 that "Li is a CCP member and loves his country," carefully disengaging Li's association with foreign media and governments (Beijing Evening News 2020). This approach again aligned well with the government's propaganda. Li's mild and cooperative approach seemingly met different needs of the public and the government, thus turning him into an icon of public trust.

The third level of trust involves the contested political trust toward the Chinese authorities. Consistent with the past literature on "hierarchical trust" discussed earlier, distinctions should be made among governments at different levels, in particular the central government and the local governments. As noted, the Chinese central government often plays a benevolent role to correct errors of local governments and solve issues for the masses in major events in which political trust is facing a challenge (Baekkeskov and Rubin 2017; Li 2013). Li's case fits this pattern as the primary challenges in this case were aimed at the local authorities. Millions of people questioned the administrative sanctions meted out against Li by the Wuhan authorities. Indeed, Li's "misbehavior" (i.e., relaying materials via WeChat) could be easily related to by the masses who echoed Li's pain and suffering. It should be acknowledged that the local governments often have their special interests in consideration, albeit they generally serve the needs of the central government. The Wuhan municipal government, for example, may well have had legitimate interests (e.g., avoiding public panic) in its effort to shut down "rumors" on the brink of an unprecedented pandemic. Cai (2022) also pointed out that the Wuhan and Hubei local governments were simply following the central government's policy to maintain stability. Nevertheless, it backfired this time. The gravity of the pandemic and people's outrage with Li's sanction drew intervention by the central government, which once again played its savior role to correct errors of the local government(s). Facing challenges this time, the Chinese authorities took prompt actions and made a series of revisions to restore public trust. First, to answer the concerns of the public, the central government stepped in, conducted prompt investigations, and corrected errors by the local authorities. With his name cleared, Li was declared a martyr and set as an exemplary medical worker. Second, measures were taken to hold the "wrongdoers" accountable. Besides sanctions against the two WPS officers who sanctioned Li, actions were taken against those who tarnished Li's reputation. For instance, the China National Intellectual Property Administration (国家知识产权局) (2020) denied 37 applications that tried to utilize Li Wenliang's name in their trademark registrations for profit, and fines were meted out against businesses that did so in places such as Shanghai and Chengdu (Sina Financial 2020). Third, proactive efforts were taken to commemorate Li and other fallen heroes. On the traditional Tomb-Sweeping Festival day (清明) in 2020, for instance, national mourning was declared and flags flew at half-staff across the country with public recreational activities closed (Su 2020). Fourth, Li's case triggered revisions to relevant regulations. In October 2020, the National Health Commission released a draft of the Amendment of the Law on Prevention and Control of Infectious Diseases (中华人民共和国传染病防治法). Among others, one proposed change is Article 36, which recommended financial rewards be given to units and individuals who spot and report potential infectious diseases. Further, it proposes that such units and individuals shall *not* be held responsible even if their reporting is ruled out after investigation. People credited this proposal (and similar proposals at the local levels) to Li Wenliang (Ye 2020).

In sum, the complex interactions among key players at these three levels of trust played a determinant role in reversing police sanction against Li and helping his ascendance as an icon of public trust and a model medical worker amid the pandemic. Nevertheless, his experience might be rather singular as a result of the convergence of multiple factors such as the occurrence of the pandemic and his personal background and death that led to the public outrage. Questions remain about whether Li's experience can be replicated.

5. Conclusion

Li's case was tragic, though it made Li world-famous. In this chapter, I focused on the legality of the police reprimand against Li and the unexpected public trust challenge in reaction to Li's sanction and death. A number of lessons can be drawn on the basis of this study. First, Li's case attests to the flexible and sometimes undefined scope of policing power in China. Chinese police still exercise a tremendous amount of power with broad discretion but receive little supervision, especially when 'minor crimes' are involved (Biddulph 2018). There is evidence that such power, in various administrative forms (e.g., contract tracing, travel restriction, quarantine), has been broadened and expanded in the name of fighting the pandemic in the last two years. Albeit the legality of Li's reprimand was challenged successfully, Li's case prompted little systemic changes regarding censorship, information control, and broad policing power. In fact, some observers raised such concerns. For instance, on December 30, 2020, one netizen publicized an article to commemorate Li's reprimand and wrote,

> The reason why we commemorate Li's reprimand, albeit the NSC dispatched an investigation team, they are here for a single case, but ignore the reprimand practice (训诫制度). As long as the practice still exits, as long as deleting people's posts, silencing people's voices, and shutting down people's accounts continue, everyone is a victim.[8]

Unfortunately, such calls would likely produce little results in the near future. It is also worth noting, as discussed earlier, that Chinese scholars have largely proposed to formalize police reprimand power (i.e., to add it to the laws and regulations explicitly) as the proper solution when they criticized the lack of legality in Li's case. The immediate effect of such formalization, if adopted, would be to strengthen such practices by the police, while its effect on protecting citizens' rights remains questionable (see similar concerns by Biddulph 2018 in her discussion of legal reforms regarding minor crimes in China).

Second, Li's case also showed the fluidity of legality in daily practice in China, subject to contest by the public and intervention by the Chinese authorities (especially the central government). Specifically, I examined trust issues at three different levels, including interpersonal trust between Li and his inner circles, Li's social trust (by the general public), and public contest of political trust (toward the authorities). Unlike the results of past survey studies on public trust (see review earlier), my case analysis showed complex interactions among trust at varying levels contingent upon the specific context and issue(s) involved. Scholars have argued that Chinese citizens in urban cities genuinely welcome more transparency and freedom of speech (Zhao and Hu 2017) and are no longer afraid of voicing their concerns and engaging in public discourse via social media (Chen 2020; Cao, Zeng, and Evans 2021). In Li's case, the immediate effect of the strong reactions by the masses to Li's sanction and death amid the pandemic secured Li's public support and helped him win his case of legality. To appease the public, the responses by the central government were strategic and took advantage of the hierarchical trust (e.g., shifting blames to local governments and agencies and correcting their mistakes) (Cao, Zeng, and Evans 2021; Yang 2021). It is worth noting that the roles played by the Chinese judiciary were very limited despite the SPC's statement on its official website in January 2020. Instead, the intervention by the central authority bypassed the judiciary in defining legality in this case. As noticed, the "rule of law with Chinese characteristics" means rule by law under the leadership of the CCP (Garrick and Bennett 2016; Trevaskes 2018). Within such a context, legality (and especially its daily operation) is subject to reinterpretation and modification to serve the best interest of the Party's ruling in contemporary China. Unfortunately, whether Li's success in contesting legality, at a great cost, can be replicated by others remains seriously questionable.

Third, Li's case showed that the Chinese authorities, both the central and local governments, are willing and ready to employ a variety of strategies to deal with public trust challenges, ranging from information control and surveillance, containment, and quarantine in the name of fighting the pandemic, prompt actions to address issues (e.g., initiating investigations and briefing the public), proactive measures to diffuse public tension (e.g., to refute rumors, to commemorate Li), and self-revisions and corrections (e.g., to discipline the "wrongdoers") if necessary. Their approach has become flexible and adaptive but remains piecemeal and responsive. They are willing to show their diligent efforts to solve issues in individual cases, but keep tight control over the power of surveillance, censorship, policing, and discipline. Ironically, it is the WeChat censorship that triggered Li's sanction and the subsequent public outrage in this case. While the sanction against Li was rescinded, information censorship and police disciplinary practices are kept intact and continued. Granted, there are red lines that cannot be crossed. In briefing its investigation, for instance, the NSC Investigation Team (2020b) emphasized that "Li is a Communist Party member and not an anti-regime figure (反体制人物)" and warned Western hostilities (敌对势力) who labeled Li the "whistleblower" for political purposes. On July 2, 2020, the China Ministry of Foreign Affairs refuted 37 untrue statements regarding China's human rights, one of which pointed out that Li was *not* the first one to report about coronavirus cases, thus not the 'whistleblower'. It echoed the message that Li was a good doctor and a CCP member, and labeling Li as an anti-regime hero was a political move (Beijing Evening News 2020). Indeed, Cao, Zeng, and Evans (2021) argued that the Chinese government redefined the meaning of hero by recognizing Li as one but carefully drawing the boundary. Criticism is allowed toward particular levels of the governments (Lorentzen 2014), but the central government still enjoys its "hierarchical trust" advantage and is willing to play the role of the savior. The central government still has the final say over what (and how) to give and what not to give in each individual case, including the bargain room on the issues of legality.

Notes

1 The screenshots of these messages are widely available online (e.g., see Liu 2020).
2 Cai (2022) questioned the choice of the NSC as the appropriate investigator of Li's case and argued that NSC's intervention, a political decision, lacked institutional bases, and the outcome of the investigation (including the NSC report) may have led to legitimacy crisis in this case.
3 See, for example, https://app.0375888.cn/zixunsudi/2020-03-03/2935.html (last visit, February 24, 2022).
4 On December 31, 2019, the Wuhan Municipal Health Commission claimed that "to date, there were no confirmed cases of 'human-to-human' contagion and no confirmed cases of medical staff being contracted," despite of 27 confirmed cases of infection (documented in the NSC investigation report). See Yang (2021) for more discussion on efforts by local officials to brush off early warnings about and play down the severity of the pandemic.
5 Li's blog page (https://weibo.com/u/1139098205?is_all=1#_loginLayer_1620974224344) showed a total of more than 1,546,000 followers (February 22, 2022).
6 The term "tree hollow" becomes popular because of a children's story titled "The King with the Donkey's Ears." In this story, a barber found out that the king has a pair of long ears but was warned to keep the secret. He had to talk to a tree hollow to release his secret and psychological pressure.
7 After learning that it is permissible to have a second child in November 2013, Li wrote on his Weibo account: "Holy, may have two now (艾玛，可以生两个了)!" Note that a "second child" policy was initially adopted in 2011 to cover couples who were both a single child. The policy was expanded in 2013 to allow couples to have a second child as long as one of the couple was a single child. It was further expanded to cover all couples in 2015.
8 http://bbs.tianya.cn/post-47-1620593-1.shtml (last visit, May 13, 2021).

References

Baekkeskov, Erik, and Olivier Rubin. 2017. "Information Dilemmas and Blame-Avoidance Strategies: From Secrecy to Lightning Rods in Chinese Health Crises." *Governance: An International Journal of Policy, Administration, and Institutions* 30 (3): 425–43.

Beijing Evening News. 2020. "37 Untrue Statements Regarding China's Human Rights, the Ministry of Foreign Affairs Refuted With Truth." July 2, 2020. https://baijiahao.baidu.com/s?id=1671082332475907737&wfr=spider&for=pc.

Biddulph, Sarah. 2018. "Punishments in the Post Re-education Through Labour World: Questions About Minor Crime in China." In *Chinese Legal Reform and the Global Legal Order: Adoption and Adaptation*, edited by Yun Zhao and Michael Ng, 15–43. Cambridge: Cambridge University Press.

Bociurkiw, Michael. 2020. "China's Hero Doctor Was Punished for Telling Truth About Coronavirus." *CNN*, February 11, 2020. www.cnn.com/2020/02/08/opinions/coronavirus-bociurkiw/index.html.

Braithwaite, John. 1998. "Institutionalizing Distrust, Enculturating Trust." In *Trust and* Governance, edited by Valerie Braithwaite and Margaret Levi, 343–75. New York: Russell Sage.

Buckley, Chris. 2020. "Chinese Doctor, Silenced After Warning of Outbreak, Dies From Coronavirus." *New York Times*, February 6, 2020. www.nytimes.com/2020/02/06/world/asia/chinese-doctor-Li-Wenliang-coronavirus.html.

Cai, Xiang. 2022. "How Politics 'Messed Up With' Institutionalization: A Case Study of the Investigation into the Death of Li Wenliang During the Initial Months of Covid-19." *Journal of Contemporary China* (online first, doi:10.1080/10670564.2022.2031000).

Cao, Xun, Runxi Zeng, and Richard Evans. 2021. "Digital Activism and Collective Mourning by Chinese Netizens During Covid-19." *China Information* (online first, doi:10.1177/0920203X211054172).

Chen, Dan. 2017. "Local Distrust and Regime Support: Sources and Effects of Political Trust in China." *Political Research Quarterly* 70 (2): 314–26.

Chen, Xiaoling. 2020. "Spaces of Care and Resistance in China: Public Engagement During the Covid-19 Outbreak." *Eurasian Geography and Economics* 61: 435–47.

China National Intellectual Property Administration. 2020. "Announcement on Collectively Rejecting 37 Trademark Applications Involving 'Li Wenliang' and Others in the Pandemic." *China Trademark* (中华商标) (February 3): 21–22.

Citrin, Jack, and Laura Stoker. 2018. "Political Trust in A Cynical Age." *Annual Review of Political Science* 21: 49–70.

Dalton, Russell. 1999. "Political Support in Advanced Industrial Democracies." In *Critical Citizens: Global Support for Democratic Government*, edited by Pippa Norris, 57–77. Oxford: Oxford University Press.

Feng, Zhixin, Athina Vlachantoni, Xiaoting Liu, and Kelvyn Jones. 2016. "Social Trust, Interpersonal Trust and Self-rated Health in China: A Multi-level Study." *International Journal for Equity in Health* 15: 180–90.

First Director. 2020. "100 Days After Li Wenliang's Passing: He Is Gone but Won't Be Forgotten." July 16, 2020. https://zhuanlan.zhihu.com/p/141487685.

Garrick, John, and Van Chang Bennett. 2016. *China's Socialist Rule of Law Reforms Under Xi Jinping*. London and New York: Routledge.

Green, Andrew. 2020. "Li Wenliang (Obituary)." *The Lancet*, 395 (10, 225) (February 29): 682.

Heberer, Thomas, and Gunter Schubert. 2011. "Political Trust and the Case of China." *Oriental Archive* 79 (2): 189–231.

Keele, Luke. 2007. "Social Capital and the Dynamics of Trust in Government." *American Journal of Political Science* 51 (2): 241–54.

King, Garry, Jennifer Pan, and Margaret Roberts. 2013. "How Censorship in China Allows Government Criticism but Silences Collective Expression." *American Political Science Review* 107 (2): 326–43.

———. 2017. "How the Chinese Government Fabricates Social Media Posts for Strategic Distraction, not Engaged Argument." *American Political Science Review* 111 (3): 484–501.

Laws, John. 2017. "The Rule of Law: The Presumption of Liberty and Justice." *Judicial Review* 22 (4): 365–73.

Lei, Ya-wen. 2020. "Revisiting China's Social Volcano: Attitudes Toward Inequality and Political Trust in China." *Socius: Sociological Research for a Dynamic World* 6: 1–21.

Levi, Margaret, and Laura Stoker. 2000. "Political Trust and Trustworthiness." *Annual Review of Political Science* 3 (1): 475–507.

Li, Lianjiang. 2004. "Political Trust in Rural China." *Modern China* 30 (2): 228–58.

———. 2013. "The Magnitude and Resilience of Trust in the Center: Evidence from Interviews With Petitioners in Beijing and a Local Survey in Rural China." *Modern China* 39 (1): 3–36.

———. 2016. "Reassessing Trust in the Central Government: Evidence From Five National Surveys." *The China Quarterly* 225: 100–21.

Li, Shaohua, and Bo Jin. 2020. "Reprimand by the Public Security Should Be Carried Out by Law." *Journal of Fuyang Normal University (Social Science)* (阜阳师范大学学报) 195 (3): 117–22.

Liu, Huaxing, and John Raine. 2016. "Why Is There Less Public Trust in Local Government Than in Central Government in China?" *International Journal of Public Administration* 39 (4): 258–69.

Liu, Mingyang. 2020. "A Conversation About the 'Rumor' with the Admonished Doctor: I Was Warning Others to Take Precautions." *Beijing News* (新京报), January 31, 2020. www.bjnews.com.cn/detail/158044099415716.html.

Lo, Alex, Lewis Cheung, Anna Lee, and Bixia Xu. 2016. "Confidence and Trust in Public Institution Natural Hazards Management: Case Studies in Urban and Rural China." *The Professional Geographer* 68 (3): 475–84.

Lorentzen, Peter. 2014. "China's Strategic Censorship." *American Journal of Political Science* 58 (2): 402–14.

Luo, Shuping. 2020. "Such A Reprimand Based on What Laws?" *Democracy and Legal System* (民主与法制) (8): 50–52.

Ma, Liang, and Tom Christensen. 2019. "Government Trust, Social Trust, and Citizens' Risk Concerns: Evidence From Crisis Management in China." *Public Performance & Management Review* 42 (2): 383–404.

Manion, Melanie. 2006. "Democracy, Community, Trust: The Impact of Elections in Rural China." *Comparative Political Studies* 39 (3): 301–24.

Mishler, William, and Richard Rose. 1997. "Trust, Distrust, and Skepticism: Popular Evaluations of Civil and Political Institutions in Post-Communist Societies." *Journal of Politics* 59 (2): 418–51.

———. 2001. "What Are the Origins of Political Trust? Testing Institutional and Cultural Theories in Post-Communist Societies." *Comparative Political Studies* 34 (1): 30–62.

National Supervisory Commission Investigation Team. 2020a. "A Report on Investigation of Doctor Li Wenliang per Request by the Masses (关于群众反映的涉及李文亮医生有关情况调查的通报)." March 19, 2020. https://baijiahao.baidu.com/s?id=1661592804127398651&wfr=spider&for=pc.

———. 2020b. "Press Conference." *Qianjiang Evening News* (钱江晚报), A5, March 20, 2020.

Phoenix New Media (ifeng.com). 2020. "More Than 1 Million Comments Were Deleted Under Li Wenliang's Blog? Sina Weibo Answered." June 20, 2020. https://news.ifeng.com/c/7xSa56uIhai.

Putnam, Robert. 1995. "Bowling Alone: America's Declining Social Capital." *Journal of Democracy* 6: 65–78.

Shi, Tianjian. 2001. "Cultural Values and Political Trust: A Comparison of the People's Republic of China and Taiwan." *Comparative Politics* 33 (4): 401–19.

Sina Financial. 2020. "Being Fined for Registering 'Huoshen Shan', 'Leishen Shan', and 'Li Wenliang' in Trademarks! The Reason Is . . ." April 25, 2020. https://baijiahao.baidu.com/s?id=1664921416982093798&wfr=spider&for=pc.

Steinhardt, Christopher. 2012. "How Is High Trust in China Possible? Comparing the Origins of Generalized Trust in Three Chinese Societies." *Political Studies* 60: 434–54.

Su, Alice. 2020. "Coronavirus Killed China's Whistleblower Doctor. Now the Virus Has Changed How the Country Can Mourn Him." *Los Angeles Times*, April 3, 2020. www.latimes.com/world-nation/story/2020-04-03/coronavirus-china-doctor-tomb-sweeping.

Su, Mu. 2021. "To Commemorate the One-year Anniversary of Li Wenliang's Death: A Healthy Society Should Not Have Just One Voice." *Medive* (医脉通), February 7, 2021. https://news.medlive.cn/all/info-news/show-176110_97.html.

Tang, Xinghua. 2020. "Regarding Wuhan's Eight Rumor Mongers, the Supreme Court Published an Article." *Securities Traders in China* (卷商中国), January 29, 2020. https://xueqiu.com/1184824257/140098158.

Tao, Ran, Fubing Su, Xin Sun, and Xi Lu. 2011. "Political Trust as Rational Belief: Evidence From Chinese Village Elections." *Journal of Comparative Economics* 39 (1): 108–21.

Tao, Ran, Dali Yang, Ming Li, and Xi Lu. 2014. "How Does Political Trust Affect Social Trust? An Analysis of Survey Data From Rural China Using an Instrumental Variables Approach." *International Political Science Review* 35 (2): 237–53.

Trevaskes, Susan. 2018. "A Law Unto Itself: Chinese Communist Party Leadership and Yifa Zhiguo in the Xi Era." *Modern China* 44 (4): 347–73.

Wang, Ke. 2021. "An Analysis on the Nature and Application of Public Security Reprimand." *Journal of Chaohu University* (巢湖学院学报) 23 (2): 31–37.

Wang, Zhengxu. 2005. "Before the Emergence of Critical Citizens: Economic Development and Political Trust in China." *International Review of Sociology* 15 (1): 147–63.

Wang, Zhengxu, and Yu You. 2016. "The Arrival of Critical Citizens: Decline of Political Trust and Shifting Public Priorities in China." *International Review of Sociology* 26 (1): 105–24.

Wong, Timothy Ka-ying, Po-san Wan, and Michael Hsiao. 2011. "The Bases of Political Trust in Six Asian Societies: Institutional and Cultural Explanations Compared." *International Political Science Review* 32 (3): 263–81.

Wu, Carry, and Rima Wilkes. 2018. "Local – National Political Trust Patterns: Why China Is an Exception?" *International Political Science Review* 39 (4): 436–54.

Wu, Jiebing, Yong Li, and Chengcheng Song. 2020. "Temporal Dynamics of Political Trust in China: A Cohort Analysis." *China Information* 34 (1): 109–36.

Wu, Xiaolong, Dali Yang, and Lijun Chen. 2017. "The Politics of Quality-of-life Issues: Food Safety and Political Trust in China." *Journal of Contemporary China* 26 (106): 1–15.

Xiao, Siyao. 2020. "A Moment Ago, Something Weird Happened Under Li Wenliang's Blog." July 4. www.tgbyex.com/xinwen/262579.html.

Yang, Jiejun. 2020. "Judgment and Application of Punishable Behavior and Administrative Punishment – Analysis on Li Wenliang's Case and Related Controversial Issues." *Administrative Law Review* (行政法学研究) (6): 64–77.

Yang, Qing, and Wenfang Tang. 2010. "Exploring the Sources of Institutional Trust in China: Culture, Mobilization, or Performance." *Asian Politics & Policy* 2 (3): 415–36.

Yang, Xiangfeng. 2021. "Domestic Contestation, International Backlash, and Authoritarian Resilience: How Did the Chinese Party-State Weather the Covid-19 Crisis?" *Journal of Contemporary China* 30 (32): 915–29.

Yang, Zhixu, and Ziqiang Xin. 2020. "Income Inequality and Interpersonal Trust in China." *Asian Journal of Social Psychology* 23: 253–63.

Ye, Zhengsong. 2020. "Breaking News! Major Revisions to the Law on Prevention and Control of Infectious Diseases, the Effect of Li Wenliang Is Obvious." *Medive* (医脉通), October 5, 2020. https://new.qq.com/omn/20201005/20201005A07QDE00.html.

Yi, Mingjia. 2020. "Discussion on the Legal Nature and Regulation for Administrative Admonition." *Journal of Ningxia Communist Party Institute* (宁夏党校学报) 22 (5): 122–28.

You, Jong-sung. 2012. "Social Trust: Fairness Matters More Than Homogeneity." *Political Psychology* 33 (5): 701–21.

Zhao, Dahai, and Wei Hu. 2017. "Determinants of Public Trust in Government: Empirical Evidence From Urban China." *International Review of Administrative Sciences* 83 (2): 358–77.

Zhong, Yang. 2014. "Do Chinese People Trust Their Local Government, and Why? An Empirical Study of Political Trust in Urban China." *Problems of Post-Communism* 61 (3): 31–44.

Zhou, Baohua, and Yuan Zhong. 2021. "Social Media, Collective Mourning and Extended Affective Space: A Computational Communication Analysis of Li Wenliang's Weibo Comments (2020–2021)." *Chinese Journal of Journalism and Communication* (国际新闻界) 3: 79–106.

Zhou, Shun, and Ruoyu Li. 2021. "The Legal Nature of Police's Admonition and its System Improvement." *Journal of Shanghai Police College* (上海公安学院学报) 31 (2): 40–59.

Zhu, Jiangnan, Jie Lu, and Tianjian Shi. 2013. "When Grapevine News Meets Mass Media: Different Information Sources and Popular Assessments of Government Corruption in Mainland China." *Comparative Political Studies* 46 (8): 920–46.

PART 4
Conclusion

13

CHINESE LAW IN A COMPARATIVE CONTEXT

Michael R. Fowler

1. Introduction

Analyzing the workings of government institutions in authoritarian and Communist societies is challenging, especially when the task includes predicting what is likely to happen in the near future. Recall Winston Churchill's remark in 1939 about the Soviet Union: "I cannot forecast to you the action of Russia. It is a riddle wrapped in a mystery inside an enigma." However, Churchill went on to suggest, "[B]ut perhaps there is a key. That key is Russian national interest" (Bailey 1968, 81). Each of the contributors here assesses a dimension of the Chinese legal system, looking to both the past and future, analyzing and predicting what is especially significant. Each reports how some aspect of law functions in contemporary China, looking to update, clarify, and sometimes re-think the conventional wisdom. The chapters sort through the rhetoric and reality of a Chinese legal system that, in becoming more modern and comprehensive, "has developed perhaps faster than any legal system in history" (Liebman 2011, 167).

Chinese Legality brings together the insights of a dozen scholars, with university affiliations in China, Taiwan, and Hong Kong as well as Australia, Great Britain, and the US, considering key questions regarding law in China. How should we think about Chinese legality? How is China's legal system evolving? What does the phrase "rule of law" mean in this context? How do the institutions of the legal system function? How does the Chinese Communist Party (CCP) interact with and influence the legislature, judiciary, procuratorate, and police?

In working to bring readers up-to-date on new developments, the prior chapters include the analysis of key provisions in the Chinese constitution, corporate law principles, and the new civil code. However, the scope of the book is by no means narrowly confined to technical legal issues. The authors touch on a variety of related matters. For example, Haig Patapan of Griffith University, Australia,

DOI: 10.4324/9781003294887-17

addresses, what the Party considers official deviance and corruption, what lessons the CCP drew from the killing of protestors in Tiananmen Square in 1989, and how the views of Mao Zedong, Deng Xiaoping, and Xi Jinping have differed in various particulars.

The different uses of law across the sweep of Chinese history gain attention too. As Shiping Hua of the University of Louisville notes in the Introduction, legality—"the quality and state of being in accordance with the law"—has often been a key to understanding particular dimensions of Chinese society. The historical dimension is especially important since, as was once written of law in socialist Yugoslavia

> even the impetus of a revolution cannot completely wipe out a pre-existing legal system, provided that the leaders of the revolution are not devoid of common sense and have a sound understanding of political realities and that the theory and the ideology with which they have been inspired have not made them pure dogmatists.
>
> *(Stjepanovic 1956, 226)*

Here, the contributing scholars consider legality via a historical lens, with references to the legal systems of imperial China; via an ideological lens, i.e., the evolution of legality within the People's Republic of China (PRC); and through a globalization lens, focusing on how law has helped China interact with an increasingly connected world. Taken as a whole, the chapters demonstrate how the role of law in the People's Republic of China today is a timely, highly significant, and often puzzling and fascinating topic, one of cardinal interest to students and scholars as well as to business executives and lawyers, diplomats, and other officials, governmental and non-governmental, with dealings regarding China.

2. The Significance of China and Chinese Law Today

The supreme importance of 21st-century China to people across the globe stands out in a host of ways, demonstrating why many want to refine their understanding of the country, its legal and political systems alike. Consider, first, foreign affairs. While China has been a nuclear power since 1964, it now appears to be looking toward what the Pentagon considers a "large-scale expansion of its nuclear forces," aiming to have 700 deliverable nuclear warheads by 2027 and perhaps 1,000 by 2030 (US Department of Defense, v, viii). Although China already has the world's largest ground forces with 975,000 active-duty personnel in combat units, the numerically largest navy with 355 ships and submarines, and the third-largest air force with over 2,800 aircraft, Xi Jinping has been at work to reform the country's armed forces with the goal of attaining a "world-class" military by 2050 (ibid., v–vi; Saunders 2019). Furthermore, the capabilities of the People's Liberation Army (PLA) have been growing in cyber warfare (Wortzel 2014) and other modern techniques.

In some ways law, both domestic and international, factors into even some of these foreign-policy matters. China's territorial claims over the Diaoyu or Senkaku Islands, administered by Japan, coupled with the air defense intercept zone it announced in 2013, are part of what the PLA has termed "legal warfare" (Ibid., x).[1] Even before losing the 2016 South China Sea case heard before the Permanent Court of Arbitration, the Chinese government announced it would not participate in the proceedings or accept and abide by the tribunal's decision.[2]

In this volume, the contribution on extraterritoriality by Zheng Sophia Tang and Xinxin Zhang of Wuhan University speaks to one development that lies right at the interstices of Chinese law and foreign policy. Here, the point I would emphasize is that, across much of the world, the extraterritorial application of a state's laws—i.e., the operation of its laws beyond its own sovereign borders—is not in and of itself controversial. For example, when a German criminal law brings German citizens to account for paying for sex in brothels abroad that use child prostitutes, people are not outraged. Instead, what has led to real legal and diplomatic disagreements involves "claims made upon the basis of the so-called 'effects' doctrine . . . where the state assumes jurisdiction on the grounds that the behaviour of a party is producing 'effects' within its territory" (Shaw 2014, 499).

What makes the subject of extraterritoriality especially sensitive in China is another matter of history, legal and diplomatic, with origins in unequal treaties and Chinese concessions to western imperial powers.[3] Since very early in the lengthy record of European commercial contacts with Asia, western governments demanded that Asian countries create legal systems that could deal fairly with the inevitable disputes that would arise when international trade and investment occurred. At one point, this became a characteristic of sovereignty that factored into international perceptions of what constituted a sovereign state (Fowler and Bunck 1996).

In particular, as Julie Bunck and I noted elsewhere:

> Throughout China citizens of Western powers enjoyed an expansive interpretation of the principle of extraterritoriality that allowed their national courts to exercise jurisdiction over any offense their nationals might be alleged to have committed in China. This essentially exempted foreigners from Chinese criminal law.
>
> *(Fowler and Bunck 1995, 94)*

We argued that

> the Western powers, intent on opening China to commerce, repeatedly failed to accord the Chinese government a monolithic chunk of sovereign rights the same as those enjoyed by other sovereign states. Restrictions on the content of their basket of sovereign rights long chafed Chinese officials and their peoples.
>
> *(Ibid., 95; see also ibid., 94–97; Fowler and Bunck 1994)*

Today, however, with the US–China trade war (Hua 2022), China has turned from criticizing extraterritorial jurisdiction to embracing it. Tang and Zhang observe, "Chinese central authorities changed the official narrative and made establishing a Chinese system of extraterritoriality one of its priorities to counteract the U.S. sanctions."

More broadly, China's future foreign-policy plans and the content of the Chinese grand strategy (Kashmeri 2019; Goldstein 2005) now stand as critically important issues in international relations. Central to such analysis is the Belt and Road Initiative, with China aiming to develop close relations "with over 70 countries in Eurasia, Middle East, and Africa, in economic-industrial and geopolitical partnerships" (Kashmeri 2019, 3, 5). Law factors into these relations, too. Sarwar Kashmeri observed:

> China is not following the American formula of constructing a vast military-industrial complex with scores of expensive military bases and treaty alliances. Instead, it is offering to help these countries finance and build roads, railways, ports, bridges, internet connectivity, energy pipelines, and power-generating equipment—the infrastructure that they need to modernize and increase their rate of growth but have not been able to afford. Instead of "forward-deploying" its military around the world, as America has done, China aims instead to forward-deploy its financing, technology, manufacturing, and construction skills to set up connectivity over land and sea with existing and future trading partners, and to lock in multiple sources for its ever-growing need for raw materials and resources.
>
> *(Ibid., 3–4)*

What can China's partners expect to happen in future legal and diplomatic affairs after coming to agreements for such aid? This remains very much an open question.

In terms of international commerce, China's weight is already exceptionally formidable. Kashmeri encapsulated China's astonishing economic rise by observing:

> Since the beginning of Deng Xiaoping's reforms, China's gross domestic product (GDP) has risen thirtyfold, and 750 million people have been lifted out of poverty—the most ever achieved during such a short period in recorded history. In four decades, China has gone from the ranks of the world's poorest countries to challenging the United States for the title of the largest economy in the world.
>
> *(Ibid., 2)*

The Chinese market features 1.3 billion consumers, ensuring the country's central economic importance in global trade. Alongside reporting that by 2021, 1.011 billion Chinese were using the Internet, Tang and Zhang point out:

"In 2010, China's total [Gross Domestic Product] GDP overtook that of Japan and became the second-largest economy in the world, and China became the world's leading exporter, a significant destination for and increasingly a source of foreign direct investment." According to Hua, the Chinese middle class alone has grown from 3.1% of China's population, or 39.1 million people, in 2000 to 50.8% of the population, or 707 million in 2018. Plainly, those interested in profiting through international commerce will often feel they must contend with China.

During the 21st century, China has become increasingly integrated into the international economic order, having joined the World Trade Organization (WTO) in 2001 and signed more than 100 international investment treaties. By 2018, exports accounted for nearly 20% of China's economy (Lateef 2019, x). Nevertheless, in recent years, China's rapid economic expansion has slowed notably, triggering discontent, including labor unrest (Lin 2017). All these developments implicate the functioning of the Chinese legal system. In the WTO accession agreement, as Ming Du of Durham University notes, China "committed to apply, implement and administer its laws, regulations and other measures relating to trade in goods and services in a *uniform, impartial and reasonable manner* at all levels of government throughout China" (Italics in original). To carry out these obligations has amounted to a formidable undertaking, as legal provisions were to be added or amended in accordance with various rule-of-law principles:

> transparency—laws must be made public and readily accessible; laws must be prospective, relatively clear, consistent, stable; laws must be enforced fairly and impartially, with the gap between the law on the books and law in practice narrow; and laws must be reasonably acceptable to a majority of the population or people affected (or at least the key groups affected) by the laws.
>
> *(Peerenboom 2006, 63–64)*

3. The Concerns of Onlookers

Yet, despite such formal legal obligations, the striking differences between government practices in China and in other advanced countries have long concerned many interacting with the Chinese. The collapse of the Soviet Union caused Chinese authorities to become even more intent on stifling dissent which might threaten their hold on power. In 1989, the Communist Party leaders responded to the unarmed students who had requested dialogue by imposing martial law; they then ordered soldiers and tanks into Tiananmen Square, with scores of protestors killed, while the Chinese legal system was implicated in the arrest and even the execution of others. Dingxin Zhao later argued,

> During the late 1980s, most urban Chinese's notions of what legitimates a state had changed from communist ideology to economic and moral performance, a notion more in accordance with the ideas found in an earlier, more

> traditional China. Those who watched the [student protest] movement were thus more receptive to culturally and morally charged rhetoric and activities, and they became highly emotional when the state reacted harshly to morally charged acts.
>
> *(Dingxin Zhao 2001, 269)*

More recently, the Chinese government in various speeches and party papers claimed to be instituting a rule of law throughout the country. Indeed, the 1999 Constitution envisioned the People's Republic "ruling the country by law" and building "a socialist country under the rule of law" (Article 5). Here again, however, the reality has at times diverged sharply from the rhetoric.[4] Professor Du observes, "Under the rule of law, the law constrains all members of society, including government actions. Rule by law, by contrast, means the state uses law to control its citizens but never allows law to be used by the people to control the state." In various particulars, rule by law has been more evident in recent years than rule of law. Consider, for instance, the tension that has long existed between the Han majority and the predominantly Muslim Uighur minority of more than eight million in northwest China (Kaltman 2007, 1). Rather than law protecting minority rights from government abuses, the state has repeatedly oppressed this large ethnic minority.

By 2021, Jeffrey Cimmino of the Atlantic Council labeled China's policy in Xinjiang "a systematic campaign of repression," arguing: "Through a combination of detention camps, mass surveillance, birth suppression, and other means, China is responsible for gross human-rights violations" (Cimmino 2021, 1). Researchers from the Australian Strategic Policy Institute, after noting claims by Chinese officials that "all 'trainees' from so-called vocational training centres had 'graduated' by late 2019," used satellite imagery to identify and map "more than 380 suspected detention facilities in the Xinjiang Uyghur Autonomous Region, highlighting 're-education' camps, detention centres and prisons that have been newly built or expanded since 2017" (Ruser 2020, 3). They concluded: "[A]vailable evidence suggests that many extrajudicial detainees in Xinjiang's vast 're-education' network are now being formally charged and locked up in higher security facilities, including newly built or expanded prisons, or sent to walled factory compounds for coerced labour assignments" (Ibid.).

Turn next to the situation in Hong Kong. The Tiananmen crackdown brought pro-democracy political activism to rise in Hong Kong, a place where civil unrest has broken out repeatedly for more than 100 years (Ng and Wong 2017, 1).[5] Incidentally, "democracy" has been labeled "a confusing word in China, where all leaders, from Mao Zedong to Hu Jintao, have claimed it for themselves" (Wu 2008, 34). In 2008, Guoguang Wu recounted:

> The Cultural Revolution is said, in Mao's terminology, to be "great democracy"; the monopolized control of public power by . . . the CCP, is claimed, in Hu's concept, as the indispensable condition for "socialist democracy"

> as it is practiced in China today. Meanwhile they score Western capitalist democracy as "fake" democracy, owing to the dominant influence of capitalists in political life, and boost "socialist democracy" as "genuine democracy," in which all people have an equal right to participate.
>
> *(Ibid.)*

For many years, scholars have noted that many mainland Chinese associate democracy with a chaotic society, totally out of step with the order and harmony that have long been notable Chinese values (Friedman 2006, 95).

The chapter on the Hong Kong protests by Stephen Ortmann of the Chinese University of Hong Kong examines another dimension of rule by law in China. With protests soaring again in 2019, the pro-democracy movement ultimately ran headlong into the Chinese regime's efforts to roll back moderate reforms across China, as Xi Jinping, in Ortmann's words, "centralized power further under his personal leadership, deepened the state's role in society, strengthened controls over ideas and financial flows, and publicly asserted Chinese power." In the Introduction, Professor Hua observes that the limited democracy previously permitted in Hong Kong was significantly diminished when China moved to ensure that only "patriots," as defined by the CCP, held office.

The new National Security Law further eroded Hong Kong's autonomy, undermining civil liberties while allowing for extraterritorial prosecutions. Professor Ortmann further notes: "Televised confessions have returned. The government has tightened limits for non-governmental organizations, arrested human rights activists, women's rights activists, and other societal actors independent of the government." After describing the establishment of supra-legal institutions created to enforce national security legal provisions, he concludes, "The Hong Kong government has used the law and other procedures to threaten or undermine various pro-democratic organizations from the media to civil society and even various businesses that have shown their support for the cause." What Ortmann calls "the more instrumental use of law in the service of the authoritarian regime" has had various consequences, including the stifling of debate before elections, the dissolution of civil-society organizations and the loss of academic freedom in universities. He concludes by predicting, "[M]any businesses that value predictability and legal certainty will likely move to Singapore or other nearby locations." A new chapter in the Chinese diaspora from Hong Kong (Siu-Lun 1999) has commenced.

All this underscores how the system of government in China has both an evolving orientation and a strikingly different ideological one than that found in many other states (Men 2007, 7–8). This is reflected in such disparate matters as the questionable independence of Chinese judges (He 2021), the Chinese law aimed at "managing" foreign non-governmental organizations (Franceschini and Nesossi 2017), and the extensive police surveillance now evident, ranging from omnipresent urban video cameras to extensive deoxyribonucleic acid (DNA) databases (Dirks 2020).[6] While at times during the reform period, especially earlier on, the Chinese government sometimes tolerated independent thinking to a degree unheard of earlier in the regime's history, it has also periodically cracked down, repressing the media, lawyers, professors, and others who were viewed as posing potential threats.

4. Comparative Political Ideologies

In his chapter, Ming Du quite appropriately labels the rule of law as an "essentially contested concept," one that means different things to different people. The same might very well be said of ideology. Malcolm Hamilton observed: "Anyone who reviews the literature dealing with the concept of ideology soon discovers that there are at least as many definitions of it as there are theorists proposing them" (Hamilton 1987, 18). And yet, as Inis Claude once wrote, "[A] word that means almost everything means virtually nothing, a conceptual tool used indiscriminately has its analytical edge irreparably dulled" (Fowler and Bunck 1995, 7).

Let me sketch out, then, my usage of this sometimes elusive term. Political ideologies are both abstract and somewhat simplified categories that reflect varied human aspirations about how a society should govern itself. A political ideology may be defined as a set of collectively held beliefs regarding a system of government: who should govern a state and why, which core political principles ought to underlie that government's conduct and policies, and what should constitute the most important state objectives. Although a political ideology describes a vision of an ideal state of affairs that is always tempered in practice by the difficulties and realities of governing, the key characteristics of an ideology can nonetheless provide a regime with legitimacy in the eyes of the public. Here, as Claude once observed, "Politics is not merely a struggle for power but also a contest over legitimacy, a competition in which the conferment or denial, the confirmation or revocation, of legitimacy is an important stake" (Claude 1988, 146).

As governments that operate under contrasting ideological orientations interact, it can be useful to recall certain of their basic differences in perspective. China's communist orientation differs fundamentally from the ideologies found in many countries with social democratic, classically conservative, or classically liberal philosophies or mixtures of these. Andrew Nathan once observed, "Similar-sounding ideas mean different things in different institutional and intellectual contexts" (Nathan 2008, 39). The preceding chapters reference such ideas as free trade, civil society, human rights, constitutionalism, separation of powers, independent judiciaries, and neo-liberal international economic policies. People who identify with different political ideologies often view such ideas through different lenses. Thus, as we take stock of the insights and lessons found in this volume, some core differences between the prominent political ideologies found among the world's sovereign states help to explain why official Chinese reasoning and actions are often at odds with those inspired by contrasting traditions of political philosophy.[7]

Consider, first, the social democracies, typified by the Scandinavian countries though encompassing others as well, especially in Europe. These feature multi-party political systems that postulate fair, competitive, democratic elections determining who governs the state. A vibrant civil society is valued to stimulate discourse and help to inform the democratic debate. A social democrat emphasizes equality, but primarily in the sense of ensuring that all of a state's citizens have equal access to that society's resources. He or she would reject the command economy of a doctrinaire Marxist state in favor of a capitalist one, but the state would step in to substantially regulate its economy, promoting equality by intervening regularly in relations among business, labor, and the public.

Social democrats endorse the idea that the state will provide considerable goods and services to the citizenry while taking on a great range of tasks such as organizing education and providing health care, day care, and elder care. Social democrats value a government that respects individual rights and liberties. The state's power and authority should be subject to certain limits, and citizens should be free in their speech and practice of religion.

Another notable political ideology, which has long resonated in Japan and various states in Latin America and elsewhere, is classical conservatism. From this perspective, the primary tasks of government are envisioned as ensuring order, whether on the streets, in the workplace, or in the home. In this status quo-oriented view of society, rather than emphasizing the value of change and social mobility, a country's traditions and history are glorified, with longstanding social and moral codes cherished. Class differences are often viewed as normal and natural. Stability is prized, and the government may endorse a religion. Each social class has its place and should accept its role in society. The government adopts the role of a wise parent, benevolently looking after the citizenry.[8] Instead of an emphasis in governance on creating and implementing upward mobility, the country's elites, who are likely to remain so over time, feel a compunction to look after those less fortunate. The political systems of conservative states range from genuine competitive democracies to more autocratic approaches, some of which may simply pay lip service to democratic ideals.

The founders of the US[9] came from a third ideological tradition, that of classical liberalism. Classical liberalism refers not to the agendas of political liberals today, but to the concepts of Enlightenment period political philosophers, such as John Locke and Adam Smith of Britain and Jean Jacques Rousseau and Baron de Montesquieu of France.

This perspective starts from the view that strong governments tend to become abusive in encroaching on the rights of the people. However, a competitive democracy lodged in a decentralized government system might counter this. So, too, might an emphasis on the rule of law in the sense that no individual, however wealthy or powerful, would be above or beyond the law's reach. Classical liberals envision a domestic economy in which the government allows creative talents to be unleashed by the state standing apart so that self-sufficient individuals can make their own decisions and use their intelligence and industriousness to prosper without government interference. In interactions abroad, free trade would be vigorously promoted with limited state intervention. Furthermore, a chief government's task is to ensure liberty, i.e., protect individual freedoms. A noted innovation of America's founders was a constitution aimed at creating a government that would operate in accordance with classically liberal precepts, coupled with republicanism and federalism.

In classical liberalism, an exceedingly important function of law is to constrain the state. Law alone does not produce a good society, which "requires a suitable combination and fruitful interaction of law *and* politics." Law is created as part of a political process. Politics is not an evil to be eliminated, and "the moderation and control of political action is the function of a legal system" (Claude 1959, 4). Freedom of speech and thought amounts to one vital aspect of a classically liberal political system. US Supreme Court Justice Robert Jackson wrote,

> If there is any fixed star in our constitutional constellation, it is that no official, high or petty, can prescribe what shall be orthodox in politics, nationalism, religion, or other matters of opinion or force citizens to confess by word or act their faith therein.[10]

Elsewhere Jackson observed,

> The danger that citizens will think wrongly is serious, but less dangerous than atrophy from not thinking at all. . . . Thought control is a copyright of totalitarianism, and we have no claim to it. It is not the function of our Government to keep the citizen from falling into error; it is the function of the citizen to keep the Government from falling into error.[11]

These classically liberal assumptions help to explain why the founders separated the legislative, executive, and judicial branches of government, so the power of each could balance and check the others. Here, US Supreme Court Justice Louis Brandeis once observed,

> The doctrine of the separation of powers was adopted by the Convention of 1787, not to promote efficiency but to preclude the exercise of arbitrary power. The purpose was, not to avoid friction, but, by means of the inevitable friction incidental to the distribution of the governmental powers among three departments, to save the people from autocracy.[12]

In stark contrast, socialist ideology has traditionally focused on governments promoting social and material equality through a powerful centralized state. Checks and balances are quite foreign to this approach. Instead, as Jing Men summarized,

> Marxism advocates class struggle and believes in the inevitable collapse of capitalism and the ultimate victory of communism. Marxism holds that the exploiting class should be overthrown by force to establish a proletarian dictatorship. Lenin further developed Marxism by taking states as the leading protagonists in the revolutionary struggle and world politics. . . . [R]evolution would first be successful in those nation-states where imperialist control is the weakest.
>
> *(Men 2007, 7–8)*

Officials motivated by a communist ideology envision one-party rule, exercise considerable control over a country's resources, and actively employ coercive power both to retain their authority and to diminish class differences while justifying their policies as actions that will ultimately help to promote the greater good in the long run. Dissenters are not to be allowed to stand in the way of the sweeping social transformations that the government envisions. And, within a Marxist society individuals and individual rights—whether to free speech, freedom of religion, a free press, or free elections—are to be subordinated to this projected equal society.

As for the role of law, constitutions are not envisioned as providing constraints on government. Louis Henkin wrote:

> Unlike the U.S. Constitution, the Chinese constitution does not claim to be a contract among the people establishing the state. . . . It is a manifesto, by the leaders to the people, describing the society that exists and its institutions, and proclaiming its values, goals, and aspirations. Like the U.S. Constitution it is largely a blueprint of government, but it provides not a blueprint for a system of government as the people prescribe it must be, but a map of a government the leadership has established, the government that is or is promised.
>
> *(Henkin 1986, 26–27)*

In certain respects, the People's Republic of China has relied on aspects of traditional Chinese history and culture that coexist comfortably with Marxist doctrine. For instance, neither individualism nor individual rights, claims, and entitlements were central to Chinese traditions. Historically in China, government legitimacy, in theory and practice, did not depend on the consent of the people; instead, the order and harmony of communities and the overall welfare of the society were greatly emphasized (Ibid., 21–22). Indeed, some have gone so far as to contend that in China, there has been a sense in which the public is expected to overlook instances of government officials violating the law. Hong Lu and Terance Miethe argued:

> [T]he cultural legacy of collectivism (i.e., the willingness to sacrifice a few for the interest of a whole community) and other cultural beliefs

> (e.g., punitive attitudes toward crime, the lack of sympathy toward criminal defendant) has allowed the Chinese to consider the lawless behavior of the government acceptable.
>
> *(Lu and Miethe 2007, 22)*

In other respects, China has long fit awkwardly into the general communist category, a fact underscored by the regime's longstanding emphasis on the singular aspects of their government system.[13] "Socialism with Chinese characteristics" is a phrase that has been both bandied about and puzzled over for many years (Mackerras, Taneja, and Young 1993). From the period of Mao Zedong's rule forward, identifying peculiarly Chinese characteristics to various aspects of governance in the People's Republic has been a significant part of its political discourse. Henkin observed:

> Western political ideas, including democracy, came to China in the nineteenth century, and socialism arrived in the mid-twentieth century. But both were laid over traditional ideas and a traditional Chinese society and were adapted to the needs of modern China as perceived by contemporary leaders so as to produce a unique Chinese blend. It is not easy to say how much of that blend is traditional China, how much is socialism, and how much is original—or how much is ideology and how much pragmatism.
>
> *(Henkin 1986, 20)*

Here, it may be worth considering the thesis that revolutionary change is more likely to succeed when it draws heavily on traditional values, serves clear popular interests, and brings about mutually beneficial outcomes (Bunck 1994, 219–21).

For an example of how China's experience exists in tension with Marxist theory, consider the doctrinal emphasis on socialism enhancing equality. In China, however, the country's economic opening brought on a society that soon became less and less equal. As early as 2006, Larry Diamond noted that "Overall, inequality in China has worsened dramatically in the past two decades." He pointed to a rising Gini coefficient in the 1981 to 1998 period, indeed the largest increase in the world during that period, and concluded: "By . . . comparative standards, income distribution in China is now worse than in Turkey and about as bad as in the Philippines and Bolivia, two countries known historically for extreme inequalities and steep class divisions" (Diamond 2006, 79). Since then, matters have gotten worse, with World Bank estimates of the Gini coefficient in 2021 placing China "among the most unequal global economies" (Calcea 2021).

Chinese communism has sometimes veered so far from traditional Marxist doctrine as to leave onlookers wondering about the country's core principles. In 1978, as part of China's economic opening, when Deng Xiaoping declared that "to get rich is glorious," he was both "injecting the power of capitalism into the Chinese economy and turning communist orthodoxy on its head" (Kashmeri 2019, 1–2).

Furthermore, with the onset of extensive economic reforms, law regained a more visible and significant role in Chinese society. For one thing, much new law was promulgated, as China looked to develop a far more comprehensive legal system, a task the government claimed had been completed in 2010.

The 1982 Constitution appeared to be a notable step in the effort to create more judicial independence as well as more separation between the party and the daily operations of government, and the 1999 Constitution went so far as to declare: "All state organs, the armed forces, all political parties and public organizations and all enterprises and institutions must abide by the Constitution and the law." As late as the end of 2012, Xi Jinping publicly termed the full implementation of the Constitution the primary task and fundamental work for constructing a socialist state. However, as Guobin Zhu of the City University of Hong Kong Law School points out, after a real academic blossoming of debate and discussion on Chinese constitutionalism in the first dozen years of the 21st century, a counter-, or anti-, constitutionalism move occurred, starting in earnest in 2013. With explicit encouragement by the Communist Party, this denied the value of constitutionalism in China.

The problem of corruption is another topic that various chapters touch on, including especially the contributions by Andrew Wedeman of Georgia State University, "Policing the Police, Party and State" and by Chun-Chih Chang of Xiamen University in China and Chien-Min Chao of the Chinese Culture University on rent-seeking bureaucrats. With their findings in mind, one might suggest that, as ideology declines in importance as a motivating factor in society, corruption is likely to increase, as officials look to use their positions, not to promote a political agenda but to get ahead financially.

Certainly, corruption has long been a major problem facing the Chinese regime. In 2008, Minxin Pei stated:

> The abuse of power for personal gain, the classic definition of corruption, today permeates nearly all layers and departments of the government. Anti-corruption investigations have ensnared officials of all ranks, from members of the powerful Politburo . . . to senior generals and commanders of the armed forces, provincial party secretaries and governors, top executives in financial institutions and state-owned enterprises, county magistrates, and village chiefs.
>
> *(Pei 2008, 229)*

With such endemic corruption threatening China's future, Pei continued:

> Politically, corruption by the members of the ruling elite undermines the legitimacy of the CCP, erodes the authority of the state, impedes the effective implementation of government policies, and fuels public resentment against the government. Economically, corruption creates distortions, increases the costs of commerce, causes waste and inefficiency, and stunts growth and

> employment. Socially, corruption exacerbates inequality, harms public safety, victimizes the poor and powerless, and increases social injustice.
>
> *(Ibid., 229–30)*

Nevertheless, in China, as in the other communist countries of Asia, political ideology—though deviated from in practice—continues to provide the regime with its *raison d'être*, its central justification for existing, as well as establishing a yardstick by which critics might judge it. David Johnson and Michelle Miao wrote,

> China, Vietnam, and North Korea are all characterized by low respect for human rights, few restraints on government power, and single-party dominance. They also remain Communist states in two important senses: the ruling party and the state are so closely connected that it makes sense to speak of a party state, and the ruling party regards itself as the vanguard of the people.
>
> *(Johnson and Miao 2016, 316)*

5. A Comparative Law Context

We have seen how those coming from different ideological orientations often bring to bear contrasting assumptions about how government should behave, what a state's chief goals should be, and how it should interact with others. One can often perceive the influence of ideology in a state's laws and in its legal institutions as well as in its foreign-policy clashes with other states. Traditionally, Marxist theory takes law to be "a product of tension and conflict between groups and individuals" (Lu and Miethe 2007, 12)—a part of capitalist society that will inevitably "wither away" under socialism. This ideology takes laws to be written to serve the vision and interests of the ruling class, often used against those of the uncooperative members of the proletariat, and formal, equal rights are seen as clouding the people's views of "substantive inequalities in social and economic relations" (Sypnowich 1990, 1–2).

The preceding chapters lay out various dimensions of how the role of law in China, its content and the functioning of its institutions, differs in important respects from those in many other countries. The Ming Du chapter, for example, shows China trying to fit into an international economic order established by governments with very different ideological orientations. For foreign businesses engaged in interactions with China as investors or trade partners, one key question stands out: how is Chinese ideology reflected in the country's corporate laws and the manner in which the state implements them? In his chapter, Jeffrey E. Thomas of the University of Missouri-Kansas City Law School points out that, because of a cultural factor—the high Chinese tolerance for centralized government—"culturally it is more difficult to hold government accountable to the law." Indeed, the CCP's dominant position within Chinese society makes the concept of accountability quite problematic. Suisheng Zhao observed:

> Although the party has lost some of its capacity to inspire or mobilize the Chinese people, it retains effective control over the military, government agencies, and some strategic sectors of the economy. With its ultimate authority over the state, the party remains a ticket that must be punched and the main avenue of upward mobility for many politically ambitious elites. Most of these elites still want to join the party in order to advance their careers.
>
> *(Suisheng Zhao 2006, "Political Liberalization," 50)*

In general, accountability might best be approached through the related, yet prior idea of duty or responsibility. Responsibility involves the assignment and the consequent acceptance of particular tasks. Accountability focuses on the evaluation of those tasks as they have been executed over a particular time period. Usually, accountability in government involves some designated supervisory entity critically appraising the effort by a subordinate body to demonstrate responsible behavior (Fowler 2009, 38–39). However, in a single-party system, assembled without separated powers or checks and balances and lacking a tradition of transparency in governance, no one can readily bring the government to account.

Larry Diamond wrote, "'Horizontal accountability' is the means by which some agencies of government hold other governmental actors, particularly the executive branch of government, accountable to the law and the public interest" (Diamond 2006, 83). But, this raises all kinds of difficulties in the Chinese case where the Party is not separated from the state. No constitutional court with supreme authority, including over the Party, exists, nor are there independent audit agencies and ombudsmen offices, independent of Party control (Ibid.). Diamond also noted, "Unless there is some degree of *vertical accountability*—unless the public has access to information and the press has freedom to investigate and expose—it is impossible to know if the agencies of horizontal accountability are doing their jobs seriously" (Ibid. Italics in original).

So, what exactly is different about Chinese law? Contrasting ideologies help to explain some differences. With the continued preeminence of the Chinese Communist Party, law is clearly not the supreme authority in Chinese society. Although law has an often notable role and a real-world significance in modern China, it is by no means the ultimate organizing principle of Chinese life. CCP decision-making can overwhelm notions of a rule of law. And, Andrew Wedeman observes that the "intertwining of the party and state" leads to possibilities for collusion, and this may further diminish efforts to establish a rule of law.

One might also observe that, although in the last 40 years or so, China has promulgated new laws in many different fields, the Chinese system operates without the voluminous precedents of past legal cases found in the common law legal systems.[14] Other scholars have noted that, with the party leadership exerting pressure on the judiciary, in some respects but not in others, ambiguities in the law provide judicial discretion that the Party can then manipulate through its influence (Trevaskes 2016, 123). In this respect, various chapters recount different ways in which the Chinese legal system has been used to buttress the current political regime. In analyzing the limited effect that international economic norms have had on the rule of law in China, Professor Du argues that "the Chinese government's conception of law remains highly instrumentalist," with complaints of the selective and inconsistent use of law and legal procedure remaining quite prevalent.

Indeed, in China, law is treated "as an elastic instrument for achieving party purposes" (Johnson and Miao 2016, 318). This, too, has roots in pre-revolutionary Chinese history. Elsewhere, Shiping Hua has contrasted the American legal system "built on such ideals as 'all men are created equal,'" with a "Chinese legal system . . . built not on ideals, but on the pragmatic consideration by elites seeking to preserve a state that was supposed to protect its people from other states" (Hua 2019, 20). In this volume, Professor Hua further notes that a tradition established as far back as the Qin dynasty law in China was to serve state objectives and strengthen state power. Haig Patapan likewise points out that Chinese history has long featured a ruler-centric definition of law: in the first instance law is wielded as an instrument of control by the ruler. Considering matters such as gun restrictions and the use of force in police detention of suspects, Suzanne E. Scoggins of Clark University examines the history of how Chinese leaders have employed the rule of law concept in different ways to try to justify state goals and attempt to achieve them.

However, if scholarly analysis is, in part, about separating matters out and determining what is distinctive, it is also, in part, about lumping things together and determining what commonalities exist. Here, in thinking about the role of law in a range of different human societies, one might also take stock of the extent to which the position of law in China parallels that in various other countries. Those who spend time studying the way that law works in diverse countries may find notable parallels to Chinese law. Indeed, in some respects, perhaps the large handful of highly advanced legal systems principally found in Europe and in what has been called "European settler states" (Watson 1992, 257), including Australia, Canada, India, and the US, are actually the exceptions.

Most human societies feature legal systems in which the rule of law, if it exists more than rhetorically, is still very much an ideal. Certain people and organizations, including government institutions, are above the law in the sense that no legal authority has the resources or willpower to enforce laws against them. In many states, the constitution is followed so long as it conforms with the regime's policies and objectives. The body of national law might affect in important ways particular legal matters, say, street crime, permits to build, or commercial disputes. But, many legal systems have proven themselves quite incapable of consistently enforcing laws against powerful actors.[15] For instance, in various countries, the legal system has not been able to bring death squad members to justice, to counter powerful organized crime syndicates, to stop forced prostitution or child abuse, or to regulate effectively major polluters.

In much of the world, then, what the law says is one factor in determining how people behave, but it is not always the leading factor, and in some sets of circumstances, it can be a remote factor indeed. To the extent that many of the country's laws are significant, they are important not because they are always enforced by a superior power but because they stand as accepted norms (Zhu 2010, 105). The law represents a consensus of some kind, and that consensus helps to shape the way people act some of the time. From this perspective, *Chinese Legality* contributes to the scholarly literature by considering which aspects of China's legal system have become accepted or are likely to become accepted over time.

6. The Legal System Today in China

So, guided by the insights of the scholars contributing to this volume, what might be concluded about the current state of the legal system in China? Years ago, Andrew Nathan wrote, "The governance reforms under way or proposed for the future aim to make the authoritarian system more fair, more effective, and more—not less—sustainable" (Nathan 2008, 39). How about with respect to the Chinese legal system? Observers identify significant problems existing in that system, but are these improving or not? In a world marked by the rapid spread of information, the content of laws and the functioning of legal institutions in China have not been static: both evidence of steps forward and of stalled progress or even sliding backward are apparent when law in China is compared to that in other countries. As a book written 35 years ago likewise concluded: "Our studies provide reasons for both hope and pessimism, and express both in varying measures" (Edwards, Henkin, and Nathan 1986, 6). And, sometimes, reasonable minds can differ on whether encouraging elements predominate or discouraging ones seem the most important.

Consider, for instance, the use of the death penalty in China. The clear global trend is toward the death penalty being abolished, sometimes in law and sometimes in practice (Lu and Miethe 2007, ix). Yet, for many years, China has employed capital punishment more vigorously than any other state (ibid., 6; Liang and Lu 2016, xi). Although exact figures are difficult to come by since "China has not published systematic national data on death sentence and execution" (Xiong 2016, 214; Lu and Miethe 2007, 2), Amnesty International has estimated that in some years in the 21st-century China executed perhaps three times as many people as all other countries combined (Liang and Lu 2016, xi).[16] Nevertheless, multiple authorities have concluded that the Chinese reliance on capital punishment has declined over the years as a consequence of certain reform efforts (Ibid., xi; Trevaskes 2016, 124–25; Xiong 2016, 214–15; Johnson and Miao 2016, 301).

Indeed, in China today, a number of new legal provisions seem aimed at enhancing the fairness of the manner in which the legal system operates. For instance, according to Bin Liang and Hong Lu, China's criminal procedure law, adopted in 2012:

> simplifies the procedure for lawyers to meet with detained clients without police supervision (e.g., Article 37), and adopts exclusionary rules against evidence illegally obtained through torture (e.g., Articles 50, 53, 54). . . . [It] stipulates that members of (ethnic) minority groups enjoy the right to use their own native language in lawsuits (Article 9).

After noting how the new law revises death-penalty procedures, the authors continued by pointing out how Article 12 of the Criminal Law restricts the potential for retroactive penal punishment.

Showing appropriate caution in light of the Communist Party's influence on legal process in China, Liang and Lu also interjected the thought: "The effect of these new measures again remains to be seen" (Liang and Lu 2016, 338). Indeed, promulgating new rights is one issue; ensuring those rights are respected in practice is another, one that requires more widespread public knowledge and vigorous legal advocacy than may be occurring. One study based on a survey of 290 lawyers indicated:

> Chinese lawyers are selective in taking on lawsuits. . . . They are more willing to represent clients in litigation pertaining to economic and civil affairs. . . . For one thing, lawyers receive high payment for lawsuits of an economic nature. More importantly, there are political risks in taking on administrative litigation and criminal cases.
>
> *(Suisheng Zhao 2006, "Introduction," xii)*

These political risks seem tied to the fact that "the government clearly is concerned about the potential for activist lawyers to increase social instability" (Peerenboom and Chen 2008, 147). Whether the reluctance to zealously defend clients is slowly changing or might change in the future is another dimension of Chinese legality that remains to be determined.

The contributors to *China Legality* likewise note the progress the Chinese legal system has made in certain respects. For instance, Ming Du argues that law in China is administered in a more transparent fashion with less meddling by local officials than was apparent in the past. Shiping Hua reports that in rule-of-law terms, World Bank data suggests some significant improvement over the last decades. Hua and Suzanne E. Scoggins both contend the police are following the laws more scrupulously than was true in the 1980s. Bin Liang of Oklahoma State University, however, in recounting the case of Li Wenliang, the inadvertent whistleblower during the pandemic, spells out various ways in which the authorities did not closely follow relevant laws in that situation.

The patterns of law in modern China are complex. They sometimes proceed in an apparently contradictory manner, perhaps coincidentally but perhaps purposefully. Sometimes, a central current can be identified, but so, too, can a counter-current lead in the opposite direction. For instance, Shiping Hua recalls that in the period after the 1989 Tiananmen Square unrest and violent reprisal "tightened political control went hand in hand with economic reform and opening up to the outside world." He then interprets the establishment of the Civil Code and the promulgating of the Fifth Amendment as another example of the regime exerting stricter political control, while simultaneously "providing some breathing space to the people in the socio-economic sphere."

In Professor Hua's contribution on new civil law developments in China, he notes that, so long as state actors are not involved, the legal system appears to be poised to protect certain rights via the new Civil Code. After four prior failed endeavors, the importance of the drafting and passage of this extensive code, featuring 1,260 provisions, divided into seven parts, including family law, tort liability, contracts, and property rights, ought not to be underestimated. One might recall that, while exiled at the end of his life, Napoleon declared: "My true glory is not to have won forty battles. . . . What nothing will efface, what will live forever, is my *Code Civil*" (Friedrich 1956, 6–7). Whether the Chinese Civil Code will be long-lived or not remains to be seen. However, as Professor Hua observes, the fact that the code was enacted is evidence that the Chinese leadership continues to want to re-orient its legal system, so it looks like those of other market economies, providing a further opening to the outside world.

Yet, while progress may be occurring in various regards, multiple problems remain to be addressed. Fifteen years ago, Randall Peerenboom summarized the "maladies of China's administrative law system" in these terms:

> a legislative system in disarray; a weak judiciary; a number of poorly trained judges and lawyers, themselves prone to corruption and professional responsibility violations; a low level of consciousness among the populace; the persistent influence of paternalistic traditions and a culture of deference to government authority; and the fallout from the unfinished transition from a centrally planned to a market economy, which has exacerbated central-local tensions and resulted in fragmentation of authority.
>
> *(Peerenboom 2006, 60–61)*

In the intervening years, certain of these flaws have been addressed, but much ground must be traversed before all of these long-lived problems vanish.

7. Conclusion

The Chinese civilization is so ancient, and law in China has been used for so long and in such different contexts, that the subject of the evolution of the Chinese legal system has been an especially fruitful area for inquiry. Western commentators are sometimes surprised to find scholars considering case records, in particular the written records of oral testimony taken from defendants, in Qing China

(1644–1912), which was marked by an unusually extensive and well-organized system of written review (Karasawa 2007, 102–3). And, Chinese lawmaking, of course, stretches far into the distant past, long before the Qing period.[17]

Indeed, the history of the Chinese legal system is a subject so long and variegated that surprisingly few issues, even of a quite fundamental nature, have been definitively resolved. To take one example, in the Introduction Shiping Hua declares, "China does not have the tradition of natural law." Yet, in a provocative philosophical interpretation, Xiusheng Liu relied on a broad definition of natural law to conclude quite the opposite:

> Since Chinese tradition does not have the idea of God or any other (lasting) idea of transcendental superhuman power with universal authority, the main stream of natural law in Chinese tradition focuses its attention on essential human perspectives, that is, it is based on a notion of human nature or a notion of the nature of society. Harmony between social and individual life, proper arrangements of social and political order, reasonable distribution of goods to meet individual and social needs . . . are not just problems to which natural law needs to supply . . . answers but also grounds on which natural law stands.

Liu then concludes:

> I contend that Chinese philosophical tradition contains the idea of natural law, although it might be disputable as to whether natural law in Chinese philosophy falls in the Western traditional version. . . . It is fairly safe to say that Taoism is a form of natural law theory. But I do not hesitate to call Confucianism or Mohism a natural law theory.
>
> *(Liu 2001, 258–59)*

We have seen, then, a book on Chinese legality returning again and again to history. The scholars who contributed to this volume place Chinese legality today in the context of China's history of law, its legal philosophers, and its schools of legal thought. The current significance of this is it helps to illuminate answers to the question: What are the principles the Communist Chinese government is likely to revert to when making key future decisions? Here, the contribution of Haig Patapan is particularly noteworthy in focusing attention on the influence on Xi Jingping and on the modern Chinese legal system of philosopher Han Fei and the Chinese legalism school that dates to "the latter half of the Warring States period (. . . 453–221 BCE), a time of war and great economic, military, and social instability."

Extensive warfare, however, marked only the latter part of this period when China was ruled by independent states. Adam Watson observed,

> The monumental Chinese achievement in the field of statecraft is usually held to be the more or less effective imperial unity that has assured domestic

> peace and order for most of Chinese history. But for five and a half crucial and creative centuries China consisted of a number of genuinely independent states.
>
> *(Watson 1992, 85)*

He went on to argue:

> The period of the warring states . . . saw the greatest creative and intellectual activity in Chinese history. Under the imperial dynasties Chinese civilization, in philosophy, literature and the arts, was very largely a continuation and refinement of what had been achieved in the centuries of multiple independence, when different communities offered a competitive range of opportunities, and men could move from one community to another.
>
> *(Ibid., 89)*

With respect to legalism Watson noted:

> The conventional use of this word to translate the Chinese *fa-chaio* gives it misleading overtones suggesting a rule of law to which kings and executive governments are subject. The law of the Chinese legalists was the will of an autocratic ruler, formulated in precise legal decrees, to which all his subjects including his officials must conform without question. A word like "authoritarian" conveys the views of this school better.
>
> *(Ibid., 90–91)*

A larger point here may be that it is easy for commentators on Chinese governance to get swept up in the regime's rhetoric, such as the "China Dream of Great Rejuvenation," aiming at restoring China to a preeminent position of world leadership. Or, they might get bogged down in what Professor Patapan refers to as "the vagaries of factional contestation and unpredictable exigencies of domestic and international politics." A more tangible signpost to assist in analyzing government actions is the fact that Chinese rulers have traditionally looked to legalism to provide guidance. This is especially so when political life has become unstable, as has often been the case in the last quarter century. Patapan elucidates how the legalism school of thought views law as an important element of a successful state, though law is perceived, first and foremost, as an instrument of control by rulers, who are themselves above the law. Patapan argues that legalism helps to explain Xi's leadership and his ambitions for modern China. Various other authors also touch on law under such past communist leaders as Mao Zedong and Deng Xiaoping, but the particular circumstance of legalism in the current era of rule by Xi Jinping gains the most attention.

In the final analysis, *Chinese Legality* examines some very fundamental questions—where and how is law important in Chinese society, where is it less important, and why? Certainly, in such a rapidly changing environment as the 21st century, the recent and probable future developments of the Chinese legal system form "a perpetually tentative undertaking; one can only cite the latest edition and anticipate the next revision."[18] While this volume does not, then, constitute a definitive, final word, the authors do very much enhance our understanding of recent and probable future developments of this supremely important legal system.

Notes

1 Larry Wortzel wrote, "[T]he combination of psychological warfare; the manipulation of public opinion, or media warfare; and the manipulation of legal arguments to strengthen China's diplomatic and security position, or what China calls 'legal warfare', join together in a comprehensive information operations doctrine" (Wortzel 2014, 1–2).
2 *In the Matter of the South China Sea Arbitration* (The Republic of Philippines v. The People's Republic of China). Permanent Ct. of Arbitration, 2016.
3 Hungdah Chiu noted, "In the nineteenth and early twentieth centuries, China was compelled to conclude with many countries treaties that provided for extraterritoriality . . . for the nationals of those countries in China, restrictive tariff regulations, territorial cessions and leases, the right to station foreign troops in China, and other humiliating infringements on sovereignty" (Chiu 1972, 243).
4 One scholar noted, "To understand China's present government and its capacity for change, . . . one must appreciate that there has often been a huge gap between practice and ideals in the PRC. The CCP has repeatedly shown a penchant for altering its practices while claiming to maintain the same ideals, or it has reformulated ideals while practice lagged behind them" (Suisheng Zhao 2006, "Political Liberalization," 43).
5 John Wong and Michael Ng observed: "On the one hand, the law constitutes an important policy tool for defining the boundaries of law and order within which the ruling authority maintains the particular economic ordering of society it desires. On the other hand, such an imagined vision for the law as social justice enables the ruled to justify trespassing those boundaries to challenge or overturn an existing political-economic ordering that is thought to be unjust" (Wong and Ng 2017, 1).
6 In positing that China's genomic data set "likely contains more than 100 million profiles and possibly as many as 140 million," Emile Dirks wrote, "In 2003, China's Ministry of Public Security began building its own forensic DNA database. Like other such databases, it contains samples taken from entire ethnic minority communities and ordinary citizens outside any criminal investigations and without proper informed consent" (Dirks 2020, 4).
7 For the thumbnail sketches of prominent political ideologies below, I am indebted to Professor Julie Bunck of the University of Louisville.
8 Yunhai Wang noted the paternalism of Japan's current capital-punishment practices: "Acting as the 'parent' of Japanese citizens, the state (the Japanese government) cannot apply the death penalty to its 'children' capriciously; at the same time, the state cannot give up the death penalty as the final tool to show its authority as a parent" (Wang 2016, 97–98).
9 Willard Mullins observed, "When persons invoke the name or recount the exploits of the founders, past and present are merged; the past is renewed in the present, even as the present draws significance from the past. By such practices, political communities celebrate the essential identity between the original act of founding and the continuing actions that extend and preserve the polity" (Mullins 1972, 505).
10 *West Virginia Board of Education v. Barnette*, 319 U.S. 624, 642 (1943).
11 *American Communications Association v. Douds*, 339 U.S. 382, 442 (1950).

12 *Myers v. United States*, 272 U.S. 52, 293 (1926) (Brandeis, J., dissenting). By autocracy is meant government at the will of a single leader "unchecked by constitutional restrictions or limitations" (Nolan and Nolan-Haley 1990, 134).
13 Indeed, pre-revolutionary Chinese civil law has been characterized as "a Western framework . . . filled with a Chinese substance" (Bourgon 2004, 85).
14 A common law legal system may be defined as one "with a common law heritage that is both accusatorial and adversarial and in which the judge does not both investigate and act as a decision maker, as in a civil law legal system" (Fowler 1998, 312).
15 Julie Bunck and I found this was true of most Central American legal systems. In our study of regional narcotics trafficking and corruption, we noted that bridge-state governments have not simply collapsed when confronted with the transit of highly profitable illegal drugs. Instead, governments have retreated, persisted, and reasserted themselves in complex and erratic patterns (Bunck and Fowler 2012, 377–78).
16 Others have suggested that judicial executions in China have amounted to four times that of all other countries combined (Johnson and Miao 2016, 301). In 2019, Amnesty International reported that for ten years it had refrained from "publishing its estimated figures on the use of the death penalty in China." The organization noted "the figures it was able to publish on China were significantly lower than the reality . . . China has yet to publish any figures on the death penalty; however, available information indicates that each year thousands of people are executed and sentenced to death" (Amnesty International 2019, 6).
17 For a work on the writing of Chinese laws in the Qin dynasty (221–207 BCE), see Caldwell (2018).
18 I borrow this phrase from Inis L. Claude, Jr., who used it in the different context of analysis of the term sovereignty (Fowler and Bunck 1995, x).

References

Amnesty International. 2019. "Amnesty International Global Report: Death Sentences and Executions, 2019." Accessed May 7, 2022. www.justice.gov/file/1272316/download.

Bailey, Thomas A. 1968. *The Art of Diplomacy: The American Experience*. New York: Appleton – Century – Crofts.

Bourgon, Jérôme. 2004. "Rights, Freedoms, and Customs in the Making of Chinese Civil Law, 1900–1936." In *Realms of Freedom in Modern China*, edited by William C. Kirby. Stanford: Stanford University Press.

Bunck, Julie Marie. 1994. *Fidel Castro and the Quest for a Revolutionary Culture in Cuba*. University Park, PA: Pennsylvania State University Press.

Bunck, Julie Marie, and Michael Ross Fowler. 2012. *Bribes, Bullets, and Intimidation: Drug Trafficking and the Law in Central America*. University Park, PA: Pennsylvania State University Press.

Calcea, Nicu. 2021. "China's Income Equality Is Among the World's Worst: The Gap Between the Rich and Poor in China Is Almost as Huge as in the US." *The New Statesman*. Accessed May 11, 2022. www.newstatesman.com/world/2021/08/china-s-income-inequality-among-world-s-worst.

Caldwell, Ernest. 2018. *Writing Chinese Laws: The Form and Function of Legal Statutes Found in the Qin Shuihudi Corpus*. New York: Routledge.

Chiu, Hungdah. 1972. "Comparison of the Nationalist and Communist Chinese Views of Unequal Treaties." In *China's Practice of International Law: Some Case Studies*, edited by Jerome Alan Cohen, 239–67. Cambridge, MA: Harvard University Press.

Cimmino, Jeffrey. 2021. "A Strategic Framework for Countering China's Human-Rights Violations in Xinjiang." *Atlantic Council*. Accessed May 5, 2022. www.jstor.org/stable/resrep33447.

Claude, Inis L., Jr. 1959. "Eleventh Report of the Commission." In *Organizing Peace in the Nuclear Age: Commission to Study the Organization of Peace*, edited by Commission to Study the Organization of Peace and Arthur N. Holcombe, 1–272. New York: New York University Press.

———. 1988. *States and the Global System: Politics, Law and Organization*. New York: St. Martin's Press.

Diamond, Larry. 2006. "The Rule of Law as Transition to Democracy in China." In *Debating Political Reform in China: Rule of Law vs. Democratization*, edited by Suisheng Zhao, 79–91. Armonk, NY: M.E. Sharpe.

Dirks, Emile, and James Leibold. 2020. *Genomic Surveillance: Inside China's DNA Dragnet*. Barton, Australian Capital Territory: Australian Strategic Policy Institute. Accessed May 6, 2022. www.jstor.org/stable/resrep25134.

Edwards, R. Randle, Louis Henkin, and Andrew J. Nathan. 1986. *Human Rights in Contemporary China*. New York: Columbia University Press.

Fowler, Michael Ross. 1998. *With Justice for All? The Nature of the American Legal System*. Upper Saddle River, NJ: Prentice Hall.

———. 2009. "Bringing the Different United Nations to Account." In *Envisioning Reform: Enhancing UN Accountability in the Twenty-First Century*, edited by Sumihiro Kuyama and Michael Ross Fowler, 37–72. New York: United Nations University Press.

Fowler, Michael Ross, and Julie Marie Bunck. 1994. "The Chunk and Basket Theories of Sovereignty." In *Community, Diversity, and a New World Order: Essays in Honor of Inis L. Claude, Jr.*, 137–44. Lanham, MD: University Press of America.

———. 1995. *Law, Power, and the Sovereign State: The Evolution and Application of the Concept of Sovereignty*. University Park, PA: Pennsylvania State University Press.

———. 1996. "What Constitutes the Sovereign State?" *Review of International Studies* 22: 381–404.

Franceschini, Ivan, and Elisa Nesossi. 2017. "The Foreign NGOs Management Law: A Compendium." In *Disturbances in Heaven*, edited by Ivan Franceschini, Kevin Lin, and Nicholas Loubere, 60–67. Canberra: Australian National University Press. Accessed May 6, 2022. www.jstor.org/stable/pdf/j.ctt1q1crrk.14.pdf?refreqid=excelsior%3A7bf25a242bca40d4001c35de0fbc29fe&ab_segments=&origin.

Friedman, Edward. 2006. "A Comparative Politics of Democratization in China." In *Debating Political Reform in China: Rule of Law vs. Democratization*, edited by Suisheng Zhao, 91–110. Armonk, NY: M. E. Sharpe.

Friedrich, C. J. 1956. "The Ideological and Philosophical Background." In *The Code Napoleon and the Common-Law World*, edited by Bernard Schwartz, 1–18. Westport, CT: Greenwood Press.

Goldstein, Avery. 2005. *Rising to the Challenge: China's Grand Strategy and International Security*. Stanford: Stanford University Press.

Hamilton, Malcolm B. 1987. "The Elements of the Concept of Ideology." *Political Studies* XXXV: 18–38.

He, Xin. 2021. "Pressures on Chinese Judges Under Xi." *The China Journal* 85 (January): 49–74.

Henkin, Louis. 1986. "The Human Rights Idea in Contemporary China: A Comparative Perspective." In *Human Rights in Contemporary China*, edited by R. Randle Edwards, Louis Henkin, and Andrew J. Nathan, 7–40. New York: Columbia University Press.

Hua, Shiping. 2019. *Chinese Legal Culture and Constitutional Order*. New York: Routledge.

———, ed. 2022. *The Political Logic of the US-China Trade War*. Lanham, MD: Lexington Books.

Johnson, David T., and Michelle Miao. 2016. "Chinese Capital Punishment in Comparative Perspective." In *The Death Penalty in China: Policy, Practice, and Reform*, edited by Bin Liang and Hong Lu, 300–26. New York: Columbia University Press.

Kaltman, Blaine. 2007. *Under the Heel of the Dragon: Islam, Racism, Crime, and the Uighur in China*. Athens, OH: Ohio University Press.

Karasawa, Yasuhiko. 2007. "From Oral Testimony to Written Records in Qing Legal Cases." In *Thinking With Cases: Specialist Knowledge in Chinese Cultural History*, edited by Charlotte Furth et al., 101–22. Honolulu: University of Hawai'i Press.

Kashmeri, Sarwar A. 2019. *China's Grand Strategy: Weaving a New Silk Road to Global Primacy*. Santa Barbara, CA: Praeger.

Lateef, Noel V. 2019. "Foreword." In *China's Grand Strategy: Weaving a New Silk Road to Global Primacy*, edited by Sarwar A. Kashmeri, ix–xi. Santa Barbara, CA: Praeger.

Liang, Bin, and Hong Lu. 2016. *The Death Penalty in China: Policy, Practice, and Reform*. New York: Columbia University Press.

Liebman, Benjamin L. 2011. "A Return to Populist Legality? Historical Legacies and Legal Reform." In *Mao's Invisible Hand: The Political Foundations of Adaptive Governance in China*, edited by Sebastian Heilmann and Elizabeth J. Perry, 165–200. Cambridge: Harvard University Press.

Lin, Kevin. 2017. "Remoulding the State Sector: Back to the 1990s?" In *Disturbances in Heaven*, edited by Ivan Franceschini, Kevin Lin, and Nicholas Loubere, 20–23. Canberra: Australian National University. Accessed May 6, 2022. www.jstor.org/stable/pdf/j.ctt1q1crrK.6.pdf?refreq=excelsior%3A7bf25a242bca40d4001e35de0fbc29fc&ab_segments=&origin.

Liu, Xiusheng. 2001. "Natural Law in Classical Chinese Philosophy." Appendix Part II. In *Natural Law Modernized*, edited by David Braybrooke, 258–94. Toronto: University of Toronto Press.

Lu, Hong, and Terance D. Miethe. 2007. *China's Death Penalty: History, Law, and Contemporary Practices*. New York: Routledge.

Mackerras, Colin, Pradeep Taneja, and Graham Young. 1993. *China Since 1978: Reform, Modernisation, and "Socialism With Chinese Characteristics."* New York: St. Martin's Press.

Men, Jing. 2007. "Changing Ideology in China and Its Impact on Chinese Foreign Policy." In *New Dimensions of Chinese Foreign Policy*, edited by Sujian Guo and Shiping Hua, 7–39. Lanham, MD: Rowman & Littlefield.

Mullins, Willard A. 1972. "On the Concept of Ideology in Political Science." *American Political Science Review* 66 (2): 498–510.

Nathan, Andrew J. 2008. "China's Political Trajectory: What Are the Chinese Saying?" In *China's Changing Political Landscape: Prospects for Democracy*, edited by Cheng Li, 25–43. Washington, DC: Brookings Institution Press.

Ng, Michael H. K., and John D. Wong. 2017. *Civil Unrest and Governance in Hong Kong: Law and Order From Historical and Cultural Perspectives*. New York: Routledge.

Nolan, Joseph R., and Jacqueline M. Nolan-Haley. 1990. *Black's Law Dictionary: Definitions of the Terms and Phrases of American and English Jurisprudence, Ancient and Modern*. St. Paul, MN: West Publishing Co.

Peerenboom, Randall. 2006. "A Government of Laws: Democracy, Rule of Law, and Administrative Law Reform in China." In *Debating Political Reform in China: Rule of Law vs. Democratization*, 58–78. Armonk, NY: M. E. Sharpe.

Peerenboom, Randall, and Weitseng Chen. 2008. "Developing the Rule of Law." In *Political Change in China: Comparisons With Taiwan*, 135–59. Boulder, CO: Lynne Rienner.

Pei, Minxin. 2008. "Fighting Corruption: A Difficult Challenge for Chinese Leaders." In *China's Changing Political Landscape: Prospects for Democracy*, edited by Cheng Li, 229–50. Washington, DC: Brookings Institution Press.

Ruser, Nathan. 2020. *Documenting Xinjiang's Detention System*. Barton, Australian Capital Territory: Australian Strategic Policy Institute. Accessed May 5, 2022. www.jstor.org/stable/resrep26125.

Saunders, Phillip C. 2019. *Chairman Xi Remakes the PLA: Assessing Chinese Military Reforms*. Washington, DC: National Defense University Press.

Shaw, Malcolm. 2014. *International Law*. 7th ed. Cambridge, UK: Cambridge University Press.

Siu-Lun, Wong. 1999. "Deciding to Stay, Deciding to Move, Deciding Not to Decide." In *Cosmopolitan Capitalists: Hong Kong and the Chinese Diaspora at the End of the 20th Century*, edited by Gary G. Hamilton, 135–51. Seattle: University of Washington Press.

Stjepanovic, Nikola. 1956. "The Code in a Socialist State." In *The Code Napoleon and the Common-Law World*, edited by Bernard Schwartz, 224–46. Westport, CT: Greenwood Press.

Sypnowich, Christine. 1990. *The Concept of Socialist Law*. Oxford: Clarendon Press.

Trevaskes, Susan. 2016. "From 'Killing Many' to 'Killing Fewer.'" In *The Death Penalty in China: Policy, Practice, and Reform*, edited by Bin Liang and Hong Lu, 123–55. New York: Columbia University Press.

US Department of Defense, Office of the Secretary of Defense. *Military and Security Developments Involving the People's Republic of China: Annual Report to Congress*. Accessed May 4, 2022. https://media.defense.gov/2021/Nov/03/2002885874/-1/-1/0/2021-CMPR-FINAL-PDF.

Wang, Yunhai. 2016. "China's Death Penalty in a State-Power-Based Society." In *The Death Penalty in China: Policy, Practice, and Reform*, edited by Bin Liang and Hong Lu, 97–122. New York: Columbia University Press.

Watson, Adam. 1992. *The Evolution of International Society*. New York: Routledge.

Wong, John D., and Michael H. K. Ng. 2017. "Introduction: Negotiating the Legitimacy of Governance." In *Civil Unrest and Governance in Hong Kong: Law and Order From Historical and Cultural Perspectives*, edited by Michael H. K. Ng and John D. Wong, 1–7. New York: Routledge.

Wortzel, Larry M. 2014. *Chinese People's Liberation Army and Information Warfare*. Carlisle, PA: Strategic Studies Institute, U.S. Army War College.

Wu, Guoguang. 2008. "Democracy and the Rule of Law in Zhao Ziyang's Political Reform." In *Zhao Ziyang and China's Political Future*, edited by Guoguang Wu and Helen Lansdowne, 32–57. New York: Routledge.

Xiong, Moulin. 2016. "The Death Penalty After the Restoration of Centralized Review." In *The Death Penalty in China: Policy, Practice, and Reform*, edited by Bin Liang and Hong Lu, 214–46. New York: Columbia University Press.

Zhao, Dingxin. 2001. *The Power of Tiananmen: State-Society Relations and the 1989 Beijing Student Movement*. Chicago: University of Chicago Press.

Zhao, Suisheng . 2006. "Introduction." In *Debating Political Reform in China: Rule of Law vs. Democratization*, vii–xv. Armonk, NY: M. E. Sharpe.

Zhao, Suisheng . 2006. "Political Liberalization Without Democratization: Pan Wei's Proposal for Political Reform." In *Debating Political Reform in China: Rule of Law vs. Democratization*, 41–57. Armonk, NY: M. E. Sharpe.

Zhu, Yuchao. 2010. "Norms, Laws, Political Accountability and China's Legal Reform – the Cases of ALL and *Xinfang* (L & V)." In *Toward Better Governance in China: An Unconventional Pathway of Political Reform*, edited by Baogang Guo and Dennis Hickey. Lanham, MD: Rowman & Littlefield.

INDEX